## THE STATUS OF THE GIRL CHILD UNDER INTERNATIONAL LAW

Clara Chapdelaine-Feliciati offers the first comprehensive study of the status of the girl child under international law. This book significantly contributes to bridging two fields usually studied separately: law and semiotics. The author engages in the novel legal semiotics theory to decode the meaning of international treaties (mainly the Convention on the Rights of the Child, Convention on the Elimination of All Forms of Discrimination Against Women, and International Covenants) and assess whether the provisions, as formulated, clearly identify the girl child and take into account the obstacles she faces as a result of sexism, childism, and intersectional discrimination. This is also the first book to apply the Significs Meaning Triad – Sense, Meaning, Significance – in international law, and Semioethics for both a diagnosis and a prognosis of problematic signs in view of modifying the wording of relevant treaties.

Clara Chapdelaine-Feliciati (DPhil in Law, University of Oxford) is an international lawyer, Associate Professor of International Law at Xi'an Jiaotong-Liverpool University, and UKHEA Senior Fellow. She has worked for the International Criminal Court, UNICEF Office of Research, youth tribunals in Paris and Montreal, British, Chinese and Canadian Universities, and provided legal expertise to governments. She authored *Feminicides of Girl Children: An International Law Approach* (Brill 2018); and received the SSHRC IDG, SSHRC Explore, and Global Impact Grant for her novel legal semiotics theory in international law.

# The Status of the Girl Child under International Law

A SEMIOETHIC ANALYSIS

CLARA CHAPDELAINE-FELICIATI
University of Oxford, Oxford, United Kingdom

CAMBRIDGE
UNIVERSITY PRESS

CAMBRIDGE
UNIVERSITY PRESS

Shaftesbury Road, Cambridge CB2 8EA, United Kingdom

One Liberty Plaza, 20th Floor, New York, NY 10006, USA

477 Williamstown Road, Port Melbourne, VIC 3207, Australia

314–321, 3rd Floor, Plot 3, Splendor Forum, Jasola District Centre, New Delhi – 110025, India

103 Penang Road, #05–06/07, Visioncrest Commercial, Singapore 238467

Cambridge University Press is part of Cambridge University Press & Assessment, a department of the University of Cambridge.

We share the University's mission to contribute to society through the pursuit of education, learning and research at the highest international levels of excellence.

www.cambridge.org
Information on this title: www.cambridge.org/9781316512784

DOI: 10.1017/9781009072120



When citing this work, please include a reference to the DOI 10.1017/9781009072120

First published 2025

*A catalogue record for this publication is available from the British Library.*

*A Cataloging-in-Publication data record for this book is available from the Library of Congress*

ISBN 978-1-316-51278-4 Hardback



The book cover painting is by Piero del Pollaiolo, *La Giustizia*, Galleria delle Statue e delle Pitture degli Uffizi, Inv. 1890 n. 496. By concession of the Ministry of Culture. Further reproduction or duplication by any means prohibited.

*This book is dedicated to girls in the Global South and the Global North, and across social classes, who pursue avenues to reclaim their human rights and fundamental freedoms in spite of the many obstacles encountered.*

# Contents

*Preface* *page* xiii
*Acknowledgements* xv
*Meaning Glossary* xvii
I Girl Child xviii
II Son Preference and Daughter Devaluation xix
III Feminicide xx
IV Female Infanticide xxi
V Prenatal Sex Selection xxii
VI Female Genital Mutilation xxiii
VII Child Marriage xxviii
VIII Forced Marriage xxix
IX Restrictive Social and Dress Codes xxx
X Sexualized Social and Dress Codes xxxi
*List of Abbreviations* xxxiii

**Introduction** 1
I The Girl Child and International Law 1
II Intersectional Identity of the Girl Child 5
III International Legal Framework and Protection of the Girl Child 6
IV Semiotics Theory 11
V Structure of the Book 12
VI Terminology Employed to Refer to the Girl Child 13

1 **Semiotics and Semioethics** 15
I Origins and Meaning 19
II Decodification Semiotics 21

III Interpretation Semiotics: Peirce's Triadic Approach 22
IV The Victoria Lady Welby Significs Theory 25
1 Sense 27
2 Meaning 33
3 Significance 38
4 The Lady Welby Legacy 39
V Semioethics and Responsibility 41
1 Ethical Responsibility 42
VI Semiotic Analysis of Treaties in English 44

**2 Definition of the Girl Child** 47
I Recognition of the Girl Child under International Law 47
1 Universalism 47
2 Qualified Universalism 50
3 Girl Child as a Separate Entity 51
II Definition of the Girl Child 56
1 Twin Pillars of Identity: Femalehood and Childhood 57
1.1 Femalehood 57
1.2 Childhood 61
2 Dimensions of Girlhood 62
3 Boundaries of Girlhood 65
3.1 Age-based and Competence-based Boundaries 65
3.2 English Definitions 68
3.2.1 Puberty 68
3.2.2 Youth 70
3.2.3 Majority 71
4 Divisions of Girlhood 72
5 Girl Expression: Semiotics of Inferiority, Subordination and Denigration 74

**3 Sexism and Childism** 77
I The Concept of Discrimination under International Law 77
II Sexism 81
III Childism 84
1 Paternalism 85
2 Child Liberationism 87
3 Protecting the Girl Child while Promoting Her Autonomy Rights 89
3.1 Eekelaar's Interests of Children Theory 89
3.2 Herring's Common Vulnerability Theory 90
3.3 Arnstein and Hart's Ladder of Participation 91
3.4 Granting Autonomy Rights at Adolescence 94

IV The Girl Child and the Private Sphere 96
V Sexism, Childism and Cultural Relativism 99
1 Global South and Global North 99
2 Cultural Relativism 101

4 **Intersectional Identity of the Girl Child** 109
I Intersectionality Method and the Girl Child 111
II Interactive Intersectional Discrimination 114
1 Son Preference and Daughter Devaluation 114
2 Sexualized Social and Dress Codes 119

5 **Identification of the Girl Child in the Convention on the Rights of the Child** 124
I Sense 124
II Meaning 126
1 Discrimination and Androcentric Wording 129
2 Unique Violations 132
III Significance 138
1 Silence and the Immediate, Dynamical and Final Interpretants 139
2 Implementation and Monitoring 144
IV Semioethics: Recommended Definition 149

6 **The Beginning of Girlhood under International Law** 154
I Sense 156
1 English Definition 158
2 CRC 159
3 ICCPR 162
4 CEDAW 166
II Meaning 170
1 CRC 170
2 ICCPR 173
3 CEDAW 175
III Significance 177
IV Semioethics 178

7 **The End of Girlhood under International Law** 180
I Sense 180
II Meaning 187
1 Terminal Point of Girlhood 187
2 Majority or Age of Majority 190

III Significance of the Absence of a Uniform Boundary 191
1 Positive Features of the CRC for Girl Children 192
1.1 Most Widely Ratified Treaty Globally 192
1.2 Unique and Comprehensive Rights 193
2 Positive Features of Majority Before Eighteen Years 199
2.1 'Childist' Provisions of the CRC 200
2.1.1 Best Interests of the Child 200
2.1.2 Parental Authority 205
2.2 Empowering Provisions of Other Treaties 209
3 Problematic Features of the Current Threshold of Majority 211
3.1 Absence of Minimum Age for End of Girlhood 211
3.2 Discrepancy between the End of Girlhood and Emancipation 214
3.2.1 Child Justice System 216
3.3 Possibility of Unequal Treatment on the Grounds of National Domicile 217
3.4 Unequal Treatment on the Grounds of Gender 221
3.5 Unequal Treatment between Girl Children within the Same Jurisdiction 223
3.5.1 Child Marriage 224
3.6 Monitoring 227
3.7 Research Data on Girls 228
IV Semioethics: Recommended Boundary 229
1 Separate Majority and the End of Girlhood 230
2 Challenges 232
3 Proposed Amendment 235

8 **Girlhood and Womanhood in the CEDAW** 238
I Sense of Woman 238
1 Definition of 'Discrimination against Women' in the CEDAW 240
2 The Life Cycle Approach 243
3 English Definition 247
II Meaning 249
1 Girls in Article 10(f) 250
2 Child Marriage: Article 16(2) 251
III Significance 252
IV Semioethics: Recommended Definition 256

**Conclusion** 258

*Bibliography* 261

I *International Treaties* 261
II *United Nations Documents* 262
III *Cases* 265
IV *Dictionaries* 265
V *Secondary Sources* 266
*Index* 285

# Preface

During my law studies at McGill University and King's College London, and while working as Child Rights Specialist-Project Officer at the UNICEF Office of Research and collaborating with the UN Committee on the Rights of the Child and the Office of the United Nations High Commissioner for Human Rights, as well as while serving in the Prosecutor's Office, Prosecution Division at the International Criminal Court, I observed that international as well as domestic institutions tended to examine children and women as homogenous groups, and noted the absence of a comprehensive study on the girl child under international law. This led me to publish an article on restorative justice and the girl child (2006), explore the status of the girl child in a PhD in Law at the University of Oxford (2016), co-found a Girls Studies Research Network (2019), write the monograph *Feminicides of Girl Children* (Brill 2018), and secure research grants, organize panels and international conferences as well as edit books on topics such as *The Sexual Exploitation of Girl Performers* (2020), *Girls' Studies: The State of the Art* (2021) and *Girls' Positionalities at the Intersection of Identity and Violence* (2023, 2025). Yet, as noted by Sohoni,

> as a woman, I, like millions of women, have been an unresolved subject of this inquiry. The girl in every woman precedes and shapes the woman in her ... My inroad into the status of girls thus began not with recent consultancies but with my girlhood.[1]

The present inquiry therefore also stems from my own girlhood and events experienced and witnessed firsthand, being raised in a family environment that incorporates both the Global South and the Global North – Brazil and

[1] Neera Kuckreja Sohoni, *Burden of Girlhood: A Global Inquiry into the Status of Girls* (Third Party Publishing Company 1995), vii.

Québec – and their respective rich traditions, beliefs and customs, and studying in varied educational systems and communities, which led me to explore the status of girls globally. The present book is up to date as concerns new publications in the field, UN treaty body general comments and recommendations, UN General Assembly Resolutions and UN Special Rapporteur reports as of autumn 2023.

# Acknowledgements

I would like to thank Jonathan Herring, who supervised my DPhil in Law on the girl child at the University of Oxford, for insightful mentorship and guidance, and his inspiring new paradigm on Vulnerability and the Law. Victoria Welby's Meaning Triad and Ponzio and Petrilli's 'semioethics' theory provided valuable frameworks to deconstruct the prevalent legal discourse and offer recommendations to empower the girl child. In the field of semiotics, I wish to thank Jamin Pelkey, Anne Wagner and José Manuel Aroso Linhares for thought-provoking conferences, roundtables and semiotic circle(s). I am indebted to significant research on girls and women by Ladan Askari, Neera Kuckreja Sohoni, Chiseche Salome Mibenge, Savitri Goonesekere, and UN Special Rapporteurs on violence against women Radhika Coomaraswamy, Rashida Manjoo and Yakin Ertürk. Thank you to my fellow Girls' Studies Research Network co-founders Deanne Williams, Desirée de Jesus, Anuppiriya Sriskandarajah, Natalie Coulter and Kisha McPherson, as well as scholars, colleagues and students in Canada, China and the United Kingdom for inspiring discussions. Special thanks to the Clara Thomas Archives and Special Collections team for their support while I consulted the Victoria Welby archives *in loco* at York University (Toronto), and Jim Dobson, Hostel Supervisor, for making my family feel so welcome during the years we lived at Exeter House, University of Oxford. Moreover, I wish to thank the Canadian Social Sciences and Humanities Research Council-SSHRC Insight Development Grant, the SSHRC Explore Grant and the Glendon Research Grant for funding my research on girls in the entertainment industry. I am very grateful to Marianne Nield, Tom Randall and Biju Singh at Cambridge University Press, for their helpful support and advice, as well as the anonymous peer reviewers at Cambridge University

Press for their valuable feedback. Lastly, I would like to thank my husband and our family for inspiration and support, my parents for instilling in me a desire for the pursuit of truth and meaning, and my late grandparents Georgina Debiagi and Francisco Feliciati, Porto Alegre, Rio Grande do Sul, Brazil.

# Meaning Glossary

The semiotic approach adopted in this book underscores that the words employed to describe the girl child and her experiences have *Meaning* and significantly impact her status internationally. Hence, before delving into our examination of the girl child, it appears pertinent to define the terminology used in this book, notably as concerns human rights violations that are either *specific to* or *predominantly* experienced by girl children. In *Grains of Sense*, Lady Victoria Welby notes the importance of glossaries to clarify the sense of terms in all literature:

> The day will surely come when every serious work will begin with a glossary of the sense or senses in which the pivot words used, the words on which the author's thought turns, are to be taken ... If a writer were expected as a matter of course to begin by telling us how he means to use his leading terms ... he could then be criticized from the point of view of comparative significance: we could ask, has he increased or diminished the expressive power of language?[1]

As recommended by Welby, our glossary thus appears before, rather than after, the book chapters. Moreover, the present section does not constitute a typical glossary but rather a 'Meaning Glossary' for in line with the semiotic approach adopted in this book, we shall also explain the *Meaning-intention* behind our selection of certain expressions over others, and incorporate scholars' conflicting views on the validity of those expressions.[2] It is hoped that this introductory semiotic study shall increase the expressive power of language in relation to the girl child, her identity and experience in the subsequent chapters.

1 Victoria Welby, *Grains of Sense* (J. M. Dent & Co 1897), 43–44.

2 The full reference of the sources cited will be provided starting from the Introduction, except for sources cited exclusively in this Meaning Glossary.

## I GIRL CHILD

The semiotic road to the definition of the girl child in international law constitutes a journey that culminates in 1) Chapters 2, 3, 4 and 5 on the status of the girl child, 2) Chapter 6 on the beginning of girlhood and 3) Chapters 7 and 8 on the end of girlhood. This book also distinguishes between the definition of the girl child in the English language and international law. The core definition of the girl child is shaped by her sex and age: she is a female and a child, that is, *a female child*. Femalehood is defined as a hybrid natural and social term. It comprises both 1) biological traits that are *unique to* and *impact* the rights of girls specifically, and 2) the social construct of females in society. For this reason, the present book refers to the biological female child, that is, a child born female, as the latter has biological traits that are unique, such as being born with female external genitalia (vulva), having a menstrual cycle, and the possibility of becoming pregnant and giving birth,[3] which make her more vulnerable to certain violations than boys (children born male), and for which she is expressly targeted, such as female infanticide, female genital mutilation, forced marriage and pregnancy, and restrictive social codes, as shall be discussed in Chapters 2, 3 and 4. Accordingly, the situation of intersex children, and persons born male who self-identify as girls, and/or partly or fully attempt to transition or undergo gender reassignment surgeries, as well as non-binary individuals, which deserves special attention and should be specifically explored,[4] is outside the purview of this book. The twin pillars of the girl child's identity are thereby femalehood and childhood; the meaning of these two semiotic signs and their impact on the identity of the girl child globally shall be examined in this book.

3 Jonathan Law and Elizabeth Martin, *Oxford Concise Medical Dictionary* (Oxford University Press 2020). For a discussion on femalehood, see Chapter 2.

4 See, for example, Jameson Garland and Santa Slokenberga, 'Protecting the Rights of Children with Intersex Conditions from Nonconsensual Gender-Conforming Medical Interventions: The View from Europe' (2019) 27 *Medical Law Review* 482; Morgan Carpenter, 'The "Normalization" of Intersex Bodies and "Othering" of Intersex Identities in Australia' (2018) 15 *Journal of Bioethical Inquiry* 487; Laetitia Zeeman and Kay Aranda, 'A Systematic Review of the Health and Healthcare Inequalities for People with Intersex Variance' (2020) 17 *International Journal Environmental Research and Public Health* 6533; Brooks Bull et al., 'Parents of Non-Binary Children: Stories of Understanding and Support' (2022) 34 *Journal of Feminist Family Therapy* 125; Alexander Kon, 'Transgender Children and Adolescents' (2014) 14 *American Journal of Bioethics* 48; Lemma, *Transgender Identities* (2021).

## II SON PREFERENCE AND DAUGHTER DEVALUATION

Son preference is defined by Special Rapporteur on Violence against Women (SRVAW) Coomaraswamy as 'the preference of parents for male children [which] manifests itself in neglect, deprivation or discriminatory treatment of girls to the detriment of their physical and mental health'.[5] The UNFPA identifies the main causes of son preference, such as 1) patrilineal households and transmission of the family name; sexist inheritance rules and land rights; patrilocal marriages, which signify that sons remain with parents, support them, and run the family business whereas daughters move into their family-in-law's home; 2) unequal marriage payments, for instance, the requirement to pay for wedding expenses and offer a dowry; 3) divorce rights; and 4) religious and traditional practices whereby only male descendants can perform rituals during the funerals of parents or ceremonies for their ancestors.[6] In this context, the birth of the girl child is viewed as a burden rather than a blessing. Gill and Mitra-Kahn explain that son preference is inextricably linked to daughter devaluation:

> [A] preference for sons *simpliciter* cannot explain the discrepancy between the actual and natural male to female ratios ... Son preference can explain missing women only when it exists alongside two further factors: daughter devaluation and a desire to intervene to avoid having daughters.[7]

They further explain that daughter devaluation comprises differential treatment once the girl child is born and throughout childhood.[8] Diamond-Smith et al. refer instead to 'daughter avoidance'.[9] The expression 'devaluation' is, however, broader as it encapsulates practices whereby girls are less cared for during their childhood as concerns food, health and education, and not solely 'avoided' through practices such as prenatal sex selection and female infanticide. Furthermore, 'daughter devaluation' best describes the broader gender-based discrimination experienced by girls in the private sphere, as described by Sohoni: '[r]earing and socialization processes flatter and reinforce the male child's self-worth and status, while consigning the girl to

5 'Cultural Practices' (2002), para. 70.

6 'Sex Imbalances' (2012), 38–39, 41, 66.

7 Aisha Gill and Trishima Mitra-Kahn, 'Explaining Daughter Devaluation and the Issue of Missing Women in South Asia and the UK' (2009) 57 *Current Sociology* 684, 686.

8 Ibid., 686.

9 Nadia Diamond-Smith et al., 'Too Many Girls, Too Much Dowry': Son Preference and Daughter Aversion in Rural Tamil Nadu, India' (2008) 10 *Culture, Health and Sexuality* 697, 706.

a confining or even a negative self-image'.[10] This book thus defines son preference and daughter devaluation as 'the neglect, deprivation or discriminatory treatment of girls to the detriment of their physical and mental health embedded in a set of sexist norms that place greater value on boys than girls, and patriarchal laws and customs leading families to rely on boys, rather than girls, for economic, religious and socio-cultural purposes'.

## III FEMINICIDE

The term 'feminicide' refers to the killings of girl children and women underpinned by misogyny and sexism. In this regard, it is distinct from the concept of homicide, which is gender-neutral.[11] The OED comprises both the terms 'femicide' and 'feminicide', although it solely defines the former, in broad terms, as 'the killing of a woman or girl' while noting that '[i]n late use often applied specifically to the misogynistic killing of a woman or women by a man'. The expression 'gendercide' is also employed to refer to a 'deliberate extermination of persons of a particular sex [or gender]'.[12] The CEDAW Committee refers to both 'femicide' and 'feminicide' as 'gender based killings of women',[13] while the Human Rights Committee only mentions 'femicide', defined as 'an extreme form of gender-based violence that is directed against girls and women'.[14] Scholars have used both the expressions 'feminicide' and 'femicide', the latter introduced by Russell at the International Tribunal on Crimes Against Women in Brussels (1976) and defined firstly as 'the murder of women by men motivated by hatred, contempt, pleasure, or a sense of ownership of women',[15] then as the misogynist killing of women by men,[16]

[10] *Burden Girlhood* (1995), 7.

[11] Rashida Manjoo, SRVAW, 'Gender-related Killings' (23 May 2012) UN Doc A/HRC/20/16, paras. 20–28.

[12] Mary Ann Warren, *Gendercide: The Implications of Sex Selection* (Rowman and Allanfield 1985), 22.

[13] CEDAW General Recommendation No. 35: 'Gender-based Violence' (2017), para. 34.

[14] ICCPR General Comment No. 36: Article 6 '(Right to Life)' (3 September 2019) UN Doc CCPR/C/GC/36, para. 61. Other treaty bodies, such as the CRC, CESCR, CRPD and CERD do not employ these expressions.

[15] Jane Caputi and Diana Russell, 'Femicide: Speaking the Unspeakable' (1990) 1 *Ms: The World of Women* 34–37, 34. For a discussion on the origins of the terms femicide and feminicide, see Myrna Dawson and Saide Mobayed Vega, 'Femicide and Feminicide: A Growing Global Human Rights Movement' in Myrna Dawson and Saide Mobayed Vega (eds.), *The Routledge International Handbook on Femicide and Feminicide* (Routledge 2023).

[16] Jill Radford and Diana Russell (eds.), *Femicide: The Politics of Woman Killing* (Twayne 1992), 3.

and finally as the killing of females by males because they are female.[17] Latin-American scholars prefer the expression 'feminicide', introduced by Lagarde, which comes from the Latin 'feminicidio', as the meaning of 'femicidio' in Spanish is broader and encompasses all homicides of women.[18] Latin-American scholars employ the term 'feminicide' to refer to the murders of women facilitated by State action or omission, notably a legal system that fails to identify, investigate, prosecute and sentence those responsible.[19] As noted by SRVAW Manjoo:

> It is argued that the term feminicide could be usefully adopted when holding governments to account at the international level, as it highlights the impunity and the institutional violence aspect of such crimes ... Institutional violence against women and their families is present in all aspects of States' responses to the killings of women. This can include: tolerance, the blaming of victims, lack of access to justice and effective remedies, negligence, threats, corruption and abuse by officials.[20]

This book thus employs the expression 'feminicide' rather than 'femicide' to underscore States parties' duty of due diligence to undertake all measures to protect girl children.[21]

## IV FEMALE INFANTICIDE

The OED describes infanticide as 'the crime of murdering an infant after its birth, perpetrated by or with the consent of its parents, esp. the mother', and

[17] Diana Russell, 'Defining Femicide and Related Concepts' in Diana Russell and Roberta Harmes (eds.), *Femicide in Global Perspective* (Teachers College Press 2001), 3.

[18] Marcela Lagarde, 'Una feminista contra el feminicidio' (2005) 278 *Revista Envio* 1; Marcela Lagarde, 'Introducción: Por la vida y la libertad de las mujeres. Fin al feminicidio' (Introduction: For the Life and Freedom of Women: End Feminicide) in Diana Russell and Roberta Harmes (eds.), *Feminicidio: Una perspectiva global* (*Femicide in Global Perspective*, Spanish Edition 2006); Manjoo, 'Gender-related Killings' (2012), para. 25; Julia Monárrez, 'Morir por ser mujeres, Femicidio/Feminicidio. La violencia máxima' (Murdered Because We are Women, Femicide/Feminicide. The Extreme Violence) (2008) 4 *Revista Mujer Salud* (Journal of Women's Health) 27. The OED notes the origin of the term feminicide as 'A borrowing from Latin, combined with an English element. Feminicide comes from the classical Latin femina (woman)'.

[19] As in the case of the murders of women in the city of Juárez, Mexico. See Victoria Sanford, 'From Genocide to Feminicide: Impunity and Human Rights in Twenty-First Century Guatemala' (2008) 7 *Journal of Human Rights* 104, 112; Cecilia Menjívar and Shannon Drysdale Walsh, 'The Architecture of Feminicide: The State, Inequalities, and Everyday Gender Violence in Honduras' (2017) 52 *Latin American Research Review* 221, 222.

[20] 'Gender-related Killings' (2012), para. 28.

[21] See Chapdelaine-Feliciati, *Feminicides Girl Children* (2018).

the Webster as 'the killing of an infant', yet both fail to specifically define 'female infanticide'.[22] The CRC Committee notes that children may be victims of infanticide, and the CRC and CEDAW Committees joint General Recommendation-Comment identifies 'infanticide' as a harmful practice,[23] as does the CRPD Committee under the section on girls with disabilities,[24] yet solely the Human Rights Committee expressly refers to 'female infanticide', and none of these committees define 'female infanticide' and 'infanticide'.[25] Muthulakshmi argues that '[t]hough there is no proper definition of female infanticide one can say that female infanticide is the practice of killing the female baby immediately after birth'.[26] Tandon and Sharma provide the following definition:

> [A] deliberate and intentional act of killing a female child within one year of its birth either directly by using poisonous organic and inorganic chemicals or indirectly by deliberate neglect to feed the infant by either one of the parents or other family members or neighbours or by the midwife.[27]

This book adopts Tandon and Sharma's definition of female infanticide as the 'intentional act of killing a female child within one year of its birth' for it encompasses all forms of murders of girl children that occur within one year of their lives and is thereby broader than the former which solely refers to the murder of the infant girl immediately after birth. Moreover, Tandon and Sharma's definition underscores the intentional aspect of female infanticide, stating that it is 'a deliberate and intentional act'.[28]

## V PRENATAL SEX SELECTION

It is noteworthy that while prenatal sex selection is widespread worldwide, this practice is not defined in the OED and the Webster. Moreover, the

[22] The OED nonetheless refers to the concept of female infanticide in a quote 'made daughters a source of weakness to the tribe, and accordingly female infanticide was largely practised' (1897, Westminster Review June 290).
[23] CRC General Comment No. 7: 'Early Childhood' (2006), para. 11; Joint CEDAW-CRC GenRec/Com: 'Harmful Practices' (2014), para. 9.
[24] CRPD General Comment No. 3 'Women and Girls with Disabilities' (25 November 2016) UN Doc CRPD/C/GC/3, para. 36.
[25] ICCPR General Comment No. 28: 'Equality between Men and Women' (2000), para. 10; also refers to 'infanticide': General Comment No. 36: Right to Life (2019), para. 20. The CERD and CESCR general comments refer neither to infanticide nor female infanticide.
[26] R Muthulakshmi, *Female Infanticide: Its Causes and Solutions* (Discovery Publishing House 1997), 20.
[27] 'Female Foeticide' (2006), 3.
[28] For a discussion on female infanticide, see Chapdelaine-Feliciati, 'Gendercide CRC' (2018).

definitions of the expressions 'prenatal', 'sex', and 'selection' do not mention the issue of prenatal sex selection, which implies that this phenomenon is not as yet fully recognized in these two major English dictionaries. The issue of prenatal sex selection is also not mentioned under the definitions of sexism and discrimination.[29] The Collins Dictionary however describes it as 'a practice of attempting to control the sex of a baby in order to achieve a desired sex, through various scientific methods',[30] yet it does not refer to a specific sex in this context, even though the vast majority of selective abortions are performed on female fœtuses.[31] The CRC Committee denounces the 'discriminatory elimination of girls before birth' without employing the expression prenatal sex selection,[32] while the Human Rights Committee expressly refers to prenatal sex selection, yet does not offer a definition.[33] Although other procedures can ensure the birth of the desired male sex – such as pre-implantation methods: sperm sorting (first, sort the sperm, and then, use it in artificial insemination or IVF procedures) and pre-implantation genetic diagnosis (IVF embryos genetically tested for sex and then implanted) – these are not accessible, due to costs and legal prohibition, to the majority of the global population.[34] This book thus focuses on prenatal sex selection perpetrated on the fœtus. In this context, prenatal sex selection comprises three elements: 1) sex diagnosis; 2) followed by abortion; 3) the fact that both occur, respectively, to *determine* if the fœtus is female and if so, to ensure *elimination* before birth. Inspired by the Collins definition and current medical procedures, this book defines the expression prenatal sex selection as 'the practice of attempting to identify if the fœtus is female, through various scientific methods, and to eliminate the latter through gender-related abortion, solely because of its sex'.

## VI FEMALE GENITAL MUTILATION

Female genital mutilation (FGM) refers to procedures involving partial or total removal of the female external genitalia or other injury to the female

[29] OED; Webster.

[30] Collins Dictionary.

[31] See Chapter 6.

[32] CRC General Comment No. 13: 'Violence' (2011), para. 16.

[33] General Comment No. 28: 'Equality between Men and Women' (2000), para. 5. The HR Committee refers to 'the high incidence of prenatal sex selection and abortion of female foetuses'. The CEDAW, CESCR, CERD and CRPD do not refer to this practice.

[34] For a description of procedures such as ultrasonography and fœtal blood analysis, see, for example, 'Sex Imbalances' (2012), 37.

genital organs for non-medical reasons.[35] It covers four categories: type I is the partial or total removal of the clitoral glans (clitoridectomy) and/or the prepuce; Type II is the partial or total removal of the clitoral glans and the labia minora, with or without excision of the labia majora (excision); Type III is the narrowing of the vaginal opening with the creation of a covering seal by cutting and appositioning the labia minora or labia majora with or without excision of the clitoral prepuce and glans (infibulation); Type IV encompasses all other harmful procedures performed on the female genitalia for non-medical purposes, for example, pricking, piercing, incising, scraping and cauterization.[36] The terminology employed to describe the practice of FGM is controversial. The earliest studies examined the ritual aspect of FGM from an anthropological perspective and employed the expression 'female circumcision'.[37] However, in the 1970s, feminist movements, stakeholders and institutions such as the Inter-African Committee on Traditional Practices pushed for the use of 'female genital mutilation-FGM' to underscore its harmful health effects and adopt a human rights perspective.[38] The international community thereafter employed 'FGM', including in the Declaration on the Elimination of Violence Against Women (1993)[39] and the Beijing Declaration (1995).[40] Presently, academics and UN agencies have differing views on the terminology. On the one hand, some academics contend that the term 'mutilation' is ethnocentric, for its failure to cover western cosmetic procedures such as labiaplasty, as well as stigmatizing and judgmental, thereby possibly re-traumatizing girls who underwent this practice and alienating communities.[41] Accordingly, they favour the expression 'female genital cutting-FGC'. UN agencies tend to use FGM and FGC interchangeably, or

35 UNFPA-UNICEF Joint Programme on the elimination of female genital mutilation: Accelerating Change, 'Measuring Effectiveness of Female Genital Mutilation Elimination: A Compendium of Indicators' (2020), 7.

36 WHO, 'FGM Clinical Handbook' (2018), 26–32.

37 Armelle Andro and Marie Lesclingand, 'Female Genital Mutilation. Overview and Current Knowledge' (2016) 71 *Population* 217, 217–24.

38 Ibid.; 28 Too Many, 'Terminology and FGM'. www.28toomany.org/thematic/terminology-and-fgm/ (accessed 13 March 2023).

39 Art. 2(a).

40 Paras. 39, 93, 107, 113, 124, 232, 259, 277, 283.

41 Lourdes Peroni, 'Violence against Migrant Women: The Istanbul Convention Through a Postcolonial Feminist Lens' (2016) 24 *Feminist Legal Studies* 49, 52: 'FGM represents the "poster child" for forms designated as harmful to women … equally intrusive female genital aesthetic surgeries, on the other hand, have not received comparable attention'; Brian Earp and Sara Johnsdotter, 'Current Critiques of the WHO Policy on Female Genital Mutilation' (2021) 33 *International Journal of Impotence Research: Your Sexual Medicine Journal* 196; Rosie Duivenbode and Aasim I Padela, 'Female Genital Cutting (FGC) and the Cultural Boundaries of Medical Practice' (2019) 19 *American Journal of Bioethics* 3.

combined as 'FGM/C', including within the same publication, often without providing a rationale for use, preference or differentiation.[42] On the other hand, several stakeholders and researchers from the Global South, including the Inter-African Committee on Traditional Practices (IAC), have argued that the adoption of expressions such as FGC by certain UN agencies emerged from lobby groups largely based in the Global North, and that it trivializes the severity of FGM and its consequences on girls and women. The IAC *Declaration on the Terminology FGM* states the following:

> An issue of concern at the 6th General Assembly ... has been attempts to dilute the terminology Female Genital Mutilation (FGM) and replace it with the following: "Female Circumcision," "Female Genital Alteration," "Female Genital Excision," "Female Genital Surgery," and more recently "Female Genital Cutting" (FGC). ... Female Genital Cutting (FGC) does not reflect the accurate extent of harm and mutilation caused by all types of FGM. This terminology has been adopted by some UN specialized agencies and bi-lateral donors ... influenced by specific lobby groups largely based in western countries ... These changes trivialize the nature of female genital mutilation and the suffering of African women and girls ... [and] ... made without consultation, [they] override the consensus reached by African women in the front line of the campaign as well as the ... millions of African girls and women who suffer in silence.[43]

Indeed, the verb 'cut' is defined in the English language as making 'an incision in or into', whereas mutilation refers to 'the severing or maiming of a limb or bodily organ', implying a more severe procedure.[44] Between 2007 and 2014, the UNFPA employed the hybrid terminology FGM/C on the grounds that it was less judgmental towards practising communities; however, it has now revisited its position and formally adopted the term FGM, noting that 'more than ever, we are at a time when the practice must be viewed from a human rights perspective and the term "mutilation" better

[42] For example, UNESCO, Plan International, and French Ministry, 'Beijing + 25: Generation Equality begins with Adolescent Girls' Education' (2020); UNDP, 'Making the Law Work for Women and Girls in the Context of HIV' (2020); WHO, 'Guidelines on the Management of Health Complications from Female Genital Mutilation' (2018); UN Women, 'Female Genital Mutilation/Cutting and Violence against Women and Girls: Strengthening the Policy Between Different Forms of Violence' (2017).

[43] Inter-African Committee, 'Declaration: On the Terminology FGM', 6th IAC General Assembly, 4–7 April 2005, Bamako, Mali' (6 April 2005).

[44] OED. It is worthy of note that the OED refers to 'mutilation', offering the following quote: 'about 25 countries in Africa engage in mutilation: an estimated 98% of women are "circumcised" in Djibouti and Somalia' (*Time*, 21 March 1994, 45/3).

describes the practice ... both in terms of the process and the outcome'.[45] UN treaty bodies have overwhelmingly adopted the expression FGM. The Human Rights Committee, CESCR and CRPD exclusively employ FGM in their general comments.[46] The CEDAW Committee initially referred to 'female circumcision' in 1990,[47] then employed 'female circumcision or genital mutilation' in 1992,[48] and since 1999, refers systematically to 'female genital mutilation'.[49] The CRC Committee's general comments also exclusively employ 'female genital mutilation'.[50] The exception is the CEDAW-CRC joint recommendation-comment that employs all three expressions – FGM, FC and FGC in one paragraph; however, it specifies that 'In the context of the present joint general recommendation/general comment [this practice] is referred to as female genital mutilation',[51] and moreover systematically uses the expression 'female genital mutilation' before and after this paragraph, which implies a preference for FGM.[52] All the CRC general comments and CEDAW recommendations adopted thereafter, that is, since 2014, exclusively employ FGM. The term FGM is currently enshrined in regional instruments such as the Protocol to the African Charter on Human and People's Rights on the Rights of Women in Africa,[53] the UN International Day of Zero Tolerance for FGM,[54] the UN Secretary General report for the elimination

45 UNFPA, 'Implementation of the International and Regional Human Rights Framework for the Elimination of Female Genital Mutilation' (2014), 12.

46 ICCPR General Comment No. 28: 'Equality between Men and Women' (2000), para. 11; CESCR General Comments No. 14: 'Health' (2000), paras. 22, 35; No. 16: 'Equal Rights Men and Women (2005), para. 29; No. 21: 'Right of Everyone to Take Part in Cultural Life' (21 December 2009) UN Doc E/C.12/GC/21, para. 64; No. 22: 'Reproductive Health' (2016), para. 29, 49, 59; CRPD General Comment No. 3: 'Women and Girls' (2016), paras. 10, 32, 37, 44.

47 CEDAW General Recommendation No. 14: 'Female Circumcision' (1990).

48 CEDAW General Recommendation No. 19: 'Violence against Women (1992), para. 20.

49 CEDAW General Recommendations: 1) No. 24: 'Women and Health' (1999), paras. 12,15, 18; 2) No. 32: 'Refugee Women' (2014), paras. 15, 26; 3) No. 34: 'Rural Women' (2016), paras. 22, 23; 4) No. 36: 'Education' (2017), paras. 53, 55; 5) No. 39: 'Indigenous Women and Girls' (2022), para. 37.

50 CRC General Comments: 1) No. 4: 'Adolescent Health' (2003), paras. 10, 24, 39; 2) No. 6: 'Unaccompanied Children' (2005), para. 74; 3) No. 7: 'Early Childhood' (2006), para. 11; 4) No. 11: 'Indigenous Children' (2009), para. 22; 5) No. 12: 'Right to be Heard' (2009), para. 120; 6) No. 13: 'Violence' (2011), para. 29; 7) No. 20: 'Adolescence' (2016), para. 27; 8) No. 21: 'Street Situations' (2017), para. 8.

51 Joint CEDAW-CRC GenRec/Com: 'Harmful Practices' (2014), para. 19.

52 Ibid., paras. 7, 57, 73, 82, 83.

53 (2003), art. 5: Elimination of Harmful Practices.

54 UN International Day of Zero Tolerance for FGM. www.un.org/en/observances/female-genital-mutilation-day (accessed 12 July 2023).

of female genital mutilations,[55] the UNGA resolution on discrimination against women and girls (2022),[56] and all UNGA Resolutions on the Girl Child.[57]

Overall, Lewis emphasizes that '[a]ppropriate terminology depends on context'.[58] Since the present book focuses on the language of rights and international treaties, we select the expression FGM in line with UN treaty bodies and several UN institutions, scholars and experts from the Global South and North.[59] Moreover, rather than employing weaker terminology – such as FGC – to avoid selective culturalization of harmful cultural practices in the Global South, this book aims to underscore the severity of *all* forms of FGM, including those originating in the Global North, such as labiaplasty and non-consensual intersex genital

55 UN General Assembly, Report of the Secretary General: 'Intensifying Global Efforts for the Elimination of Female Genital Mutilations' (26 July 2016) UN Doc A/71/209.

56 UNGA Resolution 'Elimination of All Forms of Discrimination against Women and Girls' (29 July 2022) UN Doc A/HRC/RES/50/18, preamble.

57 See, for example, Resolution 'The Girl Child' (6 January 2022) UN Doc A/RES/76/146 that employs exclusively the expression FGM: preamble, paras. 8, 30.

58 Hope Lewis, 'Female Genital Mutilation and Female Genital Cutting' (*Oxford University Press Encyclopedia of Human Rights* 2009), 203.

59 See, for example, OHCHR, 'Report: Good Practices and Major Challenges in Preventing and Eliminating Female Genital Mutilation' (27 March 2015) UN DOC A/HRC/29/20; Onyeka Okongwu, 'Are Laws the Appropriate Solution: The Need to Adopt Non-Policy Measures in Aid of the Implementation of Sex Discrimination Laws in Nigeria' (2021) 21 *International Journal of Discrimination and the Law* 26; Simon Tabe Tabe, 'Traditional Law and Discriminatory Customary Practices against Women in Cameroon: A Critical Perspective' (2020) 28 *African Journal of International and Comparative Law* 418; Taylor, *Commentary ICCPR* (2020); Leyla-Denisa Obreja, 'Intimate Partner Violence in Childhood: Human Rights Implications in Multiple Exposure Scenarios' (2019) 27 *International Journal of Children's Rights* 99; Samantha Besson and Eleonor Kleber, 'Non-Discrimination' (2019); Eric Heinze, 'The Myth of Flexible Universality: Human Rights and the Limits of Comparative Naturalism' (2019) 39 *Oxford Journal of Legal Studies* 624; Solomon Tekle Abegaz, 'The Influence of Human Rights Instruments on Children's Rights Jurisprudence: An Appraisal of the Ethiopian Federal Cassation Court' (2016) 30 *International Journal of Law, Policy and the Family* 197; Adeyemo Olaitan and Bamidele Ifeoluwayimika, 'The Menace of Domestic Violence: Improving the Lives of Women in Nigeria' (2016) 9 *African Journal of Legal Studies* 177; Sandra Fredman, 'Women and Poverty – A Human Rights Approach' (2016) 24 *African Journal of International and Comparative Law* 494; Goonesekere, 'HRs for Girls' (2014); Ertürk and Purkayastha, 'Linking Research' (2012); Jamil Ddamulira Mujuzi, 'Female Genital Mutilation in Uganda: A Glimpse at the Abolition Process' (2012) 56 *Journal of African Law* 139; Freeman et al., *Commentary CEDAW* (2012); Chi Mgbako et al., 'Penetrating the Silence in Sierra Leone: A Blueprint for the Eradication of Female Genital Mutilation' (2010) 23 *Harvard Human Rights Journal* 111; Niraj Nathwani, 'Islamic Headscarves and Human Rights: A Critical Analysis of the Relevant Case Law of the European Court of Human Rights' (2007) 25 *Netherlands Quarterly of Human Rights* 221.

mutilation,[60] and clitoridectomy procedures previously perpetrated in Europe and North America to 'cure female masturbation and hysteria'.[61] The use of the expression FGM in this book is in no way intended to stigmatize girls; rather, it aims to underscore the strength of survivors who underwent various forms of this practice and are advocating for its eradication. As for the concern that the expression FGM may alienate practising communities, it is acknowledged that stakeholders may wish to adopt other terminology in different contexts and programs. This book employs the term FGM to recognize the physical, mental, emotional and sexual impacts on girl children, in light of the UNFPA-UNICEF observation that it 'more accurately describes the practice from a human rights viewpoint'.[62]

## VII CHILD MARRIAGE

This book employs the expression 'child marriage' as defined by the CEDAW and CRC Committees: 'any marriage where at least one of the parties is under 18 years of age'.[63] Some international institutions, scholars and civil rights organizations employ child marriage interchangeably with early marriage.[64] The CRC and CEDAW Committees define 'child marriage' as a synonym to 'early marriage', and underscore that it constitutes a form of forced marriage, although the Committees allow for exceptions in the case of children aged 16 years and over who obtain approval by a Court:

> *Child marriage, also referred to as early marriage, is any marriage where at least one of the parties is under 18 years of age.* The overwhelming majority of child marriages, both formal and informal, involve girls, although at times their spouses are also under 18 years of age. A child marriage is considered to be a form of forced marriage, given that one and/or both parties have not expressed full, free and informed consent. As a matter of respecting the child's evolving capacities and autonomy in making decisions that affect her or his life, a marriage of a mature, capable child below 18 years of age may be allowed in exceptional circumstances, provided that the child is at

[60] Dianne Otto, 'Lost in Translation: Re-Scripting the Sexed Subjects of International Human Rights Law' in Anne Orford (ed.), *International Law and its others* (Cambridge University Press 2006), 318–356; Runacres and Wood, 'Cosmetic Labiaplasty' (2016); Drolet and Drolet, 'Rise Labiaplasty' (2019).

[61] First performed by British doctor Isaac Baker Brown in the 19th century, yet still practised in the USA into the 1960s: see Andro and Lesclingand, 'FGM' (2016), 220.

[62] 'FGM Elimination' (2020), 83.

[63] Joint CEDAW-CRC GenRec/Com: 'Harmful Practices' (2014), para. 20.

[64] UNFPA, 'Child Marriage in Kosovo' (2012), 1.

> least 16 years of age and that such decisions are made by a judge based on legitimate exceptional grounds defined by law and on the evidence of maturity, without deference to culture and tradition.[65]

UNICEF refers to child marriage as 'a legal or customary union between two people of whom one or both spouses is below the age of 18',[66] and the World Bank as 'a formal or informal union before the age of 18'.[67] Other terms, such as 'betrothal' or 'betrothal of a child', describe the union of child marriage; it is the act of promising a child's hand in marriage, or engagement for the ultimate intention of marriage.[68] The CEDAW under article 16(2) stipulates that the betrothal and the marriage of a child 'shall have no legal effect' and 'all necessary action, including legislation, shall be taken to specify a minimum age for marriage and to make the registration of marriages in an official registry compulsory'.

According to certain scholars, however, the expressions 'child marriage' and 'early marriage' differ slightly; while victims of early marriage may be under the age of 18, some argue that during the ages 15–17, girls are no longer considered children in some societies, and thus cannot be deemed child brides.[69] As shall be examined in Chapter 7, this book considers that girls should be covered under the umbrella of childhood until 18 years, and employs the expression child marriage, rather than early marriage, to refer to any marriage before the girl reaches her 18th birthday.

## VIII FORCED MARRIAGE

Forced marriage is a marriage in which one or two of the spouses are coerced or strongly pressured into entering a marital agreement. As stated in the Universal Declaration of Human Rights (UDHR), a consensual marriage refers to a marital union in which the 'free and full consent of the intending spouses' is present.[70] The UDHR stipulates that men and women must be 'of full age' to have the right to marry and offer their full consent.[71] A forced marriage is thus a marriage in which this consent from both parties is absent.

[65] Joint CEDAW-CRC GenRec/Com: 'Harmful Practices' (2014), para. 20 (emphasis added).
[66] UNICEF, 'Programme Brief: Child Marriage' (2012), 1.
[67] World Bank, 'Ending Child Marriage: Child Marriage Laws and Their Limitations' (2017), 1.
[68] South African Development Committee, 'Model Law on Eradicating Child Marriage and Protecting Children Already in Marriage' (2016), 8.
[69] Laura Stark, 'Early Marriage and Cultural Constructions of Adulthood in Two Slums in Dar es Salaam' (2018) 20 *Culture, Health, and Sexuality* 888, 889.
[70] UDHR, art. 16(2).
[71] Ibid., art. 16(1)(2).

Moreover, it must be noted that because children are not 'of full age', as stated in the UDHR, they cannot provide full and free consent. In many cases, child brides are not given a choice as to who they marry, and when they will marry.[72] As noted by Freeman et al., the girl child 'may be threatened with force, including death, or exile from the family if she attempts to refuse and may indeed be killed if she does so'.[73] This book thus employs the following definition of forced marriage, as stated by the CRC and CEDAW Committees:

> Forced marriages are marriages in which one and/or both parties *have not personally expressed their full and free consent to the union*. They may be manifested in various forms, including child marriage, . . . exchange or trade-off marriages [i.e. baad and baadal], servile marriages and levirate marriages [coercing a widow to marry a relative of her deceased husband]. In some contexts, a forced marriage may occur when a rapist is permitted to escape criminal sanctions by marrying the victim, usually with the consent of her family . . . Forced marriage may also be defined as a marriage in which one of the parties is not permitted to end or leave it.[74]

Accordingly, while all child marriages are deemed forced marriages,[75] not all forced marriages are child marriages, since adult women can also be pressured into or required to enter such legal arrangements.

## IX RESTRICTIVE SOCIAL AND DRESS CODES

The expression 'restrictive social codes' refers to social codes that restrict the rights of girls and women by subjecting them to the authority of a male guardian, notably concerning activities such as pursuing studies, applying for employment, administering property, opening a bank account, or travelling outside the home, thereby limiting their political, economic and mobility rights.[76] The male guardian is typically the father, husband, brother, uncle or

72 Senem Ertan and Fatma Yol, 'Forced Marriage', in Scott Romaniuk and Péter Marton (eds.), *The Palgrave Encyclopedia of Global Security Studies* (Palgrave MacMillan 2019), 2.

73 *Commentary CEDAW* (2012), 424.

74 Joint CEDAW-CRC GenRec/Com: 'Harmful Practices' (2014), para. 23 (emphasis added).

75 To the exception offered by the Joint CEDAW-CRC GenRec/Com: 'Harmful Practices' (2014), concerning 16-year-olds with approval by a court and according to specific criteria, see definition of 'child marriage' in the glossary.

76 See Chapter 3 for a discussion of the unequal rights of women and girls under domestic law globally; World Bank, 'Women, Business, Law' (2023); Human Rights Watch, 'Everything Tied to Man' (2021); UN Women, 'Women's Rights' (2020); UN Women, 'Families in Changing World' (2020); Minority Rights Group International, 'Beyond the Veil' (2019); UNFPA, 'Kingdom of Saudi Arabia: Gender Justice and the Law' (2019); UN Women,

grandfather, although it can also be the adult son; these rules, laws, policies and practices are underpinned by the notion that men are the heads of households and the legal and social guardians of women.[77] According to restrictive social codes, girl children might also be required to follow strict dress codes and hide their bodies completely or almost completely, although the two requisites are not systematically mutually inclusive.[78] This book thus employs the expression 'restrictive social and dress codes' for codes requiring girl children to follow a series of rules whereby the actions of females are controlled by male family members and/or public authorities, including the obligation to completely cover their bodies against their will. Indeed, the term 'social' refers to the notions of social structure, hence to the 'established set of customs, relationships, institutions', as well as that of social control, notably 'the control of the individual by the social group to which [s/he] belongs' and 'control by government, on behalf of society as a whole, of particular sectors of society'.[79]

## X SEXUALIZED SOCIAL AND DRESS CODES

This book employs the expression 'sexualized social and dress codes' to describe codes promoted by mainstream and social media that over-sexualize and objectify girl children as commodities and foster unhealthy beauty ideals.[80] Sexualized codes are implemented via movies, television series and programs, music, beauty pageants, fashion shows and most recently by influencers on social media, notably on the very popular platforms Instagram and TikTok.[81] While these sexualized codes originated in the Global North, notably through Hollywood, they have permeated most regions of the world with the advent of globalization, including the very successful Bollywood,

'Equality, Law, Women, Girls' (2019); World Bank, 'Ending Violence against Women and Girls' (2018).

77 Human Rights Watch, 'Everything Tied to Man' (2021), 1–2.

78 Koo and Han, 'To Veil or Not to Veil' (2018); Wheeler, 'Saudi Women Driving Change' (2020); La Fornara, 'Dress Code Restrictions' (2018); Coomaraswamy, 'Cultural Practices' (2002), para. 86.

79 OED.

80 See Chapter 4. Gerding, 'Sexualization Girls Magazines' (2018); Ortega, 'Child Models' (2014); Paccione, 'Underage Fashion Models' (2017); Darbyshire, 'Childhood Death' (2007); APA, 'Report Sexualization Girls' (2010); Behm-Morawitz, 'Sext Up KIDS' (2013).

81 Bissonette, 'TikTok Body Dissatisfaction' (2022); Kelly and Garmon, 'Child Beauty Pageants' (2016); Brown and Tiggemann, 'Attractive Images Instagram' (2016); Vandenbosch et al., 'Sexualization Music Entertainment' (2013).

Nollywood and K-pop industries.[82] These codes, combined with peer pressure, can lead girls to 'sculpt' new bodies through various forms of eating disorders and cosmetic plastic surgery, including breast implants, rhinoplasty, buttock enhancement and female genital mutilation such as labiaplasty.[83] Hence, the expression 'sexualized dress codes' encompasses the pressure to change the body *itself*, whereby girl children are compelled to carve inhuman features onto their human bodies.

[82] Jain et al., 'Sexuality Bollywood Movies' (2019); Ghaznavi et al., 'Violent but Sexy Hollywood and Bollywood' (2017); Endong, 'Pornography Objectification Nollywood' (2019); Kaya, 'Rape Prime-Time Television' (2019); Girija and Basavaraja, 'Globalization Beauty' (2019); Kim, 'K-Pop's Girls' Generation' (2017).

[83] Logrieco et al., 'Tik Tok Anti-Pro-Anorexia Videos' (2021); Kleemans et al., 'Instagram Adolescent Girls' (2018); Pilgrim and Bohnet-Joschko, 'Influencers Instagram Dieting' (2019); Wallner et al., 'Female Breast Perception' (2023); Pedalino and Camerini, 'Instagram Body Dissatisfaction' (2022); Maki et al., 'Vulva Appearance Pornography' (2023); Runacres and Wood, 'Cosmetic Labiaplasty' (2016); Drolet and Drolet, 'Rise Labiaplasty' (2019).

# Abbreviations

***International Instruments, UN Treaty Bodies, International and National Agencies***

Beijing Declaration – Beijing Declaration and Platform for Action
Beijing Rules – UN Standard Minimum Rules for the Administration of Juvenile Justice
CEDAW – UN Convention on the Elimination of All Forms of Discrimination Against Women
CEDAW Committee – Committee on the Elimination of Discrimination Against Women – CEDAW Treaty body
CERD – International Convention on the Elimination of All Forms of Racial Discrimination
CRC – UN Convention on the Rights of the Child
CRC Committee – Committee on the Rights of the Child – CRC Treaty body
CRC DGD – CRC Day of General Discussion
CRPD – UN Convention on the Rights of Persons with Disabilities
DEDAW – Declaration on the Elimination of Discrimination Against Women
ECPAT – End Child Prostitution and Trafficking
HDR – Human Development Report
HR Committee – United Nations Human Rights Committee – ICCPR Treaty body
ICC – International Criminal Court
ICCPR – International Covenant on Civil and Political Rights
ICESCR – International Covenant on Economic, Social and Cultural Rights
ICJ – International Court of Justice
ILO – International Labour Organization

ILO Minimum Age Convention – ILO Convention Concerning the Minimum Age for Admission to Employment
Marriage Convention – Convention on Consent to Marriage, Minimum Age for Marriage and Registration of Marriages
OHCHR – Office of the United Nations High Commissioner for Human Rights
OPAC – Optional Protocol to the Convention on the Rights of the Child on the Involvement of Children in Armed Conflict
OPSC – Optional Protocol to the Convention on the Rights of the Child on the Sale of Children, Child Prostitution and Child Pornography
Riyadh Guidelines – UN Guidelines for the Prevention of Juvenile Delinquency
SRCR – UN Special Rapporteur in the Field of Cultural Rights
SRRE – UN Special Rapporteur on the Right to Education
SRRH – UN Special Rapporteur on the Right to Health
SRVAW – UN Special Rapporteur on Violence Against Women, Its Causes and Consequences (until 2022)
SRVAWG – UN Special Rapporteur on Violence Against Women and Girls, Its Causes and Consequences (since 2022)
UDHR – Universal Declaration of Human Rights
UN – United Nations
UNAIDS – Joint UN Programme on HIV/AIDS
UNDP – UN Development Programme
UNESCO – UN Educational, Scientific and Cultural Organization
UNFPA – UN Population Fund
UNGA – UN General Assembly
UNGEI – UN Girls' Education Initiative
UNHCHR – UN High Commissioner for Human Rights
UNICEF – UN Children's Fund
UNODC – UN Office on Drugs and Crime
UNSG – UN Secretary General
UNTS – UN Treaty Series
UN Women – UN Entity for Gender Equality and the Empowerment of Women
Vienna Convention – Vienna Convention on the Law of Treaties
Vienna Declaration – Vienna Declaration and Programme of Action
WHO – World Health Organization

***Dictionaries***

CED – Cambridge English Dictionary

OED – Oxford English Dictionary, Second Edition (1989), Online Updated Edition

OED 1911 – Oxford English Dictionary 1911 Edition

OMD – Oxford Concise Medical Dictionary

SOEDHP – Short Oxford English Dictionary on Historical Principles

Webster – Merriam-Webster Dictionary of the English Language, Eleventh Edition (2003) Online Updated Edition

# Introduction

## I THE GIRL CHILD AND INTERNATIONAL LAW

The girl child appears, on the surface, to be sufficiently protected under international law. Her human rights and fundamental freedoms are enshrined in the UN Convention on the Rights of the Child (CRC)[1] and the UN Convention on the Elimination of all Forms of Discrimination Against Women (CEDAW),[2] the two central international treaties promoting the rights of children and women. She is also covered by international instruments referring to all members of the 'human family', such as the Universal Declaration of Human Rights (UDHR),[3] and the Twin International Covenants – the International Covenant on Civil and Political Rights (ICCPR)[4] and the International Covenant on Economic, Social and Cultural Rights (ICESCR).[5] Since the principle of non-discrimination constitutes an integral part of international law, these rights apply equally to her, regardless of her sex and age, except for certain rights which are only afforded to individuals once they reach majority or a certain age, such as the rights to vote and to be eligible for election.[6] Many girl children nevertheless experience a series of violations of the rights granted to them under international law. UN treaty bodies, such as the UN Committee on the Rights of the Child

1 CRC (New York, adopted 20 November 1989, entered into force 2 September 1990) 1577 UNTS 3.

2 CEDAW (New York, adopted 18 December 1979, entered into force 3 September 1981) 1249 UNTS 13.

3 UDHR (adopted 10 December 1948) UNGA Res 217 A (III).

4 ICCPR (New York, adopted 16 December 1966, entered into force 23 March 1976) 999 UNTS 171.

5 ICESCR (New York, adopted 16 December 1966, entered into force 3 January 1976) 993 UNTS 3.

6 CEDAW, art. 7(a).

(CRC Committee) and the UN Committee on the Elimination of All Forms of Discrimination Against Women (CEDAW Committee), underline the predicament of the girl child in their general comments and recommendations, respectively,[7] as does the UN General Assembly in its eighteen resolutions on the girl child (1996–2022).[8] The UN General Assembly notably stresses, in its 2008 general resolution on the girl child, that it is:

> [d]eeply concerned about discrimination against the girl child and the violation of the rights of the girl child, which often result in less access for girls to education, nutrition and physical and mental health care, in girls enjoying fewer of the rights, opportunities and benefits of childhood and adolescence than boys, and in leaving them more vulnerable than boys to the consequences of unprotected and premature sexual relations and often being subjected to various forms of cultural, social, sexual and economic exploitation and to violence, abuse, rape, incest, honour-related crimes and harmful traditional practices, such as female infanticide, early marriage, forced marriage, prenatal sex selection and female genital mutilation.[9]

Although the principle of non-discrimination is widely recognized under international law,[10] many unborn females are eliminated solely on the grounds of gender through prenatal sex selection, or shortly after birth, through female infanticide. In 2012, UN Women noted that 134 million females were missing globally as a result of gender-based prenatal selection and infanticide,[11] and this number is projected to reach 150 million by 2035.[12] While the girl child's right to life is protected under international

7 See Chapters 2 and 4.

8 United Nations General Assembly (UNGA) Resolutions on 'The Girl Child' (hereinafter UNGA Resolution 'The Girl Child'): 1) (15 February 1996) UN Doc A/RES/50/154; 2) (20 February 1997) UN Doc A/RES/51/76; 3) (11 February 1998) UN Doc A/RES/52/106; 4) (23 February 1999) UN Doc A/RES/53/127; 5) (25 February 2000) UN Doc A/RES/54/148; 6) (16 February 2001) UN Doc A/RES/55/78; 7) (26 February 2002) UN Doc A/RES/56/139; 8) (12 February 2003) UN Doc A/RES/57/189; 9) (26 February 2004) UN Doc A/RES/58/156; 10) (11 January 2006) UN Doc A/RES/60/141; 11) (19 February 2008) UN Doc A/RES/62/140; 12) (1 March 2010) UN Doc A/RES/64/145; 13) (27 March 2012) UN Doc A/RES/66/140; 14) (4 February 2014) UN Doc A/RES/68/146; 15) (29 February 2016) UN Doc A/RES/70/138; 16) (17 January 2018) UN Doc A/RES/72/154; 17) (22 January 2020) UN Doc A/RES/74/134; 18) (6 January 2022) UN Doc A/RES/76/146; UNGA Resolution 'International Day of the Girl Child' (30 March 2012) UN Doc A/RES/66/170.

9 UNGA Resolution 'The Girl Child' (2008), preamble.

10 For instance, the principle of non-discrimination is enshrined in arts. 2 and 26 of the ICCPR, art. 2 of the ICESCR and art. 2 of the CRC.

11 UN Women, 'Progress of the World's Women: In Pursuit of Justice' (2012), 110.

12 John Bongaarts and Christophe Guilmoto, 'How Many More Missing Women? Excess Female Mortality and Prenatal Sex Selection 1970–2050' (2015) 41 *Population and Development Review* 241.

law,[13] many girls experience a series of gender-based killings during childhood and adolescence, including honour-related killings and dowry-related killings.[14] Presently, over 58 per cent of female victims of intentional homicide are killed by a partner or member of their own family, amounting to over 50,000 deaths a year, and these figures are underrated since numerous cases go unreported.[15] Female genital mutilation (FGM), which violates the internationally recognized right to health,[16] is another widespread practice. The World Health Organization (WHO) estimates that over 200 million girls and women worldwide have experienced some form of genital mutilation.[17] Also, many girls have limited access to reproductive health care, including contraception, leading to sexually transmitted diseases and unwanted pregnancies.[18] Furthermore, although the right to education is acknowledged under international law,[19] approximately 131 million girls worldwide do not attend school,[20] and 100 million young women are unable to read a single sentence.[21] Also, while the rights to human dignity, bodily integrity and protection against material injurious to girls' well-being and physical and mental health are protected under international law,[22] the mainstream and social media promote sexualized social and dress codes, including unhealthy beauty standards such as the 'cult of thinness', which according to the WHO play a central role in the increase of eating disorders in girl children.[23] Presently,

13 The right to life is enshrined in art. 6 of the ICCPR and the CRC.

14 UN Office on Drugs and Crime, 'Global Study on Homicide: Gender-related Killing of Women and Girls' (2018): for example, female dowry deaths account for 40 to 50 per cent of all female homicides recorded annually in India: 32.

15 Ibid., 13, 31.

16 The right to health is enshrined in art. 24 of the CRC and art. 12 of the ICESCR. This book employs the expression FGM; please see glossary.

17 WHO, 'Care of Girls and Women Living with Female Genital Mutilation: A Clinical Handbook' (2018), vi.

18 UNAIDS, 'Women and HIV: A Spotlight on Adolescent Girls and Young Women' (2019), 4: '[t]wo hundred million women and girls living in developing countries who want to avoid pregnancy are not using modern methods of contraception'; WHO, 'Adolescent Pregnancy: Evidence Brief' (2019), 1.

19 The right to education is protected under arts. 28 and 29 of the CRC, and art. 13 of the ICESCR.

20 UNESCO Institute for Statistics, 'Fact Sheet No. 48' (2018), 5.

21 UNESCO and UNGEI, 'Teaching and Learning: Achieving Quality for All, Global Monitoring Report' (2013–2014), 5.

22 See for example CRC, preamble, arts. 17, 24, 29.

23 Vikram Patel, 'Gender in Mental Health Research' (WHO 2004), 20. See Katharina Pilgrim and Sabine Bohnet-Joschko, 'Selling Health and Happiness: How Influencers Communicate on Instagram about Dieting and Exercise: Mixed Methods Research' (2019) 19 *BMC Public Health* 1054; Federica Pedalino and Anna-Linda Camerini, 'Instagram Use and Body Dissatisfaction: The Mediating Role of Upward Social Comparison with Peers and Influencers

over 15 per cent of girls suffer from anorexia and bulimia nervosa or related partial or mixed eating disorders in the Global North and, with the advent of globalization, also within the middle class in the Global South.[24] Additionally, while economic and sexual exploitation is prohibited under international law,[25] the International Labour Organization (ILO) estimates that 63 million girls between 5 and 17 years are involved in child labour,[26] more than half are engaged in hazardous work and girl domestic workers are especially vulnerable to abuse and slavery-like conditions.[27] Lastly, the UN study on violence against children underscores that over 150 million girl children globally are victims of sexual violence,[28] even though this crime is expressly proscribed under international law.[29] The human rights of the girl child are thus recognized in international law and yet continuously denied at the domestic level. It is argued that this paradox is underpinned by two interrelated factors. Firstly, internationally recognized human rights are denied to the girl child because of her inferior status in society as a female and child. Secondly, the international legal framework, rather than tackling this issue, fails to take into consideration the significant obstacles girl children encounter in exercising their rights as a result of sexism, 'childism',[30] and intersectional discrimination.[31]

among Young Females' (2022) 19 *International Journal of Environmental Research and Public Health* 1543; Danielle Bissonette and Dawn Szymanski, 'TikTok Use and Body Dissatisfaction: Examining Direct, Indirect, and Moderated Relations' (2022) 43 *Body Image* 205, 206.

24 Giuseppe Logrieco et al., 'The Paradox of Tik Tok Anti-Pro-Anorexia Videos: How Social Media Can Promote Non-Suicidal Self-Injury and Anorexia' (2021) 18 *International Journal of Environmental Research and Public Health* 1041; United Kingdom Royal College of Psychiatrists, 'Position Statement on Early Intervention for Eating Disorders' (2019) PS03/19, 2. See Chapter 4 for a discussion on sexualized social and dress codes and their significance for girl children.

25 The right to protection against economic exploitation and hazardous work is enshrined in arts. 32, 34, 35, 36 of the CRC, and arts. 7, 10 of the ICESCR.

26 ILO and UNICEF, 'Child Labour Global Estimates, Trends and the Road Forward' (2020), 8.

27 ILO, 'Practical Guide to Ending Child Labour and Protecting Young Workers in Domestic Work' (2017), 137, 138, 144: violations experienced by girl domestic workers include beating, kicking, whipping, pinching, scalding, overwork, denial of food and sexual violence at the hands of men and boys in the household: 137–138, 144.

28 Paolo Sérgio Pinheiro, 'UN Study World Report on Violence against Children' (2006), 54.

29 CRC, art. 19.

30 Childism is a form of discrimination against children. See Chapter 3 and Elizabeth Young-Bruehl, *Childism: Confronting Prejudice against Children* (Yale University Press 2012), 4.

31 See Chapters 3 and 4.

## II INTERSECTIONAL IDENTITY OF THE GIRL CHILD

The girl child occupies a unique position in society as a member of both female and child identity categories. As a female, she experiences violations of rights caused by gender-based discrimination or 'sexism', and as a child, she faces abuses enabled by child-based discrimination or 'childism'. She may also encounter both forms of discrimination at one given time, or over the course of her childhood. Moreover, sexism and childism often mutually reinforce each other, thereby placing the girl child in a triple subordinate position.[32] Her inferior status in society thus leaves her particularly vulnerable to human rights violations. However, it is important to recognize that girl children are not the sole victims of human rights abuses. Numerous adult men and women, as well as boys, also suffer a series of human rights violations, such as torture, poverty, economic and sexual exploitation and restrictions to their fundamental freedoms. Each of these identity groups encounters a series of issues that are unique to them. Hence, while this book shall, where relevant, underscore the inferior status ascribed to girl children worldwide in relation to boys within the 'child' category and with regard to adult women within the 'woman' category, it does not aim to conduct 'Oppression Olympics'[33] between the girl child and other identity groups, such as adult women and boys, to determine which suffers most. We focus on the situation of the girl child while recognizing that other individuals and groups face unique violations of rights, which are outside the scope of this book. Moreover, not every girl child experiences the abovementioned human rights violations. Girls who occupy a subordinate position in a given society within a series of identity vectors – such as class, race, sexual orientation and (dis)abilities – are more likely to encounter human rights violations than their privileged counterparts. In this regard, girls with disabilities, girls infected with HIV/AIDS, lesbian girls and girls who belong to certain minority groups – such as aboriginal girls and nomadic girls – are particularly exposed. Additionally, girl children are more vulnerable to human rights abuses in certain circumstances, notably during detention, armed conflict and as refugees. Hence, each girl child encounters varying degrees of restrictions to her rights, according to her economic, social and cultural circumstances. It is nevertheless argued that the vectors of discrimination of sexism and childism impact all girl children, albeit to

32 Ibid.

33 Ange-Marie Hancock, 'When Multiplication Doesn't Equal Quick Addition: Examining Intersectionality as a Research Paradigm' (2007) 5 *Perspectives on Politics* 63, 68. See Chapter 4.

different degrees. For example, girls located in a privileged position in society on account of class, race, sexual orientation and abilities still experience sexualized social and dress codes, both in the public and private spheres, as demonstrated by the phenomenon of 'rape culture' which permeates social media platforms as well as elite boarding schools and Ivy League universities.[34] In this regard, Sohoni emphasizes that '[i]n contemporary times, no culture, country, or people can truly assert that, among them, girlhood stands tall, proud and free'.[35]

## III INTERNATIONAL LEGAL FRAMEWORK AND PROTECTION OF THE GIRL CHILD

A series of factors impede the implementation of girls' rights at the domestic level, such as the unequal distribution of resources between corporations, nations and individuals, the repercussions of past and present forms of colonization and armed conflict.[36] Within the international legal framework, four central features impact the protection of girls' rights, namely 1) the *pacta sunt servanda* principle, 2) reservations, 3) the absence of sanctions and 4) the content of treaties. This book shall focus on the fourth feature, the content of treaties, to assess whether the identification of the girl child under international law addresses the intersectional discrimination she experiences.

The first feature of the international legal framework impacting the protection of girl children is the *pacta sunt servanda* principle, whereby international treaties solely create obligations for states that consent to be bound by them. The Vienna Convention on the Law of Treaties (1969) stipulates that '[e]very treaty in force is binding upon the parties to it and must be performed by them in good faith'.[37] The consent can be expressed in several ways: '[t]he consent of a State to be bound by a treaty may be expressed by signature, exchange of instruments constituting a treaty, ratification,

[34] See Chapter 4.

[35] Neera Kuckreja Sohoni, *Burden of Girlhood: A Global Enquiry into the Status of Girls* (Third Party Publishing Company 1995), viii.

[36] See for example Subrata Sankar Bagchi and Arnab Das, *Human Rights and the Third World: Issues and Discourses* (Lexington Books 2014); Thomas Pogge, 'Recognized and Violated by International Law: The Human Rights of the Global Poor' (2005) 18 *Leiden Journal of International Law* 717; Roland Burke, *Decolonization and the Evolution of International Human Rights* (University Pennsylvania Press 2010); Gerd Oberleitner, *Human Rights in Armed Conflict: Law, Practice, Policy* (Cambridge University Press 2015).

[37] Vienna Convention on the Law of Treaties (Vienna, adopted 23 May 1969, entered into force 27 January 1980) 1155 UNTS 331 (hereinafter Vienna Convention), art. 26.

acceptance, approval or accession, or by any other means if so agreed'.[38] A treaty is binding upon the parties to it and conversely, states that are not parties to a treaty are not bound by it: '[a] treaty does not create either obligations or rights for a third State without its consent'.[39] Hence, states that are not parties to an international treaty are not required to respect, protect and fulfil the rights it enshrines. Presently, several states are not parties to key treaties such as the CEDAW, ICCPR and ICESCR,[40] and although the CRC is the most widely ratified with 196 States parties, the United States of America has still not ratified it.[41] Accordingly, girl children living in countries that are not parties to these treaties are not protected by their provisions. Moreover, many international instruments and documents relevant to the girl child, such as the Beijing Declaration[42] and UN Women conclusions on violence against women and girls,[43] do not constitute treaties and are therefore not legally binding.[44] Secondly, states can formulate reservations to exclude or significantly reduce their obligations under the treaty.[45] A substantial number of countries entered reservations to provisions enshrining critical rights for girl children. For instance, several States parties to the CRC and CEDAW specify in their reservations that they do not consider themselves bound by articles enshrining the principle of non-discrimination, notably between the sexes; equality in entering, during and at the dissolution of marriage; and the rights to participation, education and protection against violence.[46]

Thirdly, there are no international enforcement mechanisms to impose concrete sanctions on states that fail to fulfil their obligations under human rights treaties. Presently, States parties are required to submit and present their reports to the treaty body. However, this procedure does not constitute a legal

[38] Ibid., art. 11.
[39] Ibid., art. 34.
[40] See Chapter 7.
[41] See CRC, 1557 UNTS 3.
[42] The Beijing Declaration and Platform for Action, 'Fourth World Conference on Women: Action for Equality, Development and Peace' (1995) UN Doc A/CONF.177/20 and A/CONF.177/20/Add.1.
[43] Commission on the Status of Women, 'Agreed Conclusions on the Elimination and Prevention of All Forms of Violence against Women and Girls' (2013) UN Doc E/CN.6/2013/11.
[44] As defined in the Vienna Convention (1969), art. 1a): 'treaty means an international agreement concluded between States in written form and governed by international law, whether embodied in a single instrument or in two or more related instruments and whatever its particular designation'.
[45] Vienna Convention (1969), art. 2(1)(d).
[46] See Chapter 5.

course of action and is more akin to a diplomatic conversation between states and the Committee. Kelly underscores the ritualistic nature and extreme civility of these exchanges:

> One of the most striking aspects of the sessions is just how polite they are. The Committee chair warmly welcomes delegations from even the most authoritarian and brutal states. One by one, members express thanks to the delegation for coming and say that they are grateful for the delegation's efforts in preparing their reports and the responses to questions ... questions are never posed in a challenging manner. Rather they are made as suggestions, or as requests for responses to allegations that other people have made. Time after time it is stressed that the Committee is not a court. The task, everyone is told, is to promote human rights through a friendly exchange.[47]

The Committee publishes 'concluding observations' evaluating the implementation of treaty provisions at the domestic level, and provides recommendations for improvement.[48] However, states have noted that concluding observations 'are not in themselves formally binding interpretations of the treaty', and States parties that do not comply with obligations are not imposed sanctions.[49] In this regard, Fortin argues:

> [T]he absence of any supervision or coercion over this can lead to [State] reports painting an over-optimistic and complacent picture of governmental achievements. This weakening of the reporting procedure has led to many countries providing reports indicating little or no difficulty with implementing some of their most onerous obligations.[50]

Also, while concluding observations may temporarily tarnish a non-complying state's international reputation, such reports are not systematically covered by the mainstream media, especially in states with limited freedom of the press, and thereby often go unnoticed. Finally, while treaty bodies may, under certain conditions, consider complaints submitted by individuals concerning

47 Tobias Kelly, 'Two Cheers for Ritual: The UN Committee Against Torture' (2018) 9 *Humanity* 93, 95–96.

48 For example, States parties to the CRC are required, under art. 44, to submit reports to the CRC Committee on the measures they have adopted to give effect to the rights, and the latter can make suggestions and general recommendations entitled 'Concluding Observations'; CRC, art. 45(d).

49 International Law Association (ILA) Committee on International Human Rights Law and Practice, 'Final Report on the Impact of Findings of the United Nations Human Rights Treaty Bodies' (Berlin Conference 2004), para. 16.

50 Jane Fortin, *Children's Rights and the Developing Law* (3rd ed., Cambridge University Press 2009), 48.

violations of rights, their decisions are not legally binding.[51] As noted by the Office of the United Nations High Commissioner for Human Rights (OHCHR), the Committee will provide 'recommendations', and if the latter are ignored, the Committee will 'pursue' a dialogue as a follow-up, in the hopes that the State will agree to comply.[52] In this context, Simma and Alston's observation thirty-five years ago that 'the international human rights regime, even though strong on promotion, is extremely weak on what a lawyer would consider enforcement or remedies',[53] is still accurate. Presently, there is no 'international court of human rights' expressly tasked to enforce the decisions and concluding observations of human rights treaty bodies.[54]

[51] Optional Protocol to the CRC on a Communications Procedure (New York, adopted 19 December 2011, entered into force 14 April 2014) 2983 UNTS 135; Optional Protocol to the CEDAW (New York, adopted 6 October 1999, entered into force 22 December 2000) 2131 UNTS 83; Optional Protocol to the ICCPR (New York, adopted 16 December 1966, entered into force 23 March 1976) 999 UNTS 171; Optional Protocol to the ICESCR (adopted 10 December 2008; entered into force 5 May 2013) 2922 UNTS 29. See also OHCHR Human Rights Treaty Bodies – Individual Communications: '[t]he Committee's decisions represent an authoritative interpretation of the treaty concerned. They contain recommendations to the State party. When the Committee concludes that a violation of the Covenant has taken place, the State is invited to provide information, within 180 days, on the steps it has taken to implement the recommendations. The State's response is then transmitted to the complainant for comments'. www.ohchr.org/EN/HRBodies/TBPetitions/Pages/IndividualCommunications.aspx#proceduregenerale (accessed 14 June 2023).

[52] OHCHR Human Rights Treaty Bodies – Individual Communications: www.ohchr.org/EN/HRBodies/TBPetitions/Pages/IndividualCommunications.aspx#proceduregenerale (accessed 14 June 2023): '[i]f the State party fails to take appropriate action, the case is kept under consideration by the Committee under the follow-up procedure. *A dialogue is thus pursued with the State party and the case remains open until satisfactory measures are taken*' (emphasis added).

[53] Bruno Simma and Philip Alston, 'The Sources of Human Rights Law: Custom, Jus Cogens, and General Principles' (1989) 12 *Australian Year Book International Law* 82, 83–84.

[54] The International Criminal Court is restricted to the most serious crimes: genocide, crimes against humanity, war crimes and the crime of aggression: Rome Statute (Rome, adopted 17 July 1998, entered into force 1 July 2002) 2187 UNTS 3, art. 5. The International Court of Justice has not historically examined States parties failing to fulfil their obligations under international human rights treaties, and although applications were brought concerning treaties such as the International Convention on the Elimination of all Forms of Racial Discrimination (CERD) and the Convention against Torture, the process was initiated by countries, that is, states parties rather than treaty bodies, thereby failing to ensure uniformity globally, and raising the question as to whether these applications are not political in nature rather than focused on human rights more broadly, given that they are initiated by certain states against specific states and not others: Charter of the United Nations and Statute of the International Court of Justice (San Francisco, adopted 26 June 1945, entered into force 24 October 1945) 33 UNTS 993; Convention against Torture and Other Cruel, Inhuman or Degrading Treatment or Punishment (New York, adopted 10 December 1984, entered into force 26 June 1987) 1465 UNTS 85; International Convention on the Elimination of all Forms of Racial Discrimination (CERD) (New York, adopted 7 March 1966, entered into

Lastly, the content of treaties, notably the identification of the girl child and the wording of provisions enshrining her rights, is another central feature of the international legal framework. Terminology plays a central role in shaping the substance of human rights and fundamental freedoms in the international legal realm. It operates both legally, as it determines the scope of rights and corresponding duties of States parties, and symbolically, as it constitutes an apparatus of signs through which the very existence of rights becomes universally acknowledged.[55] Also, since rights are not solely given effect in courts but also in political debates and various spheres of the girl child's life, the language employed to phrase rights must be sufficiently comprehensible for the population at large, in particular non-lawyers, who come into contact with her.[56] In addition, it must be easily understood by the rights holders themselves, notably girl children, so that they may identify which actions and omissions constitute violations of their rights under the law, and accordingly, which rights may be invoked and which violations reported. In this regard, if rights are phrased in weak or general terms, States parties may misconstrue their treaty obligations and fail to implement rights properly. Moreover, the general public may misunderstand the substance of the rights of the girl child, and it may also inhibit girl children and their advocates seeking to enforce these rights. The lengthy drafting process of international human rights treaties whereby government delegations meet over the course of years, and even decades, to discuss the wording of each provision, exemplifies the crucial function of terminology within the international legal framework. As stated by

force 4 January 1969) 660 UNTS 195; see for example, 'Application Instituting Proceedings Concerning a Dispute under the Convention Against Torture and Other Cruel, Inhuman or Degrading Treatment or Punishment (Canada and the Netherlands *v.* Syrian Arab Republic), (8 June 2023) in which the applicants argue that the ICJ has jurisdiction under art. 36(1) of the ICJ Statute which states that jurisdiction of the Court 'comprises ... all matters specially provided for ... in treaties and conventions in force' and art. 30 of the Convention against Torture which provides that 'any dispute between two or more States Parties concerning the interpretation or application of this Convention which cannot be settled through negotiations shall, at the request of one of them, be submitted to arbitration. If within six months from the date of the request for arbitration the Parties are unable to agree on the organization of the arbitration, any one of those Parties may refer the dispute to the International Court of Justice' (paras. 8 and 10); see also, 'Application Instituting Proceedings containing a Request for Provisional Measures – Application of the International Convention on the Elimination of all forms of Racial Discrimination' (Armenia *v.* Azerbaijan), (16 September 2021) and 'Application of the International Convention on the Elimination of All Forms of Racial Discrimination' (Qatar *v.* United Arab Emirates), Provisional Measures, Order of 23 July 2018, I.C.J. Reports 2018 (II).

55 Clara Chapdelaine-Feliciati, 'The Sense, Meaning, and Significance of the Twin International Covenants on Political and Economic Rights' (2013) 196 *Semiotica* 326.

56 For example, teachers, doctors, law enforcement personnel and her parents or legal guardians.

Professor Maresca during the Vienna Conference on the Law of Treaties: 'diplomacy, of which treaties [are] the solemn conclusion, [is] a written art: the most eloquent oratory [is] of no avail unless the provisions agreed upon [are] satisfactorily written down'.[57] It is worthy of note that the drafting age of the CRC lasted over ten years,[58] as did that of the CEDAW.[59] The adoption process of the ICCPR and the ICESCR spanned over twenty years, twice as much as that of the CRC and CEDAW. The international community first contemplated creating the International Bill of Rights, which comprises the UDHR, ICCPR and ICESCR, at the UN Conference on International Organization in 1945.[60] The Commission on Human Rights was established two years later, and the drafting process lasted until 1966 when both Covenants were adopted. Another decade elapsed before they entered into force.[61] As shall be examined in Chapters 6 and 7, provisions concerning the boundaries of childhood and thereby girlhood were among the most controversial during the drafting of the CRC, which implies that state representatives were aware of their significance.[62]

## IV SEMIOTICS THEORY

Although the factors explored above are all significant, this book focuses on the first central element concerning the protection of the girl child: her identification under international law. The book engages in a semioethics analysis of the English text of international human rights treaties to assess whether the provisions as formulated clearly identify the girl child and take

[57] UN Conference on the Law of Treaties (Vienna, Second Session, 9 April–22 May 1969), 11th Meeting (30 April 1969) UN Doc A/CONF.39/11/Add.1, Professor Adolfo Maresca, Italy, 37, para. 26.

[58] Sharon Detrick, *The United Nations Convention on the Rights of the Child: A Guide to the Travaux Préparatoires* (Martinus Nijhoff 1992), 1: ten years from the Polish proposal in 1979 to its adoption on 20 November 1989, and an additional ten months until entering into force on 2 September 1990.

[59] While the Commission on the Status of Women prepared, in 1966, a draft *Declaration on the Elimination of Discrimination Against Women* (DEDAW) (adopted 7 November 1967) UN Doc A/RES/2263, it took eight years for the UN to appoint the working group. The CEDAW was adopted on 18 December 1979, and two more years elapsed before it came into force on 3 September 1981: see Lars Rehof, *Guide to the* Travaux Préparatoires *of the United Nations Convention on the Elimination of all Forms of Discrimination against Women* (Martinus Nijhoff 1993), 6–12.

[60] Marc Bossuyt, *Guide to the* Travaux Préparatoires *of the International Covenant on Civil and Political Rights* (Martinus Nijhoff 1987); John Humphrey, 'The International Bill of Rights: Scope and Implementation' (1976) 17 *William and Mary Law Review* 527.

[61] *Guide to the* Travaux Préparatoires (1987).

[62] Detrick, *Travaux Préparatoires CRC* (1992), 26, 100–123.

into account her unique condition. It examines the content of the two main treaties promoting girl child rights, the CRC and the CEDAW, and the Twin International Covenants, the ICCPR and the ICESCR, where relevant. This book applies the science of semiotics, which studies the meaning of signs and symbols in all forms of expression, notably language.[63] More specifically, it explores Significs theory and each of the components of The Meaning Triad devised by the foremother of modern semiotics, Victoria Lady Welby: 1) the 'sense' of the terms employed in treaties, that is, their textual meaning, 2) the 'meaning-intention', that is, the intention of the drafters of these treaties when choosing these specific terms and 3) their 'ultimate significance' in shaping the identification of the girl child.[64] It contends that the terminology employed to define the girl child does not take into consideration the obstacles she faces in exercising her rights as a result of sexism, childism and intersectional discrimination. In order to address this shortcoming, the book undertakes a semioethics approach,[65] by considering whether the content of international treaties could be modified to empower the girl child.

## V STRUCTURE OF THE BOOK

This book conducts an examination of the status of the girl child under international law. It firstly presents semiotics and intersectionality theory, and how these frameworks shall be employed to analyse the content of international treaties in relation to the girl child. It begins by exploring, in Chapter 1, the development of modern semiotics, while referring to decodification semiotics and interpretation semiotics, and offers a definition of legal semiotics. It thereafter presents Welby's Significs theory and Meaning Triad, and Ponzio and Petrilli's Semioethics approach. Chapter 2 provides a history of the recognition of the girl child in the international legal framework. It conducts an examination of the definition of the girl child in the English language and analyses her two vectors of identity: femalehood and childhood. Chapter 2 further explores the conceptions of girlhood and its dimensions, boundaries and divisions, as well as the etymology of the expression 'girl' and its semiotics of inferiority and subordination throughout history. Chapter 3

[63] See Chapter 1.
[64] Victoria Welby, *Significs and Language: The Articulate Form of Our Expressive and Interpretative Resources* (Macmillan 1911; reprint in John Benjamins, *Foundations of Semiotics* (1985)).
[65] Augusto Ponzio and Susan Petrilli, *Semioetica* (Meltemi 2003); Augusto Ponzio and Susan Petrilli, 'Semioethics' in Paul Cobley (ed.), *The Routledge Companion to Semiotics* (Routledge 2009).

discusses the concepts of discrimination, sexism, childism, the public/private divide, universalism and cultural relativism, and their significance for the girl child. Chapter 4 examines interactive intersectional discrimination. It explains the cumulative and interactive gender-based and child-based discrimination encountered by the girl child, and offers case studies of violations embedded in both sexism and childism. This book studies violations experienced by the girl child in both the Global North and Global South, which often interconnect with the advent of globalization, for example, through social media platforms such as Instagram and TikTok that promote sexualized social and dress codes.

Secondly, this book examines the delineation of girlhood under international law. Chapter 5 analyses the identification of the 'girl child' in the main treaty promoting child rights, the CRC. Chapter 6 investigates whether the boundary for the beginning of girlhood should be clearly ascertained in the international legal framework. To this effect, it examines two interconnected issues: prenatal sex selection and the right of adolescent girls to a safe abortion. Lastly, the boundary for the end of girlhood under the CRC and that separating girlhood and womanhood under the CEDAW, and their repercussions on the girl child, are analyzed in Chapters 7 and 8, respectively. We observe that female human beings located at the intersection of girlhood and womanhood may fall short of the protection of both the CRC and many provisions of the CEDAW. In these chapters, the book resorts to semioethics to consider the possibility of amending the CRC, as permitted under article 50,[66] or revising the CEDAW, as allowed for under article 26.[67]

## VI TERMINOLOGY EMPLOYED TO REFER TO THE GIRL CHILD

This book employs the expressions 'girl child' and 'girl' interchangeably as encompassing all female children. We nonetheless propose to distinguish divisions *within* girlhood and thus employ the expressions 'young girls' for prepubescent girls and 'adolescent girls' for girls who reached puberty, as the realities and obstacles faced by both subgroups can be different, such as the possibility of becoming pregnant.[68] Also, while the CRC systematically employs masculine pronouns and possessive adjectives before their feminine

[66] CRC, art. 50; see Chapters 5 and 7.
[67] CEDAW, art. 26; see Chapter 8.
[68] For a discussion on the divisions of girlhood, see Chapter 2.

counterparts in its provisions, namely 'him or her',[69] 'he or she'[70] and 'his or her',[71] this book shall instead begin with the feminine to ensure the visibility of the girl child throughout our analysis, and thus employ the formulations 'her/him', 's/he' and 'her/his'. We shall also closely examine the significance of the use of the masculine pronouns 'him' and 'he' and the possessive adjective 'his' in certain treaties.

[69] CRC, arts. 3(2), 40(2)(b)(ii).
[70] CRC, art. 29(1)(c).
[71] CRC, preamble, arts. 2(1), 3(2), 7(1), 8, 9(1), 10, 12(1), 14(2), 16(1), 17, 20(1), 22, 23(2)(3), 24(1), 25, 29(1)(c), 30, 37(b)–(d), 40(2)(b)(ii)–(iv)(vii).

# 1

# Semiotics and Semioethics

The science or doctrine of semiotics[1] has been applied throughout history to study the meaning of signs and symbols in numerous fields, such as linguistics, theology, philosophy, literature, architecture, mathematics and logic, medicine, psychiatry and psychology, economics, biology and ecology, as well as learning and education.[2] The term semiotics comes from the Greek *semeiotikos* 'significance',[3] or 'observant of signs',[4] *semeiosis* 'indication',[5] as well as *semeioun* 'interpret as a sign' and 'to signal',[6] and *semeion* 'sign'.[7] A similar word, *semeiotics*, referred to the branch of medicine dealing with the interpretation of symptoms in 1670, and earlier in 1588 under the adjective *semeiotical*.[8] The term 'semiotics' was acknowledged as the study of signs and symbols in English as early as 1641 in the works of Bishop John

1 Thomas Sebeok preferred the expression 'doctrine of signs' to the more 'ennobling terms' science or theory, in reference to John Locke's use of the expression 'doctrine' as 'a body of principles and opinions that vaguely go to form a field of knowledge': Susan Petrilli, *Sign Crossroads in Global Perspective: Semioethics and Responsibility* (Transaction Publishers 2010), 6.

2 For a discussion on semiotics in various disciplines, see Jamin Pelkey (ed.), *Bloomsbury Semiotics Anthology* (Bloomsbury 2022), and for example, Gabriele Aroni, *The Semiotics of Architecture in Video Games* (Bloomsbury Advances in Semiotics 2022); Gabriele Aroni, 'Semiotics in Architecture and Spatial Design' in Jamin Pelkey (ed.), *Bloomsbury Semiotics Anthology* (Bloomsbury 2023) 277–96; Gabriele Aroni, 'Games as Authorial Platforms? An Exploration of the Legal Status of User-Created Content from Digital Games' (2023) 36 *International Journal for the Semiotics of Law* 2021; and Robert Yelle, *Semiotics of Religion: Signs of the Sacred in Religion* (Bloomsbury Advances in Semiotics 2012).

3 *Shorter Oxford English Dictionary on Historical Principles*, Sixth Edition (2007) (SOEDHP).

4 *Chambers Dictionary of Etymology* (2002 [1988]) (Chambers Etymology).

5 *Chambers Etymology*.

6 SOEDHP.

7 *Chambers Etymology*.

8 Ibid.

Wilkins, the first secretary of the Royal Society.[9] It is presently defined as '[t]he science of communication studied through the interpretation of signs and symbols as they operate in various fields',[10] and '[t]he branch of knowledge that deals with the production of meanings by sign systems in various fields'.[11]

Law comprises infinite chains of icons and representations, or 'legisigns',[12] that underpin the foundations of society, and thus constitutes an especially pertinent area of study for semiotics. Yet scholars and semioticians have yet to agree on a definition of *semiotics-of-law, semiotics-in-law* or *legal semiotics* and often refer to these expressions interchangeably. Tiefenbrun defines *semiotics of law* as 'a specialized study of sign systems underlying legal informational exchanges', while Broekman, Mootz and Pencak refer to the subject of *legal semiotics* as 'the scientific approach that regards law as a system of signs and meanings'.[13] Some consider that legal semiotics constitutes a special branch dedicated to the study of law within the science of semiotics, others view it as a subdiscipline within legal theory and others as an interdisciplinary method to explore the legal realm.[14] Moreover, legal semiotics comprises *semiotics-of-law* and *semiotics-in-law*. Semiotics of law examines legal information exchanges via the study of sign systems, whereas semiotics in law considers law as a system of signs. The concept of legal semiotics comprises three central elements: 1) studies the legal realm as an infinite sign system, 2) offers a method or methods to perform this ambitious undertaking, which will be discussed and applied in the present book and 3) provides a common language for scholars, practitioners and the general public.[15] The 'common language' element of legal semiotics is crucial as legal terminology constitutes a language of its own – separate and yet closely connected to everyday idioms – which was until

9 Ibid.

10 *Oxford English Dictionary*, Second Edition (1989), Online Edition (OED).

11 SOEDHP.

12 See Roberta Kevelson, *Peirce, Science, Signs* (Peter Lang 1996), 51.

13 Susan Tiefenbrun, *Decoding International Law: Semiotics and the Humanities* (Oxford University Press 2010), 24; Jan Broekman, Francis Mootz III and William Pencak, 'Preface – Semiotics in the Seminar' in Jan Broekman and Francis Mootz III (eds.), *The Semiotics of Law in Legal Education* (Springer 2011), v.

14 For a discussion on the definition of legal semiotics, see Clara Chapdelaine-Feliciati, 'Semiotics in Law and Jurisprudence' in Jamin Pelkey (ed.), *Bloomsbury Semiotics Anthology* (Bloomsbury 2023); Clara Chapdelaine-Feliciati, Encyclopedia Entry 'Semiotic of Law', SEMIOTICON SEO-Semiotics Encyclopedia Online. https://semioticon.com/seo/semiotics-of-law/ (accessed 2 July 2023).

15 'Semiotics in Law and Jurisprudence' (2023), 266–69. The author wishes to thank Ulf Linderfalk for a rich discussion on the distinctions between (textual) interpretation and legal semiotics, and the latter's possible added value, as well as linguistics and legal semiotics, during her panel at the Cambridge International Law Conference, Cambridge University, Faculty of Law (2023).

recently only accessible to a privileged few. As noted by Hargitt, '[w]hile based on ordinary language, legal language is a jargon primarily characterized by a complex and specialized lexicon, which requires interpretation to be understood and often makes the language completely foreign and incomprehensible'.[16] Exploring the meaning(s) in law constitutes, for semioticians, an exercise in translation, as legal terms and concepts are not readily known by the general public and require an interpretation in layman's terms. This is particularly important in human rights law because the content of international treaties and domestic legislation should be easily accessible to all individuals so they be *informed of* and *exercise* their rights. Already in 1947, Dr Chang, the Chinese representative to the drafting committee of the UDHR (1948), underscored the importance of ensuring that international instruments are easily comprehended by all persons: '[a] declaration of human rights should be brief and readily understandable by all. It should be a document for all men everywhere, not merely for lawyers and scholars.'[17] Accordingly, the use of specialized or ambiguous terminology constitutes a critical obstacle to the realization of human rights and fundamental freedoms, especially for subordinate identity groups that do not master this language, such as girl children.

Legal semiotics therefore allows for an examination of the triadic relationship between 1) authority or 'master signifiers',[18] 2) the language of law and 3) the general public. Indeed, 'master signifiers' – notably lawyers, judges, scholars and policymakers, hence influential individuals in a given society – play a central role in constructing and interpreting the language of the law and its many meanings. Wessel argues in this regard that 'the language of international law is nothing but a rhetorical device of the powerful'.[19] As noted by Cyran:

> The reality of legal discourse is that an institution (government) is achieving its goals by using language and employing functionaries, or 'authoritative figures', [to] (sic) define meaning. The authorities consist of courts (through judges) and legislatures (through legislators). Thus, unlike in a natural

[16] Samantha Hargitt, 'What Could be Gained in Translation: Legal Language and Lawyer-Linguists in a Globalized World' (2013) 20 *Indiana Journal Global Legal Studies* 425, 427.

[17] Draft International Declaration of Human Rights, 3rd session, Third Committee, 91st meeting (2 October 1948) UN Doc A/C.3/SR.91, 48.

[18] Edward Cyran, 'Common Law Lawyers Should Mind Their Trial Practices: Understanding, Identifying, and Correcting a Semiotic Imbalance' in Jan Broekman and Francis Mootz III (eds.), *The Semiotics of Law in Legal Education* (Springer 2011), 120.

[19] Jared Wessel, 'International Law as Language – Towards a "Neo" New Haven School' (2010) 23 *International Journal for the Semiotics of Law* 123, 125.

> discourse where anyone can participate in the decision-making process of meaning through communication, in an artificial discourse, only those who communicate with the functionaries can actually influence the meaning of signs.[20]

This language, in turn, holds significant power in shaping our understanding of society. Semioticians can thereby deconstruct the 'master discourse' and its impact on the social order, especially as concerns the most vulnerable groups in society, including girl children. Wagner refers to the 'discourse of power' and the necessity to question its content and origins, especially when it creates inequalities: '[o]nce citizens become aware of the fact that they are speakers of a specific discourse, they are indeed empowered *to speak differently* – to each other as well as to their respective social institutions'.[21] Legal semiotics therefore allows for a critique of the symbols employed in legislation and courts, notably their substance and *raison d'être*. Kevelson defines legisigns as 'provisional judgements, held and acted on as if they were truths', although they are in fact the product of an 'ad hoc community that comes together out of a common purpose'.[22] As shall be examined in this monograph, there is a significant gap between, on the one hand, the 'master signifiers' in international law, that is, those who engage in the drafting of human rights treaties, notably government representatives, legal experts and UN officials, and on the other hand, the object of those treaties, thus individuals exposed to violations. Since girl children occupy a subordinate position in society on account of their sex and age, they are not only absent from the drafting process, but also oftentimes unacquainted with the content of treaties, the legal terminology and the modus operandi of treaty bodies. In many cases, they are oblivious to the international legal framework altogether. Accordingly, girl children are passive objects of the very master discourse of international law that should promote and protect their rights.

While the science of semiotics is a useful method to decode international law, legal scholars nevertheless tend to adopt a traditional approach to interpretation and often examine treaty law separately from linguistics, and even more so, from semiotics. In their interdisciplinary publication, Smolka and Pirker combine their respective fields of linguistics and law to argue that 'legal interpretation . . . should no longer be considered merely a legal afterthought –

20 'Common Law Lawyers' (2011), 118.

21 Anne Wagner, 'Promises and Prospects' in Anne Wagner and Jan Broekman (eds.), *Prospects of Legal Semiotics* (Springer 2010), vi.

22 *Peirce Signs* (1996), 51.

as if meaning were "all in the text"'.[23] Kevelson's seminal work at Penn State University, pursued successfully by Broekman, Catá-Backer and Mootz,[24] has instilled a growing awareness of the relevancy of legal semiotics within academia. Yet very few lawyers, judges and law professors engage with this science. In this regard, Tiefenbrun notes that '[s]emiotics is only at the infant stage in its adoption by the legal community as a workable theory and method'.[25] She further argues that only 'a courageous few' have delved into this doctrine.[26] The present book adopts the novel legal semiotics approach, and thus the principles and methods of the science of semiotics, to interpret and decipher the meaning of signs in the legal field, more specifically in international law. The next section will firstly present the origins of semiotics and key schools of interpretation within semiotics theory, notably decodification semiotics and interpretation semiotics as they relate to our analysis of the girl child. We shall thereafter examine the second element of legal semiotics, that is, the 'methods' or 'frameworks' employed to examine the law. For this purpose, we will describe the 'signific' and 'semioethic' methodologies applied in this book to 'decode' the provisions of international treaties and examine whether they sufficiently protect the girl child.

## I ORIGINS AND MEANING

In order to understand the concept of semiotics, it is important to examine the notions of sign and symbol. The term 'sign' is defined as '[a] basic element of communication, either linguistic (a written or spoken word) or non-linguistic (an image, article of clothing, etc.) consisting of two indivisible elements the relation between which is arbitrary (*signifiant* [signifier] and *signifié* [signified]), and which derives its meaning only from its relationship to other signs within the same sign system'.[27] Instead, the expression 'symbol' comes from the Greek *sumbolon*, a 'mark, token, watchword, outward sign' and refers to a

[23] Jennifer Smolka and Benedikt Pirker, 'International Law and Pragmatics: An Account of Interpretation in International Law' (2016) 5 *International Journal of Language & Law* 1, 2. Smolka and Pirker observe that '[i]nternational legal scholarship is focusing, more and more, on the interpretation of international law. This development had engendered a rich set of interdisciplinary approaches. The powerful and diverse international judiciary is now recognized to play the role of a veritable "law maker"... But one has to take a closer look to find scholarship that engages with linguistics': 15.

[24] See for example Jan Broekman and Larry Catá Backer (eds.), *Lawyers Making Meaning: The Semiotics of Law in Legal Education II* (Springer 2013).

[25] *Decoding International Law* (2010), 23.

[26] Ibid., 24–25.

[27] SOEDHP.

material object representing an abstract concept or quality.[28] The science of semiotics therefore examines the meaning of all forms of communication, both verbal signs, namely language, and nonverbal signs, such as images and sound, and their symbolic as well as concrete implications. In this regard, Tiefenbrun observes that the process of interpretation or 'decoding' signs constitutes a 'systematic process of finding keys to hidden codes that unlock the doors to meaning'.[29]

The origins of semiotics as a discipline in the western world can be traced back to Mesopotamia in 3000 BCE and thereafter in ancient Greece, where signs were interpreted for divinatory and medical purposes.[30] In Mesopotamia, divinatory tablets were structured along a combination of signs which allowed one to 'infer something hidden or non-present from something perceptible or present', and in Greece, signs were perceived as 'the instrument of mediation between the total knowledge of the gods and the more limited knowledge of humankind'.[31] The process of semiotics also finds its origins in medical symptomology, uncovered in the Corpus Hippocraticum, the collection of very varied texts illustrating medical theory and practice during the fifth and fourth centuries BCE,[32] which operates a threefold analysis of symptoms as signs to be interpreted in patients: 1) anamnesis (analysis of the causes), 2) diagnosis (analysis of the sickness) and 3) prognosis (oriented towards the future).[33] In fact, it is noteworthy that the Greek term *semeion* refers to both 'signs' and 'symptoms',[34] and that semiotics is described as 'the branch of medical science relating to the interpretation of symptoms',[35] for, as shall be discussed in this chapter, the doctrine of semioethics reproduces this convergence by examining signs as 'symptoms' of social illnesses within the communication order.

Semiotics has been criticized in recent years as a gnoseological science claiming neutrality and objectivity, applied to conduct an abstract and descriptive analysis of signs, that ignores the wider context in which they are created and interpreted, as is the case with the Saussurian binary model of signs which shall be examined in the next section. However, various schools of thought

28 Ibid.

29 *Decoding International Law* (2010), 24.

30 Giovanni Manetti, 'Ancient Semiotics' in Paul Cobley (ed.), *The Routledge Companion to Semiotics* (Routledge 2009), 13.

31 Ibid., 14, 15.

32 Ibid., 16.

33 'Semioethics' (2009), 150; 'Ancient Semiotics' (2009), 16.

34 OED.

35 Ibid.

emerged within what is now identified as 'modern semiotics', and which progressively addressed the reductive view of signs to acknowledge their inevitable axiological reading, from the triadic or 'interpretation approach' adopted by Peirce, Welby, Bakhtin and Rossi-Landi to the significs theory devised by Welby, and followed by Morris, which considers the relationship between signs and values. Ponzio and Petrilli expanded Welby's significs theory and Sebeok's 'Global Semiotics' to create the field of semioethics that explores the meaning of signs and language for the purpose of addressing societal issues.[36]

## II DECODIFICATION SEMIOTICS

The first phase of modern semiotics, also identified as the discipline of semiology or 'study of signs',[37] is founded upon the binary sign model elaborated by Ferdinand de Saussure in his *Cours de linguistique hénérale (Writings in General Linguistics)*, and thereafter published by students of his course in 1916.[38] The Saussurian model is binary on two counts. First, each sign is dyadic: it comprises both the sign vehicle, the 'signifier' (for example, a word) and the content of the sign, the 'signified' (the concept conveyed by the word). Each signifier may stand for more than one concept. For instance, as shall be examined in Chapter 2, the signifier 'girl' can refer to female children but also to domestic workers and even prostitutes, or simply to young women. Likewise, each signified (concept) may be represented by various signifiers (words). The concept of girlhood can be signified by the expressions 'young girls', 'teenage girls', 'teen girls', 'adolescent girls', 'young women' as well as 'youths' and 'juveniles'. The Saussurian model is also binary for signs relate to each other: the first sign is understood in relation to another sign. For example, the meaning of a word is understood by contrasting its meaning with another word, as the term 'girl' might be identified by contrasting it with 'boy', 'woman' or 'man'.

The Saussurian sign model was heavily criticized by several semioticians on the grounds that it operates an artificial 'equal exchange logic' whereby the signifier and the signified, and signs more generally, are conceived as static entities that relate to each other in a mechanical manner. In this context, signs

36 *Semioetica* (2003); 'Semioethics' (2009).

37 *Merriam-Webster Dictionary of the English Language*, Eleventh Edition (2003), Online Updated Edition (Webster). The OED defines semiology as '[t]he branch of science concerned with the study of linguistic signs and symbols'.

38 Simon Bouquet and Rudolf Engler (eds.), *Ferdinand de Saussure: Writings in General Linguistics* (Oxford University Press 2006).

are perceived as mere signals that are recognized and decoded.[39] Bakhtin and Voloshinov argued that the Saussurian matrix was too restrictive for it failed to acknowledge the central role played by the interpretant: individual and collective responses to signs. Saussure examined signs separately from the signifying process and thereby neglected to account for the 'specificity of human communication interaction … the capacity for plurilingualism or heteroglossia, for plurivocality, ambiguity, polysemy, dialogism and otherness'.[40] Indeed, the Saussurian approach was largely inspired by the School of Lausanne on pure economics and the theory of equal exchange value which considers an object of analysis outside its larger context. Consequently, it applied the categories developed by pure economics whereby laws regulating the market economy are studied outside the social relations of production and common structures. In this regard, Rossi-Landi devised the 'postal package theory',[41] to illustrate that, in his view, Saussure conceives signs as merely postal packages sent off from one postal office and received by another, and communication as solely a collection of signs assembled by the sender and identified by the receiver. Rossi-Landi stressed that under the Saussurian approach, 'the receiver needs only to register the content of the message, that is, decodify the message without interpreting it'.[42] The Saussurian model is described as 'decodification semiotics' and 'the semiotics of the code and message',[43] for it is based on the premise that signs are recognized and decoded in an objective and systematic manner.

## III INTERPRETATION SEMIOTICS: PEIRCE'S TRIADIC APPROACH

Interpretation semiotics appears to address the weakness of the binary model for it acknowledges that signs may be interpreted differently by various individuals and in different contexts. It is particularly relevant in international law because human rights treaties constitute 'signs' that may be attributed several

39 Susan Petrilli, *Victoria Welby and the Science of Signs: Significs, Semiotics, Philosophy of Language* (Transaction Publishers 2015), 151.

40 Susan Petrilli, *Sign Studies and Semioethics: Communication, Translation and Values* (De Gruyter Mouton 2014), 6; see Valentin Voloshinov, *Freudianism: A Critical Sketch* (Indiana University Press 1987 [1927]).

41 See Ferruccio Rossi-Landi, *Significato, comunicazione, e parlare comune* (Meaning, Communication and Common Speech) (Marsilio 1998 [1961]); Ferruccio Rossi-Landi, *Language as Work and Trade: A Semiotic Homology for Linguistics and Economics* (Bergin & Garvey Publishers 1983).

42 *Significs* (2015), 151.

43 Massimo Bonfantini, *Le tre tendenze semiotiche del novecento* (The Three Semiotic Trends of the Twentieth Century) (1981) 30 *Versus* 21.

meanings globally. Interpretation semiotics was developed before the Saussurian model, notably in the works of Charles Peirce and Victoria Welby, during the second half of the nineteenth century and early twentieth century, although it became commonly known much later, in the 1930s, and is therefore identified as the second phase of modern semiotics. Peirce, who is widely acclaimed as the forefather of contemporary semiotics, developed a triadic analysis of signs, inspired by the work of the Conimbricenses in the Latin Age,[44] which considers that the sign has three components: 1) the object, 2) the 'sign' or *representamen* and 3) the interpretant – that interact to create an understanding of any object, real or virtual.[45] The first sign component is the object, or 'dynamical object': the object as it is in reality, the 'material' object. The second sign component is the sign or *representamen*, that is, the 'interpreted object': the object as it is represented by the sign. Lastly, the interpretant is the meaning that is given to the object through interpretation. This triadic approach is also described as 'object-interpreted-interpretant'.[46] Hence, if one were to apply Peirce's triadism to examine the semiotics of the concept 'girl': 1) the 'real object' of study is the conceptual notion of the girl child, 2) it is represented by the word 'girl' (the sign representamen) and 3) its definitions in dictionaries and how it is understood by individuals constitute the interpretant.[47] In the Peircean perspective, every interpretant is in turn dependent upon other interpretants, for any definition is based upon the definitions of each word it comprises.[48] For example, the conceptual notion of girl child rights is defined by several representamen, such as claims, liberties, privileges, powers and immunities,[49] and each of

[44] John Doyle (ed.), *The Conimbricenses: Some Questions on Signs* (Marquette University Press 2001).

[45] Floyd Merrell, 'Charles Sanders Peirce's Concept of the Sign' in Paul Cobley (ed.), *The Routledge Companion to Semiotics and Linguistics* (Routledge 2001), 28; Charles Hartshorne and Paul Weiss (eds.), *The Collected Papers of Charles Peirce* (Harvard University Press 1931–1935); Christian Kloesel (ed.), *Writings of Charles S Peirce: A Chronological Edition* (Indiana University Press 1982–2000).

[46] Charles Hartshorne and Paul Weiss (eds.), *The Collected Papers of Charles Peirce* (Harvard University Press 1931–1935); *Sign Crossroads* (2010), 51; Nicole Everaert-Desmedt, 'Peirce's Semiotics' in Louis Hébert (dir.), *Signo* (online) (2011), 3. www.signosemio.com/peirce/semiotics.asp (accessed 12 March 2023).

[47] For a discussion on Peirce's triadism and the law, see 'Semiotics in Law and Jurisprudence' (2023).

[48] Nicole Everaert-Desmedt, 'Peirce's Semiotics' in Louis Hébert (dir.), *Signo* (online) (2011), 3. www.signosemio.com/peirce/semiotics.asp (accessed 12 March 2023).

[49] See Wesley Hohfeld, *Fundamental Legal Conceptions as Applied in Judicial Reasoning* (Yale University Press 1923). Also, for a discussion on those senses of the term, see Bernard Jackson, 'Legal Semiotics and Semiotic Aspects of Jurisprudence' in Anne Wagner and Jan Broekman (eds.), *Prospects of Legal Semiotics* (Springer 2010), 24.

these signifiers has its own definition and definitions, composed of signifiers which in turn are also defined in dictionaries. In this regard, interpretation semiotics is also referred to as 'semiosis', which is the 'process, or relation, or situation, in which something carries out the role of the sign': the sign stands for another sign, and thereby creates another sign.[50] The interpretant, that is, *definitions in dictionaries and what individuals and communities understand it to mean*, has the potential of engendering another sign indefinitely, in an 'unending chain of deferrals from one interpretant to another',[51] a phenomenon entitled 'infinite semiosis'.[52]

Peirce developed another triad comprising the immediate, dynamical and final interpretants. The immediate interpretant concerns the meaning normally given to a sign, the dynamical interpretant refers to the meaning of a sign in a specific context and the final interpretant relates to 'the sign as it appears at the extreme limits of its interpretative possibilities, that is, it concerns all those possible responses that signs may provoke in the unlimited chain of interpretants'.[53] This triad is particularly relevant for the analysis of the content of international treaties as it underscores that while a number of concepts may be universally acknowledged and understood, certain notions are interpreted differently according to various sociological, cultural, regional and economic factors. Hence, the terminology employed to define the girl child and describe her rights must be sufficiently clear so as not to be misinterpreted, especially in its extreme limits, in ways that could diminish her rights.

Although Peirce recognized the important role played by the interpretant, his triadic approach was nevertheless criticized on the grounds that it operates a unilateral and abstract analysis of signs and fails to account for human influence on the conception of signs as well as its corresponding impact.[54] Firstly, Peirce overlooked the intention behind the conception of signs and the choice of signifiers. He disregarded the motivation – what we shall refer to as 'meaning-intention' – of the master signifiers who create signs and select the representamen, as well as the power relations involved. Secondly, Peirce failed to examine the concrete and symbolic outcomes of the use of concepts and sign vehicles. While he acknowledged that signs may be interpreted differently according to various contexts, and thus shall have diverse impacts in different communities, he nevertheless neglected to account for the valutative aspect of signs: the

50 *Sign Crossroads* (2010), 49, 53.
51 Ibid., 51.
52 Susan Petrilli, *The Self as a Sign, the World, and the Other: Living Semiotics* (Transaction Publishers 2013), 21.
53 *Significs* (2015), 155.
54 *Sign Studies* (2014), 129.

repercussions of the final interpretation on human beings and society. While Peirce demonstrated interest in the relationship between signs and values in his later works,[55] his triadic approach did not encompass an ethical component, and thus disregarded the axiology of signs, that is, the theory of their value. Accordingly, this valutative aspect of semiotics was thereafter also neglected by Peircians.[56] This may appear as somewhat surprising since Peirce's research was greatly influenced by the works of Victoria Welby, who emphasized the role of interpretation in the doctrine of semiotics, and with whom he corresponded regularly over the course of decades.[57] In fact, Welby expanded the science of semiotics as conceived by Peirce to address the relation between signs and values, an approach which was thereafter followed by Charles Morris.

## IV THE VICTORIA LADY WELBY SIGNIFICS THEORY

Lady Welby occupied a privileged position within English society as the goddaughter of Queen Victoria and was, therefore, able, in spite of her subordinate status as a woman at the time, to publish many articles in newspapers and scientific journals as well as books and essays in the fields of philosophy, science, mathematics, anthropology, education and social issues, as well as share her theories through an epistolary network of over 450 leading personalities of her time.[58] Lady Welby's approach to semiotics constitutes a landmark for, in addition to studying the meaning of signs and symbols, she conceived a new discipline, coined 'significs', to explore their intentional or volitional aspect, and ultimate significance. Her definition of significs was enshrined in the 1911 edition of the *Oxford English Dictionary* (OED) as 'a proposed science and educational method based upon the importance of realizing the exact significance of terms and conceptions, and their influence on thought and life'.[59] Welby chose to name this new approach 'significs' in reference to the 'unconsciously philosophical question' which initiates the analysis of meaning: 'What does this signify?' which encapsulates questions such as '"What is the sense of . . . ?", "What do we intend by . . . ?", "What is the meaning of . . .?" (. . .) "Why do we give value to experience?"'[60] She wished to distinguish her approach from the general semiotics doctrine of her

55 'Semioethics' (2009), 151.

56 Ibid.

57 See Charles Hardwick and James Cook (eds.), *Semiotics and Significs: The Correspondence between Charles S. Peirce and Victoria Lady Welby* (Indiana University Press 1977).

58 *Sign Crossroads* (2010), 53–55; *Sign Studies* (2014), 126.

59 Oxford English Dictionary 1911 Edition (OED 1911).

60 *Sign Studies* (2014), 129–30.

time, and noted that as a new term 'significs' presented the advantage of not having been used and thus did not have technical associations, contrary to terms such as 'semantics' which refers generally to 'the study of the meaning of signs',[61] and 'sensifics' which could be associated with 'sense'.[62]

Welby's numerous travels throughout her childhood, in countries spanning four continents, such as Canada, the United States, Mexico, Italy, France, Morocco, Turkey and Syria,[63] opened her linguistic and cultural horizons, and she became aware, at a young age, of the diversity of interpretations that signs and words could have within different political, social, cultural and economic contexts. In this regard, she criticized the presumption of certain semioticians and British scholars of her time that signs have the same meaning for all individuals and interpretants. Welby coined the expression 'plain meaning' to refer to this restrictive approach:

> [w]e have been postulating an absolute Plain Meaning to be thought of, as it were, in capital letters. We have been virtually assuming that our hearers and readers all share the same mental background and atmosphere. We have practically supposed that they all look through the same inferential eyes.[64]

She was particularly concerned with the 'widespread belief that a text can evolve into a single reading, into an absolute and definitive interpretant valid for all times'.[65] As previously mentioned, her work falls within interpretation semiotics and it is noteworthy that well before Saussure's decodification semiotics, she had already identified the latter's central shortcoming: the myth of the single universal meaning of terminology.

Welby developed the *Threefold Laws of Meaning* – Sense, Meaning, and Significance – as a framework to examine the import of all forms of human expression. She explained this Meaning Triad in the following terms:

> [T]he one crucial question in all Expression, whether by action or sound, symbol or picture, is its special property, first of Sense, that in which it is used, then of Meaning as the intention of the user, and, most far-reaching and momentous of all, of implication, of ultimate Significance.[66]

61 OED.
62 *Sign Studies* (2014), 125–26.
63 *Significs* (2015), xix.
64 Victoria Welby, 'Meaning and Metaphor' (1893) 3 *The Monist* 510, 512.
65 *Sign Studies* (2014), 141.
66 *Significs and Language* (1911), 9. Welby's scientific writings are presently available in the Welby Collection, Clara Thomas Archives and Special Collections, York University Libraries (Toronto, Canada), consulted by the author *in loco*, and the Lady Welby Library at the University of London Library (United Kingdom).

Welby's theory of significs seems particularly suitable to examine the semiotics of terminology in the international legal realm as concerns girl children, for in addition to studying the sense of words, it enables an analysis of the reason behind the selection of terms to define the girl child and phrase her rights, and their ultimate significance. In this regard, it appears more appropriate than Peirce's 'immediate-dynamic-final interpretant' triad, which does not consider the 'meaning-intention' and 'ultimate significance' of signs. Welby's *Threefold Laws of Meaning* allow for the examination of the significance of terminology and thus its possible interpretations according to diverse political, economic, social and cultural factors, which is crucial when studying the content of international treaties adopted by states worldwide. This book shall therefore apply Lady Welby's Meaning Triad as a framework to examine whether the content of international law sufficiently protects the girl child.

### 1 *Sense*

The Meaning Triad comprises three levels of analysis that shall be examined in this book. The first level of meaning, *sense*, corresponds to the textual meaning of the provisions of international human rights treaties relevant to girl children. *Sense* refers to the words used to describe the girl child and the content of her rights and fundamental freedoms in treaty provisions, and what they are understood to signify within the international legal framework. This first step is reflected in the 'General Rule of Interpretation' established in the Vienna Convention on the Law of Treaties (1969) under article 31(1), which considers word analysis as the starting point of treaty interpretation: '[a] treaty shall be interpreted in good faith in accordance with the *ordinary meaning to be given to the terms* of the treaty in their context and in the light of its object and purpose'.[67] In this perspective, Welby's *sense* element corresponds to the 'textual approach' of the Vienna Convention based on the assumption that the text has an intrinsic meaning, independently from the circumstances of its drafting, similar to Saussure's equal exchange logic between the signifier (the treaty text) and the signified (the agreement between the parties). Since the Vienna Convention is the central international instrument codifying the rules of treaty interpretation, its recognition of the primacy of the text, or *sense*, is particularly relevant to our analysis. This book shall refer to the ordinary meaning of the terms employed in relevant international treaties, unless it could be argued that the drafters intended a special meaning. Indeed, article

[67] Vienna Convention (1969), art. 31(1) (emphasis added).

31(4) of the Vienna Convention places the burden of proof on those arguing that the term has a special meaning: '[a] special meaning shall be given to a term if it is established that the parties so intended'. In this regard, Gardiner contends that should the context be technical or specialized, words shall be interpreted accordingly.[68] While in fields such as intellectual property and in complex contracts, treaties should be examined in light of the special meaning of the terms employed, it is argued that human rights treaties belong to a different category. For rights to become universal, their 'representamen' and 'signifier' – the treaty provisions – must be easy to comprehend and thus accessible to all human beings, across cultures, and regardless of socio-economic status. Accordingly, provisions should be clearly formulated so that all individuals can understand their meaning, including the final interpretant(s). This concern for clarity and accessibility is embedded in the text of the UDHR,[69] and the international community thereafter avoided specialized legal terminology in human rights treaties, although as shall be discussed in the next chapters, ambiguous terms and concepts are still employed. Hence, this book shall analyze the ordinary meaning of terms in treaties relevant to the girl child, except when there is a clear indication that the drafters gave them special meaning. The sense of the terminology employed to identify the girl child and describe her rights shall be assessed by examining the definitions offered within international instruments and English dictionaries. As noted by Kadelbach: '[t]he emphasis on "ordinary meaning", understood as the common use of the term, is probably the reason for the use of dictionaries of all sorts in order to determine an everyday understanding'.[70] This book shall primarily refer to the OED and the Webster; however, it will also turn to other dictionaries providing a more comprehensive historical perspective of terms.

The examination of the sense of international treaties nevertheless involves certain limitations. Firstly, it is acknowledged that the exploration of the sense element through interpretative semiotics can become a form of infinite semiosis, since the recourse to dictionaries to elucidate the ordinary meaning of words can become a never-ending process where definitions carry out the role of the sign. As noted by Barthes, dictionaries are 'vertiginous' objects in which each word is defined in relation to other terms, which in turn are also

68 Richard Gardiner, *Treaty Interpretation* (Oxford University Press 2015), 369.

69 Following Dr Chang's interventions, see Draft International Declaration of Human Rights, 3rd session, Third Committee, 91st meeting (2 October 1948) UN Doc A/C.3/SR.91, 48.

70 Stefan Kadelbach, 'Interpretation of the Charter' in Bruno Simma et al. (eds.), *The Charter of the United Nations: A Commentary* (Oxford University Press 2012), 76–77.

defined in reference to other terminology.[71] However, in the case at hand, we shall restrict our analysis to the first and second levels of the definitions of terms examined, for instance, we shall explore 1) the terminology 'girl child' and 2) relevant terms employed to describe this concept in dictionaries, as well as pertinent synonyms and antonyms, such as woman, man and boy; however, we shall not embark on a boundless analysis of each term thereafter. Moreover, our study is not restricted to dictionaries, as it primarily focuses on definitions offered in international treaties and is thus more circumscribed.

Secondly, the 'ordinary meaning' or textual approach is complicated by the historical meaning of terminology: certain terms adopted during the drafting of the treaty might not have the same sense today, or tomorrow. In this regard, it is worthy of note that several terms referring to the child, and the girl child, have been re-examined since the drafting of relevant international instruments pertaining to children. For instance, the expression 'juvenile', employed in the UN Standard Minimum Rules for the Administration of Juvenile Justice (1985), as well as in the CRC General Comment on Juvenile Justice (2007),[72] is today recognized as having negative connotations, since the commission of an offence suddenly becomes the central identity vector defining the child, including the girl child. Accordingly, expressions such as 'girls in conflict with the law', 'young people' and 'youths' are preferred.[73] The present author recommended the use of the expression 'child justice' in 2007,[74] and the CRC Committee adopted this new terminology in its general comment replacing the expression 'juvenile justice' in 2019.[75] This book shall

[71] Roland Barthes, *Œuvres complètes* (Complete Works of Roland Barthes) (Éditions du Seuil 2002), 513.

[72] See for example the United Nations Standard Minimum Rules for the Administration of Juvenile Justice (The Beijing Rules), (adopted 29 November 1985) UN Doc A/Res/40/33; United Nations Rules for the Protection of Juveniles Deprived of their Liberty (adopted 14 December 1990) UN Doc A/Res/45/113); United Nations Guidelines for the Prevention of Juvenile Delinquency (The Riyadh Guidelines) (adopted 14 December 1990) UN Doc A/Res/45/112; CRC General Comment No. 10: Children's Rights in Juvenile Justice (25 April 2007) UN Doc CRC/C/GC/10.

[73] For a discussion on the terminology employed to refer to children in conflict with the law, see Andrew Becroft, 'Children and Young People in Conflict with the Law: Asking the Hard Questions' (2009) 57 *Juvenile and Family Court Journal* 1; Clara Chapdelaine-Feliciati, 'Child Justice in Canada and the Four Ps: Protection, Prosecution, Prevention, and Participation' (2007) 15 *Critical Criminology* 267; Gayle Rhineberger-Dunn, 'Myth versus Reality: Comparing the Depiction of Juvenile Delinquency in Metropolitan Newspapers with Arrest Data' (2013) 83 *Sociological Inquiry* 473.

[74] 'Child Justice' (2007).

[75] CRC General Comment No. 24: Children's Rights in the Child Justice System (18 September 2019) UN Doc CRC/C/GC/24: the Committee specifies that 'the term "child justice system" is used in place of "juvenile justice"' in its first footnote, and defines the 'child

thus consider historical meaning while examining treaty provisions, and notably refer to the *travaux préparatoires* to elucidate the drafters' intentions.

Thirdly, the concept of 'ordinary meaning' itself raises questions. Professor McDougal, in his legendary criticism of the textual approach during the drafting of article 31 of the Vienna Convention, questioned whether one could identify a plain meaning of words:

> In reality, words had no fixed or natural meaning which the parties to an agreement could not alter. The 'plain and ordinary' meanings of words were multiple and ambiguous and could be made particular and clear only by reference to the factual circumstances of their use.[76]

Moreover, the Special Rapporteur of the International Law Commission, Waldock, recognized that '[w]ith regard to the expression "ordinary meaning", nothing could have been further from the Commission's intention than to suggest that words had a "dictionary" or "intrinsic" meaning in themselves'.[77] This criticism of the ordinary meaning echoes Welby's concern of the 'plain meaning' of words which led her to devise her theory of significs and The Meaning Triad, notably the second and third elements of 'meaning' and 'significance'.[78] The textual approach has been criticized on the grounds that it appears to examine the text in a vacuum and fails to acknowledge the intention of the master signifiers, that is, the treaty drafters, and the role of the interpretant. During the Vienna Conference, some delegates noted that interpreting 'words in accordance with dictionary definitions ... might conflict with the will of the parties'.[79] Others observed that words could be interpreted differently by different individuals and institutions.[80] This latter

justice system' as 'the legislation, norms and standards, procedures, mechanisms and provisions specifically applicable to, and institutions and bodies set up to deal with, children considered as offenders' (para. 8); it refers for example to the 'child justice system' and 'principles of child justice' (para. 3).

76 UN Conference on the Law of Treaties (Vienna, First Session, 26 March–24 May 1968), 31st Meeting (19 April 1968) UN Doc A/CONF.39/11, Professor Myres McDougal, United States of America, 167, para. 44.

77 UN Conference on the Law of Treaties (Vienna, First Session, 26 March–24 May 1968), 33rd Meeting (22 April 1968) UN Doc A/CONF.39/11, Sir Humphrey Waldock, 184, para. 70.

78 'Meaning and Metaphor' (1893), 512–13.

79 UN Conference on the Law of Treaties (Vienna, First Session, 26 March–24 May 1968), 32nd Meeting (20 April 1968) UN Doc A/CONF.39/11, Mr Santiago Martínez Caro, Spain, 174, para. 32.

80 UN Conference on the Law of Treaties (Vienna, First Session, 26 March–24 May 1968), 31st Meeting (19 April 1968) UN Doc A/CONF.39/11, Professor Myres McDougal, United States of America, 167, para. 41. In this context, he quoted McNair's declaration that: 'it begs the question whether the words used are, or are not, clear – a subjective matter because they may be clear to one man and not clear to another, and frequently to one or more judges and not to

statement is aligned with Peirce's third triadic element: the interpretant. Peirce underscores that 'no man's interpretation of words is based on exactly the same experience among different persons'.[81] Kolb argues that the 'subject of interpretation', that is, the person or institution interpreting the treaty, is a considerable factor to consider, and notes in this regard that 'le qui l'emporte souvent sur le comment' ('the person who interprets often has precedence over the means employed to interpret', my translation).[82] As previously noted, each individual may attribute different meanings to the same sign, and the final interpretant may push this divergence to the extreme. For example, as shall be discussed in this book, certain concepts, such as the 'best interests of the child' principle enshrined in the CRC, may be perceived by certain States parties or individuals as sanctioning harmful practices, such as child marriage or FGM, in the name of the girl's 'best interests'.[83] Since the textual approach may lead to diverse interpretations, it can also allow States parties to act in bad faith when implementing treaty provisions. Hosseinnejad argues that 'to assume that words have a "plain" meaning independent from the tradition within which the word is used permits interpreters to interpret legal texts according to whatever seems suitable to them'.[84] This is particularly problematic as concerns the human rights and fundamental freedoms of the girl child since States parties may choose to interpret provisions so as not to protect her rights fully. Accordingly, in order to address these shortcomings, the present book shall examine the sense of the 'ordinary meaning' of terms under an extra-textual or 'teleological' approach which gives effect to the object and purpose of the treaty as indicated in article 31(1) of the Vienna Convention, and as supported by several of the Vienna Convention drafters.[85] In some

their colleagues', Lord Arnold Duncan McNair, *The Law of Treaties* (Oxford Clarendon Press 1961), 372.

81 *Collected Papers* (1931–1935), vol. 5, 506.

82 Robert Kolb, 'Is There a Subject-Matter Ontology in Interpretation of International Legal Norms?' in Mads Andenas and Eirik Bjorge (eds.), *A Farewell to Fragmentation: Reassertion and Convergence in International Law* (Cambridge University Press 2015) 476–77. Kolb notes for instance that states and the ICJ might adopt different approaches and notably have different agendas.

83 Ladan Askari, 'Girls' Rights under International Law: An Argument for Establishing Gender Equality as Jus Cogens' (1998–1999) 8 *Southern California Review of Law and Women's Studies* 3, explains that the interdeterminacy of this standard 'exposes it to multiple interpretations', noting that FGM could be perceived as allowing the girl child to become an accepted member of her community: 19.

84 Katayoun Hosseinnejad, 'On the Nature of Interpretation in International Law' (2015) 4 *UCL Journal of Law and Jurisprudence* 225, 240.

85 See for example Martin Ris, 'Treaty Interpretation and ICJ Recourse to *Travaux Préparatoires*: Towards a Proposed Amendment of Articles 31 and 32 of the Vienna Convention on the Law of Treaties' (1991) 14 *Boston College International and Comparative Law Review* 111, 113,

cases, it will be acknowledged that the word examined might have only one meaning, or at least, one main ordinary meaning.[86] While the treaty text is the basis of our interpretation, other elements shall also be examined to clarify the context, object and purpose of the treaty, as stated in the Vienna Convention:

> 31(2) The context for the purpose of the interpretation of a treaty shall comprise, in addition to the text, including its preamble and annexes:
>
> a) any agreement relating to the treaty which was made between all the parties in connection with the conclusion of the treaty
> b) any instrument which was made by one or more parties in connection with the conclusion of the treaty and accepted by the other parties as an instrument related to the treaty.

In the semiotic analysis conducted in this book, we shall refer to the preamble of treaties to clarify the content of provisions, where relevant. Moreover, as stipulated under article 31(2)a) of the Vienna Convention, together with the context, we shall consider 'any agreement relating to the treaty which was made between all the parties in connection with the conclusion of the treaty' and in line with article 31(3) of the Vienna Convention, we shall consider subsequent agreements 'between the parties regarding the interpretation of the treaty' and 'subsequent practice in the application of the treaty'. For example, we shall refer, where relevant, to subsequent agreements, such as the Optional Protocols to the CRC, even though the latter were not ratified by all States parties to the Convention, for they indicate an intention by several parties to address specific issues, notably children in armed conflict and sexual exploitation.[87] Finally, our analysis will not be limited to the text and the object and

115; Shabtai Rosenne, 'Interpretation of Treaties in the Restatement and the International Law Commission's Draft Articles: A Comparison' (1966) 5 *Columbia Journal of Transnational Law* 205, 221; UN Conference on the Law of Treaties (Vienna, First Session, 26 March–24 May 1968), 31st Meeting (19 April 1968) UN Doc A/CONF.39/11, Mr E. K. Dadzie, Ghana, 170, para. 70.

86 See for example UN Conference on the Law of Treaties (Vienna, First Session, 26 March–24 May 1968), 32nd Meeting (20 April 1968) UN Doc A/CONF.39/11, Professor Stanislaw Nahlik, Poland, 174, para. 23: '[o]f course, the same word might have several meanings, but that was true of certain words only. Moreover, among different meanings of a word, there was usually one which could be considered as its "ordinary meaning" or "natural meaning"'.

87 Optional Protocol to the Convention on the Rights of the Child on the Involvement of Children in Armed Conflict (OPAC) (New York, adopted 25 May 2000, entered into force 12 February 2002) 2173 UNTS 222: 173 States parties; Optional Protocol to the Convention on the Rights of the Child on the Sale of Children, Child Prostitution and Child Pornography (OPSC) (New York, adopted 25 may 2000, entered into force 18 January 2002) 2171 UNTS 227: 178 States parties. For a discussion on the OPSC, see Clara Chapdelaine-Feliciati et al., 'United Nations Handbook on the Optional Protocol to the CRC on the Sale of Children, Child Prostitution and Child Pornography' (UNICEF Office Research 2009).

purpose of the treaties examined, for we shall also consider Welby's second triadic element: the 'meaning-intention' of the parties.

## 2 *Meaning*

The second level of Welby's Triad is the *meaning* of the word employed, 'the intent which it is desired to convey – the intention of the user'.[88] This level corresponds to the intention behind the selection of a term, the 'meaning-intention'.[89] The *meaning* of terminology in international law is the intention of the drafters when choosing specific terms to describe rights as well as States parties' duties under the treaty. It shall be investigated in this book by studying the *travaux préparatoires* of international treaties, notably the CRC, CEDAW and ICCPR, which describe the negotiations leading to the selection of terminology to formulate rights during the drafting processes. The UN Institute for Training and Research (UNITAR) emphasizes that the *travaux préparatoires* enable us to:

> trace the origin of each significant word and phrase and, in addition, identify proposals which were made in the course of negotiations, but which were not implemented ... and which for this very reason can shed light – albeit sometimes a negative one – on the meaning of the text adopted.[90]

One can argue that the second triadic element 'meaning-intention' is reflected under article 32 of the Vienna Convention which stipulates that '[r]ecourse may be had to supplementary means of interpretation, including the preparatory work of the treaty and the circumstances of its conclusion'. Lauterpacht famously noted that the *travaux* constitute a fundamental element, perhaps the most important, of treaty interpretation, and is an essential tool to identify the intention of the parties.[91]

While the *travaux* offer essential insight to identify the *meaning-intention* of the drafters, they nevertheless comprise some limitations which should be acknowledged. The first issue is what we mean by *travaux préparatoires*: what is included in these documents? For instance, do they comprise the declarations of agreement, instructions to negotiators, diplomatic exchanges and

88 Victoria Welby, *What is Meaning? Studies in the Development of Significance* (Macmillan 1903; reprint in John Benjamins, Foundations of Semiotics (1983)), 5–6.

89 Petrilli, *Signifying and Understanding: Reading the Works of Victoria Welby and the Signific Movement* (De Gruyter Mouton 2009), 264.

90 *Travaux préparatoires ICCPR* (1987), xxii.

91 Sir Hersch Lauterpacht, 'De l'interprétation des traités: Rapport' (Treaty Interpretation: Report) (1950-II) 43 *Annuaire de l'Institut de droit international – Yearbook, Institute of International Law* 366, 397.

documents emanating from international agencies? It is notable that the drafters of the Vienna Convention chose not to offer a definition of the *travaux préparatoires*, so as not to restrict their content.[92] This begs the question whether the *travaux* solely incorporate discussions that occurred during official meetings, or also communications and statements made outside this context. Many negotiations occur both *behind* closed doors during private meetings and *outside* closed doors during 'informal' conversations. Indeed, as noted by Ris: 'crucial deliberations ... often occur in private and thus never appear in the negotiation record'.[93] This uncertainty as to the content of the *travaux* has the additional shortcoming that any statement made during the framing of the treaty could be considered a part of the preparatory work, including in informal settings. It also raises the following question: at which time do comments made by delegates matter? Moreover, states' interventions during official meetings can be misleading. As noted by the Brazilian delegation during the Vienna Conference:

> Although the preparatory work must undoubtedly be borne in mind, the utmost caution was necessary. States sometimes concealed their real views on the questions under discussion at conferences or resorted to friendly States to express them. A certain degree of confusion was thereby created, and gave rise to mistrust.[94]

In the case at hand, since state representatives are aware that their interventions are recorded in the *travaux préparatoires*, they may prefer not to formally disagree with a formulation of rights that would protect girl children, and instead pressure other states, including those that share common political and commercial interests, to voice their opposition. A government delegation may even request other states to present its suggestions in their own name. One must also bear in mind that since the drafting process spans over a decade, as with the CRC and CEDAW, and two decades for the Twin Covenants, several states undergo significant regime changes during these time periods.[95] The same state may send different representatives to the working group over the course of a decade or two, and in some cases, give them completely

92 Julian Davis Mortenson, 'The Travaux of Travaux: Is the Vienna Convention Hostile to Drafting History?' (2013) 107 *American Journal of International Law* 780, 807.

93 'Recourse to Travaux Préparatoires' (1991), 113.

94 UN Conference on the Law of Treaties (Vienna, First Session, 26 March–24 May 1968), 32nd Meeting (20 April 1968) UN Doc A/CONF.39/11, Ambassador Gilberto Amado, Brazil, 176, para. 53.

95 Yahli Shereshevsky and Tom Noah, 'Does Exposure to Preparatory Work Affect Treaty Interpretation? An Experimental Study on International Law Students and Experts' (2018) 28 *European Journal of International Law* 1287, 1289.

opposite instructions. This may account for the fact that some states strongly support a certain vision of human rights, or in the case at hand, of girl child rights, at the beginning of the drafting process, and thereafter adopt a completely different approach. Hence, the contributions of states may vary significantly throughout the course of treaty preparation, thereby preventing consistency and thus a reliable diagnosis of their meaning-intention.[96]

Furthermore, a state, acting in bad faith, could purposely bring out an issue during the official meetings, in the hopes that such a declaration will later be used to interpret treaty provisions. This issue was raised during the Vienna Conference: 'it was only too easy for a State wishing to evade its obligations to inject an element of uncertainty by referring to preparatory work'.[97] Hence, the *travaux préparatoires* cannot offer a complete depiction of the drafting process and must be read in light of the abovementioned limitations. In this book, we shall restrict our analysis to the discussions that occurred between the drafters as reported in the *travaux préparatoires* of the CRC, CEDAW and ICCPR, including the preliminary drafts of provisions, while acknowledging that these official documents cannot offer an exhaustive account of negotiations and debates, such as confidential agreements taking place behind closed doors, in hallways, at receptions and other informal venues.

The second issue to be considered is that the semiotic reading of the *travaux préparatoires* is affected by historical subjectivism.[98] Indeed, one cannot examine the past objectively, and reference to history in international law will inevitably be political. As noted by Klabbers:

> [W]hile relying on history, we do not adopt it wholesale: we pick out the bits and pieces, and the versions of history, that are convenient for whichever

96 It is worthy of note that in the case at hand, this problem does not apply so much to the CRC as most states sent consistently the same, or almost always the same, delegates to meetings: see Nigel Cantwell, 'Origins, Development and Significance of the United Nations Convention on the Rights of the Child' in Sharon Detrick (ed.), *The United Nations Convention on the Rights of the Child: A Guide to the* Travaux préparatoires (Martinus Nijhoff 1992), 23.

97 UN Conference on the Law of Treaties (Vienna, First Session, 26 March–24 May 1968), 31st Meeting (19 April 1968) UN Doc A/CONF.39/11, Professor Eduardo Jiménez de Aréchaga, Uruguay, 170, para. 65.

98 For a discussion on historical subjectivism and the CRC, see Clara Chapdelaine-Feliciati, 'Les réserves en droit international ont-elles des limites? Étude sémioéthique du droit à l'éducation de la Convention relative aux droits de l'enfant'(Do Reservations have Limits under International Law? Semioethic Study of the Child's Right to Education under the Convention on the Rights of the Child) (2022) 35 *Revue internationale de sémiotique juridique/International Journal for the Semiotics of Law* 309. The author wishes to thank José Manuel Aroso Linhares and Mario Ricca for judicious comments on 'semiotic transmutation', historical subjectivism and the *travaux préparatoires* during her presentation at the Conference *The Limits of Law*, Coimbra University, Faculty of Law, Portugal (2019).

> argument we happen to be making ... whereas we ignore the less useful or welcome aspects and versions ... what matters is not whether to look at history generally, but which history to look at, and whose history to look at.[99]

A semiotic analysis of the *travaux préparatoires* which were drafted over thirty (CRC) to seventy years ago (Twin Covenants) undertaken in a modern perspective may not account for the historical dynamics of that era. Likewise, such an analysis might be influenced by the semiotician's own awareness of events that took place afterwards and which were not considered by the drafters at the time. Additionally, as is the case with treaty provisions, the *travaux* may be read in contemporary or instead historical language, which adds an additional layer of interpretation. Linderfalk argues that the former refers to language conventions 'adhered to at the time the treaty is interpreted', and the latter 'adhered to at the time the treaty was concluded'.[100] In the former case, the semiotician might neglect to take into consideration the meaning of terms at the time they were selected, and in the latter, s/he might fail to examine the impact of that terminology today. The semiotician might also question whether the meaning of the terms selected was meant to evolve according to future schools of thought and international developments, or whether they were fixed once enshrined in the treaty.[101] Accordingly, a semiotic analysis of the *travaux préparatoires* constitutes a transformation or transmutation of historical documents. Moreover, the *travaux* themselves are the product of the interpretation, by their authors, of the discussions that took place during the drafting process. These authors also have a *meaning-intention* which may have influenced the final product, thereby creating a new *sense* of the *travaux préparatoires*. Consequently, a semiotic analysis involves two levels of transformation of the *travaux*: that of their authors, and that of semioticians, both acting as Peirce's 'immediate' and 'dynamical' interpretants, thereby adding their own subjective layers of interpretation.[102] In this regard, it is worthy of note that several scholars criticize the claim of objectivity in interpretation. Zarbiyev notes that '[i]nterpretation represents a danger to the

99 'Declining Travaux' (2003), 270.

100 Ulf Linderfalk, *On the Interpretation of Treaties: The Modern International Law as Expressed in the 1969 Vienna Convention on the Law of Treaties* (Springer 2007), 73. Smolka and Pirker contend that judges' decisions to analyze the former or the latter are often acted upon mechanically, without acknowledging the shortcomings of either approach, and thus often lack transparency: 'International Law Pragmatics' (2016), 3.

101 Rahim Moloo, 'Changing Times, Changing Obligations? The Interpretation of Treaties over Time', Proceedings of the Annual Meeting, American Society of International Law, 106 *Confronting Complexity* (Cambridge University Press 2012), 262–63.

102 *Collected Papers Peirce* (1931–1935); 'Peirce Concept Sign' (2001), 28.

integrity of law, implying that it does a certain level of discretion, which is antithetical to certainty that is seen as an essential part of any legal system'.[103]

The third issue to be considered is that the sense of the *travaux préparatoires* may differ when they are translated into other languages. For instance, the English version of the propositions submitted by delegates may differ from its French version, which adds another layer of uncertainty.[104] In this book, we shall thus consider these factors, and while our analysis shall be conducted in the contemporary English language, we shall also acknowledge the sense that was given to certain terms at the time they were selected by the drafters, including by referring to dictionaries. The *travaux préparatoires* nevertheless constitute an essential element of interpretation, both to elucidate the sense of the treaty text, and its meaning-intention. As regards the former, the Vienna Convention confirms that the *travaux préparatoires* constitute an element of treaty interpretation for they may assist in understanding the context or textual environment of the terms of the treaty. The decision to locate the *travaux* in article 32, separately from article 31 which enshrines the General Rule of Interpretation, constitutes a sign in itself, especially as article 32 refers to '[s]-upplementary means of interpretation', thereby implying that the *travaux* are subordinate to the text of the treaty. As previously noted, the Vienna Convention gives precedence to the textual ordinary meaning of a word rather than the intent of the drafters when elucidating the sense of the treaty. Kadelbach underscores that the ICJ, 'along the lines of the [Vienna Convention], has moved towards preference of the textual over the original intent approach'.[105] This does not signify that reference to the *travaux* is not pertinent to elucidate the sense of treaty provisions. Presently, UNITAR notes that individuals who accept professional responsibility in interpreting treaties, such as States parties, members of treaty bodies, judges and lawyers, hence the master signifiers 'will not normally feel able to rely exclusively upon the interpretation which someone else has placed upon the preparatory work'.[106] In this regard, UNITAR emphasizes that '[n]o lawyer would feel satisfied about his identification of a meaning of a treaty unless he had examined the preparatory work'.[107]

[103] Fuad Zarbiyev, 'The Cash Value of the Rules of Treaty Interpretation' (2019) 32 *Leiden Journal of International* Law 33, 37.

[104] See last section of this chapter for a discussion on authentic languages and translations of international instruments.

[105] 'Charter Interpretation' (2012), 77.

[106] *Travaux préparatoires ICCPR* (1987), xxii.

[107] Ibid., xxii. It is however noteworthy that the UN Institute for Training and Research (UNITAR) solely employs masculine pronouns to refer to lawyers, for it could imply that this profession does not encompass women.

Lady Welby's first two laws of meaning, that is, the examination of the sense of terms and the investigation of the meaning-intention of the drafters, constitute two distinct although interconnected components of the semiotic analysis, and are equally important to establish the significance of international treaties. Whereas in the rules of interpretation of the Vienna Convention, the intent of the drafters is examined solely for the purpose of identifying the sense of the treaty provisions, and solely as a subsidiary element, this book examines the *travaux préparatoires* to uncover the meaning-intention of the delegates in choosing a term as it sheds light on the power struggles between delegates – and the competing interests they may represent – in shaping the symbolic and concrete significance of treaty provisions as concerns the girl child. As noted by Klabbers:

> The *travaux préparatoires* somehow connect the stultified text of a treaty to the real world of politics, of intercourse between states with their powers and their weaknesses, their sympathies and antipathies, their motivations and intentions.[108]

The *travaux* allow us to identify treaty provisions that were reached unanimously, and those that instead triggered significant debates, in some cases, over the course of decades. This second element of The Meaning Triad is particularly useful to ascertain which girl child rights encountered the most resistance from certain States parties, and thus which are less likely to be implemented at the domestic level.

## 3 *Significance*

The third level of meaning, *significance*, is the ultimate, covert or overt, import of the language used to phrase rights under international law. Welby underscores:

> Significance is always manifold, and intensifies its sense as well as its meaning, by expressing its importance, its appeal to us, its moment for us, its emotional force, its ideal value, its moral aspects, its universal or at least social range.[109]

The significance of terminology in international law is that it moulds the substance of rights, their scope, as well as the extent of States parties' obligations. In this regard, terminology shapes the notion of rights and their potential

[108] 'Declining Travaux' (2003), 286.
[109] *What is Meaning?* (1903), 5–6.

universal recognition and implementation at the domestic level, and conversely, their possible denial, dismissal or violation. The significance of terminology shall be explored in this monograph by analyzing the consequences of the formulation of rights in treaties on their substance as well as on the corresponding obligations of States parties. We shall endeavour to answer the following questions: is the girl child clearly identified under international law? Who is protected under the umbrella of the 'girl child' identity vector? Is the boundary for the beginning, and for the end of girlhood, clearly delineated in the international legal framework? What happens to young women located at the frontiers of girlhood and womanhood? Are the rights of girl children phrased in sufficiently clear terms? Could they be (mis)interpreted by the dynamical and final interpretants? Do provisions, as formulated, take into consideration the obstacles that girl children face in exercising their rights? Do treaties tackle specific human rights abuses experienced by girl children, such as child marriage? Do treaties tend to focus only on certain forms of abuse, thereby disregarding other issues, such as the over-sexualization of girls and unrealistic beauty ideals? Are the rights phrased in a paternalistic approach or do they truly empower girl children? Do treaty provisions protect girl children in both the Global South and Global North, the West and East and across social classes? Finally, do treaty provisions address the intersectional discrimination experienced by girls on account of class, race, religion, culture, (dis)abilities and sexual orientation as well as girls in specific circumstances, such as armed conflict, detention and girl child refugees?

## 4 *The Lady Welby Legacy*

Welby's study of the meaning and value of signs was followed by Charles Morris who underscored that the science of semiotics could not be studied separately from axiology, defined as the 'study of the nature, and criteria of values and of value judgments especially in ethics'.[110] Morris argued that every sign has not only meaning in terms of 'linguistic meaning', the approach followed by Peirce and Saussure, but also an intrinsic social and ethical meaning. In this regard, he stated that: '[i]n many languages there is a term like the English term "meaning" which has two poles: that which something signifies and the value or significance of what is signified'.[111]

[110] Webster.

[111] Charles Morris, *Signification and Significance: A Study of the Relations of Signs and Values* (MIT Press 1964), vii.

Although influential, Lady Welby's contribution to the semiotics discourse was neglected, in part because she often published anonymously to ensure her work be recognized on its own merit, noting that 'the only honor she valued was that of being treated by workers as a serious worker'.[112] Moreover, when Lady Welby did sign her work, she tried to remove her title: 'may I confess that in signing my book "V Welby" I hoped to get rid as far as possible of the irrelevant associations of my unlucky title? . . . You will understand my desire to be known as simply as possible'.[113] Finally, it is noteworthy that most (male) semioticians failed to acknowledge her work in their publications, even though they underscored her influence on their discoveries within their correspondence to her.[114] For instance, although Ogden's research was significantly inspired by Welby's work – exchanging over sixty letters with her discussing significs theory, and staying at her home, with access to her library and papers – he mentions her only once and briefly in his book *The Meaning of Meaning: A Study of the Influence of Language upon Thought and the Science of Symbolism.*[115]

Victoria Welby's theory of significs nevertheless had a strong bearing on the development of legal semiotics in The Netherlands through Jacob de Haan, who applied her Meaning Triad as a framework to analyze legal language, notably in his 1916 doctoral dissertation. It is worthy of note that it took 100 years for The Meaning Triad to be applied again in the legal field, in another dissertation in law, this time at the University of Oxford, by the present author. This 100-year gap could be explained by de Haan's early departure. Although de Haan was extremely prolific in his lifetime as he held the first Chair of Legal Significs at the University of Amsterdam, published two books and over forty articles, and coined the expression 'legal significs', his work unfortunately came to an end when he moved to Jerusalem and was assassinated, on political grounds, shortly thereafter.[116]

Welby was only recently recognized as the foremother of modern semiotics, notably through the works of Thomas Sebeok and Susan Petrilli.[117] Sebeok

[112] Letter from Victoria Welby to Charles Peirce (22 December 1903), Victoria Lady Welby Correspondence, consulted at the Clara Thomas Archives and Special Collections, York University Libraries, File 1970-010/012(7), Inventory No. 443, 9.

[113] Ibid.

[114] Ibid., 63; *Sign Studies* (2014), 126–27.

[115] Charles Ogden and Ivor Richards, *The Meaning of Meaning: A Study of the Influence of Language upon Thought and the Science of Symbolism* (Harcourt 1923); See *Sign Studies* (2014), 126–27; *Significs* (2015), xxiii, 177–205.

[116] *Signifying* (2009), 757–58.

[117] See for example Sebeok's essay 'Women in Semiotics' in *Global Semiotics* (Indiana University Press 2001); *Significs* (2015).

described Welby as 'the legendary foremother and prime mover of "significs" and "sensifics" species of turn-of-the-century (and subsequent) semiotics'.[118] In fact, since Welby's *Threefold Laws of Meaning* only received attention recently by semiotic scholars, it has as yet not been formally criticized. One could argue that the weakness of Welby's theory is that while it allows for an examination of the significance of signs, and the 'deconstruction' of their content, it does not propose a methodology to modify them to avoid potential negative outcomes, thereby 'rebuilding' their structure. Welby's analysis of the value of meaning and its ultimate significance, as well as her concern for 'the effects, consequences and implications of the conjunction between signs and values for human behaviour'[119] nevertheless paved the way for the discipline of semioethics elaborated one century later, which addresses this shortcoming.

## V SEMIOETHICS AND RESPONSIBILITY

The semioethics approach was introduced by Ponzio and Petrilli in 2003. It 'critiques the reification and hypostatization of signs and values and, instead, investigates the processes that produce them'.[120] Initially coined 'ethosemiotics' by Ponzio, to refer to Aristotle's concept of ethos (ethical appeal) and 'teleosemiotics', from the term 'teleo' which signifies 'end', it was finally identified as 'semioethics' to underline the interconnectedness between semiotics and ethics.[121] This new approach expands the ancient medical semiotics of symptomology found in the Corpus Hippocraticum – which studied physical and mental symptoms in patients triadically in terms of anamnesis, diagnosis and prognosis – to examine current symptoms of the globalized world, in all fields of human behaviour, for the purpose of 1) uncovering their causes, 2) offering a diagnosis and 3) identifying potential remedies. Petrilli explains:

> [S]emioethics proposes to examine symptoms – in our case symptoms of the worldwide social malaise – generated by the current communication order and its passive reproduction. Semioethics proposes a critical reading of the world-as-it-is and is committed to the search for possible remedies and improvements.[122]

118 *Significs* (2015), xxix.
119 *Sign Studies* (2014), 127.
120 Ibid., 12; *Semioetica* (2003).
121 'Semioethics' (2009), 152–53.
122 *Sign Studies* (2014), v.

The semioethics matrix was greatly influenced by Sebeok's global semiotics theory,[123] which aims to examine signs in a multidisciplinary and holistic manner. Global semiotics is a 'metascience concerned with all academic disciplines as sign-related' that recognizes the 'universal role of signs in creating the reality of human consciousness'.[124] Petrilli notes that global semiotics 'unites what other fields of knowledge and human praxis generally keep apart either for justified needs of a specialized order, or because of a useless and even harmful tendency towards short-sighted sectorialization'.[125] The semioethics approach 'interrogates the human world today on the assumption that it is not the only possible world, that this world has not been established definitely, once and for all, by some conservative ideology'.[126] In this regard, this book adopts a semioethics approach for it does not perceive the predicament of the girl child as a fatality that cannot be addressed, nor does it consider international treaties as static entities one cannot amend to clarify the wording of rights.

## 1 *Ethical Responsibility*

The semioethics approach, in line with the global semiotics theory, underscores the responsibility of semioticians in analyzing signs and their significance. It considers that signs should be evaluated not solely for the purpose of offering a diagnosis, but also for identifying possible avenues to address societal problems and humanize the communication order. In this regard, semioethics aims for ethical responsibility:

> As a scientific method and philosophical vision of life, semiotics is adequately equipped to contribute to the quest for social change – hence the invitation to eventual 'semioticians', or if you please 'semioethicians', whether by profession or simply as actors on the stage of life, to take up the challenge.[127]

Semioethics addresses Welby's critique of semioticians who passively reproduce problematic signs and ambiguous terminology rather than attempt to question and deconstruct their meaning:

> The question is, whether this state of things is quite so inevitable as most of us seem to think. Certainly, so long as we are content to live in the fool's

[123] *Global Semiotics* (2001).
[124] *Sign Crossroads* (2010), 25, 5.
[125] Ibid., 25.
[126] 'Semioethics' (2009), 158.
[127] *Sign Studies* (2014), vii.

> paradise of supposing that only the … prejudiced … or the ignorant can possibly mistake our meaning, and that our misreading of others are simply due to their obscurity … or literary incapacity, we shall ourselves contribute to the hopelessness of the situation. But this is a subject which cannot be dealt with in an incidental way; it is rather a hope for the future, that one of the most practically serviceable of subjects – that of Meaning, its conditions and its changes – shall be seriously taken up'.[128]

The present book adopts a semioethics approach for it not only examines the *sense*, *meaning* and *significance* of provisions enshrining the rights of the girl child in international treaties, but also proposes to amend the wording of these provisions, where necessary, to strengthen the protection of the girl child. It studies the content of international human rights treaties, which constitute important elements of the communication order, to identify potential remedies to the current predicament of the girl child. It notably recommends terminology that will clarify the status of the girl child in the CRC and the CEDAW to avoid misinterpretations by States parties, international and national institutions, individuals and communities and the girl child herself. In this regard, it takes into consideration the various conceptions of girlhood worldwide stemming from sexism and childism so that the provisions of international treaties unambiguously protect the girl child. The proposed reformulation of key provisions aims to ensure that rights are clearly stated, even when read by Welby and Peirce's 'final interpretants', that is, States parties, communities and individuals who do not consider girl children as rights holders.

The semioethic theory is novel and commentators have not, as yet, developed a critique of this approach. One can identify two potential shortcomings of the semioethic approach. First, it is important to bear in mind that the first phase of semioethics whereby one detects potential weaknesses in language within the communication order, does not automatically ensure the second phase of semioethics, that is, it does not signify that one can find the proper terminology to replace it. Welby stresses that '[i]t is, unfortunately, one thing to see the needless traps of which language is full and quite another to succeed in avoiding them'.[129] Hence, while this book shall endeavour to suggest amendments to provisions to strengthen the protection of the girl child under international law, it will also underscore the limitations of those recommendations.

Second, one can contend that a potential risk of the semioethic theory would be to consider that establishing a diagnosis of the impact of signs and modifying them accordingly suffices to address social problems. Indeed, the modification of the

[128] Victoria Welby, 'Meaning and Metaphor' (1893), 512.

[129] Letter from Welby to Peirce (24 May 1903), Clara Thomas Archives, File 1970-101/021(7).

wording of provisions enshrining the rights of the girl child shall not guarantee that violations of her rights will cease. As explained in the Introduction, many factors impact the protection of girl child rights in the international legal framework. We therefore undertake a semioethic approach while acknowledging that modifying the formulation of provisions shall not in itself ensure that girls' rights be respected at the domestic level. It is nevertheless argued that a major step to advancing the rights of the girl child rests in the terminology employed to phrase her rights. Accordingly, the semioethic analysis of international law constitutes an essential endeavour to improve her condition worldwide.

## VI SEMIOTIC ANALYSIS OF TREATIES IN ENGLISH

This book conducts a semioethic analysis of the content of international treaties in English, which is one of the six official languages of the UN, along with Arabic, Chinese, French, Russian and Spanish,[130] and a working language of all UN treaty bodies.[131] It is worthy of note that English holds precedence over other official and working languages in everyday UN proceedings,[132] and that the drafting of international treaties occurs predominantly in this language.[133] Furthermore, the vast majority of doctrinal work on the interpretation of treaties is conducted in English, and several leading periodicals have recently switched

[130] UN General Assembly Resolution 2, 'Rules of Procedure Concerning Languages' (1 February 1946): '[i]n all the organs of the United Nations, other than the International Court of Justice, Chinese, French, English, Russian and Spanish shall be the official languages'; Arabic became an official language in 1973; see UNGA Res (XXVIII) (18 December 1973) 'Inclusion of Chinese among the Working Languages of the General Assembly, its Committees and its Subcommittees and Inclusion of Arabic among the Official and the Working Languages of the General Assembly and its Main Committees, Amendments to Rules 51 and 59 of the Rules of Procedure of the Assembly'. English is also one of the two languages of the ICJ. UN Charter, art. 39: 'The official languages of the Court shall be French and English'.

[131] UNGA Res 2, 'Rules of Procedure Concerning Languages' (1 February 1946): '[i]n all the organs of the United Nations … English and French [shall be] the working languages'. Most notably for our analysis, the working languages of the CRC Committee are English, French and Spanish; see 'Committee on the Rights of the Child Rules of Procedure' (18 March 2015) UN Doc CRC/C/4/Rev.4, rules 34–38 (original English); the working languages of the CEDAW Committee are the same as the official languages of the UN; see 'Rules of Procedure of the Committee on the Elimination of Discrimination Against Women' (28 May 2008) UN Doc HRI/GEN/3/Rev.3, rules 24–26; the working languages of the HR Committee are Arabic, English, French, Russian and Spanish; see 'Rules of Procedure of the Human Rights Committee' (11 January 2012) UN Doc CCPR/C/3/Rev.10, rules 28–32 (original English).

[132] See Jacqueline Mowbray, 'Language in the UN and EU: Linguistic Diversity as a Challenge for Multilateralism' (2010) 8 *New Zealand Journal of Public and International Law* 91; Anne Bayefsky, *The UN Human Rights Treaty System: Universality at the Crossroads* (Springer 2001), 106–8; Jesús Baigorri Jalón, *Interpreters at the United Nations. A History* (Universidad de Salamanca 2004), 34.

[133] Christian Tomuschat, 'The (Hegemonic?) Role of the English Language' (2017) 86 *Nordic Journal of International Law* 196, 203.

to this language in order to increase their readership and influence.[134] In this regard, Bohlander notes that 'English has become the *lingua franca* in international legal academic and practical dialogue'.[135] However, while English may occupy a privileged position within the six official languages of the UN, all are placed on an equal footing as authentic languages of the international human rights treaties examined in this volume, such as the CRC and CEDAW,[136] and to the exception of Arabic, in the ICCPR and ICESCR.[137] This signifies that the treaty text is equally authoritative in each of these languages.[138] It is acknowledged, in this regard, that the semiotic investigation of the *sense* of treaty provisions conducted in this monograph might not account for differences that exist in other authentic languages of these treaties.[139] Each language carries a unique identity and may convey concepts that cannot be fully translated or transmuted into other languages, notably across distinct legal traditions.[140] In this regard, the International Law Commission underscores:

> [F]ew plurilingual treaties containing more than one or two articles are without some discrepancy between the texts. The different genius of the languages, the absence of a complete *consensus ad idem*, or lack of sufficient time to coordinate the texts may result in minor or even major discrepancies in the meaning of the texts.[141]

134 Claude Truchot, 'The Spread of English: From France to a More General Perspective' (1997) 16 *World Englishes* 65, 66–67; Tomuschat, 'Hegemonic English Language' (2017), 213–27; Michael Bohlander, 'Language, Intellectual Culture, Legal Traditions and International Criminal Justice' (2014) 12 *Journal of International Criminal Justice* 491; Celina Frade, 'Power Dynamics and Legal English' (2007) 26 *World Englishes* 48.

135 'Language International Justice' (2014), 491.

136 CRC, art. 54: '[t]he original of the present Convention, of which the Arabic, Chinese, English, French, Russian and Spanish texts are equally authentic, shall be deposited with the Secretary-General of the United Nations'; CEDAW, art. 30: '[t]he present Convention, the Arabic, Chinese, English, French, Russian and Spanish texts of which are equally authentic, shall be deposited with the Secretary-General of the United Nations'.

137 ICCPR, art. 53(1) and ICESCR, art. 31(1) (same text): '[t]he present Covenant, of which the Chinese, English, French, Russian and Spanish texts are equally authentic, shall be deposited in the archives of the United Nations'.

138 See Vienna Convention (1969), art. 33(1): '[w]hen a treaty has been authenticated in two or more languages, the text is equally authoritative in each language'.

139 For a discussion on authentic languages and semiotics, see Clara Chapdelaine-Feliciati, 'The Semiotic Puzzle: Authentic Languages and International Law' (2020) 5 *International Journal of Legal Discourse* 317.

140 'Hegemonic English Language' (2017); Dinah Shelton, 'Reconciliable Differences? The Interpretation of Multilingual Treaties' (1996) 20 *Hastings International and Comparative Law Review* 611; 'Translation Legal Language' (2013); 'International Law Language' (2010); *Treaty Interpretation* (2015).

141 International Law Commission, Yearbook, 1966, vol II, UN Doc A/CN.4/SER.A/1966/Add.1, 225, para. 6.

The discrepancies are compounded by the number of authentic languages, time constraints and limited translation support.[142] One could surmise that if the analysis of the *sense* of provisions is circumscribed to English, it is also restricted as concerns its *significance* for the protection of the girl child. However, it is argued that the conclusions drawn from the semiotic analysis of a treaty in the English language are significant on three grounds. Firstly, it impacts States parties and individuals whose official language is English,[143] and secondly, states whose official language is a language other than the authentic languages of the treaty, as they may choose to refer to the English version. Presently, close to half of the states in the world have an official language other than the UN official languages, and nearly 4.8 billion people do not have as a mother tongue or second language any of the UN official languages.[144] Any of these States parties may refer solely to one authentic language, such as English. In this regard, if a weakness were identified in the wording of rights in English, it could impact the interpretation of human rights on any continent, even if other authentic texts did not present such a problem. Thirdly, given the equal authority of each authentic language, states whose official language is an authentic language other than English – that is, Arabic, Chinese, French, Spanish and Russian – can also choose to refer to the English version, and could thereby invoke weak wording in the English text to limit their duty to protect girl children. Hence, the English text also impacts the interpretation of the other authentic texts of the treaty even if the provisions of the latter are formulated in strong terms. At the same time, it is acknowledged that the suggestion to amend the English wording of treaties will not in itself suffice to improve the protection of the girl child in the international legal framework, for authentic texts in other languages, such as French and Spanish, could also comprise weaknesses not addressed in this book. A similar semiotic and semioethic exercise, conducted in the other authentic languages of the UN, would thus be appropriate, and could be the object of another study.

142 'Linguistic Diversity' (2010), 107; 'Reconciliable Differences' (1996), 621.

143 This is significant, given that the population of English speakers is estimated at over 387,307,788.156 worldwide: World Development Indicators (WDI) (2022) The World Bank, Total Population. https://databank.worldbank.org/reports.aspx?source=2&series=SP.POP.TOTL&country=WLD# (accessed 11 August 2023).

144 UN Department for General Assembly and Conference Management. www.un.org/dgacm/en/content/multilingualism-coordination (accessed 23 August 2023). These include states in all regions and with some of the world's highest populations, such as Brazil, Indonesia, Bangladesh and Japan.

# 2

# Definition of the Girl Child

The definition of the girl child is essential as it determines which human beings are bearers of the rights accorded to girl children under international law and which legal remedies are available to them.[1] The analysis of the status of the girl child and her rights under international law therefore requires an exploration of the definition of girl child in the international legal apparatus. One can observe that the girl child is a relatively novel concept under international law. Initially subsumed within overarching conceptual categories, the girl child has been progressively recognized over the past fifty years as a distinct rights holder under international law.

## I RECOGNITION OF THE GIRL CHILD UNDER INTERNATIONAL LAW

### 1 *Universalism*

The international community originally adopted a *universalist approach*,[2] under the International Bill of Rights, whereby general provisions recognizing human rights were considered sufficient to encompass all persons and protect marginalized groups. Its instruments – the UDHR, ICCPR and ICESCR – employ overarching terms, such as 'every human being', 'human beings', 'the human person', 'any person', 'all', 'all persons', 'no one', 'the individual', 'individuals', 'peoples', 'everyone' and 'anyone'.[3] The International Bill of

[1] Regarding children, see Geraldine Van Bueren, *The International Law on the Rights of the Child* (Martinus Nijhoff 1998), 32.

[2] Johanna Bond, 'International Intersectionality: A Theoretical and Pragmatic Exploration of Women's International Human Rights Violations' (2003) 52 *Emory Law Journal* 71, 76, 79.

[3] UDHR, preamble, arts. 1–15, 17–29; ICCPR, preamble, arts. 1, 2, 5–19, 22, 26, 27; ICESCR, preamble, arts. 5–9, 11–13, 15.

Rights enshrines the principle of non-discrimination and, notably, lists *sex* as a prohibited ground of discrimination, which appears to indicate that rights apply equally to all human beings regardless of sex. Indeed, the principle of non-discrimination is central in the UDHR, ICCPR and ICESCR, and occupies a privileged position at the beginning of each instrument.[4] Article 2 of the UDHR stipulates that the rights set out in the Declaration apply to everyone, without distinction, and provides a non-exhaustive list of prohibited grounds of discrimination, notably sex, which is pertinent to the girl child. The ICCPR specifies under article 2 that rights shall be recognized without distinction of any kind, and provides an open-ended list of prohibited grounds of discrimination, notably sex. The ICESCR incorporates the principle of non-discrimination under article 2, stressing that States parties undertake to guarantee that the rights shall be exercised without discrimination. This Covenant lists an open-ended series of grounds, notably sex. While the UDHR and ICCPR refer to a 'distinction' and the ICESCR to 'discrimination', this terminology is viewed as interchangeable for 'the clear intention behind the terms of both covenants was to exclude only arbitrary or unjust distinction or discrimination'.[5] An additional feature of the ICCPR and ICESCR, contrarily to the UDHR, is that they expressly require States parties to ensure the equal rights of men and women,[6] which can be extended by analogy to equality between boys and girls. It is worthy of note that the Twin Covenants, under their respective articles 3, refer to an 'equal right' rather than a prohibition of discrimination, and moreover, apply to all the enshrined civil and political, or economic, social and cultural rights; thus, '[a] violation of [a]rticle 3 does not depend on the violation of any other Covenant right'.[7] In addition, while articles 2 and 3 of the Twin Covenants constitute accessory prohibitions that 'can be violated only in conjunction with another substantive provision', the ICCPR also comprises a *free-standing* or autonomous guarantee of non-discrimination under article 26 for it prohibits discrimination with regard to all rights and benefits recognized by the law: 'the law shall prohibit any discrimination and guarantee to all persons equal and effective protection

[4] The principle of non-discrimination is enshrined in art. 2 of each instrument. See Chapter 3 for a discussion on the definition of discrimination under international law as it relates to the girl child.

[5] Paul M Taylor, A *Commentary on the International Covenant on Civil and Political Rights* (Cambridge University Press 2020), 67–68; Bertrand Ramcharan, 'Equality and Nondiscrimination' in Louis Henkin (ed.), *The International Bill of Rights: The Covenant on Civil and Political Rights* (Columbia University Press 1981), 259.

[6] ICCPR, art. 3; ICESCR, art. 3.

[7] Taylor, *Commentary ICCPR* (2020), 88, 104 (concerning art. 3 of the ICCPR). See Chapter 3 for a discussion on equality and non-discrimination.

against discrimination on any ground such as ... sex'.[8] In this regard, article 26 is confined neither to the rights enshrined in the ICCPR nor to the listed grounds,[9] and the Covenant thereby provides an autonomous right by prohibiting discrimination de jure (in law) and de facto (in fact) pertaining to any field regulated and protected by public authorities.[10] Article 7 of the UDHR also constitutes an autonomous clause stating that 'all are equal before the law and are entitled without any discrimination to equal protection of the law', and thereby guarantees equality before the law and in the law.[11] Although these instruments do not expressly list 'age' as a prohibited ground of discrimination, they enshrine the principle of non-discrimination in a clause that guarantees general prohibitions of discrimination, that is, with an open-ended list of grounds.[12] The Human Rights Committee notes, for example, that 'children benefit from all of the civil rights enunciated in the Covenant'.[13] The principle of non-discrimination has continued to be recognized in core international treaties, and is presently one of the most frequently proclaimed norms of the international legal apparatus.[14] In this regard, Dinstein notes that this fundamental concept should be understood as 'a general procedural legal principle permeating all substantive international human rights, collective as well as individual'.[15] Hence, under the universalist approach, the human rights and fundamental freedoms of each individual girl child are protected, and girl children as a group are encompassed within the overarching human category.[16]

[8] Taylor, *Commentary ICCPR* (2020), 60, 69.

[9] Bert Vierdag, *The Concept of Discrimination in International Law* (Martinus Nijhoff 1973), 110.

[10] ICCPR General Comment No. 18: 'Non-discrimination' (10 November 1989) UN Doc HRI/GEN/1/Rev.9, para. 12.

[11] Samantha Besson and Eleonor Kleber 'Article 2: The Right to Non-Discrimination' in John Tobin (ed.), *The UN Convention on the Rights of the Child: A Commentary* (Oxford University Press 2019), 46.

[12] The UDHR and ICCPR introduce the list of grounds by referring to 'distinction of any kind, such as race, colour, sex' and end with 'or other status': UDHR, art. 2; ICCPR, art. 2(1). The ICESCR refers to 'discrimination of any kind as to race, colour, sex' and also ends with 'or other status': art. 2(2). Besson and Kleber explain that 'the list of prohibited discrimination grounds is purely indicative and can be extended to other similar grounds': 'Non-discrimination' (2019), 46.

[13] ICCPR General Comment No. 17: 'Rights of the Child' (7 April 1989) UN Doc HRI/GEN/1/Rev.9, para. 2.

[14] Anne Bayefsky, 'The Principle of Equality or Non-Discrimination in International Law' (1990) 11 *Human Rights Law Journal* 1, 1.

[15] Yoram Dinstein, 'Discrimination and International Human Rights' (1985) 15 *Israel Yearbook on Human Rights* 11, 11.

[16] The International Bill of Rights, however, employs gender-specific masculine pronouns, an issue that shall be examined in Chapters 5 and 7.

## 2 *Qualified Universalism*

After the proclamation of the UDHR and the Twin Covenants, the international legal community questioned the 'unqualified embrace of universalism' – which assumed that human rights violations were experienced by individuals in an identical manner – and recognized the necessity of addressing specific types of discrimination.[17] This led to the adoption of the *qualified universalist approach* that considers human rights as universal while simultaneously acknowledging that individuals experience different types of human rights violations according to their membership within various identity categories.[18] Accordingly, instruments were tailored for specific categories of rights holders, notably women and children, to address their unique situation and enshrine ground-specific prohibitions of discrimination. In 1979, the CEDAW was adopted to expressly require States parties to eliminate discrimination against women in the application of the human rights and fundamental freedoms enshrined in the International Bill of Rights. The CEDAW underlines, in its preamble, that despite the various international instruments protecting human rights, which notably recognize the equal rights of men and women, extensive discrimination against women continues to exist.[19] It requires States parties to eliminate discrimination against women, as defined under article 1, concerning both civil and political, and economic, social and cultural rights.[20] As a female, one could contend that the girl child is subsumed within the generic woman class and therefore protected under the CEDAW. However, as shall be demonstrated in Chapter 8, the issue is complex, and one cannot positively assert that girls are systematically covered under the CEDAW. The CRC, the first legally binding instrument specifically acknowledging children as rights holders, was adopted a decade after the CEDAW. Although the international legal framework does not define the girl child, it offers an official description of the term 'child' in the CRC: 'a child means every human being below the age of eighteen years unless under the law applicable to the child, majority is attained earlier'.[21] As in other tailored

[17] 'International Intersectionality', 80.

[18] Ibid., 76, 155.

[19] CEDAW, preamble: '[c]oncerned, however, that despite these various instruments (the Charter of the United Nations, the UDHR, the International Covenants on Human Rights, and resolutions, declarations and recommendations adopted by the United Nations) extensive discrimination against women continues to exist'.

[20] CEDAW, art. 2: '[s]tates Parties condemn discrimination against women in all its forms, agree to pursue by all appropriate means and without delay a policy of eliminating discrimination against women'.

[21] CRC, art. 1.

treaties, the preamble of the CRC stresses that even though various instruments already protect all members of the human family, children experience serious human rights violations: 'in all countries in the world, there are children living in exceptionally difficult conditions, and ... such children need special consideration'.[22] The CRC employs the gender-neutral terms 'the child' and 'children',[23] and uses the pronouns and possessive adjectives 'his or her', 'him or her' and 'he or she',[24] thereby encompassing both boys and girls. In addition, the CRC enshrines under article 2(1) a general discrimination clause comprising a list of prohibited grounds of discrimination similar to that of the International Bill of Rights, which includes sex.[25] It places a duty on States parties to respect and enforce the rights outlined in the CRC for each child without discrimination of any kind, based either on the child or on their parents' or legal guardian's vectors of identity. This clause is thus subordinate or accessory rather than autonomous as it applies solely to articles enshrined in the CRC. Moreover, article 2(2) expressly protects children, thus including girl children, against discrimination based on their parents' activities or status. The CRC nevertheless fails to define 'child-based discrimination' or childism. Overall, article 2 remains open and cannot be restricted to some areas, such as education, and is a directly justiciable clause that girl children can invoke before domestic courts, as in the ICCPR.[26] The girl child therefore appears to be covered under the generic 'child' category within the international legal framework.

### 3 *Girl Child as a Separate Entity*

Although the girl child was already subsumed within larger categories, the international legal framework progressively referred to her as a distinct being. It is noteworthy that the term 'girl' was introduced in treaties addressing issues which predominantly affect her. The first legally binding instrument to incorporate the term 'girl' is the Marriage Convention (1962), in a provision prohibiting child

[22] CRC, preamble.

[23] The CRC employs the expression 'the child' in its preamble and arts. 1–3, 5–10, 12–32, 34, 36–41. The expression 'children' is incorporated in its preamble and arts. 3, 11, 17, 18, 20, 23, 24, 28, 33–35, 38, 40, 42.

[24] CRC, preamble, arts. 2, 3, 7, 8, 9, 10, 12, 14, 16, 17, 20, 22, 23, 24, 25, 29, 30, 37, 40.

[25] Besson and Kleber note that it constitutes a unique general non-discrimination clause in a ground-specific human rights instrument: '[u]nlike the other non-discrimination clauses in ground-specific instruments, it is not restricted to one discrimination ground only. Nor, however, is it so general that it is oblivious to the child-specific nature of the discrimination at stake': 'Non-Discrimination' (2019), 48.

[26] Ibid., 48–49; ICCPR, art. 2(1).

marriage and the betrothal of 'young girls'.[27] The second binding instrument to mention girls is the CEDAW (1979), in a single article regarding school drop-out rates, another issue predominantly faced by girl children.[28] Since then, a growing number of binding instruments have underlined the predicament of girl children. The Worst Forms of Child Labour Convention (1999) emphasizes the necessity of considering 'the special situation of girls'.[29] The Convention on the Rights of Persons with Disabilities (CRPD 2006) recognizes that 'women and girls with disabilities are often at greater risk … of violence, injury or abuse, neglect or negligent treatment, maltreatment or exploitation'.[30] Moreover, non-binding instruments, such as the Standard Rules on the Equalization of Opportunities for Persons with Disabilities (1993),[31] the UN Millennium Declaration (2000)[32] and the Declaration of Commitment on HIV/AIDS (2001),[33] specifically refer to the girl child, once again in relation to the distinct situations faced by girls, notably those living with disabilities, poverty and HIV/AIDS.

In the 1990s, the international community accorded significant attention to the girl child in a number of non-binding global policy agreements. It first employed the expression 'girl child' in 1990, which was designated the 'Year of the Girl Child'.[34] That same year, states committed themselves to 'establish policies, objectives and goals that enhance the equality of status, welfare and opportunity of the girl child' in the Declaration on Social Development of the World Summit for Social Development.[35] In addition, 1991–2000 was

[27] Convention on Consent to Marriage, Minimum Age for Marriage and Registration of Marriage (New York, adopted 10 December 1962, entered into force 9 December 1964) 521 UNTS 231, preamble: '[a]ll States … should take all appropriate measures with a view to … eliminating completely child marriages and the betrothal of young girls'.

[28] CEDAW, art. 10(f): 'the reduction of female student drop-out rates and the organization of programmes for girls and women who have left school prematurely'.

[29] Convention No. 182 Concerning the Prohibition and Immediate Action for the Elimination of the Worst Forms of Child Labour (Geneva, adopted 17 June 1999, entered into force 19 November 2000) 2133 UNTS 161, art. 7(2)(e).

[30] Convention on the Rights of Persons with Disabilities (New York, adopted 13 December 2006, entered into force 3 May 2008) 2515 UNTS 3, preamble (q).

[31] Standard Rules on the Equalization of Opportunities for Persons with Disabilities (New York, adopted 20 December 1993), (4 March 1994) UN Doc A/RES/48/96, preamble, rules 4(5), 6 (4), 9(3).

[32] United Nations Millennium Declaration (New York, adopted 8 September 2000) UN Doc A/RES/55/2, para. 19.

[33] Declaration of Commitment on HIV/AIDS (New York, adopted 27 June 2001), (2 August 2001) UN Doc A/RES/S-26/2, paras. 4, 14, 59–63, 65.

[34] Savitri Goonesekere, 'Elimination of All Forms of Discrimination and Violence against the Girl Child' (UNICEF 2006) EGM/DVGC/2006/BP.1, 6.

[35] Copenhagen Declaration on Social Development (Copenhagen, adopted 12 March 1995), (19 April 1995) UN Doc A/CONF.166/9, commitment 5 (f).

designated the 'Decade of the Girl Child' in South Asia.[36] The Vienna Declaration and Programme of Action (1993) specifically recognizes that 'the human rights of women and of the girl child are an inalienable, integral and indivisible part of universal human rights', and broadly calls upon states to 'ensure the effective protection and promotion of [the] human rights of the girl child'.[37] The CRC Committee also acknowledged her unique condition by dedicating a Day of General Discussion to the girl child in 1995, in which it recommended that the Platform for Action of the Fourth World Conference on Women, to be held the same year, reflect the situation and fundamental rights of the girl child.[38] The Platform for Action followed suit by considering the condition of the girl child as a distinct critical area of concern and reaffirming the commitment of governments to 'ensure the full implementation of the human rights of women and of the girl child as an inalienable, integral and indivisible part of all human rights and fundamental freedoms'.[39] Since 1992, the CEDAW Committee has employed the expression 'girl' in fourteen out of its thirty-nine general recommendations on topics such as violence, equality in marriage and family relations, health, education and trafficking.[40] It is worthy of note that three of its more recent recommendations

36 'Discrimination Girl Child' (2006), 10.

37 World Conference on Human Rights (Vienna, adopted 25 June 1993) UN Doc A/Conf.157/24, paras. 18, 49.

38 CRC Committee 'Day of General Discussion: The Girl Child' (21 January 1995) UN Doc CRC/C/38 (CRC DGD Girl Child), para. 299(a). Several international bodies participated in the discussion, notably the Inter-African Committee on Traditional Practices Affecting the Health of Women and Children, UNICEF, UNHCR, UNFPA, ILO, FAO, UNESCO, WHO, NGO Committee, International Abolitionist Federation, Associated Country Women of the World and Rädda Barden International.

39 Beijing Declaration (Beijing, adopted 15 September 1995) UN Doc A/Conf.177/20/Rev.1, Annex 1, paras. 259–85, 9.

40 CEDAW General Recommendations: 1) No. 19: 'Violence against Women' (11th Session 1992), paras. 15, 21; 2) No. 21: 'Equality in Marriage and Family Relations' (13th Session 1994), paras. 36, 38; 3) No. 24: 'Women and Health' (20th session 1999), paras. 8, 12, 18, 28; 4) No. 28: 'Core Obligations of States Parties under Article 2 of the CEDAW' (16 December 2010) UN Doc CEDAW/C/GC/28, para. 21; 5) No. 30: 'Women in Conflict' (1 November 2013) UN Doc CEDAW/C/GC/30, paras. 4, 7, 11, 22–24, 34–36, 38–41, 48, 50, 52, 53, 57, 58, 60–62, 65–69, 78, 81; 6) Joint CEDAW General Recommendation No. 31 and CRC General Comment No.18: 'Harmful Practices' (14 November 2014) UN Doc CEDAW/C/GC/31-CRC/C/GC/18, paras. 1, 3, 6, 9, 11, 17–25, 27, 29, 42, 53–56, 60–69, 72, 73, 77, 81–85; 7) No. 32: 'Gender-related Dimensions of Refugee Women' (14 November 2014) UN Doc CEDAW/C/GC/32, paras. 10, 26, 27, 34, 45, 46, 50, 51, 53, 63; 8) No. 33: 'Women's Access to Justice' (3 August 2015) UN Doc CEDAW/C/GC/33, paras. 1, 18, 24, 25, 35; 9) No. 34: 'The Rights of Rural Women' (7 March 2016) UN Doc CEDAW/C/GC/34, paras. 2, 8, 10, 12, 22–27, 32, 34, 38, 39, 42, 43, 75, 76, 81–85; 10) No. 35: 'Gender-based Violence against Women' (updating general recommendation No. 19), (26 July 2017) UN Doc CEDAW/C/GC/35, paras. 14, 18, 26, 28, 30, 35; 11) No. 36: 'Right of Girls and Women to

refer to 'girls' expressly in their titles,[41] demonstrating an increased concern for their predicament. The CRC Committee started referring to girls in its very first general comment, and this inclusion continued across twenty comments as regards the aims of education, HIV/AIDS, adolescent health, separated children, early childhood, children with disabilities, juvenile justice (replaced with child justice), indigenous children, the right of the child to be heard, violence, right to health, adolescence, right to play, harmful practices and the digital environment.[42] Since 2000, the Human Rights Committee has referred

Education' (27 November 2017) UN Doc CEDAW/C/GC/36, paras. 1–5, 7, 12, 13, 15, 18–25, 27–33, 35, 37–44, 46–48, 50–57, 60–72, 81–83; 12) No. 37: 'Gender-related Dimensions of Disaster Risk Reduction in the Context of Climate Change' (13 March 2018) UN Doc CEDAW/C/GC/37, paras. 2–7, 15, 19, 26, 29–32, 36, 38, 46, 55, 57, 59, 60, 62, 66, 68, 69, 75, 78; 13) No. 38: 'Trafficking in Women and Girls in the Context of Global Migration' (20 November 2020) UN Doc CEDAW/C/GC/38, paras. 1, 2, 4–7, 10, 12–22, 24, 25, 30, 31, 33, 34, 40, 42, 45, 47–50, 52, 54–56, 65–67, 71, 75, 76, 79–82, 84, 86–90, 92, 93, 95–104, 106–109, 112, 114, 117–120; 14) No. 39: 'The Rights of Indigenous Women and Girls' (31 October 2022) UN Doc CEDAW/C/GC/39 (all paragraphs except for para. 24).

[41] CEDAW General Recommendations: 1) No. 36: 'Education' (2017); 2) No. 38 'Trafficking' (2020); 3) No. 39 'Indigenous' (2022).

[42] CRC General Comments: 1) No. 1: 'The Aims of Education' (17 April 2001) UN Doc CRC/GC/2001/1, para. 10; 2) No. 3: 'HIV/AIDS and the Rights of the Child' (17 March 2003) UN Doc CRC/GC/2003/3, paras. 2, 7, 8, 17, 18, 36, 38; 3) No. 4: 'Adolescent Health and Development' (1 July 2003) UN Doc CRC/GC/2003/4, paras. 9, 20, 26, 27, 30, 31, 39; 4) No. 6: 'Treatment of Unaccompanied and Separated Children Outside Their Country of Origin' (1 September 2005) UN Doc CRC/GC/2005/6, paras. 3, 41, 47, 50, 56, 59; 5) No. 7: 'Implementing Child Rights in Early Childhood' (20 September 2006) UN Doc CRC/C/GC/7/Rev.1, paras. 24, 28, 34, 36; 6) No. 9: 'The Rights of Children with Disabilities' (27 February 2007) UN Doc CRC/C/GC/9, paras. 8, 10, 60, 79; 7) No. 10 'Juvenile Justice' (2007), paras. 8, 40, 97; 8) No. 11: 'Indigenous Children and Their Rights under the Convention' (12 February 2009) UN Doc CRC/C/GC/11, paras. 29, 61, 72; 9) No. 12: 'The Right of the Child to be Heard' (20 July 2009) UN Doc CRC/C/GC/12, paras, 4, 9, 77, 95, 97, 134; 10) No. 13: 'The Right of the Child to Freedom from all Forms of Violence' (18 April 2011) UN Doc CRC/C/GC/13, paras. 16, 19, 23, 29, 72; 11) No. 15: 'The Right of the Child to the Enjoyment of the Highest Attainable Standard of Health' (17 April 2013) UN Doc CRC/C/GC/15, paras. 9, 41, 51, 56, 60; 12) No. 16: 'On State Obligations Regarding the Impact of the Business Sector on Children's Rights' (17 April 2013) UN Doc CRC/C/GC/16, para. 19; 13) No. 17: 'The Right of the Child to Rest, Leisure, Play, Recreational Activities, Cultural Life and the Arts' (17 April 2013) UN Doc CRC/C/GC/17, paras. 3, 16, 36, 42, 47, 48, 56, 57, 58; 14) Joint CEDAW-CRC GenRec/GenCom: 'Harmful Practices' (2014), paras.1, 3, 6, 9, 11, 17–25, 27, 29, 42, 53–56, 60–69, 72, 73, 77, 81–85; 15) No. 19: 'On Public Budgeting for the Realization of Children's Rights' (20 July 2016) UN Doc CRC/C/GC/19, para. 8; 16) No. 20: 'On the Implementation of the Rights of the Child During Adolescence' (6 December 2016) UN Doc CRC/C/GC/20, paras. 5, 21, 27, 28, 30, 36, 38, 45, 48, 59, 60, 62, 69, 71, 75, 76, 81, 86; 17) No. 22: Joint General Comment No. 3 of the Committee on the Protection of the Rights of All Migrant Workers and Members of Their Families and No. 22 of the Committee on the Rights of the Child: 'General Principles Regarding the Human Rights of Children in the Context of International Migration' (16 November 2017) UN Doc CMW/C/GC/3-CRC/C/GC/22, paras. 24, 39; 18) No. 23: Joint General Comment No. 4 of the Committee on the Protection

to 'girls' in three general comments on equality between men and women, liberty and the right to life,[43] and since 1999, the CESCR has mentioned girls in eight general comments concerning pertinent rights, such as the rights to education and health, equal rights of men and women, sexual and reproductive health and the right to access and control land.[44]

The expression 'girl child' was finally established in 2000, within the Optional Protocol to the CRC on the Sale of Children, Child Prostitution and Child Pornography (OPSC), nearly a decade after its introduction within non-binding instruments. It is notable that the first legally binding instrument in which the expression 'girl child' was enshrined is once again a treaty dedicated to addressing an issue that predominantly affects girls: sexual exploitation. In this regard, the OPSC recognizes in its preamble that 'a number of particularly vulnerable groups, including girl children, are at greater risk of sexual exploitation, and that girl children are disproportionately represented among the sexually exploited'. The CRC Committee also employed the expression 'girl child' in its general comments adopted between 2006 and 2009, although it returned to using 'girl' thereafter.[45] The CEDAW Committee mentions the expression 'girl child' specifically in four recommendations,[46] and the CESCR

of the Rights of All Migrant Workers and Members of Their Families and No. 23 of the Committee on the Rights of the Child on State Obligations: 'Human Rights of Children in the Context of International Migration in Countries of Origin, Transit, Destination and Return' (16 November 2017) UN Doc CMW/C/GC/4-CRC/C/GC/23, paras. 26, 41, 44; 19) No. 24: 'Child Justice' (2019), para. 40; 20) No. 25: 'Children's Rights in Relation to the Digital Environment' (2 March 2021) UN Doc CRC/C/GC/25, paras. 11, 101.

43 ICCPR General Comments: 1) No. 28: 'Equality between Men and Women' (29 March 2000) UN Doc HRI/GEN/1/Rev.9, paras. 22, 28; 2) No. 35: 'Liberty and Security of Person' (16 December 2014) UN Doc CCPR/C/GC/35, para. 3; 3) No. 36: 'Right to Life' (30 October 2018) UN Doc CCPR/C/GC/36, paras. 8, 61.

44 CESCR General Comments: 1) No. 11: 'Plans of Action for Primary Education' (10 May 1999) UN Doc E/C.12/1999/4, paras. 3, 4; 2) No. 13: 'The Right to Education' (8 December 1999) UN Doc E/C.12/1999/10, paras. 16, 50, 55; 3) No. 14: 'The Right to the Highest Attainable Standard of Health' (11 August 2000) UN Doc E/C.12/2000/4, para. 22; 4) No. 16: 'The Equal Rights of Men and Women in the Enjoyment of All Economic, Social and Cultural Rights' (11 August 2005) UN Doc E/C.12/2005/4, paras. 21, 27, 30; 5) No. 22: 'Sexual and Reproductive Health' (2 May 2016) UN Doc E/C.12/GC/22, paras. 2, 28, 30, 48; 6) No. 24: 'Business Activities' (10 August 2017) UN Doc E/C.12/GC/24, paras. 9, 21; 7) No. 25: 'Science and Economic, Social and Cultural Rights' (30 April 2020) UN Doc E/C.12/GC/25, paras. 31, 32, 52; 8) No. 26: 'Land and Economic, Social and Cultural Rights' (24 January 2023) E/C.12/GC/26, para. 14.

45 CRC General Comments: 1) No. 7: 'Early Childhood' (2006), paras. 11, 36; 2) No. 10: 'Juvenile Justice' (2007), paras. 6, 40; 3) No. 12: 'Right to be Heard' (2009), para. 77.

46 CEDAW General Recommendations: 1) No. 21: 'Equality' (1994), para. 36; 2) No. 24: 'Women and Health' (1999), paras. 6, 12, 15; 3) No. 25: 'Temporary Special Measures' (13th session 2004), paras. 19, 26; 4) No. 33: 'Access Justice' (2015), para. 24.

uses the term in its general comment on non-discrimination,[47] whereas the Human Rights Committee's general comments exclusively refer to 'girls', not to the 'girl child'.[48] Furthermore, the UN General Assembly adopted eighteen resolutions concerning the girl child between 1996 and 2022, thus averaging one resolution per year during a span of twenty-five years.[49] Each resolution underscores some of the violations experienced by girl children and provides recommendations. In 2011, the UN General Assembly designated 11 October as the 'International Day of the Girl Child', to be observed every year beginning in 2012, and invited Member States, international organizations and civil society to raise awareness of the situation of girls around the world.[50] In 2022, the UN Human Rights Council extended the mandate of the Special Rapporteur on violence against women, its causes and consequences, under the title of 'Special Rapporteur on Violence against *Women and Girls*, Its Causes and Consequences', demonstrating a concern for the gender-based violence uniquely experienced by girl children.[51]

## II DEFINITION OF THE GIRL CHILD

Although the girl child is acknowledged in international law, she remains undefined. There is presently no universal definition of the girl child and not a single instrument in the international legal apparatus offers a description of the expressions 'girl' and 'girl child'.[52] Moreover, none of these instruments classify the expressions 'man', 'woman', 'boy' and 'girl', and thereby appear to assume that these four identity groups are defined a priori. Since the girl child is not defined in the international legal framework, this section explores the description of the girl child in the English language, notably in English dictionaries. It analyses two vectors of identity of the girl child: femalehood and childhood. Moreover, it discusses the semiotics of inferiority, subordination and denigration associated with the expression 'girl child' throughout history.

47 CESCR General Comment No. 20: 'Non-Discrimination in Economic, Social and Cultural Rights' (2 July 2009) UN Doc E/C.12/GC/20, paras. 8, 11.

48 See ICCPR General Comments mentioning girls in earlier notes.

49 UNGA Resolutions 'The Girl Child', see Introduction.

50 UNGA Resolution 'International Day of the Girl Child' (30 March 2012) UN Doc A/RES/66/170, paras. 1, 2.

51 UNGA Resolution 'Mandate of Special Rapporteur on Violence against Women and Girls, Its Causes and Consequences' (18 July 2022) UN Doc A/HRC/RES/50/7 (emphasis added), para. 2.

52 This book examines the semiotics of terminology in English, one of the six official languages of the UN: see Chapter 1.

The actual origin of the expression 'girl' is unknown.[53] Along with 1,000 other English words, such as 'man' and 'boy', the source of the term 'girl' remains obscure to this day.[54] The expression 'girl' was first recorded in the English language in the Middle Ages, when it was used to designate a child of either sex and a young person,[55] as exemplified by the expression 'knave girl' for the boy child.[56] Sohoni remarks that '[t]he irony in this uncertain but gender-neutral interpretation of the linguistic beginning of girlhood is poignant'.[57] The term 'girl' was given the current meaning of 'female child' near the end of the fourteenth century to distinguish female children from male children.[58] The expression 'girl child' is recorded as early as 1755 in the Johnson Dictionary of English Language.[59]

### 1 *Twin Pillars of Identity: Femalehood and Childhood*

The most recent editions of the OED and the Webster offer several parameters for the definition of the girl child: the primary description is that of 'a female child; a young or relatively young woman',[60] and 'a female child; a young unmarried woman',[61] respectively. The core definition of the girl child is shaped by her sex and age: she is a female and a child.[62] The twin pillars of girlhood are thereby femalehood and childhood.

#### 1.1 Femalehood

Femalehood is described as a hybrid natural and social term. The OED defines it first and foremost in terms of biology as 'a person of the sex that can bear offspring; a woman or a girl' and 'a female animal (including the human being considered as an animal species)', more specifically as

53 OED: 'Origin Unknown'; *The Oxford Dictionary of English Etymology* (Oxford Clarendon Press 1966): 'certainty (as to origin) is not attainable on the evidence'.

54 Anatoly Liberman, *An Analytic Dictionary of English Etymology: An Introduction* (University of Minnesota Press 2008), 94–100.

55 Chambers Etymology; OED.

56 Morris Dictionary of Word and Phrase Origins: A Comprehensive Reference Book on the Origins and Meanings of Thousands of Words and Expressions, Presented with Wit and Authority (2nd ed., Harper Collins 1988).

57 *Burden Girlhood* (1995), 14.

58 OED.

59 OED; Johnson Dictionary of English Language (1755): 'child, ... A girl child'.

60 OED; SOEDHP.

61 Webster.

62 Sohoni underscores that the parameter 'female child' is a valid biological fact: *Burden Girlhood* (1995), 1.

'producing gametes (ova) that can develop into a new individual, usually (but not always) after fertilization by a male gamete (as a spermatozoon)'.[63] According to the *Oxford Concise Medical Dictionary* (OMD), femalehood is biologically characterized by being born with female external genitalia, that is, a vulva comprising '[t]wo pairs of fleshy folds – the labia majora and labia minora – [that] surround the openings of the vagina and urethra and extend forward to the clitoris', ovaries that will produce ova and a uterus (womb) which is 'the part of the female reproductive tract that is specialized to allow the embryo to become implanted in its inner wall and to nourish the growing fetus from the maternal blood'; by developing, during puberty, 'the appearance of secondary sexual characteristics [e.g. growing of breasts in girls], and in girls by the start of menstruation' and by the possibility of becoming pregnant and giving birth.[64] It is notable that in these definitions, female biological traits and girlhood are inextricably linked.[65] The OMD also defines women as having two X chromosomes in contrast to men who have one X and one Y chromosome. It defines a sex chromosome as 'a chromosome that is involved in the determination of the sex of the individual. Women have two X chromosomes; men have one X chromosome and one Y chromosome'. Femalehood is secondly defined, in the OED, as 'a quality, attribute etc; peculiar to or characteristic of a woman or women' and 'designating something to which femaleness is attributed, typically on the basis of some perceived or assigned quality associated with the female sex'. The concept of femalehood thus comprises both a natural or biological feature – sex – and the social construction attached to it – gender. Indeed, sex refers to 'either of the two main categories [male and female] into which humans and many other living things are divided on the basis of their reproductive functions' and gender is 'the state of being male or female as expressed by social or cultural

[63] OED: The term 'male' is also predominantly defined in terms of biological traits as 'designating the sex which can beget, but not bear, offspring' and 'producing gametes (such as spermatozoa) that can fertilize female gametes (ova)'.

[64] OMD, see entries 'vulva', 'uterus (womb)', 'breast', 'ovary', 'puberty', 'menstruation', and 'pregnancy'. Pregnancy is defined as 'the period during which a woman carries a developing fetus, normally in the uterus'. The OMD further explains: '[d]uring pregnancy, menstruation is absent, there may be a great increase in appetite, and the breasts increase in size; the woman may also experience morning sickness. These and other changes are brought about by a hormone (progesterone) produced by the ovary and later by the placenta'.

[65] See, for example, puberty defined in the OMD as 'the time at which the onset of sexual maturity occurs and the reproductive organs become functional. This is manifested in both sexes by the appearance of secondary sexual characteristics (e.g. deepening of the voice in boys; growth of breasts in girls) and in girls by the start of menstruation. These changes are brought about by an increase in sex hormone activity due to stimulation of the ovaries and testes by pituitary hormones'.

distinctions and differences, rather than biological ones; the collective attributes or traits associated with a particular sex'.[66] This definition aligns with that given by feminist legal scholars who observe that gender refers to 'the social construction of differences between women and men and ideas of "femininity" and "masculinity" – the excess cultural baggage associated with biological sex',[67] and that 'every person and every existing social structure contributes to it, including the law'.[68] In this regard, the OED notes that 'the word sex tends now to refer to biological differences, while gender often refers to cultural or social ones'.

Hence, while sex is the biological attribute that differentiates females from males, gender refers to the social construction of both sexes in a given society: the characteristics ascribed to them and their corresponding privileged or subordinate social status. Yet the categorization of individuals according to their sex has been criticized by several scholars on the grounds that males and females do not always constitute clear-cut biological categories, arguing that 10 per cent of the population has chromosomal variations that do not fully match the female and male categories, and that some children have physiological attributes that place them in neither category, notably intersex children.[69] Accordingly, the division of individuals into two sexes has been signalled as not accounting for those who do not fit within either category or those who instead have attributes of both sexes, and finally those who self-identify as non-binary, or as both sexes or different sexes at a given time or throughout the life cycle.[70] However, the description of the biological features of each sex should not be overlooked. Firstly, biological females (persons born female)[71] have biological traits that are unique and make them more vulnerable to certain violations than biological males (persons born male), and for

66 OED.

67 Hillary Charlesworth, 'Feminist Methods in International Law' (1999) 93 *American Journal of International Law* 379, 379.

68 Marsha Freeman, Christine Chinkin and Beate Rudolf (eds.), *The UN Convention on the Elimination of All Forms of Discrimination Against Women: A Commentary* (1st ed., Oxford University Press 2012), 147.

69 Lena Gunnarsson, 'A Defense of the Category "Women"' (2011) 12 *Feminist Theory* 23, 29.

70 See, for example, Leslie McCall, 'The Complexity of Intersectionality' (2005) 30 *Signs: Journal of Women in Culture and Society* 1771, who argues that '[t]here are no longer two genders but countless ones, no longer two sexes but five': 1778.

71 It is worth mentioning that some trans activists, including scholars, argue that the expression 'born female' should be replaced by 'assigned female at birth – AFAB' for they consider that sex is assigned by a doctor at birth, and would not constitute a biological reality. See Christine Harb et al., 'Motivators and Barriers to Accessing Sexual Health Care Services for Transgender/Genderqueer Individuals Assigned Female Sex at Birth' (2019) 4 *Transgender Health* 58; Jessica Clarke, 'Sex Assigned at Birth' (2022) 122 *Columbia Law Review* 1821.

which they are expressly targeted. For example, being born with external female genitalia (the vulva), which is identifiable at birth, makes girls vulnerable to the practices of female infanticide and female genital mutilation, and once reaching puberty, the development of a menstrual cycle and the possibility of getting pregnant[72] lead to practices of child marriage and restrictive social codes that predominantly affect girls, as shall be discussed in this book. Also, the practice of prenatal sex selection is perpetrated on the female fetus because of her two X chromosomes.[73] In these situations, the girl child's parents and wider family do not consider whether she will 'self-identify' as a boy, a man or a non-binary person and/or undergo gender reassignment surgeries in the future; her membership in the girlhood category is identified exclusively on account of her biological traits. This female/male binary distinction is also significant for it has formed the basis of the social construction of females in society. Indeed, biological traits ascribed to the female sex such as inferior physical strength and weakness, especially during the menstrual cycle and when pregnant, were – and still are – employed in patriarchal societies as justifications for limiting the autonomy rights of women in both the public and private spheres. The social construction of femalehood as a weak, emotional and irrational sex has historically created a vicious cycle whereby women were not granted the same political, economic and legal rights as men, and thereby not given the opportunity to demonstrate their rational capacity, which further strengthened the argument that they were naturally ill-fitted for rational decision-making. As noted by Mill:

> The subjection of women to men being a universal custom, any departure from it quite naturally appears unnatural ... They have always hitherto been kept, as far as regards spontaneous development, in so unnatural a state, that their nature cannot but have been greatly distorted and disguised.[74]

The characteristics ascribed to the female sex on the grounds of biological and physical features are thereby employed to support the social construction of the female gender as inferior, irrational and weak. This dynamic shall also be observed as concerns the social construction of childhood. The present book thus adopts the OED definition of femalehood in terms of both biological traits and a social construct when referring to the girl child. It is acknowledged that intersex children and persons born male who self-identify as girls or as non-binary, and/or partly or fully attempt to transition as female through

72 OMD.

73 OMD.

74 John Stuart Mill, *The Subjection of Women* (Longmans, Green, Reader and Dyer 1869), 23, 104–5.

gender reassignment surgeries, also face unique challenges, which should be specifically explored, and are outside the purview of this book.[75]

### 1.2 Childhood

As with femalehood, the concept of childhood is a hybrid natural and social term. It is constructed upon both the unique biological traits of children that distinguish them from adults and the conception of children in a given society. The definition of 'child' in the English language reproduces this hybrid qualification. The main description of child is that of 'a young person of either sex, usually one below the age of puberty, a boy or girl',[76] and 'a young person of either sex, esp. between infancy and youth'.[77] This definition is notable on two grounds. Firstly, it describes childhood with reference to a state or age,[78] rather than specific social characteristics or constructions. Secondly, the term child as defined clearly encompasses both females and males, whereas it was historically employed to refer exclusively to the male infant, to describe 'an unborn or newly born human being; a fetus; an infant ... In early use occasionally contextually: a male infant'.[79] Conversely, it was also historically employed to describe the female infant, that is, 'a baby girl', especially in regional English and Irish English, with the OED offering the following quote: '[c]hild, still used in its old sense of 'girl', and pronounced cheel',[80] and employed as opposed to boy: 'Is it a boy or a child?'[81] The concept of 'child' is also defined in terms of its social construct as 'a person who has [or is considered to have] the character, manners, or attainment of a child'.[82] In this regard, Archard states that 'just as sex is biological and gender is social, it will be argued that physical immaturity is a natural fact whereas "childhood" is a social construct'.[83]

The concept of childhood refers to the notion that children and adults have distinct characteristics placing them in two different social categories. Historically, both eastern and western traditions acknowledged that children and adults differ on certain grounds, although the barrier separating these

75 See glossary definition of Girl Child.
76 OED. The Webster also refers to 'a young person especially between infancy and puberty'.
77 Webster.
78 OED.
79 OED.
80 OED: '[f]ormerly more widespread in English regional use in western varieties as far as north of Lancashire; now apparently restricted to the south-west'; N. Rogers *Wessex Dial* 75/1 (1979).
81 OED: W. W. Gill, *Manx Dial* II 32 (1934).
82 OED.
83 David Archard, *Children: Rights and Childhood* (Routledge 2015), 30.

categories differed.[84] In fact, the 'girl child category' as opposed to the adult woman has credible grounds. Physical and cerebral differences do exist between girls and adult women, and the categories of childhood and adulthood are thus not solely social, but also based on natural facts. In this regard, Archard stresses: 'children are not a natural kind, but "childhood" is not merely a social construct'.[85] Yet while there is an agreed-upon notion that children are distinct from adults, the conceptions of childhood, that is, the various perceptions of what distinguishes children and adults, vary greatly globally.[86] Hence, childhood cannot be examined as a universal and natural category but rather as a social construction which differs across history, cultures and socio-economic environments. In this regard, James and Prout argue that childhood is a shifting social and historical construction, and accordingly, all accounts of childhood should be evaluated in their proper temporal and social context.[87] The construction and various conceptions of childhood constitute a theoretical frame that is central to an examination of the girl child's identity as they shape her legal and social status. Archard contends that the conceptions of childhood vary in three respects: 1) boundaries, 2) dimensions and 3) divisions. The boundary of childhood refers to the barrier at which it ends, the 'extent of childhood'.[88] The dimensions of childhood comprise the moral, juridical, metaphysical and political aspects under which childhood is considered distinct from adulthood, and finally, the divisions of childhood refer to the subcategories or phases within childhood.[89] The issue, however, is to determine whether the dimensions, boundaries and divisions of girlhood reflect the actual physical and cognitive attributes of girl children, including those of girls located at the frontier of womanhood.

## 2 *Dimensions of Girlhood*

In his historical analysis of the construction and reconstruction of childhood, Hendrick underscores that 'each construction sought to mould "childhood" as a singular noun; the plural posed too many conceptual and political

[84] Ibid., 23–33.

[85] Ibid., 31.

[86] Archard notes that: '[t]he concept of childhood requires that children be distinguishable from adults in respect of some unspecified set of attributes. A *conception* of childhood is the specification of those attributes': Ibid., 32.

[87] Allison James and Alan Prout, 'Re-presenting Childhood' in Allison James and Alan Prout (eds.), *Constructing and Reconstructing Childhood: Contemporary Issues in the Sociological Study of Childhood* (Routledge 2015), 214.

[88] *Childhood* (2015), 35.

[89] Ibid., 35–40.

problems'.[90] Accordingly, master signifiers – political and religious leaders, psychologists and educationalists – have aimed to shape a universal conception of childhood. The modern conception of childhood is often characterized by a developmental approach with universal features involving teleology, necessity and endogeneity.[91] Indeed, current theories on child rights are greatly influenced by psychological theorists such as Piaget and Freud who conceived childhood as a stage in human development.[92] The developmental approach is teleological in that it views adulthood as an end to be reached, the 'telos'.[93] The second feature of the developmental approach is the necessity for the child to go through each stage to progress to the next. Finally, the development of the child is endogenous for it is 'self-propelled and inevitable: it derives its motive force from structures, functions and processes which are rooted within the child's nature', and the latter is 'genetically inherited and biologically fixed'.[94] This model thus considers that both nature and nurture influence the development of the girl child: 'the environment tends to be viewed only as the occasion for and scene of personal change'.[95] Although child theorists in the twentieth and twenty-first centuries have departed to a certain extent from the developmental approach,[96] this theory has nevertheless significantly shaped the modern construction of childhood. On the one hand, it could be argued that it has positively influenced childhood theories for it recognizes that children develop skills progressively through stages and thereby do not constitute a homogenous class. As a result, developmental theories support the notion that adolescent girls should be granted more autonomy rights than very young girls. On the other hand, its view of adulthood as the normative status and its presumption that adults constitute perfected versions of children have supported the concept of childism.[97]

The distinction between the concept and conceptions of childhood is of particular relevance in the analysis of the status of the girl child under

90 Harry Hendrick, 'Constructions and Reconstructions of British Childhood: An Interpretative Survey, 1800 to the Present' in Allison James and Alan Prout (eds.), *Constructing and Reconstructing Childhood: Contemporary Issues in the Sociological Study of Childhood* (Routledge 2015), 50.

91 *Childhood* (2015), 45–49.

92 Ibid., 44–46.

93 Ibid., 45–46. Adulthood is considered the 'ideal end-state' and the norm from which children depart until they acquire the necessary competencies.

94 Ibid., 47.

95 Ibid.

96 See Chapter 3.

97 See Chapter 3. In this regard, Archard underscores that under the developmental approach, '[c]hildhood in relation to adulthood mirrors the primitive in relation to the civilized and the modern, the primate in relation to the properly human': *Childhood* (2015), 48.

international law. While the concept of childhood is recognized worldwide – as illustrated by the almost universal ratification of the CRC as the central instrument protecting children's rights – its conceptions, that is, the distinct interpretations of its dimensions, divisions and boundaries according to a series of historical, cultural and socio-economic factors, have a considerable bearing on the protection of child rights internationally. As noted by Cipriani:

> Predominant conceptions of childhood in large part determine questions of rights, legal status, parental authority, and governments' power to intervene – including which legal rights children may or may not be able to assert for themselves.[98]

Furthermore, the present book argues that the conceptions of girlhood may vary distinctly from those of boyhood as concerns dimensions, divisions and boundaries, and thereby significantly impact the status of the girl child. Sexism is very present globally and women and girls are still accorded fewer rights than men and boys on the grounds of alleged emotional, intellectual and physical weaknesses.[99] In this regard, as concerns dimensions, boys might be perceived as possessing more cognitive abilities than girls, and granted more autonomy rights or allowed to pursue education at a higher level than girls. The divisions and boundaries might accordingly differ between girlhood and boyhood. For instance, societies might consider that boys are more mature than girls and therefore reach adolescence or adulthood earlier. Conversely, in a paternalistic society, girls might be conceived as more nurturing than boys and stripped of their 'child' status at a younger age than boys in order to marry and start a family, leading to distinct age thresholds globally for girls and boys.[100] In this regard, Sohoni observes that the age parameters of girlhood are varied and conflicting globally:

> The age parameters of girlhood are ambiguous – girlhood ranges from age 0 to a flexible ceiling extending to age 20 – depending on various cultural, legal, political, civil, or religious dictates. Often in the same country, a girl is considered a minor on the basis of one law but an adult according to another. Her adult status entitles her to vote or to run for public office, and may commence at a different age than her lawful maturity in terms of her right to inheritance or property ownership; her right to work; right to marry; right to choose abortion; or even her right to drive a motorized vehicle. Then again,

98 Don Cipriani, *Children's Rights and the Minimum Age of Criminal Responsibility: A Global Perspective* (Ashgate 2009), 16.

99 See Chapter 3.

100 See Chapters 4 and 7.

the confusion may be compounded by varying age limits in each piece of legislation with respect to girls and boys.[101]

### 3 *Boundaries of Girlhood*

One of the illustrations of the complexity of delineating girlhood and womanhood is the issue of identifying a specific barrier separating these two identity categories, and the varying legal thresholds for distinct rights both *within* and *between* states globally. Every girl child is unique and acquires mental and physical competencies throughout the life cycle. One cannot claim that girls as a class lack cognitive abilities or that every adult woman is a perfectly rational being.[102] As noted by Lansdown, each child has circumstances impacting the development of varied abilities: 'children in different environments and cultures who are faced with diverse life experiences will acquire competencies at different ages, and their acquisition of competencies will vary according to circumstances'.[103] Girls will develop mental and physical competencies at distinct times according to their upbringing as well as socio-economic, cultural and personal circumstances. The key question is which parameter should be applied to determine this boundary.

#### 3.1 Age-based and Competence-based Boundaries

The current boundary of girlhood is usually delineated at a specific age. The parameter of age may seem arbitrary for it implies 'the absurd idea that every single individual on the stroke of midnight acquires, all at once and totally, the abilities associated, conventionally, with a particular age'.[104] Accordingly, granting girls autonomy rights at a specific age may appear inappropriate. Since every girl child acquires competencies at a different pace according to her circumstances, the parameter of age appears to penalise girls, notably adolescent girls, who have the required competency, while unfairly favouring adult women who instead still show immaturity, except for women who, according to a medical diagnosis, do not possess the minimum competency for legal capacity, such as those suffering from dementia. Hence, it could be argued that the end of girlhood should be established on a case-by-case analysis of each girl's competence. Herring observes that a standard of

[101] *Burden Girlhood* (1995), 1–2.
[102] See Chapter 3 for a discussion on Herring's Common Vulnerability Theory.
[103] Gerison Lansdown, *The Evolving Capacities of the Child* (UNICEF 2005), ix.
[104] *Childhood* (2015), 84–85.

competence 'treats each person as an individual, rather than relying on stereotypical assumptions about age'.[105] In this regard, the Gillick competence test established by the House of Lords in the United Kingdom is notable on two grounds. Their Lordships adopted a developmental view of childhood by underscoring the 'developing decision-making powers of children',[106] and thus recognized that older children should be granted more autonomy rights than infants or young children. Moreover, the House of Lords held that a child is able to take responsibility for making her/his own decisions when s/he reaches a sufficient understanding and intelligence, and thus, once a child demonstrates the ability for rational thinking, the denying of autonomy rights is no longer validated. While the decision concerned medical treatment, Lord Scarman implied that the Gillick test could be applied to all matters concerning the child: 'parental right yields to the child's right to make his own decisions when he reaches a sufficient understanding and intelligence to be capable of making up his own mind on the matter requiring decision'.[107]

Conversely, the competence-based criterion for the end of girlhood is characterized by three central weaknesses. Firstly, it does not offer an objective standard but rather depends upon a criterion of 'competence' established in the law within each state, and its subsequent interpretation by a judge or a professional. The competence test can therefore appear subjective in that it rests on the various conceptions of childhood, and moreover girlhood, in each nation, as well as those of individuals in a position of authority. The Gillick case illustrates the issue of subjectivity, for the same test was subsequently interpreted by courts as signifying that while a child could demonstrate the competency to consent to medical treatment, his or her refusal of consent could be overridden by the provision of a doctor or another valid consent,[108] thereby establishing an 'asymmetry between consent and refusals', referred to as a 'retreat from Gillick'.[109] Cave and Wallbank argue that, according to the retreat from Gillick, the decision of the minor to consent or refuse treatment

[105] Jonathan Herring, 'Children's Rights for Grown-ups' in Sandra Fredman and Sarah Spencer (eds.), *Age as an Equality Issue: Legal and Policy Perspectives* (Hart 2003), 160.

[106] Rachel Taylor, 'Reversing the Retreat from Gillick? R (Axon) v. Secretary of State for Health' (2007) 19 *Child and Family Law Quarterly* 81, 82.

[107] Gillick v. West Norfolk and Wisbech Area Health Authority (1986) AC 112, 186. Lord Scarman's androcentric phrasing in this context is notable.

[108] Stephen Gilmore and Jonathan Herring, 'No is the Hardest Word: Consent and Children's Autonomy' (2011) 23 Child and Family Law Quarterly 3, 3–4; Re R (A Minor) (Wardship: Consent to Treatment (1992) Fam 11; Re W (A Minor) (Medical Treatment: Court's Jurisdiction) (1993) Fam 64.

[109] Emma Cave and Julie Wallbank, 'Minors' Capacity to Refuse Treatment: A Reply to Gilmore and Herring' (2012) 20 *Medical Law Review* 423, 424.

shall be solely considered as a demonstration of competence if it coincides with the 'ideal desire autonomy',[110] described by Coggon as the universal standards established by a given society or community in which the child lives, and not according to her/his 'best desire autonomy' which reflects 'a persons's overall desire given by his own values'.[111] The competence test might therefore be influenced by a society's perception of a 'good' decision rather than the actual cognitive abilities of an individual girl child. This test may appear arbitrary for it depends on which professional or judge applies her/his interpretation of competence. Moreover, one can contend that if a single test was reinterpreted within the same jurisdiction, the United Kingdom, and within a short period of time (eight years), the criterion of competence is likely to vary significantly between nations according to political, social, economic and cultural factors, as well as the individual opinions of the judiciary and other professionals asked to evaluate the competency of girl children. Societies might have different conceptions of distinct groups of children on account of gender, race, class, religion, sexual orientation and abilities. The conception of competence in a given society could be strongly influenced by adults' desire to control girls within the private and public spheres, rather than actual abilities. Cipriani argues that 'children's competence – or how adults interpret and depict children's competence – proves to be an exceptionally political question that determines rights and policies for children'.[112] For example, the criterion to demonstrate competency might be exceedingly demanding in order to prevent girl children from acquiring autonomy rights. Conversely, states could intentionally consider that a minimum standard of competency suffices to reach adulthood, thereby removing their obligation to provide for and protect girl children at a young age. The competence test might be additionally subjective in a society that conceives the dimensions of boyhood and girlhood differently. This is particularly problematic where sexism intersects with childism, for the criteria of a competency test might be tailored to favour boys, and moreover, adults in a position of authority might overestimate the performance in a given test of boys, which would penalize girls. Also, it would be difficult to establish a universal criterion for competence which takes into consideration the distinct realities of girls located at the intersection of various identity vectors, such as class. For instance, while a girl child belonging to a privileged socio-economic class might demonstrate excellent

[110] Ibid., 444–45.

[111] John Coggon, 'Varied and Principled Understandings of Autonomy in English Law: Justifiable Inconsistency or Blinkered Moralism?' (2007) 15 *Health Care Analysis* 235, 240.

[112] *Minimum Age* (2009), 16.

cognitive abilities, both verbal and written, she might not possess the required skills to survive in an underprivileged neighbourhood, and vice versa. Hence, the criteria to evaluate the competence of girl children would have to acknowledge the distinct skills developed within extremely different contexts.

Secondly, the competence test fails to offer a clear and predictable parameter. Fortin argues that the concept of Gillick competence is characterized by its uncertainty, and notably the difficulty of applying it within the family unit:

> By making an adolescent's legal capacity hinge on notions as debatable as understanding and maturity fundamentally hampers its effectiveness as a means of settling internal family conflicts. Parents struggling to impose restrictions on recalcitrant adolescents may find it impossible to retain their objectivity when deciding whether their offspring can comply with Lord Scarman's test of capacity.[113]

Instead, the age parameter offers certainty for children and adults as to when they shall be granted specific rights. Herring notes that '[t]he age criterion … makes it easier for citizens who will be able to plan their lives on the basis that they are or are not to be assessed competent, rather than having to establish their competence on each new occasion'.[114] Thirdly, it would be very difficult and impractical for states, both in terms of financial and human resources, to conduct nationwide surveys and interviews of every girl child throughout girlhood to establish whether she reached the competence criterion. Hence, the age parameter and the competence test fail to offer a boundary for the end of girlhood that would be both objective and predictable as well as fair and adapted to the actual cognitive and physical abilities – and in fact to the idiosyncrasy – of each individual girl child.

## 3.2 English Definitions

In the English language and in the law, several parameters are offered for the end of childhood and thus girlhood: puberty, youth, adolescence, majority and adulthood, which shed light on – yet further complicate – the frontiers of girlhood.

### 3.2.1 Puberty

The OED and the Webster offer two distinct outer boundaries for girlhood in their definitions of 'child': 1) puberty[115] and 2)

[113] *Children's Rights* (2009), 94.

[114] 'Children Rights Grown-ups' (2003), 161.

[115] OED: 'a young person of either sex, usually one below the age of puberty, a boy or girl'. The Webster also refers to 'a young person especially between infancy and puberty'.

youth.[116] The parameter of puberty raises four issues. Firstly, while the process of puberty, defined in the OED as 'the period of life during which a young person reaches sexual maturity and becomes capable of reproduction', occurs within generally agreed age limits, each girl child reaches this development at a different time.[117] Accordingly, this definition allows for inconsistencies worldwide, both within and between states. This parameter is further complicated by the OED which refers to 'the age of puberty', implying that puberty hits at a specific age, whereas the Webster mentions the notion of puberty as not age-bound, and the OMD as 'a time at which the onset of sexual maturity occurs and the reproductive organs become functional', thus time-bound yet not age-bound. Secondly, the OED definition of child implies that girls are no longer children once they reach puberty, which can occur very early, in some cases as early as eight years old for early signs, and ten for procreation.[118] In this regard, it is notable that the 1911 edition of the OED specified that puberty was reached under the law in England at fourteen years for boys and twelve years for girls,[119] and the Webster presently stipulates that 'the age at which puberty occurs [is] often construed legally as 14 in boys and 12 in girls'. Thirdly, the OED identifies puberty as the boundary for both the end of childhood and the beginning of adolescence, since the latter is defined as 'the *period following the onset of puberty* during which a young person develops from a child into an adult'.[120] According to this definition, an adolescent girl is no longer a girl child. Fourthly, although the OED offers puberty as the boundary for the end of childhood, it provides a different parameter for the beginning of adulthood: 'having reached the age of maturity'. Maturity here refers to both physical and mental maturity: 'the state of being physically and mentally mature'.[121] The distinct parameters of 'puberty' – which is based solely on physical attributes – for the end of childhood, and instead that of 'maturity' for the beginning of adulthood, could thereby imply that a girl child who is capable of procreation, yet who has not attained mental maturity or the 'age of maturity', falls outside the realms of both childhood and adulthood. The definition of adulthood as reaching 'the age of maturity' also implies that

116 Webster: 'a young person of either sex, esp. between infancy and youth'.

117 UNFPA, 'The State of the World Population: How Our Future Depends on a Girl at This Decisive Age' (2016), 81; UNESCO, 'Good Policy and Practice in Health Education: Puberty Education & Menstrual Hygiene Management' (2014), 10; Getachew Mullu Kassa et al., 'Prevalence and Determinants of Adolescent Pregnancy in Africa: A Systematic Review and Meta-Analysis' (2018) 15 *Reproductive Health* 195, 196.

118 'Future Depends Girl' (2016), 81.

119 Puberty was defined in this context as '[b]eing functionally capable of procreation'.

120 OED (emphasis added).

121 OED.

maturity is tied to a specific age, yet the dictionary does not provide a specific number. Moreover, the legal definition of 'adult' provided in the OED further complicates the frontiers of childhood and adulthood, for it refers to a person who 'has reached the age of majority', thereby indicating that majority and adulthood coincide.

3.2.2 Youth As previously noted, the Webster defines a child as a 'young person of either sex, esp. between infancy and youth'. It describes 'youth', in turn, as 'the period between childhood and manhood'.[122] This definition is problematic because it implies that 'childhood' and 'youth' constitute two mutually exclusive periods of life, and therefore 'children' and 'young people' are two distinct identity groups. Consequently, according to the Webster, one cannot be a girl child and a young person at the same time. Yet, the Webster refers to a child as 'a young person' in this definition, which implies that a girl child is also a young person, and thus girlhood and youth coincide, which appears to contradict the definition of youth. Furthermore, this definition does not provide an age at which 'youth' begins and ends, and the boundaries separating childhood, youth and adulthood are therefore left ambiguous. The Webster also offers the following definition of child: 'a young person especially between infancy and puberty', which implies, as in the OED, that the parameter for the end of childhood is puberty, rather than youth. Since the Webster applies both puberty and youth as the frontiers of childhood, this could imply that they coincide, that is, puberty and youth happen at the same time. The Webster nevertheless specifies that childhood occurs '*especially* between infancy and puberty',[123] and thus the former could end after puberty. To make matters more complicated, the Webster also defines youth as 'the period between childhood and maturity', and thereby provides three distinct categories: 1) childhood, 2) youth and 3) maturity, which appears to indicate, once again, that childhood and youth constitute mutually exclusive categories. Moreover, maturity is defined in the Webster as 'the state of being fully developed in the body *or* the mind',[124] which implies that youth terminates as soon as either physical or mental maturity is reached. Instead, the term adult is described as one who is 'fully developed and mature', without qualifying the 'either-or' physical and mental abilities. Hence, as previously noted, if youth terminates at physical maturity and adulthood begins at full physical as well as

[122] It is noteworthy that the Webster offers an androcentric definition of youth by referring to 'manhood' instead of using gender-neutral terms such as 'adulthood'.

[123] Emphasis added.

[124] Emphasis added.

mental maturity, girls who reach physical but not mental maturity would not fall under either category.

3.2.3 Majority As noted in Section 3.2.1, the term adult refers to a person that 'has reached the age of majority'.[125] Majority is defined as '[t]he state of being of full age' in the OED, and 'the age at which full civil rights are accorded' in the Webster. These definitions indicate that majority is attained when a young person is granted civil and political rights, notably legal capacity. The Dictionary of Legal Terms defines majority as 'the age when a person is considered legally responsible for all his or her activities and becomes entitled to the legal rights held by citizens generally'.[126] According to this definition, the girl child, upon reaching majority, is granted all legal rights, such as civil and political as well as economic, social and cultural rights. In contrast, the OED refers to a minor as one who has not 'attained full age', the Webster as 'not having reached majority' and the *Dictionary of Legal Terms* as the 'condition of being under legal age'.[127] Hence, the concept of minority is described *in relation to* and *as opposed to* majority. It is worthy of note, from a semiotic perspective, that the term 'minority' is associated with negative attributes. For example, the OED describes it as 'the condition or fact of being smaller, inferior, or subordinate in relation to something else', and the Webster as 'inferior in importance', which as shall be examined in the next section, is also the case for the expression 'girl'. Hence, girls are qualified by two expressions, 'minority' and 'girlhood', that further propel their inferior status in society. Overall, one can observe that the main definitions of majority and minority are age-bound rather than competence-bound, as they refer to '[t]he state of being of full age' and 'legal age'.

The definitions of majority raise several questions. First, does 'full age' mean that the girl, once exiting minority, will be granted all 'adult' rights at once? The term minor is nonetheless defined as 'a person who is not yet old enough to have the rights of an adult',[128] which clarifies a number of issues, notably that minority and adulthood constitute two separate categories, and thereby implies that one is granted rights at majority. Moreover, by referring to 'a person who is not yet old enough', this definition implies that minority ends when reaching a certain age, instead of through other means such as entering marriage or puberty. Second, while the OED refers to 'the age of majority' and

125 OED.

126 Steven Gifi, *Barron's Dictionary of Legal Terms: A Simplified Guide to the Language of Law* (1993).

127 *Dictionary of Legal Terms* (1993).

128 Webster.

the *Dictionary of Legal Terms* to the 'legal age', which age is inferred in these definitions? Since the parameter for the end of childhood in the OED is puberty rather than majority, girls who attained puberty *before* maturity and thus majority might belong neither to childhood nor adulthood. Additionally, it is notable that there is a lack of uniformity across definitions within the same dictionary, and that none offers a set age. The definitions provided by English dictionaries thus tend to obfuscate, rather than clarify, the outer limits of girlhood.

## 4 *Divisions of Girlhood*

One cannot contend that girls lack rational autonomy until the very day they reach adulthood. Psychological studies demonstrate that '[t]he standard indices of physical maturation can be reached at different stages',[129] and the abilities of an adolescent girl are distinctly more developed than those of an infant. Placing all girls under a certain age threshold in the social category of 'children' might therefore appear artificial, which leads us to an exploration of subcategories within girlhood. In Roman Law, childhood was divided into infancy, pre-puberty and minority, while in developmental psychology, girlhood is divided into early childhood (i.e. preschool), middle childhood (school age) and adolescence (puberty),[130] or into specific age groups: below 0, 0–1, 2–5, 6–10, 11–14, 15–19.[131] According to medical classifications, childhood ends at puberty, and is followed by different stages of adolescence, namely early adolescence (10–13 years), mid-adolescence (14–15 years) and late adolescence (16–18 years), the latter described by Guercio as the period during which girls 'begin to behave similarly to adults, and develop their own distinct identities, opinions and ideas'.[132] The CRC Committee provides three divisions of childhood, in line with developmental psychology. First, 'early childhood', which is 'at birth and throughout infancy; during the preschool years; as well as during the transition to school', and while noting that this transition usually occurs from 4 to 7 years depending on the State party,

[129] *Childhood* (2015), 31.

[130] Jean Piaget, *Science of Education and the Psychology of the Child* (Viking 1970); Jean Piaget et al., *Epistemology and Psychology of Functions* (Reidel Publishing Company 1977); see also Laura Guercio, 'Establishing the Social and Legal Categories for "Girls" and "Girl Children"' (2022) 28 *Violence against Women* 1842.

[131] *Burden Girlhood* (1995), 2.

[132] 'Girls and Girl Children' (2022), 1849–50; Eric Hazen et al., 'Child, Adolescent and Adult Development' in Theodore Stern et al. (eds.), *Massachusetts General Hospital Comprehensive Clinical Psychiatry* (Elsevier 2016); Karen Marcdante et al., 'Overview and Assessment of Adolescents' in Karen Marcdante et al. (eds.), *Nelson Essentials of Pediatrics* (Elsevier 2018).

the Committee offers 'the period below the age of 8 years' as a working definition.[133] Second, 'middle childhood' identified *a contrario* as distinct from the other two divisions, and third, 'adolescence', defined in the CRC Committee general comment on adolescent health as 'a period characterized by rapid physical, cognitive and social changes, including sexual and reproductive maturation; the gradual building up of the capacity to assume adult behaviours and roles involving new responsibilities requiring new knowledge and skills', and while the Committee does not provide the boundary for the beginning of adolescence in this context, it does mention its outer limit: 18 years.[134] In a more recent general comment on adolescence, the Committee specifies that it 'does not seek … to define adolescence, but instead focuses on the period of childhood from 10 years until the 18th birthday to facilitate consistency in data collection', and thus offers 10–18 years for adolescence.[135] These divisions follow research in the field of psychology demonstrating that children, both girls and boys, progressively develop intellectual capacities, reaching a level of rational thinking during adolescence.[136] In this regard, Guercio observes that '[p]hysical and psychological differences between a female child who has not yet reached puberty, *girl child*, and a female person who is no longer a child but not yet an adult, *girl*, also entail a different assessment of the effects of actions committed against them, or by them', and thereby considers whether the violence committed against a six-year-old girl has the same effect as that committed against a sixteen-year old.[137] She thus suggests the subcategories 'girl child' to refer to prepubescence and 'girl' to adolescence, to tend to their respective needs.[138] While this proposal is interesting, as it is indeed important to distinguish between the realities of a prepubescent girl and an adolescent girl, the terminology suggested by Guercio can be problematic as it would imply that the 'girl child' expression only refers to girls before puberty, and would thereby exclude adolescent girls. Moreover, since the international legal framework has only recently recognized the girl child identity group, and employs the expressions 'girl child' and 'girl' interchangeably, Guercio's divisions might further confuse the 'girl child' category under international law. We thus suggest maintaining the approach adopted in international law and employing the expressions 'girl child' and 'girl' as encompassing all female children. We nonetheless propose to

[133] CRC General Comment No. 7 Early Childhood (2006), para. 4.

[134] CRC General Comment No. 4 Adolescent Health (2003), paras. 1, 2.

[135] CRC General Comment No. 20 Adolescence (2016), para. 5.

[136] *Childhood* (2015), 84, 88.

[137] 'Girls and Girl Children' (2022), 1846, 1850 (emphasis added).

[138] Ibid., 1850.

distinguish divisions *within* girlhood and employ the expressions 'young girls' for prepubescent girls and 'adolescent girls' for girls who reached puberty, as the realities and obstacles faced by both subgroups can be very different, as astutely explained by Guercio.

## 5 *Girl Expression: Semiotics of Inferiority, Subordination and Denigration*

While the current definition of girlhood is founded on femalehood and childhood, it is noteworthy that the term 'girl' has historically been correlated with social inferiority and subordination, as demonstrated by its parameters in English dictionaries. The expression 'girl' has been used to refer to female domestic servants since the second half of the seventeenth century;[139] in fact, English dictionaries still offer descriptions such as 'female servant' and 'maid' or 'assistant',[140] and note that the term 'girl' has been employed to designate a 'black female servant or domestic employee' chiefly in South Africa, and previously in the United States, stressing that the use of the term 'girl' in this manner is derogatory and offensive.[141] Moreover, the term 'girl' has been used to refer to female prostitutes for over 350 years.[142] Numerous expressions, such as 'girls of the game', and later 'girls of ease' and 'girls about [the] town' are recorded as designating female individuals who sell their bodies.[143] As seen in Stoddard's *Poems*: 'Men hurry by with a stealthy glance, Women pass with their eyes cast down; Even the children seem to know The shameless girl of the town'.[144] It is notable that English dictionaries still identify, after the 'female child' and 'female servant' initial definitions, the concept of a girl with that of a female 'prostitute'.[145] In addition, the adjective 'girlish' in the SOEDHP and the noun 'girlie' in the Webster are both employed as alternative expressions for pornography: 'publication, entertainment, etc featuring young women, usually naked or semi-naked, in erotic contexts'[146] and 'featuring scantily clothed girls'.[147] The pornographic industry currently uses the expression 'girls' rather than 'women' when referring to the reified female

[139] Chambers Etymology; OED.
[140] Webster; OED; SOEDHP.
[141] OED.
[142] The OED traces this description back to the second half of the seventeenth century.
[143] OED.
[144] OED, Richard Henry Stoddard, *Poems* (1880, 243).
[145] OED; Webster.
[146] SOEDHP.
[147] Webster. The Webster 1995 edition described it as 'featuring nude or nearly nude women or pictures of them: a girlie magazine or show'.

human beings it sells and supplies to customers, as girls are more highly valued 'sexual products' than adult women.[148]

The expression 'girl' has also historically designated unmarried women. In the 1911 edition of the OED, 'girl' was described as a 'female child, unmarried woman', and the Webster still defines her in this manner. This designation is problematic on two grounds. First, it enshrines the notion that unmarried females constitute a distinct class of adult females who have not earned their status as 'women'. Second, it is inaccurate to link singlehood to girlhood, for, as noted by Sohoni in her criticism of the Webster definition of 'girl', many girl children are in fact married, including at a young age.[149] The compounds offered in the OED, such as 'girl-bride', 'girl-wife', 'girl-mother' and 'girl-widow' demonstrate the historical recognition, in the English language, of the young character of married female beings, who were, and still are to this day, children.[150] Although the OED departed from this designation, the Webster still defines 'girl' as an unmarried woman, thereby enshrining the wrongful association between youth and celibacy criticized by Sohoni. The expression 'girl' has also referred to someone's partner or wife, a 'girlfriend' and 'sweetheart',[151] which is not problematic *per se*; however, it is noteworthy that the term 'girl', rather than 'woman', is used for romantic purposes, which raises the question how young the girl child is pictured to be. Moreover, 'girl' is often employed in these contexts to refer to a person solely in relation to a man. For instance, 'best girl' refers to a 'man's favourite female companion', and 'girl Friday' to 'a female friend, esp. a person's (a young man's) usual or preferred female companion or sexual partner', which underlines the sexual nature of the relationship.[152] English dictionaries thereby perpetuate the 'phallocentric tradition' whereby girls are traditionally defined as 'man's other'.[153] Freeman

[148] Valeria Rubattu et al., 'Cam Girls and Adult Performers are Enjoying a Boom in Business' (2023) 12 *Social Sciences* 62. For example, the GirlsDoPorn.com website, accused of featuring trafficked girls and sexual assault, and which was also hosted on the very prolific Pornhub international website as a premium partner: see Sylvia Rodeschini, 'New Standards of Respectability in Contemporary Pornography: Pornhub's Corporate Communication' (2021) 8 *Porn Studies* 76; Timothy Lee, *Arstechnica*, 'GirlsDoPorn Website Goes Offline After $13M Judgment, Criminal Charges' (16 January 2020). https://arstechnica.com/tech-policy/2020/01/girlsdoporn-website-goes-offline-after-13m-judgment-criminal-charges/ (accessed 4 June 2023).

[149] *Burden Girlhood* (1995), 1.

[150] OED.

[151] The Oxford and Webster dictionaries offer this parameter, although not as their official definition of the girl expression.

[152] SOEDHP.

[153] Ian Bryan and Julie Wallbank, 'The Lore of Sexual Difference in Social and Legal Discourse on "Date Rape"' (2004) 15 *Law and Critique* 183, 185–86.

et al. note that '[d]uring the long history of humanity – with the rare exception of a few matriarchal cultures – "woman" has always been and is persistently constructed as "the other", that is: not-a-man'.[154] In this regard, it is notable that Johns Hopkins University in the United States adopted this approach in its glossary definition of 'lesbian' as a 'non-man attracted to non-men', which it thereafter removed after eliciting significant criticism that the university was 'erasing women'.[155]

Finally, the expression 'girl' is also employed to describe adult women and men in a pejorative manner. The OED underscores that 'girl' was 'attested earlier in (often derogatory) reference to women with respect to their occupational or social status'.[156] The complex association with inferiority of the term 'girl' when employed to refer to women is illustrated by the fact that while women may still use it *between each other*, in a context of friendship and/or collegiality, it can be perceived as a derogatory appellation when used by a man. The term 'girl' also designates adult men of weak character and inferior status and can be employed with a homophobic underlying tone. The term 'girl' may identify a weak or effeminate man or 'oversensitive man',[157] and prison inmates who are sexually subservient to dominant and abusive detainees.[158] Hence, one can observe that the expression 'girl' is associated with subordination on account of class, profession, race and marital status, as well as solely in reference to the male comparator, or in a derogatory manner towards adult women and men. The presence of these definitions in the latest editions of the OED and the Webster is significant for it demonstrates that the notion of inferiority still permeates the concept of the girl child, thereby reflecting, within the language of dictionaries and everyday discourse, the inferior status ascribed to girl children worldwide.

[154] *Commentary CEDAW* (2012), 146.

[155] See Evelyn Okpanachi et al., *Newsweek*, 'I'm a Woman. Don't Call me a Non-Man' (14 June 2023). www.newsweek.com/johns-hopkins-women-transgender-non-binary-1806627 (accessed 19 June 2023); Valerie Richardson, *The Washington Times*, 'Johns Hopkins Removes Glossary that Defines "Lesbian" as "Non-Man" after Uproar' (14 June 2023). www.washingtontimes.com/news/2023/jun/14/johns-hopkins-removes-glossary-defines-lesbian-non/ (accessed 19 June 2023).

[156] OED.

[157] OED; SOEDHP.

[158] OED.

# 3

# Sexism and Childism

The situation of the girl child is unique for her two vectors of identity, femalehood and childhood, place a double burden of discrimination on her. As a female, she encounters gender-based discrimination called sexism, and as a child, she undergoes child-based discrimination, a novel concept termed 'childism'.[1] A semioethic analysis of the international legal apparatus must therefore conduct an examination of whether treaties protecting the girl child take into consideration the obstacles she faces in exercising her rights as a result of sexism and childism.

## I THE CONCEPT OF DISCRIMINATION UNDER INTERNATIONAL LAW

Before examining the sexism and childism experienced by girls specifically, it is important to explore the twin concepts of equality and discrimination, which are positive and negative statements of the same principle. Indeed, as noted by Besson and Kleber: 'one is treated equally when one is not discriminated against, and one is discriminated against when one is not treated equally'.[2] Equality law distinguishes between formal equality, which treats

[1] *Childism* (2012), 4.

[2] 'Non-Discrimination' (2019), 57. See Chapter 2 for an examination of non-discrimination in the International Bill of Rights, CEDAW and CRC. For a discussion on the principle of non-discrimination more broadly, see for example Shreya Atrey, *Intersectional Discrimination* (Oxford University Press 2019); Sandra Fredman, *Discrimination Law* (Oxford University Press 2011); Tarunabh Khaitan, *A Theory of Discrimination Law* (Oxford University Press 2015); 'Equality and Non-Discrimination' (1981); Wouter Vandenhole, *Non-Discrimination and Equality in the View of the UN Human Rights Treaty Bodies* (Intersentia 2005); Dinah Shelton, 'Prohibited Discrimination in International Human Rights Law' in Aristotle Constantinides and Nikos Zaikos (eds.), *The Diversity of International Law* (Martinus Nijhoff 2009); Olivier de Schutter, *International Human Rights Law* (Cambridge University Press

everyone equally, and substantive equality, which considers that differential treatment may be justified for persons who are not similarly situated. Formal equality and substantive equality are rooted in the principles of Aristotelian philosophy, whereby 'equality and justice require like things to be treated in a like manner, while unlike things are to be treated in an unlike manner'.[3] Formal equality refers to the first aspect, also known as 'sameness', 'similarly situated' and 'identical treatment approach', which 'focuses on the content of laws and practices and their even-handed application'.[4] Instead, substantive equality, also known as the 'difference approach',[5] refers to the second Aristotelian principle which recognizes that the equal treatment of privileged and subordinate groups might in fact lead to de facto inequality. Fredman underscores in this regard that '[w]here equal treatment leads to disadvantage ... it may be necessary to treat [this group] differently in order to achieve equalities of outcome'.[6] Substantive equality thus examines the concrete implications of laws, policies and practices. Indeed, general provisions ensuring formal equality may fail to take into account the obstacles the girl child faces in exercising her rights as a result of sexism, childism, or a combination of both. Fredman advocates for transformative equality, which involves a paradigm shift in considering structural inequality. For example, as concerns sexism, she argues for systemic changes in the established order rather than simply improving women's status in a male-defined world.[7] Direct discrimination against girl children occurs when they experience differential treatment expressly on the grounds of sex and/or age, for example, when girls are not entitled to education on equal terms with boys, or to reproductive health on equal grounds with boys or adult women under the law. Indirect

2014); Daniel Moeckli, 'Equality and Non-Discrimination' in Daniel Moeckli et al. (eds.), *International Human Rights Law* (Oxford University Press 2018). See also Vierdag, *Discrimination International Law* (1973), which identifies four elements of unequal legislative treatment: 1) denial of a right to some that is accorded to others, 2) diminution of a right for some while it is fully accorded to others, 3) imposition of a duty on some that is not imposed on others and 4) imposition of a duty on some that is not imposed as heavily on others: 44.

3 Andrew Byrnes and Puja Kapai, 'Article 1' in Patricia Schulz et al. (eds.), *The UN Convention on the Elimination of All Forms of Discrimination against Women and its Optional Protocol: A Commentary* (2nd ed., Oxford University Press 2022), 82.

4 Ibid.

5 Ibid., 83.

6 Sandra Fredman, 'Engendering Socio-Economic Rights' (2009) 25 *South African Journal on Human Rights* 410, 419. For an analysis of the four overlapping dimensions of substantive equality: redistribution, recognition, transformation and participation, see *Discrimination Law* (2011).

7 Sandra Fredman, 'Beyond the Dichotomy of Formal and Substantive Equality: Towards a New Definition of Equal Rights' in Ineke Boerefijn et al. (eds.), *Temporary Special Measures: Accelerating De Facto Equality of Women under Art 4 CEDAW* (Intersentia 2003), 115.

discrimination occurs when seemingly gender and child-neutral norms or practices actually penalize or disproportionality affect girls de facto, for example, when restrictions on reproductive health concerning the entire population actually impact girls more than boys, men or even adult women.

While the principle of non-discrimination is fundamental under international law, it is not defined in the international legal apparatus. The UDHR, ICCPR and ICESCR neither define the term discrimination nor indicate what constitutes discrimination.[8] The international legal framework solely identifies specific grounds of discrimination, such as racial discrimination in the International Convention on the Elimination of All Forms of Racial Discrimination (CERD),[9] and discrimination against women in the CEDAW.[10] Instead, the CRC does not define the concept of discrimination against children.[11] However, the Human Rights Committee provides a definition of discrimination, which although not legally binding, offers guidance on the interpretation of this notion under the ICCPR:

> [A]ny distinction, exclusion, restriction or preference which is based on any ground such as race, colour, *sex*, language, religion, political or other opinion, national or social origin, property, birth or other status and which has the purpose or effect of nullifying or impairing the recognition, enjoyment or exercise by all persons, on an equal footing, of all rights and freedoms.[12]

It is worthy of note that the definition offered by the Human Rights Committee lists 'sex' as a prohibited ground of discrimination, but not 'age', and thereby appears to cover the gender-based rather than child-based discrimination experienced by the girl child. The Human Rights Committee recognizes both formal and substantive equality, noting that the enjoyment of rights and freedoms on an equal footing does not signify identical treatment in every instance, and specifically refers to the prohibition of the death sentence on persons below 18 years in this context.[13] It underscores that States parties have a negative as well as positive duty to address discrimination: the obligation of States parties is not limited to that of prohibiting discriminatory acts, for

8 For example, ICCPR General Comment No. 18 Non-Discrimination (1989), para. 6: '[t]he Committee notes that the Covenant neither defines the term "discrimination" nor indicates what constitutes discrimination'.

9 CERD, art. 1.

10 CEDAW, art. 1. See Chapter 8 for a discussion on the concept of 'discrimination against women' under international law as it pertains to the girl child.

11 The CRC Committee also fails to provide a definition in its general comments, see 'Non-Discrimination' (2019), 58.

12 ICCPR General Comment No. 18 Non-Discrimination (1989), para. 7 (emphasis added).

13 Ibid., para. 8.

they may be required to take affirmative action to address factors perpetuating discrimination.[14] As concerns equality between men and women, the Human Rights Committee further notes that '[t]he State party must not only adopt measures of protection, but also positive measures in all areas so as to achieve the effective and equal empowerment of women'.[15] Besson expands on Bayefsky's analysis of the principle of non-discrimination under international law, and considers that the definition of discrimination provided by the Human Rights Committee comprises four elements: 1) the differentiation of similar situations or the similar treatment of different situations, 2) the absence of legitimate ends, 3) the lack of proportionality of means to ends and 4) the use of suspect classifications.[16] Besson's analytical framework is relevant to the girl child whose experience satisfies the four elements, for instance, as concerns female infanticide.[17] First, female infanticide constitutes an intentional unjustified distinction: killing a female child because of her gender. Second, there is an absence of legitimate ends. Besson notes that the justification of the distinction should be assessed in relation to the aims and effects of such a measure, bearing the principles which normally prevail in a democratic society.[18] There is a non-reasonable relationship of proportionality between the desire not to raise a female child and killing her once she is born.[19] Moreover, Bayefsky stresses that some grounds are more suspect than others, such as discrimination on the basis of sex, which is the case at hand.[20] As this book conducts a semiotic examination of concepts, we shall turn to the definition of discrimination in the English language. The OED defines discrimination firstly as making a distinction: 'the action of perceiving, noting, or making a distinction between things' and 'the power or faculty of observing differences accurately, or of making exact distinctions; discernement'. The sixth OED definition however relates to its legal meaning as 'unjust or prejudicial treatment of a person or group, especially on the grounds of race,

[14] Ibid., para. 10: 'the principle of equality sometimes requires … affirmative action in order to diminish or eliminate conditions which cause or help to perpetuate discrimination prohibited by the Covenant'.

[15] ICCPR General Comment No. 28 Equality between Men and Women (2000), para. 3.

[16] 'Equality International Law' (1990); Samantha Besson, 'The Principle of Non-Discrimination in the Convention on the Rights of the Child' (2005) 13 *International Journal of Children's Rights* 435.

[17] See glossary definition of female infanticide; for a discussion on female infanticide under the CRC, see Chapdelaine-Feliciati, 'Deconstructing the Convention on the Rights of the Child: Semiotics, Significs and Semioethics of Gendercide' (2018) 7 *Cambridge International Law Journal* 29.

[18] 'Non-Discrimination CRC' (2005), 436.

[19] See glossary definition of Son Preference and Daughter Devaluation.

[20] 'Equality International Law' (1990), 18–24.

gender, sexual orientation' and in relation to positive discrimination as 'favourable treatment of a person or group, in order to compensate for disadvantage or lack of privilege'. It is contrasted with the definition of equality as 'the condition of having equal dignity, rank, or privileges with others; the fact of being on an equal footing'.[21] Accordingly, in line with the Human Rights Committee and OED definitions, this book considers 'the unjust or prejudicial treatment'[22] of girls on the grounds of sex and age, 'nullifying or impairing the recognition, enjoyment or exercise', on an equal footing with other identity groups, namely boys, women and men, of their international human rights and freedoms.[23]

## II SEXISM

The term sexism was not enshrined in the 1911 edition of the OED, which appears to imply that this phenomenon was not yet acknowledged. Sexism was originally defined as 'the state or condition of belonging to the male or female sex',[24] and thus referred to membership to the male or female sex rather than to a form of discrimination. The concept of sexism is presently defined in English dictionaries as 'prejudice, stereotyping, or discrimination, typically against women, on the basis of sex',[25] and 'prejudice or discrimination based on sex, especially: discrimination against women'.[26] These definitions are noteworthy on three grounds. Firstly, both definitions define sexism as a prejudice or discrimination on the basis of sex and do not refer to the concept of 'gender'. Secondly, they expressly refer to discrimination against women, rather than 'discrimination against female beings', or 'discrimination against women and girls', and thereby do not clearly state whether sexism covers both adult women and girls, an issue that shall be examined in the CEDAW.[27] Thirdly, these definitions refer to discrimination *against women* rather than against men, which may reflect a historical pattern whereby sexism has, and still is, usually a discrimination against females rather than males. It is important to bear in mind that gender stereotypes also have a negative impact on boys, who are still experiencing the societal pressure to 'man up' at a young age and are thereby prevented from expressing emotions and seeking help if

[21] OED.
[22] OED.
[23] ICCPR General Comment No. 18 Non-Discrimination (1989), para. 7.
[24] OED.
[25] OED.
[26] Webster.
[27] See Chapter 8.

needed.[28] A problematic consequence of sexism for boys is illustrated by the social stigma encountered by male victims of sexual assault within their communities when reporting these crimes.[29] Many male survivors of sexual violence internalize the gender myth that as males they should have been able to defend themselves against their aggressor, which leads to additional guilt and trauma, and reluctance to report the crime. In this regard, Dorais deplores that even today, '[t]he violation of a male is often seen, by aggressor and victim alike, as a symbolic defeat and emasculation'.[30] Another significant consequence of gender stereotypes concerning masculinity is that boys are over-represented in child labour, and required to work in hazardous conditions in much greater numbers than girls in factories and farms, thereby placing them at greater risk of accidents leading to injury and death.[31]

The impact of the social construction of females as the weak sex is nevertheless particularly significant for girls. Sexism is still prevalent globally, both de facto and de jure, as many states enshrine discriminatory provisions against girls and women in their legislation.[32] Overall, nearly 2.4 billion women do not have the same legal rights as men under domestic law globally.[33] Presently, in 69 states, women face significant obstacles to employment, such as the inability to choose *whether* to work, and the absence of laws against discrimination and sexual harassment in the workplace.[34] Moreover, a woman's testimony does not carry the same evidentiary weight in court as that

28 See for example Wayne Martino and Bob Meyenn, *'What About the Boys?': Issues of Masculinity in Schools* (Open University Press 2001); Matthew Oransky and Jeanne Marecek, '"I'm not Going to be a Girl": Masculinity and Emotions in Boys' Friendships and Peer Groups' (2009) 24 *Journal of Adolescent Research* 218.

29 UNICEF, 'Research on the Sexual Exploitation of Boys: Findings, Ethical Considerations and Methodological Challenges' (2020), 5; 'Study Violence Children' (2006), 55; Michel Dorais, *Don't Tell: The Sexual Abuse of Boys* (McGill-Queen's University Press 2002), 17.

30 *Don't Tell* (2002), 113.

31 'Child Labour' (2020), 8: Presently, 97 million boys and 63 million girls are involved in child labour, thus over one thirdmore boys.

32 See for example UN Women, 'Women's Rights 25 Years After Beijing' (2020); UN Women, 'Families in a Changing World' (2020); WHO and UNICEF, 'Protect the Progress: Report on the Every Woman Every Child Global Strategy' (2022); UNICEF, 'Gender Equality: Global Annual Results Report 2021' (2022). Freeman et al. observe that in several states 'official laws and policies attribute different (unequal) rights and responsibilities to men and women on the basis of gender stereotypes' and/or 'officially recognize the validity of customary or religious laws in the constitution and/or state (federal) laws, even when such laws are contrary to the principle of sex equality': *Commentary CEDAW* (2012), 154.

33 World Bank, 'Women, Business and the Law' (2023), 12.

34 Ibid., 25; see also OECD, 'A Long Way before Turning Promises into Progress: Discriminatory Laws and Social Norms Still Hamper Gender Equality' (2019); Infrastructure and Cities for Economic Development (ICED), 'Violence against Women and Girls, Infrastructure and Cities' (2017).

of a man in 48 states.[35] UN Women underscores that women cannot, on an equal basis with men, be the head of the household in 31 states, pursue a trade or profession in 18 states, inherit equally as a spouse in 36 states, apply for a passport in 37 states, nor travel outside the home in 17 states.[36] In this regard, 55 states limit women and girls' mobility rights,[37] and some states recently adopted legislation to further restrict their freedoms.[38] These figures are indicative of broad expressions of sexism, and while they also cover discrimination against adult women, Sohoni rightfully observes that '[w]hen the woman is unequal to the man, the girl is unequal to the boy as well'.[39] Also, since many girls marry before reaching 18 years, the lack of protection of 'married women' impacts girls as young brides in the private sphere.[40] In its 2023 study, the World Bank notes that married girls and women are required, under the law, to obey their husbands in 18 states,[41] and remain unable, in the same way as their husbands, to obtain a divorce in 46 states, or to remarry in 68 states.[42] Also, 28 states fail to offer legal protection against domestic violence.[43] Furthermore, 111 states do not criminalize marital rape,[44] and the perpetrators of rape are exempt from criminal charges if they marry their victim in 54 states.[45] Finally, all girls – both married and unmarried – do not have the same right to inheritance as boys in 41 states.[46]

35 OECD, 'SIGI Global Report: Transforming Challenges into Opportunities' (2019), 154; see also European Union, 'Discriminatory Laws Undermining Women's Rights' (2020), 21.

36 UN Women, 'Equality in Law for Women and Girls by 2030: A Multistakeholder Strategy for Accelerated Action' (2019), 16; see also World Bank, 'Ending Violence against Women and Girls: Global and Regional Trends in Women's Legal Protection against Domestic Violence and Sexual Harassment' (2018), 8–9.

37 'Women, Business, Law' (2023), 24; see also Human Rights Watch, 'Everything I Have to Do is Tied to a Man' (2021); Minority Rights Group International, 'Beyond the Veil: Discrimination against Women in Iran' (2019); UNFPA, 'Saudi Arabia, Gender, Law' (2019).

38 See for example Saudi Arabia Personal Status Law enacted in March 2022 (Royal Decree M73) which reintroduced restrictions on married women's ability to choose where to live and travel, and requires that they obey their husbands: 'Women, Business, Law' (2023), 23.

39 *Burden Girlhood* (1995), vii.

40 UNICEF notes that 12 million girls are married in childhood each year, and unless the rates of child marriage decline faster globally, 150 million more girls are likely to be married by 2030: Claudia Cappa, 'New Global Estimates of Child Marriage' (UNICEF 2018), 5; UNICEF, 'Progress for Every Child in the SDG Era' (2018), 65.

41 'Women, Business, Law' (2023), 29.

42 Ibid.

43 Ibid.; see also Human Rights Watch, 'World Report: Events' (2021), 32.

44 'Women's Rights' (2020), 22.

45 UNFPA, 'My Body is My Own: Claiming the Right to Autonomy and Self-determination' (2021), 48.

46 'Women, Business, Law' (2023), 34; see also Rangita de Silva de Alwis, 'End All Forms of Discrimination against Women and Girls with Disabilities and Enhance the Participation of

## III CHILDISM

The concept of childism is very novel and defined neither in dictionaries nor under international law. In *Childism: Confronting Prejudice against Children*, psychoanalyst Young-Bruehl defines childism as 'a belief system that constructs its target group, "the child", as an immature being, produced and owned by adults who use it to serve their own needs and fantasies'.[47] A perfect illustration of childism is the exploitation of child performers by 'stage parents' who use them to fulfil their own ambitions for money and fame; in its extreme form, childism is expressed through the sexual violence and exploitation of children by paedophiles who use the latter as objects to 'fulfil their fantasies'. Childism differs from ageism, which is discrimination against people of a particular age, as the latter applies to any person, young or old, who experiences discrimination, whereas the former is *child-specific*. It is noteworthy that the OED expressly refers to discrimination against the elderly and not against children, in its definition of ageism: 'prejudice or discrimination on the grounds of a person's age; age discrimination, esp. against the elderly', thereby implying that ageism does not comprise prejudice against the young, notably children. Childism is therefore a form of prejudice solely based on one's membership to the social grouping 'children'.

Childism is underpinned by the assumption that children are inferior to adults on three grounds: 1) intellectually, since they are perceived as incapable of rational thinking and deemed too 'emotional'; 2) morally, for they are considered devoid of a moral compass and 3) physically, as they are thought unable to accomplish things on their own. Childism is often accompanied by the language of vulnerability which, as Herring notes, tends to essentialise children: '[c]hildren are classified as bound together in their weakness, innocence, and vulnerability. That fails to recognize the diversity of children and their range of childhood experiences'.[48] Under a 'childist' approach, children are perceived as the property of adults instead of persons, as objects of the law instead of subjects of the law and as a collective and undifferentiated class instead of individuals.[49] In this regard, it is worthy of note that the term 'child' is associated with negative connotations in the English language, as the OED also describes a child as 'a person who has (or is considered to have) the

Women with Disabilities in Inclusive Innovation' (2019), 4; UNICEF, 'A New Era for Girls: Taking Stock of 25 Years of Progress' (2020), 6.

47 *Childism* (2012), 36.

48 Jonathan Herring, 'Vulnerability, Children, and the Law' in Michael Freeman (ed.), *Law and Childhood Studies: Current Legal Issues* (Oxford University Press 2012), 249.

49 'Child Justice' (2007), 281.

character, manners, or attainment of a child, usually with negative connotations; an immature, irresponsible, or childish person'.[50] Initially coined by psychiatrists Pierce and Allen in the 1970s, who modelled it on racism, childism was thereafter paralleled to sexism by Alderson and Goodwin in the 1990s.[51] The latter referred to childism while comparing adults' paternalistic attitude towards children to that of men with women at the end of the nineteenth century. Alderson and Goodwin underscored the novelty of this concept by noting that 'childism is so endemic and accepted that we do not yet have a word for it'.[52] Childism significantly impacts the rights of girl children. The CRC Committee notes that children, including girls, are 'powerless within their families, and often voiceless and invisible within society',[53] and moreover, that young children 'have been regarded as undeveloped, lacking even basic capacities for understanding, communicating and making choices', and thereby denied the right to participation.[54] In this regard, the Committee deplores that respect for the young child's agency as a participant in family, community and society is 'frequently overlooked, or rejected as inappropriate on the grounds of age and immaturity'.[55]

### 1 *Paternalism*

As is the case with sexism, childism is underpinned by paternalism, defined as 'a behaviour, by a person, organization or state, which limits some person or group's liberty or autonomy for their own good', and a 'policy or practice of restricting the freedoms and responsibilities of subordinates or dependents in what is considered or claimed to be in their best interests'.[56] For instance, under a paternalistic approach, females are perceived as weak and vulnerable and the restriction on their rights to freedom of expression and movement, or employment, is thereby undertaken 'in their best interests'. Although Alderson and Goodwin refer to the behaviour which took place over a century ago, as previously mentioned, paternalism towards women is still present in many

50 OED. The quote selected in the OED is also noteworthy: '[t]he French, always treated as children, are, in political matters, children still' (Henry Thomas Buckle, *History of Civilization in England Part I*, ix, 576, 1857).

51 Chester Pierce and Gail Allen, 'Childism: The Basic Oppression' (1975) 5 *Psychiatric Annals* 266; Priscilla Alderson and Mary Goodwin, 'Contradictions within Concepts of Children's Competence' (1993) 1 *International Journal of Children's Rights* 303.

52 'Contradictions' (1993), 309.

53 CRC General Comment No. 7 Early Childhood (2006), para. 14.

54 Ibid.

55 Ibid.

56 OED.

nations, where the mobility rights of female human beings, and their ability to occupy positions of authority, such as that of a judge, are restricted.[57] Likewise, paternalism towards children is underpinned by the vulnerability rhetoric,[58] and may occur with a view to protecting them 'from the dangers that are posed by the world, adults, other children, and themselves'.[59] In the former case, the inferiority of females is based on assumptions about their sex, whereas in the latter, they are justified by the young age of children. Within paternalism, some child theorists argue that adolescents should be granted rights but that the State should still hold the power to protect them against 'foolish, self-destructive choices'.[60] This approach is qualified liberal paternalism or justified paternalism, as children are allocated rights within a supervisory environment. However, in its most extreme forms, as evidenced in the Massachusetts legislation during the seventeenth century, paternalism can lead to the legitimization of life-threatening physical chastisement of children, and the death penalty for insubordinate children for the purpose of strengthening the authority of parents to raise their child properly and to teach other children not to misbehave, for their 'own good'. Indeed, the 1646 Stubborn Child Statute of the Commonwealth of Massachusetts legalized capital punishment of disobedient children on the complaint of their parents.[61] It is therefore sometimes difficult to determine whether one adopts a paternalist approach in view of protecting girls from harm, or whether it is entrenched in a desire for control, or even in the actual hatred of 'girl children' as an identity group. In the eighteenth century, the phenomenon of outright aversion towards children came to be recognized in the English language with the expression *misopedia*, which signifies 'hatred of children', modelled as it was on other Greek-derived group-hatred words such as misogyny, and it was employed to describe child-based oppressive behaviour.[62]

57 'Women, Business, Law' (2023); 'Equality, Law, Women, Girls' (2019); Radhika Coomaraswamy, SRVAW, 'Cultural Practices in the Family That Are Violent Towards Women' (31 January 2002) UN Doc E/CN.4/2002/83, para. 84; Nazila Ghanea, 'Rights, Women and Human Rights Change in Iran' in Mavis MacLean and John Eekelaar (eds.), *Managing Family Justice in Diverse Societies* (Hart 2013), 249; Human Rights Watch, 'Everything Tied to Man' (2021); Minority Rights Group International, 'Beyond the Veil' (2019); UNFPA, 'Saudi Arabia, Gender, Law' (2019).

58 'Vulnerability' (2012), 243.

59 'Children's Rights Grown-ups' (2003), 150.

60 *Children's Rights* (2009), 28.

61 Steven Mintz, 'Children, Families and the State: American Family Law in Historical Perspective' (1992) 69 *Denver University Law Review*, 635, 640.

62 *Childism* (2012), 5.

The first and major criticism of childism and paternalism is that they tend to underestimate the cognitive abilities of children as a class. While an infant may not have the ability to exercise autonomy rights, older children are often closer to adults in terms of cognitive and physical abilities than to toddlers. The second criticism rests in the belief underpinning childism that granting autonomy rights to children might in fact threaten their interests. Locke argued that providing a child 'unrestrained liberty, before he has reason to guide him, is not the allowing him the privilege of his nature to be free; but to thrust him out amongst brutes'.[63] However, it could equally be argued that denying a child autonomy rights might render her/him vulnerable to abuses perpetrated by adults who have authority over her/him, and who are considered to act in the child's best interests, notably parents, educators and respected community members. Children raised in a paternalistic environment may not have the opportunity to develop the necessary skills to make informed decisions and protect their rights, and might be ill-equipped to exercise their rights once they reach adulthood. In this regard, Fortin notes:

> [I]t is unrealistic to argue that a child who is protected throughout from responsibility and from participation in important decisions regarding his or her upbringing will become a confident young person and responsible citizen.[64]

### 2 *Child Liberationism*

At the other end of the spectrum of paternalism, child liberationists argue that children should be granted the same rights as adults.[65] Child liberationism, a child rights movement developed in the 1970s, questions the presumption that children do not have the required cognitive abilities to make decisions. Child liberationists, such as Holt and Farson, argue:

> '[C]hildishness', connoting vulnerability, frailty and helplessness, is not a natural quality of children but rather an ideological construct which helps to support the denial of their proper rights. The innocence and incompetence of children is not a biological fact, but a projection onto young humans of our own adult needs. We want children to be helpless so that we can help

[63] John Locke, 'Two Treatises of Government' in Ian Shapiro (ed.), *Two Treatises of Government and A Letter Concerning Toleration* (Yale University Press 2003 [1689]), 126.

[64] *Children's Rights* (2009), 7.

[65] 'Children's Rights Grown-ups' (2003), 152.

> them; we need them to be dependent so that we can exercise authority over them. 'Cute' is the archetypal adjective of this oppressive ideology.[66]

Moreover, Farson contends that childhood is a modern invention created to legitimize the segregation of children from adults whereby the latter are granted power and decision-making over the former.[67] In his view, children are under an apartheid regime in which their civil rights are denied on the grounds of age, as was the case in South Africa and the United States as concerns race, and as is the case in several states in which women and girls are removed or restricted from fully participating in the public sphere.[68] Child liberationists argue that paternalism both devalues child competencies and exaggerates adult capacities for rational thinking. They contend that few adults 'consenting to medical treatment or people making financial decisions are able to make a fully informed decision or to act on the basis of a rational decision-making process', and yet their decisions are not questioned or overruled by authority.[69] In his monograph on the moral status of human beings, Dwyer argues that children are in fact *superior* to adults on a series of grounds, such as aliveness, potential for future life and eventually realizing any advantages of adult life.[70] He considers that greater weight should be given to children's interests than to the identical interests of adults, even when adults have as much at stake.[71] While Dwyer supports age minimums, he solely refers to some activities such as drinking and driving.[72] It is notable that he also proposes a linguistic change whereby the terms 'child' and 'adult' would be replaced by 'young' or 'old', to avoid the respective pejorative and honorific connotations,[73] thereby acknowledging the semiotic impact of terminology on the social construction and conceptions of childhood and adulthood. Overall, child liberationists argue that paternalism purposefully devalues the cognitive abilities of children to legitimize the power exercised upon them by adults, as sexist traits accorded to females on account of their sex are employed to justify male domination.

The inherent weakness of the child liberationists' argument is that it tends to exaggerate the mental and physical abilities of children, especially young

66 *Childhood* (2015), 67–68; Richard Farson, *Birthrights* (Macmillan 1974); John Holt, *Escape from Childhood: The Needs and Rights of Children* (Penguin 1974).
67 *Childhood* (2015), 27.
68 See Section II on sexism.
69 'Vulnerability' (2012), 250.
70 James Dwyer, *Moral Status and Human Life: The Case for Children's Superiority* (Cambridge University Press 2011), 181.
71 Ibid., 188–89.
72 Ibid., 191.
73 Ibid.

children, to justify granting equal rights to children and adults. Indeed, if young children who have not yet acquired rational thinking are granted full autonomy rights, they could make decisions that are not in their best interests and that would negatively affect their livelihood and future. The distinction between childhood and femalehood rests in the fact that the natural attributes of the former comprise a scientifically acknowledged immaturity and limitation of cognitive and physical abilities, especially during early childhood and infancy, which could validate restrictions on their autonomy rights, whereas the biological traits of females do not establish a difference with males as concerns competency and rational thinking. Hence, while creating a distinction of rights between males and females constitutes unjust discrimination, certain restrictions on children's freedoms could be justified in certain contexts. In addition, when using an extreme child liberationist approach, the State might remove its protection of children on the grounds that the latter are sufficiently responsible and independent, and thus able to fend for themselves. Conversely, denying children their autonomy rights might place them in a vulnerable position vis-à-vis adults who have authority over them and who abuse it, as in cases of physical, sexual and emotional violence. One must therefore strike a balance between the paternalist and the child liberationist approaches, and thus between granting all the rights of adults to girl children – including very young girl children – and the need to protect girls from themselves, other children and adults.

## 3 *Protecting the Girl Child while Promoting Her Autonomy Rights*

The tension between paternalism and child liberationism lies in the difficult balance between protecting the girl child, especially at an early age, for instance against exploitation and violence from adults and other children, while ensuring that her autonomy rights are not curtailed in the process.

### 3.1 Eekelaar's Interests of Children Theory

A number of methodologies were devised to delineate the competing rights and interests of children. Eekelaar identifies three types of interests: 1) basic, 2) developmental and 3) autonomy, and stresses that in case of conflict, the former two should prevail.[74] He employs the expression 'interests' rather than

[74] John Eekelaar, 'The Emergence of Children's Rights' (1986) 6 *Oxford Journal of Legal Studies* 161, 170–71.

'rights', for the former is a precondition of the latter's recognition.[75] According to Eekelaar's approach, if the girl child, in exercising her autonomy or participation interests, threatens her own basic interests – notably as concerns the rights to food, housing and clothing, or developmental interests, such as rights to education and socialization – she should not be granted the right to autonomy. Eekelaar nevertheless underscores that although subordinate to the other two, autonomy interests are also very important and thus 'where they [autonomy rights] may be exercised without threatening these two interests, the claim for their satisfaction must be high'.[76] He suggests a path towards the granting of autonomy rights: '[t]his recognition of the autonomy interests of children can be reconciled with their basic and developmental interests only through the empirical application of the concept of the acquisition of full capacity', noting that the test should be whether the child demonstrates intellectual understanding as well as emotional maturity.[77] However, since it is difficult to identify when one achieves maturity, Eekelaar proposes to favour the basic and developmental interests over the autonomy interests until a child reaches a defined age.[78]

## 3.2 Herring's Common Vulnerability Theory

Herring recognizes that whilst children are indeed vulnerable, so are adults, as 'children's vulnerability is, in essence, no different from that faced by adults', and therefore devised what could be termed the 'common vulnerability theory'.[79] As is the case with sexism that negatively impacts girls and boys, both girls and adult women are penalized by childism within the female category. Childism is underpinned by the conceptual dichotomy between childhood and adulthood, according to which girls are perceived as vulnerable while women (and men) are viewed as perfectly rational and independent, and thus as not needing societal assistance. This is prejudicial to adult women as well as adult men. Herring's vulnerability theory underscores that all individuals – children and adults alike – need support from their communities and broader society, and that everyone can be at times vulnerable.[80] This theory resonates with the OED quote under the definition of child: 'Men

[75] Ibid., 169.
[76] Ibid., 171.
[77] Ibid., 181.
[78] Ibid.
[79] 'Vulnerability' (2012), 244.
[80] Ibid.

are but Children of a larger growth.'[81] In this context, Herring criticizes society's paradigm of the male adult as 'the businessman in a suit'.[82] All individuals, regardless of age, need society to ensure, through laws and policies, protection against exploitation, for instance as regards employment, property purchase or rental, marriage and separation. Adults also need a support system to assist in balancing their work and personal lives, notably to raise children or take care of elders. In this regard, social services such as daycare, universal health care and education, as well as consumer and tenant associations, are crucial. Herring explains that all individuals, whether they belong to subordinate or privileged identity groups, are dependent on others, for vulnerability is an 'inherent human characteristic'.[83] Since the central weakness of paternalism and child liberationism is that they, respectively, *under* and *over* estimate the mental and physical abilities of girl children to justify distinct or equal treatment with adults, the common vulnerability approach operates a paradigm shift. The objective is not to focus on adults' or children's superiority, but rather on how children and adults both experience physical, social and structural vulnerability in various situations throughout the life cycle. This book thus examines the girl child from a common vulnerability approach: we recognize that vulnerability is 'the normal state for people to be in',[84] and the focus then shifts to how individuals of all ages, including girls, can be assisted and empowered in developing their constantly evolving capacities in various fields.

## 3.3 Arnstein and Hart's Ladder of Participation

Arnstein's ladder of citizen participation for adults,[85] and its adaptation by Hart for children,[86] as well as Shier's tool for practitioners working with children,[87] provide models of progressive participation in which both adults and children can be assisted in making informed decisions in a series of areas, such as medical treatment, education and work. This approach is underpinned by the notion that rational autonomy is acquired through participation

81 OED; John Dryden, *All for Love* (1678), Act IV, 46.

82 'Vulnerability' (2012), 244.

83 Ibid., 250.

84 Ibid., 258.

85 Sherry Arnstein, 'A Ladder of Citizen Participation' (1969) 35 *Journal of the American Institute of Planners* 216.

86 Roger Hart, *Children's Participation, from Tokenism to Citizenship* (UNICEF 1992).

87 Harry Shier, 'Pathways to Participation: Openings, Opportunities and Obligations: A New Model for Enhancing Children's Participation in Decision-making' (2001) 15 *Children and Society* 107.

and that individuals, regardless of age, need support throughout the life cycle. Indeed, one can argue that any important choice requires information and guidance. Shier devised an enabling model of child participation which comprises five progressive steps: 1) listening to children, 2) supporting them in expressing their views, 3) taking their views into account, 4) involving them in decision-making and 5) sharing power and responsibility with them in decision-making.[88] It is argued that we could add a sixth level of participation, once the prior levels have been achieved: 6) the child reaches a decision on her/his own.[89] Fortin explains:

> [O]n attaining [the age of 18], adolescents are expected to make an immediate successful transition from the legal status of childhood to responsible citizenship. Giving them a chance to develop the skills needed for adulthood is therefore essential.[90]

Hence, rather than waiting for the girl child to acquire the necessary capacities to make informed decisions, Shier's model provides a framework whereby she is supported to develop abilities from an early age. Accordingly, she can exercise her autonomy rights as soon as possible, while benefiting from guidance in the process. The concept that children need to be treated as rational beings as early as possible was already entrenched in the writings of Locke, who argued:

> It will perhaps be wondered, that I mention reasoning with children: and yet I cannot but think that the true way of dealing with them. They understand it as early as they do language; and, if I misobserve not, they love to be treated as rational creatures, sooner than is imagined.[91]

Smith contends that the age at which one participates is hardly an issue, for once they are properly supported, even very young children can participate in important ways.[92] The CRC Committee supports this view, noting that: 'the child is able to form views from the youngest age, even when she or he may be unable to express them verbally'.[93] It underscores that states should show respect for all forms of communication, and notably nonverbal forms of

88 Ibid., 110.

89 'Child Justice' (2007), 282.

90 *Children's Rights* (2009), 90.

91 John Locke, 'Some Thoughts Concerning Education' in John William Adamson (ed.), *The Educational Writings of John Locke* (Cambridge University Press 2011 [1922], [1693]), 64, para. 81.

92 Anne Smith, 'Interpreting and Supporting Participation Rights: Contributions from Sociocultural Theory' (2002) 10 *International Journal of Children's Rights* 73, 84.

93 CRC General Comment No. 12 Right to be Heard (2009), para. 21.

communication 'including play, body language, facial expressions, and drawing and painting, through which very young children demonstrate understanding, choices and preferences'.[94] The CRC Committee places the burden of proof on the State to demonstrate that the child lacks the capacity to participate. It notes that 'States parties should presume that a child has the capacity to form her or his own views and recognize that she or he has the right to express them; it is not up to the child to first prove her or his capacity'.[95] It is worthy of note that the CRC Committee employs the feminine pronoun before the masculine pronoun in this sentence, which strengthens the visibility of the girl child.

The paradigm shift whereby the vulnerability of both children and adults is embraced, and the models of participation empowering all human beings to make informed decisions and exercise their autonomy rights, are particularly relevant in light of the interdependence and indivisibility of human rights.[96] The recognition of girl children's autonomy and participation rights strengthens the exercise of other human rights. The first three levels of Shier's model, whereby girls are listened to and supported in expressing their views from an early age, and such views are taken into account, even in small everyday decisions, enable them to develop communication skills and bolster their confidence. Girl children are therefore more likely to report violations, especially to reliable and trustworthy adults and children, as they know that they will be listened to. In fact, knowledge of one's rights is a precondition for exercising those rights, and thus if girls are to report violations, they must be aware that they have a right to protection in the first place. Moreover, if girls are given a voice in society, adults are less likely to prey on them for fear of being denounced and prosecuted. In this regard, Harris argues that 'it is precisely because children have been treated as children and not as equals that they have been fair game for adults, exploited, abused, and even tortured and arbitrarily done to death'.[97] As concerns the last three levels: 4) involving children in decision-making, 5) sharing power and responsibility in decision-making and 6) children reaching a decision on their own, it is argued that if girl children are involved in policy-making concerning girls' rights, they may provide invaluable input which will not only impact their own lives, but that of other girls as well. As noted in Chapter 1, girls are rarely involved in policy-making, notably at the international level. During the CRC drafting, child

94 Ibid.

95 Ibid., para. 20.

96 Vienna Declaration (1995), art. 5.

97 John Harris, 'Liberating Children' in Michael Leahy and Dan Cohn-Sherbok (eds.), *The Liberation Debate: Rights at Issue* (Routledge 1996), 136.

participation was limited to some states referring to opinions from youth organizations, and Swedish and Canadian children listening to debates of the working group on some occasions. Lopatka, the Chairman-Rapporteur of the CRC Working Group, observed that children were mostly invited to celebrate the adoption of the CRC in New York, and that 'the children gathered there were obviously delighted to join in the celebrations making a historic moment'.[98] From a semiotic perspective, if we replace 'children' with any other adult identity group, based on sex, race, religion or abilities, this 'participation' in drafting and negotiating the terms of a treaty pertaining to their own rights would appear very limited, if not tokenistic.

Moreover, the participation approach allows for a reconciliation of Eekelaar's three types of interests. The autonomy interests of the girl child can be reinforced by the levels identified in Shier's tool, and thereby further strengthen her basic and developmental interests rather than conflict with them. Girls are in turn able to participate actively in their own protection. It is nevertheless important to underscore that the CRC Committee and scholars such as Hart and Shier refer to the ability of children to express their views – not to their legal right to make final decisions concerning their lives, and notably to be granted all 'adult' rights in the political, economic and legal spheres such as voting, running for office, owning and administering property or heading a household.

## 3.4 Granting Autonomy Rights at Adolescence

While the previous section examined concrete means of assisting girl children, including during early childhood, in developing their competency, it is nevertheless difficult to gather a universal acceptance that young girls possess the required cognitive abilities to make rational and informed decisions. The situation differs as concerns adolescent girls. In this regard, Archard suggests a compromise position: a presumption that adolescent children possess rational autonomy, and that they should accordingly have the right to self-determination. Rational autonomy has three components: 1) rationality, 2) maturity and 3) independence. Rationality is described as:

> the forming of generally reliable beliefs about one's surroundings, having a relatively coherent set of desires and consequently being able, in the light of

[98] OHCHR, 'Legislative History of the Convention on the Rights of the Child' (2007), xl. Lopatka explains that the work was performed by government delegations: '[i]t is obvious that the Convention on the Rights of the Child, like any other international human rights treaty, is an accomplishment of the government representatives of all States concerned': Ibid.

> these desires and beliefs, to order one's preferences consistently between alternative possible courses of action.[99]

The second component, maturity, refers to emotional balance and relative stability and the third component, independence, according to Kant's conception of 'capability of self-maintenance', could be understood in the larger sense as the ability to have a mind of one's own and make choices that do not simply follow the example of others.[100] One could argue that many adults never acquire this capacity, as demonstrated by extreme consumerism and the reckless replication of social trends, notably on social media. Already during the Enlightenment, Locke argued that as children acquire the capacity to reason, the authority of parents should be lessened: '[i]f therefore a strict hand be kept over children from the beginning . . . and if, as they grow up to the use of reason, the rigour of government be, as they deserve it, gently relaxed'.[101] The same reasoning is echoed in the Gillick case. Fortin supports this view:

> [T]here are fundamental differences between childhood thought, preoccupied as it is with practical issues to do with the here and now, and adolescent thinking which is much more sophisticated. Adolescents are increasingly able to cope with abstractions and to distinguish between the real and concrete and the abstract or possible. They become aware of their own thought processes and become self-reflective, even introspective.[102]

However, one could criticize Archard's recommendation on the grounds that he does not clarify whether the beginning of adolescence should be established at a set age, or whether competence tests should be performed on children when they approach this period in terms of age and physical development, or when they demonstrate cognitive abilities, for instance in an educational setting. Fortin suggests the age of 14 years as one at which 'a considerable degree of maturation may have occurred', and she quotes the British Royal College of Psychiatrists (BRCP) which states that '[g]enerally the frontal lobes are felt to mature at approximately 14 years of age'.[103] Lindley instead suggests 13 years as the age at which children are 'very likely to have sufficient stability and conceptual competence to be able to have the objectives of a plan of life' and that laws concerning children should be liberalized at

[99] *Childhood* (2015), 88.
[100] Ibid., 89–91.
[101] 'Some Thoughts Education' (1693), 33, para. 41.
[102] *Children's Rights* (2009), 83.
[103] Royal College of Psychiatrists, *Child Defendants* Occasional Paper OP 56 (United Kingdom 2006), 38; *Children's Rights* (2009), 83.

that age.[104] However, while psychological studies are most valuable, it is difficult to determine a specific age at which adolescence begins that would be universally accepted. Chapters 7 and 8 shall suggest possible age limits as concerns the boundaries of adolescence and the end of girlhood in the CRC and the CEDAW.

## IV THE GIRL CHILD AND THE PRIVATE SPHERE

At the heart of the discussion on sexism and childism lies the issue of defining boundaries between the public and private spheres. Historically, the State has been reluctant to 'interfere' in the private sphere and protect girl children against various forms of emotional, sexual and physical violence perpetrated by the father, husband or other male or female family members, within the home.[105] Feminists have criticized the public/private division on the grounds that it constitutes an artificial and political construct rather than a natural distinction.[106] Askari underscores the gendered division of these two spheres, thereby decoding the 'sense' attributed to each:

> The demarcation between the public and private spheres is a gendered one, for the public sphere is the male sector, as the locus of reason and power encompassing the workplace, law, politics and economics. The private sphere of the home and children is the female sector. It is associated with emotion, the opposite of reason, and it serves to oppress women and girls. Not only are activities in the private sphere valued less, but the private sphere receives little international and domestic protection, which leaves women and children, particularly girls, vulnerable to abuse.[107]

[104] Richard Lindley, 'Teenagers and Other Children' in Geoffrey Scarre (ed.), *Children, Parents and Politics* (Cambridge University Press 1989), 92.

[105] As noted by Gill, female family members, such as the mother-in-law, can be the main perpetrators of violence and discrimination against young brides and daughters: see Aisha Gill et al., 'Violence between Female In-laws in India' (2013) 14 *Journal of International Women's Studies* 147.

[106] See for example Paulina García-Del Moral and Megan Dersnah, 'A Feminist Challenge to the Gendered Politics of the Public/Private Divide: On Due Diligence, Domestic Violence, and Citizenship' (2014) 18 *Citizenship Studies* 661; Ivana Radačić, 'Human Rights of Women and the Public/Private Divide in International Human Rights Law' (2007) 3 *Croatian Yearbook of European Law and Policy* 443. Boyd contends that it 'denotes ideological division of life into apparently opposing spheres of public and private activities, and public and private responsibilities': Susan Boyd, 'Challenging the Public/Private Divide: An Overview' in Susan Boyd (ed.), *Challenging the Public/Private Divide: Feminism, Law and Public Policy* (Toronto University Press 1997), 8.

[107] 'Jus Cogens' (1998), 22–23.

Herring notes that the public/private divide is characterized by the notion that the law should not and in fact cannot properly intervene in the private sphere, unlike public areas of life where legal regulation appears more appropriate.[108] In international law, the complex unequal power relations in the private life embedded in sexism that impact women and girls have been disregarded in favour of a focus on state agents in the public sphere.[109] As concerns children, Van Bueren argues that on a global scale, the public/private divide regards 'the family as akin to a tiny state in which parents are absolute monarchs'.[110] Minow describes the legal framework as one which:

> assigns child-care responsibilities to parents, and thereby avoids public responsibility for children. Public power becomes relevant only in exceptional circumstances, when parents default. The government is not supposed to 'intervene' in the private realm of the family, where children's needs and interests are managed by their parents.[111]

Scholars have contended that this division is actually underpinned by a reluctance of the State to allocate resources to raise and protect children rather than an actual concern for the privacy of families.[112] Several paternalists support the public/private divide on the grounds that state intervention delegitimizes parental authority, notably the ability of parents to discipline the girl child for her own good and make decisions in her best interests. They further argue that the State should not grant children autonomy rights for it would endanger the family unit.[113] In fact, some paternalists challenge the very notion that children are rights holders, arguing that parents and legal guardians should act as their legal agents.[114] Other arguments have been put forward by feminist and child rights theorists to challenge the notion that children are rights holders. Fortin stresses that 'a rights approach focuses on the wrong things, downplaying the relationships which underlie the reality of daily life'.[115] It could be argued that a rights approach is inherently individualistic and fails to acknowledge the interconnectedness of human beings in

108 'Children's Rights Grown-ups' (2003), 150.

109 Yakin Ertürk and Bandana Purkayastha, 'Linking Research, Policy and Action: A Look at the Work of the Special Rapporteur on Violence against Women' (2012) 60 *Current Sociology* 142, 143.

110 *International Law Child* (1998), 72.

111 Martha Minow, 'Rights for the Next Generation: A Feminist Approach to Children's Rights' (1986) 9 *Harvard Women's Law Journal* 1, 7.

112 *Children's Rights* (2009), 323.

113 Ibid., 8–9.

114 Ibid., 2–30.

115 Ibid., 10.

society, including within the family unit. In this perspective, some argue that the concept of children as rights holders fails to acknowledge that human beings also have duties as members of society. Laws notes that '[a] society whose values are defined by reference to individual rights is by the very fact already impoverished. Its culture says nothing about individual duty – nothing about virtue'.[116] Yet however imperfect, the rights approach is still supported by many scholars, such as Fortin, who 'conclude that it is better to be a rights-holder than to "depend on the kindness and favors of others"'.[117]

It is nonetheless important to ensure that individuals and their families are protected against extreme state control and intervention. For instance, totalitarian regimes throughout history were characterized by state interference within the private lives of families and communities whereby governments took children from their parents, or set them against their parents and siblings, for political and ideological purposes. In this regard, a certain distinction between the public and private spheres is legitimate. However, many families that appear loving and caring might hide the worst forms of abuse, and parents and husbands who are well-respected members of their community and never committed criminal offences might resort to extreme forms of violence, such as sexual violence and honour-related killings against the girl child. It is therefore very difficult to identify abuse in the private sphere. Fortin warns against a hands-off presumption that treats the family as 'a state within a state', for abuse can occur in 'perfectly normal looking houses'.[118] In this regard, Baroness Hale of Richmond underscores states' duty of due diligence to protect and care for children who 'often need a great deal of state interference if they are to survive, let alone thrive'.[119] The challenge rests in identifying the degree of state intervention that will strike a balance between respecting the privacy rights of individual members of the family, notably parents, and protecting vulnerable family members, such as women, children and especially girl children.[120] Hence, while extreme state intervention within the private sphere violates liberty and privacy rights, the *laissez-faire* approach,[121] which interprets the sanctity of the family unit as a prohibition for the State to

[116] Sir John Laws, 'The Limitations of Human Rights' (1998) *Public Law* 254, 255.

[117] *Children's Rights* (2009), 11.

[118] Ibid., 9, 552.

[119] Baroness Brenda Hale of Richmond, 'Understanding Children's Rights: Theory and Practice' (2006) 44 *Family Court Review* 350, 351.

[120] See *Children's Rights* (2009), 550: 'the . . . control necessary to prevent all ill-treatment would involve an unacceptable interference with the upbringing of many thousands of children, the majority of whom are perfectly well cared for by loving parents'.

[121] *Children's Rights* (2009), 9.

grant rights to girl children or to interfere within the private sphere to protect their rights, renders the latter extremely vulnerable to a series of violations of rights, including death. Ertürk and Purkayastha describe this dichotomy as an 'ideological barrier to the human rights system from responding to the violations of rights experienced by women in private life' enabling the 'hegemony of the male head of the household'.[122] This is why the mandate of the Special Rapporteur on violence against women was a milestone as the first monitoring of human rights violations experienced by women and girls in the private sphere.[123] Hence it is contended that girls should have their human rights protected both within the public and private spheres, otherwise they might experience abuse in either context. In this regard, the reluctance of many states to interfere within the private sphere to protect vulnerable members of a given family against domestic violence or other forms of exploitation and abuse is problematic for the girl child, as shall be examined in Chapter 4.

## V SEXISM, CHILDISM AND CULTURAL RELATIVISM

### 1 *Global South and Global North*

When examining sexist or childist practices experienced by the girl child globally, it is important to consider debates concerning universalism and cultural relativism. Before delving into an analysis of cultural relativism, as this book adopts a semiotic perspective, it is essential to examine the conceptual notions of the Global South and the Global North. 'Global South' is currently defined in the English language as 'the countries of the world which are regarded as having a relatively low level of economic and industrial development, considered collectively; contrasted with Global North'.[124] The OED further notes that 'the majority of these countries are typically located to the south of more industrialized nations'. Global North as a definition is its mirrored reflection as 'the countries of the world which are characterized by a high level of economic and industrial development, considered collectively; contrasted with Global South', with the additional clarification that 'the majority of these countries are typically located to the north of less industrialized nations'.[125] The conceptual dichotomy between Global North and Global South stems in large part from recent European colonialism and US imperialism. In fact, it is worthy of note that the OED refers to the British

[122] 'Linking Research' (2012), 145.
[123] Ibid., 143.
[124] OED.
[125] OED.

Empire in its definition of imperialism: 'the principle of policy of empire; the advocacy of holding political dominion or control over dependent territories (in 19th century British politics) the principle or policy of seeking or allowing the extension of the British Empire to protect trade and investments', and in its second definition as 'the extension and maintenance of a country's power or influence through trade, diplomacy, military or cultural dominance', while expressly referring to 'the influence and control of the United States over other countries'.

The previous expressions 'developed', and 'developing' countries, or 'third world' countries are recognized as entailing negative connotations and were thus replaced by Global South and Global North. Sohoni underscores the paternalistic wording of the *Oxford Concise Dictionary* definition of a 'developing' country as 'a poor or primitive country that is developing better economic and social conditions', noting that it involves, 'a simplistic, condescending and arbitrary approach'.[126] She equally criticizes the definition of 'developed country' as the latter implies 'a state of perfection', which no state has yet achieved.[127] The 'third world' expression has also been described as 'demeaning, historically inaccurate, exclusionary and negativistic' and applied indiscriminately to very diverse states globally.[128] While Global South and Global North do not entail the same connotations *per se*, their common parameter – economic and industrial development – appears very restrictive to evaluate a country's overall performance globally. As noted by Sohoni, other yardsticks could be considered, such as social rather than economic development, and spiritual instead of material development:

> There is development in a historical and culture sense which is associated with such countries as China, Egypt, and India, whose historical presence and wealth go back several centuries, as against such countries as the United States, which, although industrially and technologically advanced, are still in their comparative infancy.[129]

Moreover, the Global South umbrella, just like its predecessors 'third world' and 'developing' states, does not account for many internal variations between states across regions such as Latin America, Asia and Africa.[130] Lastly, this dichotomy has become inadequate to refer to many states from the 'Global South' that

[126] *Burden Girlhood* (1995), 3.
[127] Ibid., 2–3.
[128] Ibid., 3–4.
[129] Ibid., 3.
[130] Mathew Zachariah, 'Letter to the Editor' (1992) 36 *Comparative Education Review* 551, noting that: 'over one hundred countries on three continents as well as many on islands; it encompasses people of astonishingly diverse ethnic origins and cultural histories': 552.

presently have significant powerful economies, such as the BRICS (Brazil, Russia, India, China and South Africa), whereas several so-called Global North states are experiencing economic crises, with exponentially growing poverty levels in North America and Western Europe, and a significant increase in violence against girls and women in the public sphere, including on public transportation.[131] This book therefore employs the expressions Global South and Global North to refer to countries that were, respectively, associated, in the last centuries, with lower and higher levels of economic and industrial development on account of colonialism and imperialism, while acknowledging, as noted by Sohoni, that the economic and industrial development parameter is very restrictive, and moreover, that the South-North sweeping categories do not account for the many internal distinctions across states, nor for the significant changes that currently place some states in the opposite category.

## 2 *Cultural Relativism*

Several scholars and activists have criticized international institutions for perpetrating a form of imperialism or neocolonialism stemming from the Global North; they argue for instance that the human rights and fundamental freedoms enshrined in international treaties are formulated in individualistic language and employ the male and western model of the 'human being', and accordingly, that these standards are not appropriate in a non-western Global South context.[132] Scholars further contend that western actors have 1) essentialized cultures in the Global South as inherently harmful to women and girls, while disregarding their symbolic role, and moreover 2) neglected violations stemming from the Global North, while downplaying important contributions to human rights from states in the Global South.[133] These critiques have valid foundations. Firstly, many human rights treaty provisions

[131] See for example Peter Lowe, 'The Rise of the BRICS in the Global Economy' (2016) 41 *Teaching Geography* 50; María José González Moreno et al., 'Fear for All Women: European Women's Fear of Harassment and Aggression in Public Spaces' (2022) 37 *Journal of Interpersonal Violence* 160; Louise Pedersen, 'Moving Bodies as Moving Targets: A Feminist Perspective on Sexual Violence in Transit' (2020) 3 *Open Philosophy* 369; Nicola Roberts et al., 'Gendered Landscapes of Safety: How Women Construct and Navigate the Urban Landscape to Avoid Sexual Violence' (2022) 22 *Criminology and Criminal Justice* 287.

[132] 'Linking Research' (2012), 143, 147–48; Radhika Coomaraswamy, 'Women and Children: The Cutting Edge of International Law' (2015) 30 *American University International Law Review* 1.

[133] 'Linking Research' (2012), 148; Coomaraswamy explains for example that populations in South Africa and Latin America spurred the UN to address issues of apartheid and disappearances; hence, '[t]o ignore this history is to belittle the struggle of so many people and groups around the world': 'Cutting Edge' (2015), 24, 26.

are formulated with a 'western male' in mind and fail to address obstacles unique to girls in exercising their rights.[134] International institutions, both the UN and NGOs, are often funded by states and corporations in the Global North, and as noted by Coomaraswamy, these donors come with a set agenda that shapes priorities 'sometimes unhelpful in fighting for issues of human rights and social justice in a given context'.[135] Secondly, the western individualistic model has demonstrated several weaknesses. A key example is the treatment of elderly individuals in the Global North who are often institutionalized in nursing homes – and thereby excluded from their families and broader communities – and where severe abuse has been reported, including physical, sexual and psychological violence and neglect.[136] Instead, from a cultural standpoint, in societies associated with the Global South, elderly parents and relatives are often housed with family in intergenerational homes, and involved in their community; their wisdom and experience are valued rather than dismissed, and shared with future generations.[137] Thirdly, it is noticeable that violations of girls' rights stemming from the Global North are often dismissed. The vast majority of studies on the girl child, including within UN institutions, focus on practices such as FGM and child marriage, while neglecting violations originating in the Global North, such as sexualized social and dress codes. As observed by Ertürk and Purkayastha, the latter 'are rarely seen as cultural phenomena, but are regarded as questions of market dynamics and free choice'.[138] This has led to an argument in favour of cultural relativism, defined firstly as 'the theory that there are no objective standards by which to evaluate a culture and that a culture can only be understood in terms of its own values and customs', and secondly as 'the idea

[134] Askari notes that '[i]ssues at the core of human rights predominantly pertain to male (white, Western and liberal) concerns and experiences since men dominate the national and international legal orders and political structures': 'Jus Cogens' (1998), 12. See Chapter 5.

[135] 'Cutting Edge' (2015), 15.

[136] See for example Lee Friedman et al., 'Physical Abuse of Elderly Adults: Victim Characteristics and Determinants of Revictimization' (2017) 65 *Journal of the American Geriatrics Society* 1420; Janne Myhre et al., 'Elder Abuse and Neglect: An Overlooked Patient Safety Issue. A Focus Group Study of Nursing Home Leaders' Perceptions of Elder Abuse and Neglect' (2020) 20 *BMC Health Services Research* 199.

[137] See UN Population, 'Living Arrangements of Older Persons Around the World' (2019): '[l]iving with a child or with extended family members was the most common living arrangement among older persons in Africa, Asia and Latin America and the Caribbean': 1.

[138] 'Linking Research' (2012), 148–49. In this regard, Rao notes that feminists should be wary of defending practices such as dangerous cosmetic surgery in the Global North 'on the grounds of seemingly culture-free concepts of individual autonomy and freedom of choice': Arati Rao, 'The Politics of Gender and Culture in International Human Rights Discourse' in Julie Peters and Andrea Wolper (eds.), *Women's Rights, Human Rights: International Feminist Perspectives* (Routledge 1995), 171.

that a culture can only be evaluated in its own terms rather than objectively'.[139] Yet cultural relativism has also been invoked to justify the perpetuation of practices embedded in sexism and childism such as FGM and child marriage, on the grounds of culture and tradition, or to downplay their severity and impact on girls, including as concerns the terminology employed to refer to these practices.[140] Rao observes that 'extreme and wide-ranging human rights violations, by both governments and extra-constitutional groups, have continued to be defended, and even justified, on the grounds of cultural difference'.[141]

Feminist scholars, mostly from the Global South, underscore that the concept of culture has varied meanings.[142] Rao devised a four-step test to assess claims made on behalf of cultural relativism that is especially relevant to the girl child: '[f]irst, what is the status of the speaker? Second, in whose name is the argument from culture advanced? Third, what is the degree of participation in culture formation of the social groups primarily affected by the cultural practices in question? Fourth, what is culture, anyway?'[143] It is notable that in relation to the first three questions, the claims of culture concerning girls are usually made 1) by powerful adults, often men, 2) who argue that discriminatory practices embedded in sexism and childism are beneficial to girls and the larger community in terms of tradition and identity, 3) whereas girls who experience these practices are not actively involved in shaping the culture invoked. Rao notes that 'mainstream human rights discourse continues to rely on the pronouncements of heads of states or high ranking government ministers, and this often amounts to hearing the oppressor's voice in lieu of the victim's'.[144] Most notably, Rao guards against self-proclaimed and privileged feminists who may refer to culture on behalf of others, such as girl children, yet because of identity vectors such as class, are not themselves experiencing the negative attributes of the very practices promoted:

> When women's groups or individual women talk about culture, we must remind ourselves that there can never be a purportedly popular notion of

139 OED.

140 'Linking Research' (2012), 147–54; 'Gender and Culture' (1995); see also glossary definition of FGM.

141 'Gender and Culture' (1995), 167.

142 See for example 'Gender and Culture' (1995); 'Cutting Edge' (2015); Savitri Goonesekere, 'From Social Welfare to Human Rights for Girls – A Path to Achieving Gender Equality' (2014) 10 *International Journal of Law in Context* 478; 'Jus Cogens' (1998); 'Linking Research' (2012).

143 'Gender and Culture' (1995), 168.

144 Ibid., 170: Rao refers for example to Kenyatta's argument that FGM binds and unifies a community, to which she notes that 'we are compelled to question the politics of such a claim, particularly when it is made by a male national leader on behalf of the social group most directly affected by the practice: women'.

> culture that is unmediated by the positionality of the speaker; we must look at the claim for exemption on cultural grounds in relation to the axes of class, ethnicity, race, sexuality, age.[145]

Rao acknowledges the evolving nature of culture as 'a series of constantly contested and negotiated social practices whose meanings are influenced by the power and status of their interpreters and participants'.[146] In this regard, she emphasizes the role of master signifiers, and their possible *meaning-intention,* in shaping and delineating the content of culture.[147] More specifically, she unveils the subjective nature of cultural relativism under international human rights law:

> The notion of culture favored by international actors must be unmasked for what it is: a falsely rigid, ahistorical, selectively chosen set of self-justificatory texts and practices whose patent partiality raises the question of exactly whose interests are being served and who comes out on top.[148]

Rao's test can be paralleled to Welby's *Threefold Laws of Meaning* employed in this book. Indeed, she examines: 1) the *sense* of declarations and arguments made on behalf of culture, and deconstructs the *sense* of culture itself, 2) the *meaning-intention* of master signifiers when employing the conceptual notion of 'culture' as a static entity, and most importantly 3) the *significance* of such interpretations for the broader community, including the final interpretants, and the persons affected by these definitions, in the case at hand, the girl child. Goonesekere further explains how culture and tradition can be instrumentalized by master signifiers for their own benefit rather than that of those impacted, namely girl children:

> States Parties use the argument of respect for culture and religion, as well as legal pluralism and diversity of legal traditions and courts, to justify gender-based discrimination and deny the universality of women's human rights.

145 Ibid., 171.
146 Ibid., 173.
147 Rao notes: '[w]ithout questioning the political uses of culture, without asking whose culture this is and who its primary beneficiaries are, without placing the very notion of culture in historical context and investigating the status of the interpreter, we cannot fully understand the ease with which women become instrumentalized in larger battles of political, economic, military, and discursive competition in the international arena': Ibid., 174. The question is thereby *who* speaks on behalf of a culture, usually 'states and other power blocs' rather than the communities, see 'Linking Research' (2012), 147. This view is supported by Freeman et al. who note that 'culture should not be seen as having a particular essence which is monolithic, static, and unchangeable. Since the content of each culture is constructed by human beings, its structure and content is subject to continuous change': *Commentary* CEDAW (2012), 150.
148 'Gender and Culture' (1995), 174.

> Scholarship from the global south and some feminist discourse also criticise norms of universality in human rights as Western cultural imperialism that is insensitive to the importance of the ethics of care and communitarian values. *The transformative nature of custom, and the manner in which custom and religion have been manipulated to create discrimination and disadvantage against women, is not understood or recognised.*[149]

This leads us to Rao's fourth question: 'What is culture, anyway?' In the English language, this concept is defined as 'the distinctive ideas, customs, social behaviour, products, or way of life of a particular nation, society, people, or period'.[150] It is worthy of note that the OED employs the following quote: '[t]hey're Englishifying him completely! They're deliberately leading him away from his culture and his family and his religion',[151] thereby underscoring the notion of cultural imperialism, and using the British Empire as a case in point. Culture is also defined as 'a way of life or social environment characterized by or associated with the specified quality or thing; a group of people subscribing or belonging to this'.[152] Ertürk offers a comprehensive and holistic definition of culture that shall be employed in this book:

> [T]he set of shared spiritual, material, intellectual and emotional features of human experience that is created and constructed within social praxis. As such, culture is intimately connected with the diverse ways in which social groups produce their daily existence economically, socially and politically. It therefore embraces both the commonly held meanings that allow for the continuation of everyday practices as well as the competing meanings that galvanize change over time.[153]

Scholars from the Global South have also argued that cultural relativism is often promoted by certain Global North scholars and activists who speak *for* rather than *with* them, and thereby reproduce colonialist approaches of infantilization. As discussed in the glossary definition of FGM, the Inter-African Committee on Traditional Practices noted that advocacy for the use of the expression 'FGC' instead of FGM on the grounds that it was more 'inclusive' actually emerged from lobby groups in the Global North.[154] The

[149] 'HRs for Girls' (2014), 481 (emphasis added).

[150] OED.

[151] Zadie Smith, *White Teeth* (2001), xii, 245.

[152] OED.

[153] Yakin Ertürk, SRVAW, 'Intersections between Culture and Violence against Women' (17 January 2007) UN Doc A/HRC/4/34, para. 17.

[154] Inter-African Committee, 'Declaration Terminology FGM', 6th IAC General Assembly, 4–7 April 2005, Bamako, Mali' (6 April 2005): '[t]his terminology has been adopted by some UN specialized agencies and bi-lateral donors … influenced by specific lobby groups largely based

Global North speaking *for* rather than *with* the Global South also occurs in other contexts. For example, while several Global North states 'fund international aid' for the Global South, France still imposes its CFA franc as the currency in fourteen African countries, and the US dollar is employed as the currency for commercial exchanges in Africa, which are certainly neocolonialist and imperialistic practices.[155] Most importantly, a central problem is that under a cultural relativist perspective, girls who belong to specific cultures may not be granted the same rights as other girls globally. In other words, such an approach can actually reproduce and amplify the hierarchy between girls in the Global North as 'privileged' and those in the Global South as 'oppressed'.[156] Coomaraswamy underscores the risks of idealizing customs and traditions that are harmful to girls in the name of cultural relativism, noting:

> Communities may be the most oppressive structure that women and girls face in their lives. Communities may have an ideology of subordination with regard to women and girls, may effectively control their emotional and sexual expression, and, in some instances, may also sanction violence against them. Romanticizing the community, even if it is for fighting the good battle against imperialism, is always problematic.[157]

She guards against the instrumentalization of concepts such as imperialism and colonialism by master signifiers to deny human rights to girls and women.[158] In this regard, Askari argues for the recognition of gender equality

in western countries. . .These changes trivialize the nature of female genital mutilation and the suffering of African women and girls'.

[155] See Yasser Louati, TRT World, 'CFA Franc: The "Colonial Currency" Keeping 14 African Nations on a Leash' (2022). www.trtworld.com/opinion/cfa-franc-the-colonial-currency-keeping-14-african-nations-on-a-leash-12781184 (accessed 29 July 2023); Eswar Prasad and Vera Songwe, 'Monetary Meld: A Currency Union Encompassing All of West Africa Promises Benefits but Faces a Multitude of Obstacles' (International Monetary Fund [IMF] 2021); Kemoe Laurent and others, 'African Currencies are under Pressure amid Higher-for-Longer US Interest Rates' (IMF Blog, 15 May 2023). www.imf.org/en/Blogs/Articles/2023/05/15/african-currencies-are-under-pressure-amid-higher-for-longer-us-interest-rates (accessed 29 July 2023).

[156] In this regard, Coomaraswamy underscores that '[t]hough at the macro-level, the argument of double standards appears forceful, it is never an answer for the individual demands of victims, many of whom I have met in person and whose suffering and need for remedy far outweigh purely intellectual claims searching for an elusive global balance of power': 'Cutting Edge' (2015), 24.

[157] Ibid., 25.

[158] Coomaraswamy notes that 'colonialism and imperialism are also terms of bluster, a way in which nations and societies attempt to obfuscate grave injustices of their own making by forging superficial solidarity with those who oppose imperialism just for the sake of it': Ibid., 28.

as a peremptory norm of international law based on its consistency as the right to cultural life is constantly evolving:

> What constitutes a right to cultural life can vary from generation to generation. In contrast, the basic components of gender discrimination are static. Irrespective of time and place, gender discrimination will always connote notions of superiority and inferiority. Because culture is dynamic, its meaning as a peremptory norm could change from generation to generation and from place to place.[159]

One must attempt to strike a delicate balance between universality and relativity, promoting inclusiveness and openness, as explained by Ertürk and Purkayastha:

> The challenge is to respect diverse cultures while developing strategies to resist oppressive practices in the name of culture and to uphold universal human rights standards while rejecting ethnocentric rulings.[160]

Hence, rather than essentializing and conceptualizing cultures as fixed realities that entail specific violations, this book acknowledges that discriminatory practices permeate all societies and thereby the overall human experience. We echo Rao's advice that '[w]e need to listen with care, but also with skepticism, to sweeping definitions of this thing called culture, forged as they are in a world of constantly expanding difference and complexity'.[161] Accordingly, the present book adopts a universal and inclusive approach whereby all violations of the rights of girl children are considered serious, whether they emerged or are perpetrated in the Global South or Global North. For example, in the glossary discussion on the expression FGM, we explained that rather than applying weaker terminology to refer to serious practices affecting girls for cultural relativist purposes, this book employs the expression FGM to *also* include mutilations perpetrated in the Global North, such as labiaplasty and non-consensual intersex gender reassignment.[162] This

[159] 'Jus Cogens' (1998), 35.

[160] 'Linking Research' (2012), 149.

[161] 'Gender and Culture' (1995), 171. For example, when discussing violence against women, Ertürk and Purkayastha underscore that 'there is a continuing normalization of violence against women, so that it is very much infused and ingrained in our historical memories, our values, our language across cultures, in varying degrees and forms': 'Linking Research' (2012), 147.

[162] See glossary, and for example Sean Runacres and Paul Wood, 'Cosmetic Labiaplasty in an Adolescent Population' (2016) 29 *Journal of Pediatric and Adolescent Gynecology* 218; Caroline Drolet and Anne Drolet, 'Self-Objectification, System Justifying Beliefs, and the Rise of Labiaplasty' (2019) 32 *Social Justice Research* 318; Melinda Jones 'Intersex Genital Mutilation – A Western Version of FGM' (2017) 25 *International Journal of Children's Rights* 396.

book adopts the same approach with regard to all violations encountered by girl children, from sexualized social and dress codes to child marriage, since the semioethic objective of our study is to identify terminology in international law that will address obstacles to the realization of the rights of *all* girl children. Moreover, this book does not simply focus on violations of girl child rights which are manifestations of sex and child-based discrimination.[163] We explore the broader notions of sexism and childism and how they interact and permeate every aspect of a girl's life, thereby placing her in a subordinate position globally. Furthermore, we emphasize that many traditions and customs from the Global South and Global North have positive features that should not be eliminated on account of universalism, for example, celebrations of milestones in a girl's life, such as reaching adolescence, pursuing studies, and once attaining adulthood, possibly marriage and motherhood (if she so chooses), and participating in funeral rituals of loved ones, are essential components of the life cycle and should be maintained as long as they do not entail violations of her rights, and if so, could still be adapted accordingly.[164] The present analysis is based on the premise that girls should be entitled to rights and opportunities, *because* and *regardless* of their many identity vectors.

[163] As noted by Rao, '[w]e need to problematize all of culture ... When we limit our inquiry to egregious violations, we limit our capacity to ameliorate human pain to just that one instance of "bad" cultural practice': 'Gender and Culture' (1995), 174.

[164] For example, including girls in funeral rites to honour their loved ones, and within societies that practice FGM at puberty, replacing this practice with other rituals and celebrations.

# 4

# Intersectional Identity of the Girl Child

The two vectors of discrimination experienced by the girl child – sexism and childism – intersect, cumulate and interact. An analysis of her situation thus requires an exploration of the intersectionality paradigm. The intersectionality theory has been applied in the past few years to study the condition of the girl child by scholars such as myself in specific contexts related to restorative justice, armed conflict, culture and international law.[1] Initially coined by Crenshaw in the late 1980s, intersectionality theory originated from critical race studies, and focused on the intersection between gender and racial discrimination.[2] According to intersectionality theory, the tendency to treat the two vectors of identity of the girl child, femalehood and childhood, as mutually exclusive categories tends to focus the attention on the most privileged members of each group – boys and adult women – while masking the

1 See in chronological order: Clara Chapdelaine-Feliciati, 'Restorative Justice for the Girl Child in Post-Conflict Rwanda' (2006) 7 *Journal of International Women's Studies* 14; Jewel Amoah, 'The World on Her Shoulders: The Rights of the Girl Child in the Context of Culture and Identity' (2007) 4 *Essex Human Rights Review* 1; Annalijn Conklin and Benjamin Mason Meier, 'A "Vector" of Rights Approach for Public Health: Towards an Intersectional Human Rights Framework for Considering the Prevention and Treatment of Harms to Girl Child Soldiers' (2008) 13 *Australian Journal of Human Rights* 65; Nura Taefi, 'The Synthesis of Age and Gender: Intersectionality, International Human Rights Law and the Marginalization of the Girl Child' (2009) 17 *The International Journal of Children's Rights* 345; 'Girls and Girl Children' (2022); see also Chiseche Salome Mibenge, *Sex and International Tribunals: The Erasure of Gender from the War Narrative* (University of Pennsylvania Press 2014), for an important analysis of the intersectional identity of the girl child and her victimization during armed conflict, crimes against humanity and genocide, including the Rwandan genocide.

2 Kimberlé Crenshaw, 'Demarginalizing the Intersection of Race and Sex: A Black Feminist Critique of Antidiscrimination Doctrine, Feminist Theory and Antiracist Politics' (1989) *University of Chicago Legal Forum* 139; Kimberlé Crenshaw, 'Mapping the Margins: Intersectionality, Identity Politics, and Violence Against Women of Color' (1991) 43 *Stanford Law Review* 1241.

unique oppression experienced by the subordinate members of these groups, in the case at hand, girl children. Crenshaw underscored that the single-axis framework of anti-discrimination law in the United States tended to obfuscate intragroup differences between white and black women on the one hand, and black men and women on the other hand, and thereby ignored the multiple oppression experienced by black women, as illustrated by the General Motors case. In this case, the black women's claim of discrimination was denied on the basis that they could neither demonstrate racism nor sexism, since neither black men nor white women were discriminated by the company. The court, examining the two types of discrimination separately, failed to recognize that black women had in fact experienced double discrimination.[3] The heightened discrimination encountered by black female workers in this case is explained by the double jeopardy concept. Developed in the late 1970s to characterize dual discrimination based on racism and sexism, this theory emphasizes that individuals with multiple subordinate identities, in the case at hand the girl child, are subjected to more discrimination than those with a single subordinate identity, namely boys (childism) and adult women (sexism).[4] The double jeopardy theory comprises the additive model and the interactive model. Firstly, as argued in the additive model, the girl child encounters two distinctive forms of oppression which are summed together, and she is thus more vulnerable to human rights violations than boys and adult women. Indeed, the girl child simultaneously experiences the matrix of domination of manhood and adulthood within both the female and child identity categories. The interactive model has a different approach; it considers that a person's subordinate identities interact in a synergetic way.[5] According to the interactive model, the girl child not only undergoes dual discrimination, but these axes of subordination interact and strengthen each other. As Connell et al. state in relation to class and gender: the two categories 'abrade, inflame, amplify, twist, negate, dampen and complicate each other'.[6] Hence, the gender discrimination experienced by the girl child as a female weakens her already vulnerable status as a child, and the child-based discrimination she encounters as a child increases the likelihood of gender-based violations.

3 'Demarginalizing' (1989), 140. DeGraffenreid *v*. General Motors Assembly Div 413 F Supp 142 (E D Mo 1976).

4 Valerie Purdie-Vaughns and Richard Eibach, 'Intersectional Invisibility: The Distinctive Advantages and Disadvantages of Multiple Subordinate-Group Identities' (2008) 59 *Sex Roles* 377.

5 Ibid., 378.

6 Robert Connell et al., *Making the Difference: Schools, Families and Social Division* (Routledge 1982), 182.

## I INTERSECTIONALITY METHOD AND THE GIRL CHILD

Although intersectionality theory provides an extremely useful conceptual framework to examine the dynamic relationship between gender and child-based discrimination, it is important to address 'a number of paradoxes embedded in its literature',[7] and their impact on our analysis of the girl child. Accordingly, two central weaknesses are examined: 1) the use of fixed categories and 2) the double jeopardy model. The first limitation of intersectionality, which was identified by anti-categorical and anti-essentialist theorists, is that it relies on fixed identity categories, such as sex and age, without acknowledging the shortcomings of these classifications. The anti-categorical complexity theory challenges the 'singularity, separateness and wholeness' of social categories, and considers that such classifications constitute artificial and simplistic constructs which fail to address the complexity of the human experience.[8] It underlines that different experiences, identities and social locations may not fit into any single 'master' category unless one imposes 'a stable and homogenizing order on a more unstable and heterogeneous social reality'.[9] Anti-categorical theorists argue that fixed identity categories are artificial and fail to acknowledge each individual's unique situation. For instance, as noted in Chapter 2, the binary division of human beings into 'females' and 'males' has been criticized as not accounting for individuals who do not fit neatly into either category on account of biological or other attributes, or who throughout a lifetime, and in different circumstances, may identify more with one gender or the other.[10] Moreover, as concerns childhood and adulthood, the parameters for the beginning and the end of childhood are still inconsistent worldwide, and the conceptions of childhood vary across regions and cultures.

Another criticism of intersectionality theory is the notion that social groupings reflect a common essence, which could erroneously suggest that categories constitute unitary and internally homogenous entities.[11] Anti-essentialist theorists underscore that intersectionality theory tends to essentialize the identified subordinate group, for instance, girl children, and disregard the differences between members of that social category. Most notably, Nash considers that since Crenshaw emphasizes the vectors of race and gender, she ignores the ways in which the existence of each individual black woman is

[7] Jennifer Nash, 'Re-Thinking Intersectionality' (2008) 89 *Feminist Review* 1, 3.
[8] 'Complexity Intersectionality' (2005), 1778.
[9] Ibid., 1777.
[10] Ibid., 1778.
[11] 'International Intersectionality' (2003).

complicated by class, nationality, language, ethnicity and sexuality, and hence fails to capture the diversity of black women's experiences.[12] In this regard, an essentialist approach to intersectionality theory may assume that girl children constitute a static entity and thereby disregard additional forms of oppression experienced by members of the girl child category, such as racism, poverty and homophobia, and the advantages of girls who belong to privileged social groups, according to their class, sexual orientation or able-bodiedness.[13] Nash also criticizes Crenshaw for not addressing 'the ways in which race and gender function as social processes in distinctive ways for particular black women in varying historical moments' and argues that instead she has treated race and gender 'as trans-historical constants that mark *all* black women in similar ways'.[14] However, categories are not merely conceptual in character for they constitute concrete distinctions in the public and private realms. As discussed in Chapter 2, classifications, such as sex and age, are essential to study relationships of inequality and their impact on subordinate groups, in the case at hand the girl child. While classifications may at times appear artificial and restrictive, they nevertheless impact the status of the girl child and therefore cannot be disregarded. A girl child may not self-identify with her categorization as a female and a child, yet she is perceived as such under legal, social and cultural parameters. Additionally, since the girl child encounters discrimination specifically because of her membership within the 'female' and 'child' social categories, one must acknowledge the existence of such classifications to address the differential treatment she experiences. Lastly, if one were to adopt a strict anti-categorical approach, all classifications would be dismissed for one cannot fully separate all the myriad intersections that constitute an individual's identity. Indeed, even the most specific subcategory cannot fully capture a girl's idiosyncrasy. In its exploration of the intersectional discrimination of the girl child, this book therefore employs a strategic essentialist and inter-categorical approach,[15] by acknowledging her vectors of femalehood and childhood, whilst noting that such classifications are hybrid biological and social constructs. It adopts an inter-categorical approach for it focuses on girl children as a whole and examines the relationships between this social category and other identity groups, such as adult women and boys, and not between groups of girl children. In this regard, this book does not follow an intra-categorical approach which focuses 'on particular social groups

[12] 'Re-Thinking Intersectionality' (2008), 9.
[13] Ibid., 10.
[14] Ibid., 7.
[15] 'Complexity Intersectionality' (2005), 1773.

at neglected points of intersection [such as girl children] in order to reveal the lived experience within such groups [for instance, distinctions between various groups of girls]'.[16] We consider that girl children share a common position while noting that they do not constitute a static or monolithic group.[17] Each girl child may encounter discrimination on grounds other than gender and age, such as race, class, ethnic origin, religion, sexual orientation and disabilities, and one must therefore acknowledge the situation of specific groups of girls who are particularly vulnerable to violations of human rights as a result of multiple forms of discrimination, notably lesbian girl children, girls living with HIV/AIDS, girls with disabilities, girls belonging to certain minority groups, such as aboriginal girls and nomadic girls, and girl children living in special circumstances, notably girls in detention, girls in armed conflict and girl child refugees. However, since gender and age are the vectors of identity shared by the girl child category as a whole, we shall primarily focus on their corresponding forms of discrimination.

The second main weakness of intersectionality theory concerns the double jeopardy model, which has been criticized as limitative on three grounds. First, it does not acknowledge 'the many complex ways that people with intersecting identities are interdependent with those who share one or more of their disadvantaged identities'.[18] For instance, since the girl child is usually economically and socially dependent on her family, if the latter experiences discrimination in employment or housing, she is likely to be further marginalized. Second, the double jeopardy model may conduct 'Oppression Olympics' or a score-keeping contest whereby each group – in this case, adult women, boys and girls – competes for the mantle of 'most oppressed', rather than joining forces to promote equality for all.[19] Lastly, since there is no universal metric of oppression, it is practically impossible to proclaim that a specific identity or multiple burdened group experiences the most oppression.[20] Indeed, it is difficult to quantify distinct forms of oppression into a single measure. In this regard, Purdie-Vaughns and Eibach note that 'the question "(w)hose group suffers most?" is one that science ultimately cannot answer'.[21] Hence, while the vectors of gender and child-based discrimination experienced by the girl child cumulate and interact and thereby place her in a unique position, this book does not purport to dismiss the importance of

16 Ibid., 1774.
17 'Category Women' (2011), 33.
18 'Intersectional Invisibility' (2008), 380.
19 'Multiplication' (2007), 68.
20 'Intersectional Invisibility' (2008), 380.
21 Ibid.

violations of rights suffered by human beings belonging to privileged identity groups, such as adult men, or individuals with a single subordinate identity, such as adult women and boys.[22]

## II INTERACTIVE INTERSECTIONAL DISCRIMINATION

The girl child experiences multiple discrimination, which refers to a situation, or phenomenon, where a person is discriminated against on several different grounds at different times,[23] since she may encounter discrimination on the grounds of her gender and age on different occasions throughout her childhood. Additionally, she faces compound discrimination, which captures more specific situations in which several grounds of discrimination add to each other,[24] when sexism and childism cumulate at one particular instance. Lastly, the gender-based and child-based vectors of discrimination also interact with each other in such a way that they are indivisible, leading to violations that trigger a series of additional encroachments on girls' rights to the extent that it is difficult to determine which breach is the cause and which is the consequence of the violation. We call this phenomenon 'interactive intersectional discrimination'.

### 1 *Son Preference and Daughter Devaluation*

The phenomenon of son preference and daughter devaluation is embedded in sexism whilst fortified by childism.[25] Son preference is firstly underpinned by sexism leading to prenatal sex selection, female infanticide, and should the girl child live, neglect throughout childhood, including undernourishment, less medical treatment in hospitals than boys and inadequate clothing during winter.[26] The girl child also has productive burdens within the family, such as caring duties and household chores, that are not shared equally with boys. The ILO emphasizes that in many countries, girls assume a disproportionate share

22 See Chapter 3.

23 Hege Skjeie and Trude Langvasbråten, 'Intersectionality in Practice? Anti-Discrimination Reforms in Norway' (2009) 11 *International Feminist Journal of Politics* 513, 514.

24 Ibid.

25 See glossary.

26 UNICEF, 'Children, Food, Nutrition' (2019), 59, 84. The UNFPA estimates that nutritional anemia affects half of all girls in the Global South: 'Young People: Forging the Future' (2011), 2; 'Cultural Practices' (2002), para. 77; UNICEF, 'Gender Counts – East and Southeast Asia: A Quantitative Assessment of Gender Equality and Its Impact on Girls and Boys' (2019), 67; Syed Manzoor Ahmed Hanifi et al., 'Where Girls are Less Likely to be Fully Vaccinated than Boys: Evidence from a Rural Area in Bangladesh' (2018) 36 *Vaccine* 3323, 3328.

of the costs borne by the household, which may reach 43 hours per week, even for girls as young as five years old.[27] Sohoni coined the expression 'unenumerated and unremunerated' work to refer to the list of care and household burdens shouldered by girl children.[28] These manifestations of son preference are in turn strengthened by childism as adults have parental authority over their children and are presumed to act in their best interests. Accordingly, many health-related deficiencies – including those leading to death, which are caused by malnutrition and the refusal of parents to take their daughter to the hospital and provide her with adequate medication – go unnoticed.[29] In addition, the burden imposed on girls to perform a series of household duties is seldom questioned, unless it reaches extreme proportions.[30] Consequently, a vast array of infringements that do not constitute obvious breaches of rights are either disregarded or undetected. And even violent acts, such as female infanticide, are often insufficiently investigated and classified as accidents and natural deaths or not prosecuted.[31] The practice of son preference resulting in malnutrition, lack of medical care and the double burden of girlhood, undermines the likelihood of girl children obtaining an education. Indeed, a hungry or sick girl is less able to learn and succeed in school. Moreover, the responsibility to fulfil significant household responsibilities leaves the girl child tired and with less time to dedicate to her studies.[32] The girl child's limited education prevents subsequent access to well-remunerated employment once she becomes an adult. Her restricted potential for economic empowerment causes parents to rely on sons for financial support, which accounts for the practice of son preference, resulting in malnutrition and limited access to health services for the girl child and the requirement for her to perform significantly more household chores than her brothers to counterweigh the 'economic liability' she constitutes. Hence, the practice of son preference and daughter devaluation reduces the prospects of

[27] 'Ending Child Labour by 2025: Review of Policies and Programmes' (2017), 21. ILO notes that over 21 hours per week is 'the threshold beyond which initial research suggests household chores begin to negatively impact on the ability of children to attend and benefit from school': 'Ending Child Labour' (2017), 21.

[28] *Burden Girlhood* (1995), 13.

[29] 'Children, Food, Nutrition' (2019), 84; 'Gender Counts' (2019), 67.

[30] 'Ending Child Labour' (2017); 'New Era Girls' (2020), 16.

[31] Usha Rana, 'Increased Female Criminality in India: A Statistical Perception' (2016) 5 *Journal of Global Research and Analysis* 221, 222; 'Gendercide CRC' (2018); Gendercide Watch, 'Case Study: Female Infanticide' (2007), 6; Ranjani Murthy, 'Fighting Female Infanticide by Working with Midwives: An Indian Case Study' (1996) 4 *Gender and Development* 20, 24.

[32] UNICEF notes in this regard that 'it is the amount of time spent on chores that can curtail girls' opportunities to enjoy the pleasures of childhood, including time to play, build social networks and focus on their education': 'New Era Girls' (2020), 16.

education for the girl child, which in turn further amplifies the practice of son preference itself, coming full circle.

Furthermore, the limited potential for economic development of the girl child caused by her lack of education tends to confine her identity to that of a future wife and mother, whose reproductive role is emphasized. The future husband and family-in-law thereby require the family of the girl child to demonstrate her chastity, which leads to various forms of social control, such as FGM, child marriage, restrictive social and dress codes and the threat of honour-related killings, all of which limit the likelihood of premarital and extramarital sex. Each of these infringements initiates other breaches of human rights. For instance, unlike male circumcision, FGM is embedded in sexism and usually performed to ensure a girl child's chastity, both before and during marriage, and thus her husband's paternity of their children.[33] The authority of parents over their daughter, which is a result of childism, further enables them to have her mutilated without consulting her or obtaining her consent. FGM has various short and long-term negative consequences on the girl child's physical and mental health. The short-term effects include severe pain, haemorrhage, severe bleeding, abscesses, ulcers, tetanus, gangrene, urine retention, damage to the bladder and other organs and shock, leading to death.[34] The long-term effects comprise hepatitis and HIV, infertility, excessive scar tissue, serious psychological trauma, as well as severe pain during sexual intercourse, extremely painful menstruation and complications during childbirth, including obstetric fistula often leading to death.[35] The reluctance of the public sphere to intervene on this issue, which is another consequence of childism as it intersects with cultural relativism, is demonstrated by the fact that in spite of progress in awareness-raising, FGM is presently neither banned nor criminalized in many countries, and is often tolerated in those in which it is prohibited.[36]

33 Joint CEDAW-CRC GenRec/Com: 'Harmful Practices' (2014), para. 19. It significantly diminishes or eliminates sexual pleasure and often causes severe pain during intercourse, which curtails the likelihood of extra-conjugal sexual activities, although it also seriously reduces the desire for conjugal ones, notably causing dyspareunia, orgasmic delay and anorgasmia: James Whitehorn et al., 'Female Genital Mutilation: Cultural and Psychological Implications' (2002) 17 *Sexual and Relationship Therapy* 161, 166.

34 'FGM Clinical Handbook' (2018), 87, 115, 155, 239.

35 Ibid; 'Cultural Practices' (2002), para. 15; Jugal Kishore, *The Vanishing Girl Child* (Century Publications 2005), 64.

36 See glossary discussion on FGM. See also Thomas Reuters Foundation, 'The Law and FGM: An Overview of 28 African Countries' (2018): in the 28 countries where this practice is endemic, only two – Kenya and Uganda – directly criminalize the practice with punishments, and in most countries, the number of prosecutions is low, while sentences are lenient and often suspended: 11, 28, 31, 57; twenty-two of these countries adopted laws to prohibit FGM,

Child marriage predominantly affects girls for it is a strategy serving three purposes underpinned by sexism. First, it aims to assure the girl child's chastity: the younger the girl, the less likely she is to have had sexual experiences. The same requirement is not imposed on boys who may therefore marry at a later age. Second, child marriage aims to ensure that the girl child will provide children to her husband and thus the younger she marries, the more reproductive years she will have to 'offer'. Third, as noted by Askari, it is easier for the husband and family-in-law to 'train' a young girl to obey their rules and 'mould' her into a submissive wife, for she is less likely to have developed 'a personality or identity of her own', and be aware of equality concepts and other paradigms of thought.[37] The ability of parents and the extended community to either force her into a marriage or manipulate her into one through social and emotional pressure is reinforced by childism whereby the girl child is under her parents' authority and they are presumed to act in her best interests by the community, society and the girl child herself. Child marriage in turn increases the prospect of a series of violations, such as sexual, physical and emotional violence. Married girls are particularly vulnerable to sexual assaults on the premise that marriage offers the husband a permanent right of access to conjugal relations.[38] Additionally, married girls on all continents are submitted to numerous forms of physical violence, such as 'pushing, shaking, slapping, punching, biting, kicking, dragging, strangling, burning, and threatening/attacking with a weapon'.[39] Child marriage also leads to infringements on the right to education, as well as the right to health, such as complications in pregnancy and while giving birth, including death.[40]

Restrictive social and dress codes also impact girls significantly. Whereas many girl children are not allowed, either under domestic law or by their family and larger community, to leave the home unaccompanied by a male guardian: a husband, father or brother, or to pursue an education, extracurricular activities or part-time employment,[41] the same is not true for boys, who

yet fail to directly criminalize and punish those involved. Two of these countries have not yet adopted legislation against this practice: 11, 22.

[37] Ladan Askari, 'The Convention on the Rights of the Child: The Necessity of Adding a Provision to Ban Child Marriages' (1998–1999) 5 *ILSA Journal of International and Comparative Law* 123, 126.

[38] 'Cultural Practices' (2002), para. 101.

[39] 'Study Violence Children' (2006), 58.

[40] 'Cultural Practices' (2002), para. 56; World Bank, 'Disease Control Priorities, Reproductive, Maternal, Newborn, and Child Health' (2016); Save the Children, 'Global Childhood Report' (2019), 14.

[41] See Chapter 3, Section II: Sexism; 'Cultural Practices' (2002), para. 84; *Commentary CEDAW* (2012), 424.

can occupy public spaces without being escorted by a close female relative, and participate in many activities not available to girl children. The girl child may also be required to abide by strict dress codes and hide her body completely or almost completely.[42] Coomaraswamy stresses the health hazards connected with these dress codes, such as asthma, high blood pressure, hearing or sight problems, skin rashes, hair loss and a general decline in mental condition.[43] In this regard, Rao observes that 'through their clothing and demeanor, women and girls become visible and vulnerable embodiments of cultural symbols and codes'.[44] In addition, many girls are considered 'unclean' during their menstrual cycle and thereby isolated in outhouses and prevented from coming into the house, prohibited from eating certain kinds of food, and not allowed in public places throughout that period.[45] Restrictive codes are strengthened by childism and the public/private divide, for the State may be reluctant to intervene, especially if the girl's parents or legal guardians contend that these codes constitute an obligation falling under cultural or religious upbringing. As noted by Taylor, '(t)he law does little to regulate the decisions made by parents concerning their children's religious upbringing, only interfering in those decisions in rare cases of a serious threat of harm to the child'.[46] Also, legal guardians may use status offences, such as curfews and the criminalization of acts of vagrancy and running away, which are entrenched in childism, either to strengthen the sexist practices imposed on their daughters in the private sphere by threatening to contact law enforcement personnel should they misbehave, or to locate them should they disobey strict curfews or socialize with friends outside the family's parameters of approval. As noted by the CRC Committee, '[i]t is particularly a matter of

42 'Cultural Practices' (2002), para. 86; Gi Yeon Koo and Ha Eun Han, 'To Veil or Not to Veil: Turkish and Iranian Hijab Policies and the Struggle for Recognition' (2018) 24 *Asian Journal of Women's Studies* 47; Deborah Wheeler, 'Saudi Women Driving Change? Rebranding, Resistance, and the Kingdom of Change' (2020) 11 *Journal of the Middle East and Africa* 87; Lisa La Fornara, 'Islam's (In)compatibility with the West?: Dress Code Restrictions in the Age of Feminism' (2018) 25 *Indiana Journal of Global Legal Studies* 463.

43 'Cultural Practices' (2002), para. 87.

44 'Gender and Culture' (1995), 169.

45 'Cultural Practices' (2002), para. 85; UNICEF, 'Gender Programmatic Reviews in UNICEF Officers in South Asia – Afghanistan, Bangladesh, Bhutan, Maldives, Nepal, Sri Lanka' (2019), 16; UNICEF, 'WASH in Schools Empowers Girls' Education' (2013), 42; UNICEF, 'Guidance on Menstrual Health and Hygiene' (2019), 13, noting that '[a]dolescent girls may face stigma, harassment and social exclusion during menstruation'.

46 Rachel Taylor, 'Parental Responsibility and Religion' in Rebecca Probert, Stephen Gilmore and Jonathan Herring (eds.), *Responsible Parents and Parental Responsibility* (Bloomsbury 2009), 124. Taylor notes that '(r)eligious upbringing may involve restriction or obligation in a wide range of aspects of the child's life, such as his or her diet and clothing': 128.

concern that girls … are often victims of this criminalization'.[47] Restrictive social and dress codes strengthen gender stereotypes requiring an obedient and submissive girl child and thereby fortify justifications for sexual and physical violence, penal sanctions and honour-related killings against girls who do not abide. These strict protocols limit the girl child's freedom of expression and movement as well as her participatory rights,[48] which in turn weaken her ability to succeed in her studies, notably to enter post-secondary education, and thus to achieve economic growth. Goonesekere underscores that these restrictive codes negatively impact several rights of girl children, from education to agency, and future employment:

> When extremist fundamentalist religious movements that seek to deny women's rights also perpetrate violence against girls who claim education rights, or impose dress codes that can limit their right to education, they also deny girls agency and capacity to claim public space through career development.[49]

Special Rapporteur Muñoz Villalobos also stresses that discriminatory social and cultural practices and restrictions on the rights to freedom of expression and movement negatively impact gender equality in education.[50] In this regard, Terre des hommes observes that 'an entire generation of girls is at risk of being excluded from the job market or of being forced into low-skilled labour'.[51] Hence, the lack of potential for economic development of the girl child strengthens a series of sexist practices against her which diminish her prospects of economic empowerment, coming once again full circle.

### 2 *Sexualized Social and Dress Codes*

Sexualized social and dress codes are ensconced in both sexism and childism. The media, especially in the Global North, increasingly portrays girl children as reified sexual beings.[52] Girls wearing heavy makeup, provocative clothing

[47] CRC General Comment No. 10: 'Juvenile Justice' (2007), para. 8.

[48] 'Gender Counts' (2019), 115.

[49] 'HRs for Girls' (2014), 489.

[50] Vernor Muñoz Villalobos, SR Education, 'Girl's Right to Education' (8 February 2006) UN Doc E/CN.4/2006/45, para. 57.

[51] Terre des Hommes, INDIFESA Campaign, 'The Condition of the Girl Child Worldwide' (2019), 15.

[52] Elizabeth Behm-Morawitz, 'Sext up KIDS: How Children are Becoming Hypersexualized' (2013) 7 *Journal of Children and Media* 530; Kelli Ortega, 'Striking a Pose: Protecting the Welfare of Child Models' (2014) 35 *Cardozo Law Review* 2535; Anais Paccione, 'On Trend:

and adopting flirtatious and suggestive poses are prevalent in advertisement, television programmes, movies, magazines, music videos – including those targeted for children – and most importantly, social media platforms such as TikTok and Instagram.[53] The mainstream and social media also promote unhealthy beauty standards, including through so-called social media 'influencers'.[54] The female ideal body advertised is a physical anomaly: she has very thin legs and arms and a tiny waist, yet voluminous breasts, and her face has very delicate features and a tiny nose, yet very large lips. This issue is also present in the Global South, for instance in the very popular Bollywood and K-pop industries, which increasingly over-sexualize women and girls and promote a fair complexion and cult of thinness, entailing significant cosmetic surgery, especially in actresses and singers, respectively.[55] Sexualized social and dress codes have three interrelated adverse consequences for girl children. Firstly, unrealistic beauty models undermine girl children's self-esteem,

Continuing the Effort to Inspire Fashion Industry Reform and Protect Underage Fashion Models' (2017) 41 *Seton Hall Legislative Journal* 417; Philip Darbyshire, 'Childhood: Are Reports of Its Death Greatly Exaggerated?' (2007) 11 *Journal of Child Health Care* 85; Valerie Walkerdine, 'Popular Culture and the Eroticization of Little Girls' in Henry Jenkins (ed.), *The Children's Culture Reader* (New York University Press 1998); Reesa Sorin, 'Changing Images of Childhood – Reconceptualizing Early Childhood Practice' (2005) 1 *International Journal of Transitions in Childhood* 12; American Psychological Association, 'Report of the APA Task Force on the Sexualization of Girls' (2010).

53 Speno Gerding and Jennifer Stevens, 'Sexualization, Youthification, and Adultification: A Content Analysis of Images of Girls and Women in Popular Magazines' (2018) 95 *Journalism and Mass Communication Quarterly* 625; Laura Vandenbosch et al., '"I Might Get Your Heart Racing in My Skin-Tight Jeans": Sexualization on Music Entertainment Television' (2013) 64 *Communication Studies* 178; Jessica Kelly and Lance Garmon, 'Perceptions of Child Beauty Pageants and Their Impacts: What Really Lies Behind the Tiara?' (2016) 24 *Atlantic Journal of Communication* 201; Zoe Brown and Marika Tiggemann, 'Attractive Celebrity and Peer Images on Instagram: Effect on Women's Mood and Body Image' (2016) 19 *Body Image* 37.

54 'Influencers Instagram Dieting' (2019); 'Instagram Body Dissatisfaction' (2022); 'TikTok Body Dissatisfaction' (2022).

55 Parul Jain et al., 'Sexuality and Substance Abuse Portrayals in Item Songs in Bollywood Movies' (2019) 17 *South Asian Popular Culture* 15; Jannath Ghaznavi et al., 'Increasingly Violent but Still Sexy: A Decade of Central Female Characters in Top-Grossing Hollywood and Bollywood Film Promotional Material' (2017) 11 *International Journal of Communication* 23; Floribert Patrick Endong, 'Pornography and Objectification of Women in Nollywood Films: A Study of Nigerian Actresses' Perception of Acting Sex and Nudity Scenes' (2019) 20 *Journal of International Women's Studies* 58; Şehriban Kaya, 'Gender and Violence: Rape as a Spectacle on Prime-Time Television' (2019) 58 *Social Science Information* 681; K Girija and G Basavaraja, 'Globalization and Commodification of Beauty – How Setting Beauty Standards have Violated Women's Rights?' (2019) 8 *Political Science* 37; Gooyong Kim, 'Between Hybridity and Hegemony in K-Pop's Global Popularity: A Case of Girls' Generation's American Debut' (2017) 11 *International Journal of Communication* 2367.

leading to depression and digitized dysmorphia.[56] In order to meet these ideals, girls have to sculpt their bodies through aesthetic plastic surgery and life-threatening eating disorders, notably anorexia and bulimia nervosa.[57] This book therefore employs the expression 'dress codes' to encompass the requirement to change the body *itself*, whereby girls are compelled to carve inhuman features onto their human bodies through eating disorders and cosmetic surgeries, including rhinoplasty, breast implants, buttock surgery and female genital mutilation such as labiaplasty.[58] The reification of girls, notably the reduction of their human identities to their physical attributes, is a manifestation of sexism for it confines girls into sexually stereotyped social roles. These sexual codes are also an expression of childism whereby adults use girl children to serve their own interests, for example, parents and managers of girl celebrities who over-sexualize them to obtain money and fame.[59] Secondly, girl children integrate these standards of behaviour and emulate the sexualized images of girls promoted in the media. As a result, many girls provide sexualized presentations of themselves on social networks and platforms, such as Instagram and TikTok,[60] and/or take part in virtual sex-related activities, such as sexting, that is, sending sexual messages or images of themselves to others.[61] Thirdly, sexualized social and dress codes treat girls as commodities and therefore exacerbate sexual exploitation and violence

56 Valeria Verrastro et al., 'Fear the Instagram: Beauty Stereotypes, Body Image and Instagram Use in a Sample of Male and Female Adolescents' (2020) 15 *Qwerty - Open and Interdisciplinary Journal of Technology, Culture and Education* 31; Mariska Kleemans et al., 'Picture Perfect: The Direct Effect of Manipulated Instagram Photos on Body Image in Adolescent Girls' (2018) 21 *Media Psychology* 93.

57 'Tik Tok Anti-Pro-Anorexia Videos' (2021). Anorexia and bulimia nervosa are mental disorders characterized by an unrealistic fear of weight gain and a distortion of body image.

58 Veya Seekis and Grace Barker, 'Does #beauty have a Dark Side? Testing Mediating Pathways between Engagement with Beauty Content on Social Media and Cosmetic Surgery Consideration' (2022) 42 *Body Image* 268; Christoph Wallner et al., 'Digital Media Play a Key Role in Influencing Female Breast Perception' (2023) 26 *Cyberpsychology, Behavior and Social Networking* 11; Samantha Maki et al., 'An Analysis of Vulva Appearance in Video Pornography' (2023) 27 *Sexuality and Culture* 310; 'Cosmetic Labiaplasty' (2016); 'Rise Labiaplasty' (2019).

59 'Striking a Pose' (2014); 'Underage Fashion Models' (2017); 'Changing Childhood' (2005), 17; 'Childhood: Its Death' (2007), 89; Christine Tamer, 'Toddlers, Tiaras, and Pedophilia? The Borderline "Child Pornography" Embraced by the American Public' (2011) 13 *Texas Review of Entertainment and Sports Law* 85.

60 'TikTok Body Dissatisfaction' (2022) note that 'many of these dance trends tend to be provocative in nature including suggestive music, sexualized dance moves, and clothing that highlights certain body parts including crow-tops, low-cut shirts or bras, and tight-fitting leggings': 206; 'Sexualization Girls' (2010), 9.

61 Jessica Ringrose et al., 'A Qualitative Study of Children, Young People and "Sexting": A Report Prepared for the National Society for the Prevention of Cruelty to Children' (Institute of

against them by peers and adults, including via online pornography.[62] Adarsh and Sahoo explain that pornography containing abuse, rape and child sex is associated with the normalizing of this behaviour, and that pornographic material, as currently presented, 'rewires' the brains of consumers.[63] Although girls are not the main consumers of these pornographic semiotic signs, they experience their *significance* onto their own bodies during sexual intercourse when their male partners reproduce 'sexual templates shaped by mainstream online violent pornography'.[64] The objectification of girls dehumanizes them in the eyes of others and leads to the acceptance of rape myths and sex role stereotypes, to the extent that sexual violence perpetrated against them by peers, notably boys, and adults, is banalized, a phenomenon described as 'rape culture'.[65] UNICEF reveals that nine million adolescent girls between the ages of fifteen and nineteen years experience forced sex in a given year. Most of the sexual coercion is perpetrated by peers, including the intimate partner.[66] In this regard, Goonesekere notes:

> [T]he commodification of women as sex symbols, combined with the misuse of communication technology, has contributed to sexual violence and harassment, spreading macho values and attitudes, even as international and national norms emphasise the importance of gender equality. The public receives a barrage of 'double messages' on women and gender relations.[67]

Education London, King's College London & LSE 2012); End Prostitution and Child Trafficking (ECPAT), 'Protecting Children from Online Sexual Exploitation' (2016), 4.

62 Fritz et al. note that 45 per cent of Pornhub and 35 per cent of Xvideo.com scenes, two popular platforms globally, contained at least one act of physical aggression – the most common of which were spanking, slapping and gagging – and that 'women were the target of nearly 97% of all physically aggressive acts in the samples from both sites': Niki Fritz et al., 'A Descriptive Analysis of the Types, Targets, and Relative Frequency of Aggression in Mainstream Pornography' (2020) 49 *Archives of Sexual Behaviour* 3041, 3046, 3047. *La Presse* observes that violent and degrading material against women and girls is still omnipresent on Pornhub, and even recommended via algorithms to its users: Tristan Péloquin, 'Pornographie: Une sorte d'éducation au viol' (A Kind of Education in Rape) (10 June 2023). www.lapresse.ca/actualites/2023-06-10/pornographie/une-sorte-d-education-au-viol.php (accessed 13 July 2023).

63 Himani Adarsh and Swapnajeet Sahoo, 'Pornography and Its Impact on Adolescent/Teenage Sexuality' (2023) 5 *Journal of Psychosexual Health* 35, 37. See also Michael Flood, 'The Harms of Pornography Exposure among Children and Young People' (2009) 18 *Child Abuse Review* 384.

64 Gail Dines, 'Growing Up with Porn: The Developmental and Societal Impact of Pornography on Children' (2017) 2 *Dignity: A Journal of Analysis of Exploitation and Violence* 1, 2, 4.

65 Roxanne Harde, 'Girls and Rape Culture' (2021) 14 *Girlhood Studies* vii; Sophie Maddocks, 'Feminism, Activism and Non-Consensual Pornography: Analyzing Efforts to End "Revenge Porn" in the United States' (2022) 7 *Feminist Media Studies* 1641.

66 UNICEF, 'A Familiar Face – Violence in the Lives of Children and Adolescents' (2017), 7.

67 'HRs for Girls' (2014), 490.

This culture of violence against girls also permeates elite boarding schools, where girls belonging to a privileged social class are victimized by their male peers, and is pursued in higher education, as demonstrated by numerous sexual assault cases reported in universities, including Ivy League universities in North America.[68] Finally, sexualized social and dress codes increase the demand for sex trafficking and child pornography of girl children: sex trafficking of girls currently represents 16 per cent of all forms of human trafficking worldwide, and 72 per cent of trafficked girls are sold for sex trafficking.[69] Hence, the single infringement of girls' rights – sexualized social and dress codes – leads to an unending chain of violations that permeate girls across social class, race and abilities. It is thus argued that the girl child experiences a cycle of violations underpinned by sexism and childism which individually and collectively lead to or exacerbate other gender and child-related breaches of her rights. The girl child therefore experiences a triad of discrimination – sexism, childism and interactive gender and child-based discrimination – that generates a series of violations of her international human rights and fundamental freedoms. The interplay of these multiple interactions places her in a uniquely subordinate position. The semioethics analysis in the next chapters therefore investigates whether international treaties take into consideration this triadic discrimination.

[68] *The Independent*, 'St Paul's: Rape Trial "Reveals Culture of Sexual Conquests" at Elite Boarding School Attended by John Kerry' (19 August 2015). www.independent.co.uk/news/world/americas/st-pauls-rape-trial-reveals-culture-of-sexual-conquests-at-elite-boarding-school-attended-by-john-kerry-10462132.html (accessed 26 June 2023); Charlene Muehlenhard et al., 'Evaluating the One-in-Five Statistic: Women's Risk of Sexual Assault While in College' (2017) 54 *Journal of Sex Research* 549; Jennifer Steinhauer and David Joachim, *The New York Times*, '55 Colleges Named in Federal Inquiry into Handling of Sexual Assault Cases' (1 May 2014). www.nytimes.com/2014/05/02/us/politics/us-lists-colleges-under-inquiry-over-sex-assault-cases.html?_r=0 (accessed 4 June 2023).

[69] UNODC, 'Global Report on Trafficking in Persons' (2020), 33, 36, 49. Sex trafficking has also been reported on online pornography platforms: Noel Titheradge and Rianna Croxford, *BBC News*, 'The Children Selling Explicit Videos on OnlyFans' (27 May 2021). www.bbc.com/news/uk-57255983 (accessed 3 July 2023); Marisa Lati, *Washington Post*, 'Pornhub Profits from Rape, Child Pornography and Sex Trafficking, Dozens of Women Allege in Lawsuit' (18 June 2021). www.washingtonpost.com/business/2021/06/18/pornhub-lawsuit-rape-child-porn-sex-trafficking/ (accessed 3 June 2023); 'GirlsDoPorn Criminal Charges' (2020); Nicholas Kristof, 'Opinion: The Children of Pornhub' *The New York Times* (4 December 2020). www.nytimes.com/2020/12/04/opinion/sunday/pornhub-rape-trafficking.html (accessed 16 May 2023). See also Grazia Giammarinaro, Special Rapporteur on Trafficking in Persons, Especially Women and Children, 'Report' (6 April 2020) UN Doc A/HRC/44/45; Mama Fatima Singhateh, Special Rapporteur on the Sale and Sexual Exploitation of Children, Including Child Prostitution, Child Pornography and Other Child Sexual Abuse Material, 'Impact of Coronavirus Disease on Different Manifestations of Sale and Sexual Exploitation of Children' (22 January 2021) UN Doc A/HRC/46/31.

# 5

# Identification of the Girl Child in the Convention on the Rights of the Child

Although the international legal framework does not define the girl child, it offers an official description of the term 'child' in the CRC: 'a child means every human being below the age of eighteen years unless under the law applicable to the child, majority is attained earlier'.[1] This definition is characterized by its silence as concerns the girl child, and the absence of specific boundaries for the beginning and the end of girlhood. This chapter shall conduct a semiotic examination of the identification of girlhood under the CRC by applying Welby's Meaning Triad to decode 1) the *sense* or textual meaning of provisions, 2) the *meaning-intention* of the CRC drafters or 'master signifiers' and 3) the ultimate *significance* of the terminology adopted in these provisions for girls globally.[2]

## I SENSE

The CRC employs the expression 'child', which is gender-neutral, and uses both masculine and feminine pronouns and possessive adjectives, thereby encompassing girls and boys.[3] Accordingly, the girl child appears protected under the Convention. However, the CRC does not refer to the girl child in the definition of child nor in any provision. The silence as to the girl child in the CRC constitutes a sign or symbol in itself. A semiotic analysis must consider not only the actual *existing* signs but also, equally significant, the *absence* of signs in a given context. Silence is considered in terms of textual

[1] CRC, art. 1.

[2] The beginning and the end of girlhood shall be explored in Chapters 6 and 7, respectively.

[3] See Chapter 2, Section I: Recognition of the Girl Child under International Law. The adjective 'gender-neutral' is defined as 'suitable for, applicable to, or common to both males and females': OED.

silence, as in treaties and treaty body documents, as well as silence by action and inaction, silence in speech and the issue of acquiescence or objection.[4] Welby dedicated significant research to the *significs of silence* in communication, noting that silence often is not less significant than words themselves 'for whether positive or negative, excessive or deficient, present or absent even, our words are of moment always'.[5] In international law, master signifiers spend decades negotiating the terms employed in provisions, and equally important, those that *shall not be included* in the semiotic space that constitutes the treaty. The absence of a given expression constitutes a sign as significant as the presence of other terms in the treaty. In relation to feminist legal theory, Waring observes that 'one of the tricks of the questions of gender and international law is to hear what is in the silence, because international law and the law of human rights concerning gender is about silences. That is what we are listening for'.[6] It is argued that the absence of any reference to the girl child in the CRC, which is the main instrument protecting child rights, constitutes an important sign that should not be ignored, for it provides an indication of her current subordinate status under international law. As noted by Sohoni: '[c]hildhood is politically mute and girlhood is culturally mute, as well. It is this veil of silence that needs to be lifted if any corrective affirmative action is to occur'.[7] This silence is compounded by the Convention's systematic use of masculine pronouns and possessive adjectives *before* their feminine counterparts.[8] Indeed, such an order of appearance throughout the CRC is problematic for it could be interpreted as signifying that the Convention prioritizes the boy child. Of particular concern is the precedence of masculine pronouns and possessive adjectives in provisions significant to the girl child, notably those enshrining three of the four general principles of the Convention, namely 1) non-discrimination, 2) the best interests of the child and 3) the right to participation.[9] Moreover, it is worthy of note that contrarily

4 The author wishes to thank fellow speakers at the International Roundtable for the Semiotics of Law at the KU Leuven Law Faculty (2021), including Jan Broekman, Frank Fleerackers and Larry Catà Backer, for insightful explorations of the various forms of silence unveiled by legal semiotics.

5 *Significs and Language* (1911), 40.

6 Marilyn Waring, 'Gender and International Law: Women and the Right to Development' (1989) 12 *Australian Yearbook of International Law* 177, 178.

7 *Burden Girlhood* (1995), viii.

8 CRC, preamble, arts. 2, 3, 7, 8, 9, 10, 12, 14, 16, 17, 20, 22, 23, 24, 25, 29, 30, 37, 40. See Chapter 2.

9 CRC, art. 2(1): 'discrimination of any kind, irrespective of the child's or *his or her* parent's'; art. 3(2): 'States Parties undertake to ensure the child such protection and care as is necessary for *his or her* well-being'; art. 12(1): 'the child who is capable of forming *his or her* own views' (emphasis added).

to other treaties, such as the ICCPR and ICESCR, that enshrine a provision protecting equality of rights between men and women,[10] the CRC does not dedicate an article to the equality of rights between boys and girls. Article 2 of the CRC prohibits discrimination between children, notably on the grounds of 'sex':

> Art 2(1) States Parties shall respect and ensure the rights set forth in the present Convention *to each child* within their jurisdiction without discrimination of any kind, irrespective of the child's ... race, colour, *sex*, language, religion, political or other opinion, national, ethnic or social origin, property, disability, birth or other status.[11]

Yet one can observe that sex is mentioned among a long list of prohibited grounds, including language, religion, property and disability, and appears third, after race and colour, thus in a less prominent manner than within article 3 of the Twin Covenants. Accordingly, 'women' are more visible in the Twin Covenants than 'girls' in the CRC. This is especially notable given that the CRC dedicates special provisions to protect certain groups of children, such as children with disabilities and refugee children,[12] which begs the question as to why it is silent regarding the girl child. The invisibility of the girl child is further exacerbated by the CRC's failure to refer to important issues that are either specific to or predominantly affect her, such as feminicide, FGM and child marriage.[13] In this regard, Askari notes that '[t]he gender-neutral language of international law translates to gender bias in practice'.[14]

## II MEANING

The *travaux préparatoires* reveal that the girl child was overlooked during the drafting of the CRC.[15] A proposal to take the situation of the girl child into

[10] ICCPR, art. 3: '[t]he States Parties to the present Covenant undertake to ensure the equal right of men and women to the enjoyment of all civil and political rights set forth in the present Covenant'; ICESCR, art. 3: '[t]he States Parties to the present Covenant undertake to ensure the equal right of men and women to the enjoyment of all economic, social and cultural rights set forth in the present Covenant'.

[11] Emphasis added.

[12] CRC, arts. 23 (children with disabilities) and 22 (refugee children).

[13] For an examination of the CRC's failure to refer to female infanticide and gendercide, see 'Gendercide CRC' (2018).

[14] 'Jus Cogens' (1998), 13.

[15] *Travaux préparatoires CRC* (1992); 'History CRC' (2007). It is worthy of note that some drafters proposed to add a 'glossary' of the terms employed in the Convention, arguing that it would be 'of great help for a correct understanding of the legal and practical effects of its

account and expand her rights was made too late in the process to be incorporated in the Convention.[16] Lopatka however notes that in the earlier stages, when the Commission on Human Rights shared the first Polish draft with member states and international and non-governmental institutions, '[t]he need to guarantee the equal rights of girls was also strongly emphasized'.[17] In addition, participants of the European Conference on the Rights of the Child in Warsaw (1979) underscored the importance of ensuring equal education for girls:

> Where it has not yet been realized both in law and in fact, priority should be given, within the available resources, to *equating education for girls and women* with that of boys and men, in all fields and at all levels.[18]

Moreover, during the drafting of the preamble, the International Planned Parenthood Federation suggested to add the following paragraphs expressly protecting girls:

> Protection of the educational rights of adolescent girls: 'Adhering to the principle that the right to education should be fully realized on the basis of equal opportunity and correspondingly that *girls should not suffer discrimination* as a result of marriage, pregnancy and/or exigencies of childcare'.
>
> Compensation for the *historical priority given to the rights of boys*: 'Recognizing that the health risks confronting girls demand that emphasis be placed on protecting their rights comparable to the *priority historically and universally awarded the rights of young males*'.[19]

Shortly thereafter, during the technical review, UNESCO criticized the silence in the CRC concerning equality between girls and boys:

> It seems to us that among the many positive principles and values conducive to the child's development, as included in the text, *the principle of equality is largely ignored*. It is particularly essential when it comes to *equal treatment of boys and girls within and outside of the family*. Since much of the later discrimination of girls can be traced back to their unequal treatment in early

provisions', which is aligned with Welby's recommendation and which we adopt in this book under our Meaning Glossary: see 'History CRC' (2007), 166.

16 'Jus Cogens' (1998), 14.

17 Adam Lopatka, OHCHR, 'History CRC' (2007), xxxviii: thus, before the second amended version in 1979.

18 Statement of Principles on the Legal Protection of the Rights of the Child, principle 8 (23 February 1979) UN Doc E/CN.4/L.1428 (emphasis added).

19 UN Doc E/CN.4/1988/WG.1/WP.2, 4, 6 (emphasis added); 'History CRC' (2007), 288.

> years, it is suggested that the element of equality *be inserted into the Preamble as their basic right.*[20]

These statements and proposals are notable on two grounds. Firstly, they demonstrate an awareness of the unique predicament of girl children. Secondly, they imply a *meaning-intention* to expressly address the discrimination experienced by girls in relation to boys, including in exercising their rights to health and education. Most notably, UNESCO recommended to enshrine the equal treatment of girls in the very preamble of the CRC, and thus as an interpretative principle of the Convention.[21] It is nevertheless worthy of note that these proposals mostly came from agencies rather than state representatives or members of the drafting committee and were not adopted. The United States did suggest to add 'the equal rights of men and women' in the preamble, based on the second preambular paragraph of the UN Charter, yet other representatives considered it 'unnecessary', arguing that 'the reference to the dignity and worth of the human person in the original text [was] sufficient'.[22] UNESCO nonetheless successfully recommended to remove the word 'brotherhood' which was present in the preambular paragraph of the revised Polish draft:

> Considering that the child should be fully prepared to live an individual life in society, and brought up in the spirit of the ideals proclaimed in the Charter of the United Nations, and in particular in the spirit of peace, dignity, tolerance, freedom and *brotherhood.*[23]

It suggested to replace 'brotherhood' with 'equality and solidarity' in the revised sentence 'and in particular in the spirit of peace, dignity, tolerance, freedom, *equality and solidarity*'; indeed the expression 'brotherhood' could be interpreted as *exclusive* of girls.[24] The situation of girl children was also emphasized during the drafting of other provisions. For example, when examining States parties' duty under article 24 on the right to health to 'develop the system of health protection so that medical assistance and care shall be open to all children', the International Federation of Women in Legal Careers suggested to add the sentence: 'to all children without any form of discrimination,

20 UN Doc E/CN.4/1989/WG.1/CRP.1, 10–12 (emphasis added); 'History CRC' (2007), 290–91.

21 UN Doc E/CN.4/1989/WG.1/CRP.1, 10–12; 'History CRC' (2007), 290–91.; Vienna Convention (1969), arts. 31 and 32; see Chapter 1.

22 Report of the Working Group, UN Doc E/CN.4/1347, para. 244 (1979); 'History CRC' (2007), 282.

23 UN Doc E/CN.4/1349 (emphasis added); 'History CRC' (2007), 284.

24 UN Doc E/CN.4/1989/WG.1/CRP.1, 10–12 (emphasis added); 'History CRC' (2007), 290–91.

*particularly discrimination based on sex*'.[25] This proposal was especially relevant given that girls still receive less healthcare than boys globally.[26] Additionally, during the drafting of article 19 on protective measures for children, the Branch for the Advancement of Women emphasized the unique violence experienced by girls and women within the private sphere:

> *[T]he abuse* (physical and sexual) *perpetrated by males* (father, brother) *against girls and young women*, who, for obvious reasons do not denounce such facts, has been an expanded practice *within the family*.[27]

It thereby recommended to add the phrase 'including when necessary removing a child into protective custody'.[28] This proposal was pertinent as it acknowledged the issue of the public/private divide and the intersectional discrimination experienced by girls within the private sphere.

### 1 *Discrimination and Androcentric Wording*

It is worthy of note that the CRC initially adopted an androcentric approach for it exclusively employed masculine pronouns and possessive adjectives, as is the case in the International Bill of Rights. The first draft of the definition of child employed the gender-specific masculine pronouns and possessive adjectives 'he' and 'his':

> According to the present Convention a child is every human being from the moment of *his* birth to the age of 18 years unless, under the law of *his* state, *he* has attained *his* age of majority earlier.[29]

New Zealand criticized this approach and proposed the term 'child' instead to prevent the CRC from 'perpetuating sex-role stereotyping':

> [W]hile we recognize the claims of customary international legal usage, we would prefer that the use of 'his' throughout the text of the draft convention be replaced by 'the child', or by the plural 'children'. It would be unwise for a convention of this type to be open to criticisms of *perpetuating sex-role stereotyping*.[30]

As for article 2 enshrining the principle of non-discrimination, the then article 1 of the first Polish draft already mentioned 'sex' in third position, after race

25 UN Doc E/CN.4/1984/WG.1/WP.4 (emphasis added); 'History CRC' (2007), 585.
26 See Chapters 3 and 4.
27 UN Doc E/CN.4/1989/WG.1/CRP.1, 25 (emphasis added); 'History CRC' (2007), 520.
28 Ibid.
29 *Travaux préparatoires* CRC (1992), 115 (emphasis added).
30 UN Doc E/CN.4/1324/Add.5 (emphasis added); 'History CRC' (2007), 660.

and colour, followed by a long list of prohibited grounds, and moreover employed notable androcentric phrasing:

> Article 1: Every child, without any exception whatsoever, shall be entitled to the rights set forth in this Convention, without distinction or discrimination on account of race, colour, sex, language, religion, political or other opinion, national or social origin, property, birth or other status, *whether of himself or of his* family.[31]

Moreover, the then article X solely referred to racial and religious discrimination, not that based on sex, and employed androcentric phrasing:

> Article X: The child shall be protected from practices which may foster racial, religious or any other form of discrimination. *He* shall be brought up in a spirit of understanding, tolerance, friendship among peoples, peace and universal *brotherhood*, and in full consciousness that *his* energy and talents should be devoted to the service of *his* fellow *men*.[32]

In this regard, New Zealand recommended that:

> discrimination on the grounds of sex be specifically stated in the first sentence of article X. *Practices fostering discrimination on the basis of sex are often unrecognized* and it is necessary to emphasize that sex is as much a ground for discrimination as race and religion so that sex discrimination can be recognized and steps taken towards elimination.[33]

New Zealand thus acknowledged the importance of featuring sex as a prohibited ground of discrimination and ensuring it is not secondary to other forms of discrimination, such as those based on race or religion. The Food and Agriculture Organization (FAO) stressed that the CRC should comprise provisions to prevent discrimination against female children concerning food and education.[34] It is noteworthy that the FAO referred to 'female children' even though the international community had been using the term 'girl' for decades. Norway recommended the use of the noun 'child' in its plural form throughout the convention, noting that 'by the use of "children" and, consequently, "they", "them" and "their", the terms "he", "whom" and "his" could be avoided, and the equal status of the two sexes would appear more clearly'.[35] In 1979, some representatives underscored that the Convention should deal

[31] UN Doc E/CN.4/1292, 124–25 (emphasis added); 'History CRC' (2007), 314.
[32] Ibid. (emphasis added).
[33] UN Doc E/CN.4/1324/Add.5 (emphasis added); 'History CRC' (2007), 318.
[34] UN Doc E/CN.4/1989/WG.1/CRP.1, 8; 'History CRC' (2007), 331.
[35] (27 December 1978) UN Doc E/CN.4/1324; 'History CRC' (2007), 60.

with children as a group and that this aspect would be emphasized by using the term 'children' throughout the Convention 'so there would be no discrimination between sexes'.[36] In 1984, the Australian representative stated that her government 'would propose *the removal of all sexist language* from the current draft of the convention – a reflection of her delegation's concern that the rights incorporated should apply equally to every child in every society'.[37] The issue of androcentrism in international documents was expressly raised at the 1987 UNESCO general conference by certain states such as Nordic countries and Canada, two years before the adoption of the CRC, and the UN thereafter adopted a resolution inviting the director-general to:

> adopt a policy related to the drafting of all the Organization's working documents aimed at avoiding, to the extent possible, the use of language which refers explicitly or implicitly to only one sex except where positive measures are being considered.[38]

The working group of the CRC, after the first reading of the Convention, requested the UN Secretariat to conduct a technical review of the draft to ensure consistency in the text concerning the use of key terms and gender-neutral language, as well as between different language versions.[39] For example, the drafters noted that it was necessary to 'take care that the language utilized did not imply any kind of discrimination, as certain forms of expression that could, in English, exclude women from the provisions of the draft convention'.[40] During this period, many experts and UN agencies provided recommendations, and expressly endorsed gender-neutral language.[41] For example, UNESCO remarked that 'insufficient attention has as yet been accorded in this text to the need for gender-neutral language'.[42] UNICEF suggested either the use of both the masculine and feminine pronouns, the use of the plural, omission of the pronouns, or repetition of the noun, and also considered the impersonal pronoun 'its', yet observed that:

> it is grammatically incorrect to use an impersonal pronoun to refer to something possessed by a person as opposed to a thing. In addition, it is not

36 (12 March 1979) UN Doc E/CN.4/L.1468; 'History CRC' (2007), 69.

37 (26 March 1985) UN Doc E/CN.4/1985/SR.53/Add.1, para. 120 (emphasis added); 'History CRC' (2007), 131.

38 UNESCO, 'Guidelines on Gender-Neutral Language' (1999), 4–5; Resolution 24/C 14.1.

39 (15 October 1988) UN Doc E/CN.4/1989/WG.1/CRP.1; 'History CRC' (2007), 187.

40 (6 April 1988) UN Doc E/CN.4/1988/28; 'History CRC' (2007), 167.

41 Such as UNESCO, UNICEF, ILO, FAO; 'History CRC' (2007), 188.

42 (15 October 1988) UN Doc E/CN.4/1989/WG.1/CRP.1; 'History CRC' (2007), 188.

> common usage, not commonly used in legislative drafting, and, arguably, is *demeaning or even dehumanizing*.[43]

It is worthy of note that the representatives of UNICEF conducted a 'semiotic' examination of the possessive pronoun 'its', demonstrating their awareness of the significance of words, and even pronouns, on the conceptions of childhood and the realization of child rights. Finally, the working group concluded that 'it would appear that the use of both the masculine and the feminine pronouns is best suited to achieve this purpose [gender-neutral language]',[44] and adopted a gender-neutral approach.[45] It recommended that 'the words "he", "him", or "his", wherever they appear in the text, be immediately followed by the words "or she", or "or her", as appropriate. Similarly, the word "its" may be replaced by "his or her"'.[46] However, the *travaux* do not shed light on the *meaning-intention* behind the decision to systematically employ the masculine before the feminine pronoun, which regrettably reproduces the precedence attributed to males in androcentric language.

## 2 *Unique Violations*

It is worthy of note that in contrast with the CEDAW, the CRC drafters chose not to refer to specific violations experienced by girl children, and moreover, solely discussed the issue of FGM in this context. During the drafting of article 24 on the right to health, the issue of traditional practices was raised by several state representatives. The first draft of then article IV originally did not mention traditional practices, and read as follows:

> The child shall enjoy the benefits of social security. He shall be entitled to grow and develop in health; to this end, special care and protection shall be provided both to him and to his mother, including adequate prenatal and post-natal care. The child shall have the right to adequate nutrition, housing, recreation and medical services.[47]

43 Ibid. (emphasis added).

44 (14 November 1988) UN Doc E/CN.4/1989/WG.1/CRPD.1/Add.1; 'History CRC' (2007), 192.

45 *Travaux préparatoires CRC* (1992), 138. See for example art. 3 of the CRC on the best interests of the child: '[t]he Working Group had before it a text (contained in document E/CN.4/1989/WG.1/WP.2) of the paragraph as adopted during the first reading incorporating suggested revisions on gender-neutral language'.

46 (14 November 1988) UN Doc E/CN.4/1989/WG.1/CRPD.1/Add.1; 'History CRC' (2007), 192.

47 UN Doc E/CN.4/1292, 124; 'History CRC' (2007), 580.

When commenting on the first Polish draft, Sweden noted:

> Medical attention and care as well as a healthy physical environment are important prerequisites for the sound development of the child. These matters should be developed in a more elaborate way than in principle 4 of the 1959 Declaration. It is important, for instance, to prevent children from being subjected to *practices which involve physical abuse and affect their present and future health or well-being.*[48]

The International Federation of Women in Legal Careers thereafter suggested a new article on the sources of damage to children's health, including 'traditional practices affecting health', and expressly pertaining to FGM:

> To adopt clearly defined national policies for the abolition of the *sexual mutilation of female babies and children* ... so as to inform public and practitioners alike of the *multiple dangers of such practices* for the children's *physical and mental health.*[49]

One can observe that the federation recognized both the physical and the psychological and emotional damages of FGM on girl children. Yet in 1985, the NGO Group suggested the broader terminology 'traditional practices harmful to their health':

> The States Parties to the present Convention shall undertake to protect children from any medical investigation or treatment detrimental to their physical or psychological health and development, and to take all appropriate and necessary measures to prevent children being subjected to *traditional practices harmful to their health.*[50]

The NGO Group thus chose not to refer specifically to sexual mutilation, nor to violations specific to girls. The following year, Rädda Barnen, on behalf of the informal NGO Group, suggested similar terminology:

> The States Parties to the present Convention shall seek to eradicate *traditional practices harmful to the health* of children and shall take all appropriate action including necessary legislative, administrative, social and educational measures to ensure that children are not subjected to such practices.[51]

When this proposal was thereafter discussed, two approaches were considered. On the one hand, the United Kingdom warned that 'the concept of traditional

[48] UN Doc E/CN.4/1324 (emphasis added); 'History CRC' (2007), 582.
[49] UN Doc E/CN.4/1984/WG.1/WP.4 (emphasis added); 'History CRC' (2007), 586.
[50] UN Doc E/CN.4/1985/WG.1/WP.1 (emphasis added); 'History CRC' (2007), 587.
[51] UN Doc E/CN.4/1986/39, paras. 50–51; 'History CRC' (2007), 592.

practices might possibly be interpreted more widely than the authors intended', and thus recommended that the wording be tightened to clarify the intention. It also questioned whether the expression 'traditional practices harmful to the health of children' actually meant 'female circumcision'.[52] It is worthy of note that the United Kingdom acknowledged the importance of clarifying the *meaning-intention* behind traditional practices in this context. On the other hand, Senegal systematically pushed to ensure FGM would not be expressly mentioned in the provision. Senegal firstly resorted to cultural relativism and 'counselled prudence when dealing with issues that entailed differences in cultural values, and emphasized the dangers of forcing practices into clandestinity if they were prohibited by State legislation'.[53] The Canadian representative proposed a compromise by adding 'seriously' before 'harmful':

> [W]hile the comments of the representative of Senegal should be taken very seriously, she wondered whether some of his concerns and those of the United Kingdom delegation might be met by the following changes to the tabled proposal: to add 'seriously' before 'harmful', 'by all appropriate means', after 'seek' ... and 'including female circumcision' after 'traditional practices' to give some clear content to the draft article.[54]

Australia supported this suggestion. Senegal offered another wording that still failed to mention FGM or practices concerning girls:

> The States Parties to the present Convention shall seek, as far as possible, to take effective and appropriate measures to combat traditional practices that affect the health of children.[55]

Canada considered that the word 'affect' was too weak and proposed it be replaced with 'seriously harm'; it also recommended that the word 'seek' be replaced with 'more forceful language'. While Senegal insisted on keeping the term 'affect', Australia suggested to add 'adversely affecting', and France proposed 'prejudicial', which was approved by Senegal.[56] Numerous state representatives insisted on expressly mentioning FGM. The Italian representative, referring to the 1985 Nairobi World Conference, underscored the seriousness of FGM:

> [F]emale circumcision was practiced on children without their consent, often in unsanitary circumstances and caused great suffering. She recognized

[52] UN Doc E/CN.4/1987/25, paras. 28–39; 'History CRC' (2007), 592.
[53] UN Doc E/CN.4/1987/25, paras. 28–39; 'History CRC' (2007), 592.
[54] UN Doc E/CN.4/1987/25, paras. 28–39; 'History CRC' (2007), 593.
[55] UN Doc E/CN.4/1987/25, paras. 28–39; 'History CRC' (2007), 593.
[56] Ibid.

> the importance of plurality of cultures but nevertheless appealed for changes in attitudes which would eliminate this problem.[57]

The United Kingdom and the United States both insisted that the concept of female circumcision be added at the end of the proposal: the United Kingdom proposed 'in particular, female circumcision', and the United States 'including, for example, female circumcision'. The strength of both proposals is that they provided a non-exhaustive list of references to harmful traditional practices, thereby allowing other violations, such as female infanticide and child marriage, to be prohibited under article 24. The US representative underscored the *meaning-intention* behind this proposal:

> [T]he amendment was designed to ensure that the Group would *explicitly address* the traditional practice of greatest concern and *would give greater content* to the phrase 'traditional practices'; in addition, he argued that adding this phrase would demonstrate that the practices to be abolished were those of a *serious nature*.[58]

Contrarily, siding with Senegal, the International Movement for Fraternal Union Among Races and Peoples rejected specific references to FGM, noting that 'there were other "traditional practices" which were also harmful such as preferential care, including feeding, for male children'.[59] This comment was in fact very pertinent and begs the question as to why the drafters did not elect to list more practices in this provision, following the Fraternal Union's point. As noted by Askari: '[o]ther harmful traditional practices [than FGM], such as son preference and female infanticide, detrimental to the life and health of girls, were not even discussed in the drafting process'.[60] The representative of Senegal read an amended proposal as follows:

> The States Parties to the present Convention shall seek to take all effective and appropriate measures with a view to abolishing *traditional practices that affect the health* of children.[61]

Canada agreed with this suggestion on the understanding that 'the term traditional practices included all those practices outlined in the 1986 report of the Working Group on Traditional Practices affecting the Health of Women and Children'.[62] It is however unfortunate that Canada failed to

57 Ibid.
58 Ibid. (emphasis added).
59 Ibid.
60 'Jus Cogens' (1998), 14.
61 UN Doc E/CN.4/1987/25, paras. 28–39; 'History CRC' (2007), 593 (emphasis added).
62 UN Doc E/CN.4/1987/25, paras. 28–39; 'History CRC' (2007), 594.

specifically mention the practices in question. The report of the working group on traditional practices affecting the health of women and children does refer to a broad list of practices, including:

> female circumcision, other forms of mutilation (facial scarification), forced feeding of women, early marriage, the various taboos or practices which prevent women from controlling their own fertility, nutritional taboos and traditional birth practices.[63]

The report also referred to 'dowries in certain regions of the world, crimes of honour and the consequences of preferential treatment for male children',[64] and gave priority consideration to 1) female circumcision, 2) traditional birth practices and 3) preferential treatment for male children.[65] The Working Group on Traditional Practices Affecting the Health of Women and Children expressly mentioned that it did not intend to solely focus on FGM.[66] Canada's broader interpretation of traditional practices as per the working group was supported by Japan, Sweden and Venezuela.[67] Moreover, the Netherlands insisted on keeping the US proposal that expressly referred to 'female circumcision'. Yet the Senegalese representative 'stated his objection to such a wording being introduced into the text of the provision'. Finally, the working group adopted the proposal from Senegal, while replacing 'that affect' with 'prejudicial'.[68] This thorough negotiation is very instructive from a semiotic perspective. The delegates clearly understood the significance of the words *present* in the provision, and those who wished to keep the expression 'female circumcision' underscored the importance of naming this violation of girls' rights. The United States noted that such wording would recognize that FGM is a practice of a 'serious nature'. Equally important is the representative of Senegal's reluctance to name FGM, and the arguments he put forward as well as the many amended proposals he brought forth that shared a common feature: the *absence* of the term FGM. Another interesting element is that the two sides of the argument appeared to be, on the one hand, numerous states, primarily from the Global North, notably Australia, Canada, Italy, Japan, Sweden, Venezuela and the Netherlands, and powerful nations at the time, such as the United States and the United Kingdom, whereas on the other hand, the only nation formally opposing any reference to FGM was

63 (4 February 1986) UN Doc E/CN.4/1986/42, para. 18.
64 Ibid.
65 Ibid., para. 22.
66 Ibid., para. 16.
67 UN Doc E/CN.4/1987/25, paras. 28–39; 'History CRC' (2007), 594.
68 UN Doc E/CN.4/1987/25, paras. 28–39; 'History CRC' (2007), 594.

Senegal, and yet the latter nevertheless emerged victorious. Although the Fraternal Union's point supported Senegal in not mentioning FGM, the Union's legitimate concern that the provision emphasized only one violation and thereby obscured others, could have been addressed by naming other prejudicial practices. For example, Canada's suggestion to refer to the Nairobi Conference could have been applied to list a series of violations. It is also pertinent to mention that during the 1988 session of the Working Group on Slavery, a suggestion was made 'that the concept of "mutilation" should be included as one of the practices that ought to be specifically forbidden and that an express prohibition of the use of children for medical experimentation should also be included in the draft convention', which would have further supported the addition of FGM as a prohibited practice in the Convention.[69] Moreover, near the end of the drafting, Mrs Warzazi, a renowned expert who served both in the Working Group on Traditional Practices Affecting the Health of Women and Children, and as Special Rapporteur on Traditional Practices Affecting the Health of Women and the Girl Child, noted that '[t]he physical and psychological health of millions of girls were threatened by traditional practices which Governments should do everything possible to eliminate',[70] thereby underscoring the plight of girls and the seriousness of the abovementioned practices. She was moreover a representative of Morocco, a Global South nation, and thus not perceived as western or biased in this context. This begs the question as to why, during the drafting of the CRC, Global North and powerful nations relinquished their proposal to expressly name FGM and accepted that of a single, Global South nation – Senegal. This could be explained by the drafting procedure of the CRC whereby decisions were taken by consensus rather than voted upon. Accordingly, the wording of provisions had to be agreed upon by all members, and a single delegate could significantly slow down the process, while certain proposals were abandoned altogether, even when supported by a significant majority.[71] Or it could be that Senegal's argumentation was persuasive, including in light of cultural relativism. Rao's culture test applies interestingly to the Senegalese representative's argumentation who spoke on behalf of a

69 UN Doc E/CN.4/1989/WG.1/CRP.1, 10; 'History CRC' (2007), 598.

70 (15 November 1989) UN Doc A/C.3/44/SR.37; 'History CRC' (2007), 244. See for example, (4 February 1986) UN Doc E/CN.4/1986/42, para. 6; Halima Embarek Warzazi, UN Special Rapporteur on Traditional Practices affecting the Health of Women and the Girl Child, 'Ninth and Final Report on the Situation Regarding the Elimination of Traditional Practices Affecting the Health of Women and the Girl Child'(11 July 2005) UN Doc E/CN.4/Sub.2/2005/36.

71 'Origins CRC' (1992), 22.

community about a practice that impacted girls. Perhaps this decision raises the question of whether discussions occurred outside formal meetings that were accordingly not included in the *travaux*. Was Senegal actually voicing the opinion of other states, or even, other Global North nations? Were some compromises agreed upon concerning other provisions of the CRC of greater concern to the abovementioned nations, whereby the issue of girls and FGM would be sacrificed on the altar of other priorities? At this point, we are entering the realm of conjectures, yet this negotiation certainly constitutes a unique outcome from an international relations and international law perspective. Finally, an interesting observation is that the drafters chose to refer to 'traditional practices' mostly stemming from the Global South, rather than all harmful practices specific to girls and boys, thereby neglecting those originating in the Global North, such as sexualized social and dress codes, which were already present in the 1980s through advertisement, television, films, fashion shows and beauty pageants. Perhaps had this inclusive and comprehensive approach been adopted, the drafters might have agreed to expressly mention other specific violations, such as FGM. The outcome is that none of the infringements specific to girls were expressly prohibited. Askari offers insight into the drafters' possible *meaning-intention* stemming from an overall lack of familiarity and concern for issues specific to girl children:

> This oversight regarding inclusion of rights particular to girls, signifies a lack of familiarity, appreciation and sensitivity by the drafters to the wide spectrum of human rights violations suffered only by girls'.[72]

In this context, Welby's explanation that '[s]ilence is often a most significant declaration, and a most misleading one',[73] is appropriate to describe the *meaning-intention* behind the CRC master signifiers: a combination of indifference and an actual desire, by some, to remove any reference to violations predominantly or exclusively experienced by the girl child.

## III SIGNIFICANCE

The absence of any reference to the girl child in the CRC is problematic in terms of protection, monitoring and implementation. Yet before delving into a semiotic examination of the significance of textual signs in the Convention, it is important to make a clarification. Many scholars in the field of child rights tend to adopt an interpretative approach to treaty provisions that favours an

[72] 'Jus Cogens' (1998), 14–15.
[73] *Significs and Language* (1911), 41.

increased protection of rights bearers, for example by referring to legal doctrine or treaty body general comments produced to strengthen state obligations. And many of these scholars come from an Anglo-Saxon and Global North background, and cite one another in an infinite semiosis that further propels their perception.[74] The present book instead explores all the ramifications of signs, including at their extreme limits, and refers for this purpose to scholars and experts from various regions and cultures globally, and states' views that represent different regions, cultures and beliefs.

### 1 *Silence and the Immediate, Dynamical and Final Interpretants*

The significance of a sign in Welby's Meaning Triad can be paralleled to Peirce's 'final interpretant', that is, the sign as it appears at the extreme limits of its interpretative possibilities.[75] Peirce, in a letter to Welby in which he underscored the connections between his 'immediate-dynamical and final interpretant' Triad and Welby's Meaning Triad, argued that in both cases, the third level underscores the creative potentialities of signs and the effect the sign may produce in diverse contexts.[76] Hence, a single sign may be interpreted differently, especially at its extreme limits, and the silence concerning the girl child in the Convention may reinforce States parties' failure to protect her rights.[77] In this perspective, it is argued that since sexism is prevalent worldwide,[78] the gender blind language of the CRC,[79] coupled with the

[74] See for example Tobin who acknowledges in his edited Commentary on the Convention on the Rights of the Child that 'the contributors to this collection largely come from Western Europe, North America, and Australia. This is largely due to my limited ability to travel which has meant that my contacts in children's rights have been limited to these regions. It is recognized that scholars, advocates, and policy makers from other regions – Africa, the Middle East, Latin America, Asia, and Eastern Europe – already have made and will continue to make a significant contribution to the understanding of the Convention': John Tobin, 'Introduction: The Foundation for Children's Rights', *The UN Convention on the Rights of the Child: A Commentary* (Oxford University Press 2019), 20.

[75] See Chapter 1.

[76] *Correspondence Peirce Welby* (1977), 109–10.

[77] Besson and Kleber observe the same phenomenon for child rights, noting that 'experiences with … international human rights instruments have revealed that the absence of explicit references to children's perspectives tend to make them *invisible in practice*, even when situations of vulnerability are addressed': 'Non-Discrimination' (2019), 69–70 (emphasis added). They note in this context the importance of art. 7 on children with disabilities in the CRPD, which begs the question as to why the CRC drafters did not dedicate specific provisions to girls, whereas some of its provisions focus on specific groups of children, such as children with disabilities under art. 23.

[78] See Chapter 3.

[79] 'Jus Cogens' (1998), 13.

absence of any reference to the girl child nor to issues specific to her or predominantly experienced by her, may reinforce the priority allocated to boys over girls at the domestic level. The use of gender-neutral language in a world in which boys and girls are treated equally might not appear problematic *per se*, especially since the CRC mentions neither girls nor boys. However, several States parties to the CRC do not consider that girls and women are holders of all human rights, and grant fewer rights to girls than boys at the domestic level.[80] UN human rights treaty bodies underscore that girls and women still have unequal rights under domestic law with regard to inheritance, property and land rights. The CESCR notes in its 2023 general comment that 'States should . . . monitor and regulate customary law, which in many countries has an important role in governing land, to protect the rights of women and girls who are affected by traditional inheritance rules of male primogeniture',[81] and the CEDAW Committee underscores in its 2022 general comment the discrimination of Indigenous women and girls in inheritance laws,[82] the capacity to conclude contracts[83] and the transmission of their nationality and Indigenous status to their children.[84] The UN General Assembly, in its 2022 resolution on the girl child, emphasizes that girls still experience discrimination in domestic law, and urges states to review 'remaining laws that discriminate against women and girls in order to modify or abolish them' including as concerns 'impunity for perpetrators of and ensuring the availability of appropriate penalties for crimes of sexual violence committed against the girl child'.[85] In this regard, it is worthy of note that a significant number of states entered reservations to the main international treaty promoting gender equality, the CEDAW, including provisions pertaining to 1) equality in

80 See Chapter 3; 'Women, Business, Law' (2023); 'Equality, Law, Women, Girls' (2019). See also CRC Concluding Observations Pakistan (11 July 2016) UN Doc CRC/C/PAK/CO/5, para. 18b): 'girls are entitled to only half of the inheritance provided to boys'.

81 CESCR General Comment No. 26: 'Land' (2023), para. 14; see also para. 13, footnote 12, referring to traditional practices 'depriving women of their inheritance and property rights', and to its Concluding Observations Concerning Benin (27 March 2020) UN Doc E/C.12/BEN/CO/3, Cameroon (25 March 2019) UN Doc E/C.12/CMR/CO/4, Niger (4 June 2018) UN Doc E/C.12/NER/CO/1, South Africa (29 November 2018) UN Doc E/C.12/ZAF/CO/1, and the Central African Republic (4 May 2018) UN Doc E/C.12/CAF/CO/1.

82 CEDAW General Recommendation No. 39: 'Indigenous Women and Girls' (2022), para. 21: '[i]nheritance laws – in both the State and Indigenous legal systems – frequently discriminate against Indigenous women'.

83 Ibid.: '[i]n many parts of the world, Indigenous women lack the capacity to conclude contracts and administer property independent of their husband or a male guardian'.

84 Ibid.: 'many laws still discriminate against Indigenous women and girls in relation to the transmission of their nationality and Indigenous status to their children when they marry non-Indigenous persons'.

85 UNGA Resolution 'The Girl Child' (2022), para. 21.

marriage and family relations, comprising the right to choose a family name, profession and occupation, and the right to decide on the number and spacing of children;[86] 2) freedom of movement and the right to choose a residence and domicile[87] and 3) with respect to their nationality and that of their children.[88] Many states also entered reservations to article 2, a central CEDAW provision stipulating that 'States Parties condemn discrimination against women in all its forms, agree to pursue by all appropriate means and without delay a policy of eliminating discrimination against women', and expressly concerning: 1) equality before the law, 2) the right to vote, 3) property rights and 4) the equal value of testimony for men and women, thereby unambiguously disclosing their *meaning-intention* not to grant equal

[86] CEDAW, art. 16; see for example in alphabetical order: Algeria, Bahrain, Bahamas (withdrawn 2011), Bangladesh specifically 16(1)c): 'the same rights and responsibilities during marriage and at its dissolution', Brazil (withdrawn 1994), Egypt, France specifically 'concerning the right to choose a family name' (withdrawn 2013), Iraq, Jordan notably 16(1)g): 'the same personal rights as husband and wife, including the right to choose a family name, a profession and an occupation', Kuwait specifically 16(f): 'concerning the same rights with guardianship of children', Lebanon, Luxembourg specifically art. 16(1)g): 'the Convention shall not affect the right to choose the family name of children' (withdrawn 2008), Libya, Malaysia, Maldives, Mauritania, Mauritius (withdrawn 1998), Monaco specifically art. 16(1)g): reservation 'regarding the right to choose one's surname' (withdrawn 2017), Morocco (withdrawn 2011), Niger (expressly refers to the right to 'decide freely and responsibly on the number and spacing of their children'), Oman, Qatar, Republic of Korea art. 16(1)g) – initially also c), d) and f) but withdrawn in 1991, Syrian Arab Republic, Tunisia (withdrawn 2014) – its reservation expressly referred to 'the acquisition of property through inheritance', United Arab Emirates, Switzerland (withdrawn 2013), Thailand (withdrawn 2012): 1249 UNTS 13.

[87] CEDAW art. 15(4): according 'men and women the same rights with regard to the law relating to the movement of persons and the freedom to choose their residence and domicile': Algeria, Bahrain, Brazil (withdrawn 1994), Jordan (expressly declared that 'a woman's residence and domicile are with her husband', withdrawn 2009), Morocco, Niger (only for married women), Qatar, Syrian Arab Republic (the latter expressly refers to 'freedom of movement'), Tunisia (withdrawn 2014), Turkey (withdrawn 1999) – other States parties, such as France, noted in their objections that such a reservation 'which seeks to deprive married women of the right to choose their residence and domicile, is contrary to the object and purpose of the Convention': 1249 UNTS 13. Some States parties, such as Israel, India and Singapore, chose the 'laissez-faire' or 'non-interference' approach concerning women and girls living or 'belonging' to cultural and religious communities.

[88] CEDAW art. 9 on (1) granting women equal rights with men to acquire, change or retain nationality, and (2) with respect to the nationality of their children: exclusively art. 9(2): Algeria (withdrawn 2009), Bahamas, Bahrain, Brunei and Democratic People's Republic of Korea (withdrawn 2015), Egypt (withdrawn 2008), Jamaica (withdrawn 1995), Jordan, Kuwait, Lebanon, Liechtenstein (withdrawn 1996), Monaco, Morocco (withdrawn 2011), Oman, Qatar, Republic of Korea, Saudi Arabia, Syrian Arab Public, Thailand (withdrawn 1992), Tunisia (withdrawn 2014); also concerning art. 9(1): Fiji (withdrawn 2000), Iraq (also acquiring nationality, withdrawn 2014), Malaysia (withdrawn art. 9(1), 1998), Turkey (concerning 9(1), withdrawn 2008), United Arab Emirates (also art. 9(1)).

rights to women and girls at the domestic level.[89] Some States parties expressed reservations specifically for provisions pertaining to inheritance,[90] and the betrothal of girls.[91] The CEDAW Committee recognizes the significance of these 'reservations' as problematic signs indicating States parties' *meaning-intention* to negate equal rights to women and girls under domestic law. The Committee expressed 'concern in relation to the significant number of reservations that appeared to be incompatible with the object and purpose of the Convention' and adopted two general recommendations requesting these reservations be reconsidered.[92] In his examination of reservations to the CRC, Schabas underscores that the high rate of reservations to the CEDAW was described as 'the most extreme case' compared to other human rights treaties.[93] The CEDAW Committee employed the strong terminology 'with alarm' to criticize reservations to article 16 on marriage and family relations, thus in the private sphere:

> The Committee has noted *with alarm* the number of States parties which have entered reservations to the whole or part of article 16, especially when a reservation has also been entered to article 2, claiming that compliance may

89 See for example CEDAW, art. 2: Algeria, Bahamas (concerning art. 2(a) that requires states to embody the principle of equality of men and women in legislation), Bahrain (remained after revision in 2014), Bangladesh (remained after revision in 1997), Democratic People's Republic of Korea (withdrawn 2015), Egypt, Lesotho, Micronesia (concerning 2(f) that requires states to modify customs and practices which constitute discrimination against women), Morocco, New Zealand (Cook Islands (2)f), Syrian Arab Republic, Malaysia (concerning 2(f), withdrawn 1998); art. 15(2) on the capacity to conclude contracts and administer property: Turkey (withdrawn 1999); art. 15(3) on contracts restricting the legal capacity of women (Belgium, withdrawn 2002); art. 15(2) concerning testimony and the right to conclude contracts: UAE. Moreover, Kuwait entered a reservation regarding art. 7 'in as much as the provision contained in that paragraph conflicts with the Kuwaiti Electoral Act, under which the right to be eligible for election and to vote is restricted to males'. Several member states also made broad reservations referring to domestic law and/or religious law.

90 For example, Libya expressly referred to art. 2 'relating to determination of the inheritance portions of the estate of a deceased person, whether female or male'; Niger to art. 2)d) and f) referring to 'customs and practices which constitute discrimination against women, particularly in respect of succession' and 'social and cultural patterns'; Qatar to 15(1) on equality before the law: 'in connection of matters of inheritance and testimony'; and UAE to art. 2(f) on 'the rules of inheritance'.

91 Malaysia initially entered a reservation concerning art. 16(1)a) that enshrines the same right to enter into marriage (withdrawn 1998), and to art. 16(2) which stipulates that 'the betrothal and the marriage of a child shall have no legal effect, and all necessary action, including legislation, shall be taken to specify a minimum age for marriage and to make the registration of marriages in an official registry compulsory' (withdrawn 2010). In this context, Malaysia noted that according to 'the laws of Malaysia the age of limit for marriage for women is sixteen and for men is eighteen'.

92 CEDAW General Recommendations No. 4: 'Reservations' (6th session, 1987), para. 3; No. 20: 'Reservations to the Convention' (11th session, 1992). Several States parties objected to the abovementioned reservations to the CEDAW: 1249 UNTS 13.

93 William Schabas, 'Reservations to the Convention on the Rights of the Child' (1996) 18 *Human Rights Quarterly* 472, 474.

> conflict with a commonly held vision of the family based, inter alia, on cultural or religious beliefs or on the country's economic or political status.[94]

It also expressed concern for reservations relating to equality in the public sphere, namely political rights, and required States parties to 'explain the reason for, and effect of, any reservations … and in their reports include a timetable for their removal'.[95] As for the CRC, some States parties entered reservations pertaining to article 2, which enshrines the principle of non-discrimination and lists prohibited grounds such as sex, and moreover reserved the right not to apply equal rights in marriage and inheritance.[96] Hence, one can observe that several interpretants, including CRC and CEDAW States parties, have clearly demonstrated that they do not consider girls and boys equal under the law, and the invisibility of the girl child in the CRC should therefore not be disregarded. Olsen argues that '(t)o the extent that the Convention deals with children as unspecified, unsituated people, it tends in fact to deal with white, *male*, relatively privileged children'.[97] Askari goes further by explaining that such terminology discriminates against girls:

> The gender-neutral language of international law as employed by the CRC, intended to protect boys' and girls' rights equally, in reality, discriminates

[94] CEDAW General Recommendation No. 21: 'Equality Marriage' (1994), para. 41 (emphasis added).

[95] CEDAW General Recommendation No. 23: 'Political and Public Life' (16th session, 1997), para. 44.

[96] For example, Malaysia expressed a reservation according to which art. 2 of the CRC would only be applicable if 'in conformity with the Constitution, national laws and national policies of the Government of Malaysia', and Qatar replaced a general reservation in 2009 with a reservation solely concerning two provisions, including art. 2 (non-discrimination), thereby expressly choosing to limit the implementation of the principle of non-discrimination. Moreover, Tunisia entered a reservation 'with regard to the provisions of article 2 of the convention, which may not impede implementation of the provisions of its national legislation concerning personal status, particularly in relation to marriage and inheritance rights'. This reservation, withdrawn by Tunisia in 2008, implies a meaning-intention not to recognize equality in the law between the sexes, especially given the specific reference to marriage. Also, as in the CEDAW, several CRC member states made broad reservations referring to domestic law and/or religious law, to which other member states objected: 1577 UNTS 3. For a discussion on reservations to the CRC, see Marie-Françoise Lücker-Babel, 'Les réserves à la Convention des Nations Unies relative aux droits de l'enfant et la sauvegarde de l'objet et du but du traité international'(Reservations to the UN Convention on the Rights of the Child and Safeguarding the Object and Purpose of the International Treaty) (1997) 8 *European Journal of International Law* 664; 'Réserves CDE' (2022). Schabas notes that the principle of non-discrimination has sometimes been categorized as a norm of *jus cogens* and that 'any reservation to [these norms] would be necessarily without effect': 'Reservations CRC' (1996), 480.

[97] Frances Olsen, 'Children's Rights: Some Feminist Approaches to the United Nations Convention on the Rights of the Child' (1992) 6 *International Journal of Law, Policy and the Family* 192, 195 (emphasis added).

> against girls. The use of an umbrella term such as 'child' ignores the additional special provisions that need to be made solely for girls.[98]

These authors' criticisms are still applicable today as the CRC provisions enshrining rights and fundamental freedoms have not been modified since the Convention's adoption. The gender blind language of the CRC and its silence regarding the girl child could be interpreted by States parties, communities and individuals who act as the immediate, dynamical or final interpretants – such as those that entered reservations pertaining to gender equality, and/or that discriminate against girls de jure and/or de facto under domestic law – as signifying that they are not required to grant her the same rights as boys under the Convention. Or it could be construed as meaning that States parties' duty of due diligence does not encompass the protection of the girl child against violations that are unique to or affect her significantly more than boys. Presently, several States parties fail to offer protective measures against the violence perpetrated on girls and women in domestic law, thus de jure, as their legal systems and governments may lack capacity or political will.[99] And even when such measures are adopted de jure, law enforcement is often weak – in terms of resources and training – and fails to investigate, prosecute and severely sentence perpetrators; girls are thereby not protected de facto.[100] In this regard, Askari emphasizes that the absence of specific references to violations in the CRC enables states to consider that the latter do not constitute practices prejudicial to girls, and concludes:

> The CRC's near universal ratification and the fast rate with which it went into force have served to over shadow the fact that the CRC is deficient especially in its protection of girl children. The CRC is lacking and prejudicial because it excludes certain violations which predominantly affect girls.[101]

## 2 *Implementation and Monitoring*

The invisibility of the girl child and of the issues pertaining to her in the CRC also impacts monitoring. It is reflected in CRC Committee general comments

98 'Jus Cogens' (1998), 14.

99 'Cutting Edge' (2015), 8; 'Linking Research' (2012), 150–52. See Chapter 3.

100 'HRs for Girls' (2014), 486; 'Gendercide CRC' (2018); Clara Chapdelaine-Feliciati, *Feminicides of Girl Children in the Family Context: An International Human Rights Law Approach* (2018).

101 'CRC Child Marriage' (1998), 137. Askari also provides the example of child marriage: '[u]nfortunately, because CRC article 24(3) fails to expressly mention child marriage as one of the traditional practices to which it is referring, many States Parties can choose to deny that the practice of child marriage falls under the provisions of article 24(3)': 'CRC Child Marriage' (1998), 130.

that examine children as a homogenous group and fail to study the unique condition of girl children, including with regard to issues that may impact girls differently than boys, such as the implementation of the Convention, the best interests of the child and corporal punishment.[102] Moreover, several general comments that mention the girl child or her special predicament only do so briefly, not systematically, and in some cases only in general terms.[103] While the principle of non-discrimination is usually present, intersectionality theory is mentioned in solely four out of twenty-five general comments, and sex or gender is not systematically examined.[104] Moreover, only five additional general comments refer to multiple discrimination pertaining to sex and

[102] For example, while many CRC general comments refer to girls, the following do not mention her, nor her special circumstances: 1) No. 2: 'The Role of Independent National Human Rights Institutions in the Promotion and Protection of the Rights of the Child' (15 November 2002) UN Doc CRC/GC/2002/2; 2) No. 5: 'General Measures of Implementation of the Convention on the Rights of the Child' (27 November 2003) UN Doc CRC/GC/2003/5; 3) No. 8: 'The Right of the Child to Protection from Corporal Punishment and Other Cruel or Degrading Forms of Punishment' (2 March 2007) CRC/C/GC/8; and 4) No. 14: 'The Right of the Child to Have His or Her Best Interests Taken as a Primary Consideration' (29 May 2013) CRC/C/GC/14; 5) No. 21: 'Children in Street Situations' (21 June 2017) UN Doc CRC/C/GC/21: solely mentions, in a footnote, that the quotes cited in the general comment include that of a 'girl from India'.

[103] See Chapter 2, Section III: Girl Child as a Separate Entity. For example, General Comment No. 19: 'Public Budgeting' (2016) mentions her once: 'the consultation included contributions from boys and girls', para. 8. While this general comment offers a good balance between referring to feminine and masculine pronouns and possessive adjectives (see paras. 52 and 53), it regrettably does not pay attention to issues uniquely experienced by girls in budgeting and the implementation of girl child rights at the domestic level.

[104] The Joint CEDAW-CRC GenRec/Com: 'Harmful Practices' (2014) refers expressly to gender and age, para. 6: 'sex- and gender-based discrimination intersects with other factors that affect women and girls'; para. 15: 'harmful practices … are grounded in discrimination on the basis of, among other things, sex, gender and age'; para. 55(e): 'legislation addresses … including discrimination on the basis of sex, gender, age and other intersecting factors'; as does the Joint Principles Migration No. 22 (2017), para. 16: 'data should be disaggregated by nationality … gender, age'; para. 23: 'special attention should be paid to gender-specific and any other challenges and vulnerabilities that may intersect'; and No. 21: 'Street Situations' (2017) mentions intersectionality and gender, para. 26: '[c]hildren can face multiple and intersecting forms of discrimination, for example, on the basis of gender'. However, No. 20: 'Adolescence' (2016), para. 21, mentions intersectionality without listing either sex or age. Also, No. 21: 'Street Situations' (2017) mentions 'gender' as it intersects with age, and notes that children are not a homogenous group, and are in fact diverse, including in terms of age and sex (para. 6), gender (para. 8), and recommends 'gender-sensitive responses' (para. 58) yet does not refer to 'girls', their unique needs nor explains what these gender sensitive responses entail, even though street girls' experiences are different than those of street boys, including increased sexual violence and prostitution. See for example 'Child Justice' (2007): during the author's legal clinic with street youth in Montreal, Canada, the observed survival rate of girls living on the street before becoming sex trafficked was much shorter than boys – on average two days.

age, and/or girls.[105] It is worthy of note that the CRC Committee overwhelmingly employs masculine pronouns and possessive adjectives before their feminine counterparts in its general comments, with the exception of those on 1) the right to be heard, 2) harmful practices, 3) business and 4) public budgeting.[106] Moreover, some general comments *exclusively and systematically* employ the masculine before the feminine, such as those on 1) AIDS, 2) early childhood, 3) corporal punishment, 4) Indigenous children, 5) violence, 6) the best interests of the child, 7) the right to leisure, and the Committee appears to have reinstated this approach in its more recent general comments on 8) adolescence, 9) principles of migration, 10) state obligations regarding migration and 11) child justice, which is concerning as these issues are experienced differently by girls and boys.[107] In fact, whereas the original general comment on juvenile justice employed the feminine before the masculine in some circumstances, its replacement on 'child justice' systematically refers first to the masculine before the feminine.[108] Hence, while the CRC Committee decision to employ the expression 'child justice' instead of 'juvenile justice' in its revised general comment (2019), as recommended by

[105] In addition to the abovementioned, see CRC General Comments: 1) No. 1: 'Education' (2001), para. 10; 2) No. 3: 'HIV/AIDS' (2003), para. 17: 'gender differences … may impact on the access'; 3) No. 7: 'Early Childhood' (2006), para. 11: 'young children who suffer multiple discrimination (e.g. … gender) are especially at risk'; 4) No. 9: 'Disabilities' (2007), para. 10: '[g]irls with disabilities are often even more vulnerable to discrimination due to gender discrimination'; para. 79: 'multiple forms of discrimination, particularly refugee and internally displaced girls with disabilities, who are more often than boys subject to abuse'; 5) No. 11: 'Indigenous Children' (2009), para. 29: 'indigenous children who may face multiple facets of discrimination … Particular attention should be given to girls in order to ensure that they enjoy their rights on an equal basis as boys'.

[106] CRC General Comments: 1) No. 12: 'Right to be Heard' (2009); 2) Joint CEDAW-CRC GenRec/Com: 'Harmful Practices' (2014); 3) No. 16: 'Business' (2013); 4) No. 19: 'Public Budgeting' (2016).

[107] CRC General Comments: 1) No. 3: 'HIV/AIDS' (2003); 2) No. 7: 'Early Childhood' (2005); 3) No. 9: 'Corporal Punishment' (2007); 4) No. 11: 'Indigenous Children' (2009); 5) No. 13: 'Violence' (2011); 6) No. 14: 'Best Interests Child' (2013); 7) No. 17: 'Right Leisure' (2013); 8) No. 20: 'Adolescence' (2016); Joint CRC-CMW General Comments: 9) No. 22: 'Principles Migration' (2017); 10) No. 23: 'State Obligations Migration' (2017); 11) No. 24: 'Child Justice' (2019).

[108] CRC General Comment No. 10: 'Juvenile Justice' (2007), para. 40: '[p]rofessionals and staff should act under all circumstances in a manner consistent with the child's dignity and worth … which promotes the child's reintegration and **his/her** assuming a constructive role in society … States parties can and should try to establish and observe higher standards … and the involvement of the child and **her/his** parents in the judicial process'; para. 44: '[i]t is equally obvious that the child has the right to be heard directly and not only through a representative or an appropriate body if it is in **her/his** best interests … In other words, the child must be given the opportunity to express **his/her** views freely, and those views should be given due weight in accordance with the age and maturity of the child' (emphasis added).

the author,[109] is definitely an improved semiotic sign for children generally, its failure to offer an equal representation of feminine and masculine identifiers constitutes a regression for the girl child. In this regard, Goonesekere notes:

> The gender-neutral approach of the CRC Committee represents a lost opportunity to address discrimination against girl children, as the starting point of gender-based discrimination, and carry forward the agenda of substantive equality for women in a holistic manner within countries.[110]

The invisibility of the girl child in the Convention is also mirrored in international studies and state reports to the CRC Committee that fail to offer sex-disaggregated data for children.[111] As a result, the situation of the girl child and the violations she experiences become invisible in the data, and thereby in the very monitoring of the implementation of children's rights. In the 1990s, Sohoni observed the disregard for girls in UN-sponsored development strategies, noting that:

> the development phenomenon is neither uniform nor egalitarian – it is sexist . . . Inevitably, girls have received the fewest benefits from development planners and processes on account of both their age and gender. They are twice denied and in a worse position than even women.[112]

This situation is still present today, as the UN General Assembly notes, in its 2022 resolution on the girl child, that it is '(d)eeply concerned (. . .) about the continuing lack of recent information and statistics, disaggregated by sex, age . . . on the status of children, including girls . . . which are necessary to inform appropriate policy responses by Member States and the United Nations system'.[113] Also, the CRC Committee's decision to allocate a day of general discussion to the girl child in 1995, and yet neglect to explore her situation in a general comment is notable, especially since other issues examined in days of general discussion were thereafter addressed in general

[109] 'Child Justice' (2007).

[110] 'HRs for Girls' (2014), 483.

[111] 'Discrimination Girl Child' (2006), paras. 55, 58; UNICEF, 'Improving Data for Women and Children: Guidance on Strengthening Administrative Data Systems for Gender Statistics' (2022): '[g]ender data are frequently neither collected in a timely nor regular manner': 5. Also, UNICEF stresses that 'while gender is acknowledged as an under-researched though important aspect of violence against children, data have seldom been disaggregated by the gender of the child': 'Study on Violence Against Girls: Report of the International Girl Child Conference' (2009): 16.

[112] *Burden Girlhood* (1995), 1.

[113] UNGA Resolutions 'The Girl Child', preamble. The 2022 UNGA Resolution on the Girl Child also '[c]alls upon States to strengthen research, data collection and analysis on the girl child, disaggregated by household structure, sex, age': para. 28.

comments.[114] The Committee itself underscored on the day of general discussion on the girl child that the CRC was 'undoubtedly (…) the most widely accepted framework for action in favour of the fundamental rights of girls'.[115] Accordingly, a general comment clarifying States parties' duty of due diligence to respect, protect and fulfil her rights under the Convention would have been especially opportune. In this regard, Goonesekere notes that the CRC Committee has failed to interpret the meaning of article 2 on non-discrimination in a special general comment on girl children.[116] The CEDAW and CRC Committees' decision to co-author a general recommendation/comment on harmful practices, which it revised in 2019,[117] and yet not on the girl child specifically – even though these two committees are ideally equipped to offer an intersectional examination of her status based on sex and age – is also worthy of note. Already in 1995, the CRC Committee, in its day of general discussion on the girl child, underscored 'the complementary and mutually reinforcing nature' of the CRC and CEDAW,[118] and argued that these two instruments should constitute an essential framework to promote and protect the fundamental rights of girls.[119] Moreover, in their joint recommendation/comment on harmful practices, the two committees note that they have 'an overlapping mandate and … shared commitment' and underscore the objective of their joint comment 'to clarify the obligations of States parties to the Convention by providing authoritative guidance on legislative, policy and other appropriate measures that must be taken to ensure full compliance with their obligations under the Conventions'.[120] This begs the question as to why these two committees focused solely on harmful practices, and have not, as yet, produced implementation guidelines in a special general recommendation/comment on the girl child. The result is that States parties in their reports, and the CRC Committee in its concluding observations and

[114] See for example Days of General Discussion: 'The Rights of Children with Disabilities' (6 October 1997) UN Doc CRC/C/69; 'Children Living in a World with HIV/Aids (5 October 1998) UN Doc CRC/C/80; 'The Rights of Indigenous Children' (3 October 2003) 34th Session CRC Committee; 'Implementing Child Rights in Early Childhood' (22 September 2004) UN Doc CRC/C/SR.979); 'The Right of the Child to be Heard' (29 September 2006) 43rd Session CRC Committee; 'Rights of All Children in the Context of International Migration' (28 September 2012) 61st Session CRC Committee; 'Digital Media and Children's Rights' (12 September 2014) 67th Session CRC Committee; all of which became general comments.

[115] CRC DGD Girl Child (1995), para. 278.

[116] 'HRs for Girls' (2014), 483.

[117] Joint CEDAW-CRC GenRec/Com: 'Harmful Practices' (2014).

[118] CRC DGD Girl Child (1995), para. 282.

[119] Ibid., para. 299.

[120] Joint CEDAW-CRC GenRec/Com: 'Harmful Practices' (2014), paras. 1, 2.

comments, fail to systematically explore the situation of girl children. In this regard, Goonesekere notes the following:

> Where Concluding Comments refer to the reality of gender-based discrimination against girls, they do not focus on the achievement of a norm of substantive equality. They merely address specific issues relevant to girls, such as denial of educational opportunity, sexual abuse, violence and trafficking.[121]

Hence, one can argue that the semiotic sign of silence concerning the girl child in the CRC has had infinite semiotic ramifications since its adoption nearly thirty-five years ago.

## IV SEMIOETHICS: RECOMMENDED DEFINITION

We have observed that while the CRC defines childhood, it fails to mention the girl child and violations specific to her, both in its definition of child and provisions enshrining key child rights. Also, the Convention systematically gives precedence to masculine pronouns and possessive adjectives. According to a semioethics approach, semioticians may attempt to remove or replace problematic forms of expression in the communication order to address broader social issues. In the case at hand, the elusive sign is silence as the *intentional* and *volitional* absence of a significant identity group: the girl child. Hence the present challenge is not to *remove* but rather *add* signs, or more accurately, terminology, to ensure that the girl child and the issues she experiences are visible in the CRC. After careful consideration, one could propose to specify, in article 1 on the definition of 'child', that this identity group comprises both girls *and* boys to underline that girls are undoubtedly rights holders under the Convention. This book thus proposes to amend the definition of 'child' enshrined under article 1 of the CRC by inserting the terms 'girl and boy' after 'a child means every human being', and moreover, to add the sentence: '[t]he rights in the present Convention apply equally to the girl-child and the boy-child'.[122] We suggest to use a dash rather than a comma between 'every human being' and 'girl and boy' to ensure that 'child' definitely encompasses girls and boys. This punctuation is inspired by the CRC General Comment No. 3: 'children – girls and boys – . . .'.[123] We also recommend to

[121] 'HRs for Girls' (2014), 483.

[122] We suggest to hyphenate 'girl-child' and 'boy-child' to ensure that the provision cannot be read as signifying that girl and child or boy and child constitute two separate entities, see 'Gendercide CRC' (2018), 47–50.

[123] CRC General Comment No. 3: 'HIV/AIDS' (2003), para. 38.

refer to girls before boys in this amended provision since many States parties have indicated in their reservations to the CRC and CEDAW that they do not intend to grant equal rights to girl children, and as several States parties accord fewer rights to females than males under domestic law.[124] The CRC Committee already refers to girls before boys in some general comments.[125] It is noteworthy that some Global North states have moved from binary gender-neutral language (s/he, she/he, him/her, her/his) to non-binary terminology, such as 'they', to include intersex children, and one could thus argue that 'child' is more appropriate than an express reference to the binary concepts of girls and boys.[126] If sexism were no longer an international issue, the gender-neutral term 'child' could be interpreted as inclusive of all children, regardless of sex, worldwide. However, this is not the case. As previously discussed, girls experience both de jure and de facto discrimination in many CRC States parties.[127] Hence, the absence of any reference to girls in the CRC could be interpreted as supporting the view that 'child' is exclusive of girls. In fact, it is argued that the gender-neutral term 'child' could be interpreted as exclusive of both girls and intersex children for states that do not recognize equality between boys and girls under domestic law.[128] In this regard, we propose to alternate, throughout the CRC, the pronouns and possessive adjectives which currently all employ the masculine before the feminine, with versions beginning instead with the feminine. We also suggest the use of a slash rather than 'or' to unambiguously cover girls and boys,

[124] See Section III on Significance and Chapter 3.

[125] See for example General Comments: 1) No. 3: 'HIV/AIDS' (2003), paras. 7, 8, 17, 36, 38; 2) No. 4: 'Adolescent Health' (2003), paras. 20, 26, 28, 30, 39; 3) No. 12: 'Right to be Heard' (2009), paras. 95, 97, 134; 4) No. 13: 'Violence' (2011), paras. 19, 72; 5) No. 15: 'Health' (2013), paras. 9, 60; 6) No. 17: 'Right Leisure' (2013), paras. 48, 57, 58; 7) Joint CEDAW-CRC GenRec/Com: 'Harmful Practices' (2014), paras. 55, 67; 8) No. 20: 'Adolescence' (2016), paras. 38, 45, 69, 76; 9) Joint CRC-CMW No. 23: 'State Obligations Migration' (2017), paras. 41, 44.

[126] See for example Canada with the New Child, Youth and Family Services Act of Ontario, S.O. 2017, c. 14 – Bill 89.

[127] See Chapter 3.

[128] The issue of intersex children, persons who self-identify as another gender, or as non-binary, or who underwent sex reassignment surgeries would require a tailored examination that is outside the purview of this book, as explained in the glossary definition of Girl Child. In recent years, the UN adopted Resolution 'Human Rights, Sexual Orientation and Gender Identity' (2 October 2014) UN Doc A/HRC/RES/27/32 and scholars drafted the non-binding 'Yogyakarta Principles on the Application of International Human Rights Law in Relation to Sexual Orientation and Gender Identity' (March 2007). For a discussion on this issue, see Michael O'Flaherty and John Fisher, 'Sexual Orientation, Gender Identity and International Human Rights Law: Contextualizing the Yogyakarta Principles' (2008) 8 *Human Rights Law Review* 207.

namely 'her/him' and 'her/his' that would alternate with 'him/her' and 'his/her', and to systematically employ the inclusive 's/he'. The objective of this proposal is not to make the boy child invisible, but rather to clarify the presence of both girls *and* boys in the CRC. While girls would be mentioned first under article 1 to compensate for their current inferior status in society, the possessive adjectives and pronouns would alternate the feminine and masculine and thereby ensure equal visibility.[129] The amended article 1 would therefore read as follows:

> For the purposes of the present Convention, a child means every human being – *girl and boy* – below the age of eighteen years unless under the law applicable to the child, majority is attained earlier. *The rights in the present Convention apply equally to the girl-child and the boy-child.*[130]

The proposed modifications could be effected according to article 50 of the CRC which enables States parties to amend the Convention.[131] An amendment to the CRC may be proposed by any State party, and it shall enter into force when it has been approved by the UN General Assembly and accepted by a two-thirds majority of States parties according to CRC article 50 (1), (2). Once the amendment enters into force, it is binding on those States parties that have accepted it (CRC, article 50(3)).[132] While this provision requires that a certain procedure be followed, it has already been employed to amend article 43(2) of the CRC, whereby the word 'ten' was replaced with 'eighteen' for the number of experts (members) of the CRC Committee,[133] and could be employed again to improve the substantive content of the Convention.

It is acknowledged that a CRC general comment, or a joint CEDAW-CRC recommendation/comment on the girl child would be relevant as an initial

[129] CRC, preamble, arts. 2, 3, 7, 8, 9, 10, 12, 14, 16, 17, 20, 22, 23, 24, 25, 29, 30, 37, 40.

[130] Emphasis added.

[131] CRC, art. 50; 'The Vienna Convention' (1969) stipulates that a treaty may be amended by agreement between the parties, and provides rules for such amendments, which are applicable unless the treaty provides otherwise: see arts. 39–41.

[132] CRC, art. 50: '(1) Any State Party may propose an amendment and file it with the Secretary-General of the United Nations ... (2) An amendment adopted ... shall enter into force when it has been approved by the General Assembly of the United Nations and accepted by a two-thirds majority of States Parties. (3) When an amendment enters into force, it shall be binding on those States Parties which have accepted it, other States Parties still being bound by the provisions of the present Convention and any earlier amendments which they have accepted'.

[133] Amendment to Article 43(2) of the Convention on the Rights of the Child (New York, adopted 12 December 1995, entered into force 18 November 2002) 2199 UNTS 210; Proposed Amendment to Article 43(2) of the Convention on the Rights of the Child (6 December 1995) UN Doc CRC/SP/1995/L.1.Rev.1.

step to clarify states' obligations under these treaties. However, it is contended that a general comment would not in itself suffice to address the silence concerning girls in the Convention. As previously noted, while these general comments and recommendations provide helpful guidelines in the interpretation and implementation of rights, they solely constitute secondary soft law instruments that are not legally binding on States parties.[134] Moreover, general comments and recommendations constitute distinct documents from the treaty, and the immediate, dynamical and final interpretants who do not have specific training in international law, notably members of the general public, may not know that the Convention should be read in light of the guidelines adopted in these soft law documents. In fact, they may not be aware of these general comments' very existence. Instead, from a legal semiotics perspective, the proposed amendment to article 1, with the accompanied alternate female and male pronouns and possessive adjectives throughout the CRC, provides two important enhancements. Firstly, once ratified by member states, this amendment would enshrine a duty of due diligence to adopt all measures to respect, protect and fulfil the rights of the girl child under the Convention and address issues uniquely or predominantly affecting her. Secondly, this proposed amendment would hold a symbolic value. It would guarantee the visibility of the girl child in the CRC and send a clear semiotic sign to all interpretants – the immediate, dynamical and final interpretants – that girls are rights holders on an equal basis with boys under the Convention. The silence concerning the girl child would thus be filled with her distinct and unequivocal presence in the most ratified international treaty protecting children's rights, and thus increase her visibility globally. Lastly, from a semioethic perspective, it would be helpful to consider amending other provisions of the CRC to expressly mention issues predominantly or exclusively experienced by girls, as recommended by Askari, such as child marriage. In this regard, one could consider referring expressly to feminicide, for example, including female infanticide, under article 6 of the CRC (the right to life) and providing a list of measures that States parties should adopt, such as ensuring the investigation, prosecution and severe sentencing for those

[134] Helen Keller and Leena Grover, 'General Comments of the Human Rights Committee and Their Legitimacy' in Helen Keller and Geir Ulfstein (eds.), *UN Human Rights Treaty Bodies: Law and Legitimacy* (Cambridge University Press 2012), 129–30; Alston observes in this regard that some governments have criticized general comments as representing an 'unacceptable attempt to attribute to treaty provisions a meaning which they do not have': Philip Alston, 'The Historical Origins of the Concept of "General Comments" in Human Rights Law' in Laurence Boisson de Chazournes and Vera Gowlland-Debbas (eds.), *The International Legal System in Quest of Equity and Universality* (Kluwer 2001), 764.

crimes.[135] One could also consider mentioning FGM, as suggested by several CRC drafters,[136] and moreover adding 'sexualized social and dress codes' such as cosmetic plastic surgery under article 24 (harmful and/or traditional practices). This examination should be expanded to cover other issues, a study which is outside the purview of the present book and could be explored in future publications.

135 'Gendercide CRC' (2018) and *Feminicides Girl Children* (2018).

136 See Section II on *Meaning-intention*; 'CRC Child Marriage' (1998): '[e]ven if the CRC is modified to include a provision against child marriage, it will still remain lacking and discriminatory toward girl children because it also does not contain a provision directly addressing female circumcision': 125.

# 6

# The Beginning of Girlhood under International Law

The definition of child in the CRC delineates the boundary for the beginning of girlhood under international law. While several legal scholars have explored the lower frontier of childhood,[1] and the issue of the unborn and the right to abortion,[2] the present chapter examines the beginning of girlhood as it impacts two issues faced by the girl child: the prenatal sex selection (PSS) of female fetuses, and the girl's right to a safe abortion.[3] The first manifestation of the interactive discrimination experienced by the girl child – sexism and childism – occurs before her birth, through the prenatal selection of the unborn female on the grounds of gender.[4] As previously noted, this practice is still prevalent, notably in South Asia, South Caucasus and the Balkans, where an estimated 1.8 million girls 'go missing' because of sex-selective

[1] See for example *International Law Child* (1998), David Archard and John Tobin, 'Article 1: The Definition of a Child' in John Tobin (ed.), *The UN Convention on the Rights of the Child: A Commentary* (Oxford University Press 2019).

[2] See for example Kate Greasley, *Arguments about Abortion: Personhood, Morality, and Law* (Oxford University Press 2017); Rita Joseph, *Human Rights and the Unborn Child* (Martinus Nijhoff 2009); Christina Zampas and Jaime Gher, 'Abortion as a Human Right – International and Regional Standards' (2008) 8 *Human Rights Law Review* 249; Philip Alston, 'The Unborn Child and Abortion under the Draft Convention on the Rights of the Child' (1990) 12 *Human Rights Quarterly* 156.

[3] The absence of a beginning point for childhood also impacts neonate testing, the eligibility to damages for children injured in the womb by mothers who consumed drugs and alcohol and inheritance rights; see *International Law Child* (1998), 33. However, these issues are not girl-specific as they concern all children – boys and girls alike – and shall therefore not be examined in this book.

[4] As posited by Alston regarding the terms 'fetus' and 'unborn child' in his analysis of the unborn child and the CRC, the use of the expressions 'unborn female', 'female unborn', 'unborn girl', 'fetus', 'female fetus' and 'unborn' in this chapter 'does not imply recognition of the position that for legal purposes, a fetus is a child *per se*': 'Unborn Child' (1990), 156.

practices.[5] The Asian Centre for Human Rights observes that 117 million girls are missing in Asia due to PSS,[6] and 15.8 million girls have gone missing in India due to this practice since 1990.[7] In this regard, Sohoni observes that prebirth and early years 'reflect the years of the girl's greatest vulnerability and risks to her survival'.[8] PSS of the female unborn is a discriminatory practice for it is performed expressly on account of gender. In addition, PSS may constitute a violation of the right to bodily integrity of the pregnant girl child or woman who bears the female fetus. Indeed, gender-selective abortions are often imposed on the pregnant girl or woman by the husband and family-in-law. Sumner observes:

> Women are often subservient to the powerful husband and mother-in-law and her fear that she might be replaced by a younger, more fertile woman who can bear sons drives her to determine the sex of the child and abort any female fetuses.[9]

This is particularly problematic when the methods employed, such as the ultrasound, only enable sex identification after three months of pregnancy, and the girl child or woman is therefore required to undergo a second-trimester abortion.[10] Tandon and Sharma underscore that should she refuse the sex-selective abortion, it is the very life of the pregnant girl child or woman that may be threatened by her husband and family-in-law.[11] At the same time, restrictions upon PSS may lead the girl child, including through pressures from her husband and family-in-law, to resort to unsafe abortions, which constitute a threat to her right to health, and even life. Presently, induced abortion is highly restricted by law in 125 countries.[12] A recent study indicates that 45 per cent of the 55.9 million abortions undergone by girls and women

5 World Bank, 'Preventing More "Missing Girls": A Review of Policies to Tackle Son Preference' (2018), 2. See Introduction and Chapter 4.

6 Asian Centre for Human Rights, 'Female Infanticide Worldwide: The Case for Action by the UN Human Rights Council' (2016), 2.

7 Population Research Institute, 'Sex-Selective Abortion in India: Estimates on the Occurrence of Sex Selective Abortion in India and Some Possible Solutions to Eliminate the Practice' (2019), 12.

8 *Burden Girlhood* (1995), 2.

9 Molly Sumner, 'The Unknown Genocide: How One Country's Culture is Destroying the Girl Child' (2009) 15 *International Journal of Nursing Practice* 65, 66.

10 UNFPA, 'Sex Imbalances at Birth: Current Trends, Consequences and Policy Implications' (2012), 37.

11 Sneh Lata Tandon and Renu Sharma, 'Female Foeticide and Infanticide in India: An Analysis of Crimes against Girl Children' (2006) 1 *International Journal of Criminal Justice Sciences* 1, 2.

12 Guttmacher Institute, 'Abortion Worldwide 2017: Uneven Progress and Unequal Access' (2017), 21.

worldwide are unsafe and lead to a high mortality rate.[13] Special Rapporteur on the Right to Health, Grover, notes that whereas abortion is one of the safest medical procedures for the pregnant woman or girl when performed by trained personnel in appropriate conditions, unsafe abortions account for nearly 13 per cent of all maternal deaths globally.[14] Another five million women and girls suffer a series of health injuries caused by unsafe abortions, 'including haemorrhage; sepsis; trauma to the vagina, uterus and abdominal organs; cervical tearing; peritonitis; reproductive tract infections; pelvic inflammatory disease and chronic pelvic pain; shock and infertility'.[15] In this context, Grover stresses:

> [C]riminal prohibition of abortion is a very clear expression of State interference with a woman's [or girl child's] right to sexual and reproductive health because it restricts a woman's [or girl child's] control over her body, possibly subjecting her to unnecessary health risks.[16]

The denial of access to safe abortions impacts girls specifically. Coomaraswamy explains that '[t]he inability to control the very functions that differentiate women biologically from men is in itself a violation of human rights'.[17] One can thus argue that such restrictions constitute a violation of the principle of non-discrimination regarding girls' rights to life and health on the grounds of sex. The key question is whether the definition of child in the CRC addresses these two interconnected issues affecting the unborn and the pregnant girl child.

## I SENSE

In its definition of child, the CRC does not specify whether childhood begins at conception, during pregnancy, or at birth:

> For the purposes of the present Convention, a child means *every human being below the age of eighteen years* unless under the law applicable to the child, majority is attained earlier.[18]

[13] Ibid., 5, 9, 32–33.

[14] Anand Grover, Special Rapporteur on the Right to Health, 'The Right of Everyone to the Enjoyment of the Highest Attainable Standard of Physical and Mental Health' (3 August 2011) UN Doc A/66/254, paras. 25, 32.

[15] Ibid., para. 25.

[16] Ibid., para. 27.

[17] 'Cultural Practices' (2002), para. 95.

[18] CRC, art. 1 (emphasis added).

The interpretation of the beginning of girlhood is thereby left to States parties. Furthermore, the terms 'unborn', 'fetus' and 'embryo' are absent from the Convention. Consequently, one cannot claim that the unborn female is comprised in the 'child' category and protected against gender discrimination under the CRC. However, in its preamble, the CRC states the following:

> Bearing in mind that, as indicated in the Declaration of the Rights of the Child, 'the child, by reason of his physical and mental immaturity, needs special safeguards and care, including appropriate legal protection, before as well as after birth'.[19]

This could imply that childhood begins before birth. Nevertheless, as shall be discussed in the *meaning-intention* section of this chapter, the drafters of the CRC specified that this preambular paragraph does not have any legally binding or interpretative implications on the determination of the beginning of childhood.[20] It therefore appears that States parties may determine that childhood begins at birth. In this regard, Archard and Tobin explain that 'a principled interpretation of article 1 leads to the unequivocal view that as a minimum, childhood begins at birth'.[21]Alston further contends that the CRC does not protect the right to life of the unborn:

> [N]either the text of the Convention itself, nor any of the relevant circumstances surrounding its adoption, lend support, either of a legal or other nature, to the suggestion that the Convention requires legislation to recognize and protect the right to life of the fetus.[22]

The CRC Committee, in its working definition of early childhood, states that this period includes 'all young children: *at birth* and throughout infancy',[23] and specifies in its comment on health that '[c]hildhood is a period of continuous growth *from birth* to infancy'.[24] In fact, the Committee refers to children 'aged 0–18 years' in its comment on violence against children.[25] Hence, the Committee appears to indicate that childhood begins at birth. The

[19] CRC, preamble quotes the Declaration of the Rights of the Child (New York, adopted 20 November 1959) UN General Assembly Resolution 1386 (XIV), which was not gender-neutral, hence the use of 'his' rather than 'his/her'.

[20] *Travaux préparatoires CRC* (1992), 110.

[21] 'Definition Child' (2019), 24.

[22] 'Unborn Child' (1990), 177–78.

[23] CRC General Comment No. 7: 'Early Childhood' (2006), para. 1: '[t]he Committee's working definition of "early childhood" is all young children: at birth and throughout infancy; during the preschool years; as well as during the transition to school' (emphasis added).

[24] CRC General Comment No. 1: 'Health' (2013), para. 20 (emphasis added).

[25] CRC General Comment No. 13: 'Violence' (2011), para. 72.

Committee plays a central role in the legal interpretation of the CRC, and this statement could therefore imply that birth constitutes the parameter for the beginning of childhood, although, as previously discussed, general comments are not legally binding. The Convention nonetheless requires States parties to ensure 'appropriate pre-natal and post-natal health care for mothers' under article 24, which could imply the protection of the unborn child, or simply a concern for the health of the mother or that of the 'future' child to be healthy *if* born. The CRC Committee also recognizes the right to prenatal and postnatal health care 'for mothers and infants', and prenatal care exclusively for the child: 'prenatal care for children', which implies that the child could be unborn.[26] Since the CRC, and the international legal framework more generally, do not establish a beginning point for girlhood, we shall explore English definitions.

### 1 *English Definition*

The OED and the Webster provide many definitions of 'child'. The main description does not specify when childhood begins: 'a young person of either sex, usually one below the age of puberty, a boy or girl',[27] and 'a young person of either sex, esp. between infancy and youth'.[28] However, both dictionaries offer another definition suggesting that the term 'child' includes the fetus: '(t) he unborn or newly born human being; fetus, infant',[29] and 'an unborn or recently born human being: fetus, infant, baby'.[30] Moreover, the OED definition of infant is that of 'a child during the earliest period of life (or still unborn)'. Conversely, the OED also provides a definition of childhood indicating that it begins at birth: '(t)he state or stage of life of a child; the time during which one is a child; *the time from birth* to puberty'.[31] Additionally, the notion of infancy is defined in the SOEDHP as 'a child during the earliest period of life *after* birth',[32] thereby specifying that birth is the parameter for the beginning of childhood, yet also as 'or (now rare) in the womb'. One can observe that the definitions of 'childhood' under international law and English dictionaries do not provide a uniform boundary for its beginning, and accordingly, one cannot establish whether girlhood commences at conception,

[26] CRC General Comments No. 7: 'Early Childhood' (2006), para. 27; No. 9: 'Disabilities' (2007), para. 53.
[27] OED.
[28] Webster.
[29] OED.
[30] Webster.
[31] Emphasis added.
[32] Emphasis added.

during pregnancy or at birth. The next section shall thus explore whether the CRC, ICCPR, CEDAW and their respective treaty bodies provide clarifications concerning PSS and the girl's right to a safe abortion.

## 2 *CRC*

The CRC does not mention PSS in any provision. One could however argue that PSS constitutes a discriminatory practice prohibited under article 2 as regards sex. Yet article 2 states that the rights enshrined in the CRC shall be conferred without discrimination 'to each child':

> Art 2(1) States Parties shall respect and ensure the rights set forth in the present Convention *to each child* within their jurisdiction without discrimination of any kind, irrespective of the child's ... sex.[33]

Hence, the provision solely applies to the child, and one cannot assert that the unborn is a child and is comprised in the 'child' category. Indeed, article 2 does not prohibit discriminatory practices generally, but solely if they concern 'children'. Moreover, as previously mentioned, the CRC Committee specifies that according to its working definition of early childhood, 'young children' refers to children 'at birth and throughout infancy',[34] which indicates that the Committee does not consider that the unborn is comprised in the 'child' category. The CRC Committee nonetheless expressly lists 'selective abortions' as forms of discrimination against girl children in the same general comment on early childhood:

> Right to non-discrimination. Article 2 ensures rights to every child, without discrimination of any kind. The Committee urges States parties to identify the implications of this principle for realizing rights in early childhood: (b) Article 2 also means that particular groups of young children must not be discriminated against. (i) *Discrimination against girl children* is a serious violation of rights, affecting their survival and all areas of their young lives as well as restricting their capacity to contribute positively to society. They may be victims of *selective abortion*, genital mutilation, neglect and infanticide, including through inadequate feeding in infancy.[35]

From a semiotics perspective, the location of the expression 'selective abortion' is notable: it is placed within a sub-paragraph specifying that discrimination against girls is 'a serious violation of rights', itself comprised

[33] Emphasis added.
[34] CRC General Comment No. 7: 'Early Childhood' (2006), para. 1.
[35] Ibid., para. 11(b)(i) (emphasis added).

within a paragraph stating that article 2 prohibits discrimination against particular groups of young children. Accordingly, one can infer from this statement that the CRC Committee considers that selective abortions constitute a form of discrimination prohibited under article 2 of the Convention. Moreover, the Committee specifies that 'girls' might be victims of selective abortions, thereby implying that the unborn female could be considered a 'girl' or a 'young girl' within the 'early childhood' division. Additionally, while the Committee does not refer expressly to PSS in its more recent general comment on violence, it does mention 'the discriminatory elimination of girls before birth', and refers to eliminated unborn females as 'girls', which could imply that it considers unborn females as 'girl children' under the Convention.[36] In this context, the Committee also underscores how PSS negatively impacts the lives of the girls who are born:

> The social costs arising from a demographic imbalance due to the *discriminatory elimination of girls before birth* are high and *have potential implications for increased violence against girls* including abduction, early and forced marriage, trafficking for sexual purposes and sexual violence.[37]

The CRC Committee mentioned this issue in its concluding observations and expressly requested States parties to prevent PSS and develop strategies to address its underlying socio-cultural factors.[38]

The CRC Committee has also had an ambiguous approach to the girl's right to a safe abortion. In its general comment on adolescent health, the Committee requires States parties to:

> develop and implement programmes that provide access to sexual and reproductive health services, including family planning, contraception and *safe abortion services where abortion is not against the law*, adequate and comprehensive obstetric care and counselling.[39]

One can observe that the Committee does not recognize the girl's right to a safe abortion *per se*, but only 'where abortion is not against the law', thus leaving this determination to each State party. The Committee also requires

[36] CRC General Comment No. 13: 'Violence' (2011), para. 16.

[37] Ibid. (emphasis added). For a discussion on the impact of prenatal sex selection and female infanticide on the sex trafficking of girls and child marriage, see Clara Chapdelaine-Feliciati, 'Sex Trafficking of Girl Children: A Legal Semiotics Study of the Convention on the Rights of the Child' in Sarah Marusek and Anne Wagner (eds.), *Research Handbook on Legal Semiotics* (Elgar Publishing 2023).

[38] See for example CRC Concluding Observations India 1) (7 July 2014) UN Doc CRC/C/IND/CO/3-4, paras. 33–34; 2) (23 February 2000) UN Doc CRC/C/15/Add.115, para. 49.

[39] CRC General Comment No. 4: 'Adolescent Health' (2003), para. 31 (emphasis added).

states to reduce maternal mortality in adolescent girls, 'particularly caused by . . . unsafe abortion practices',[40] yet does not specify that safe abortion services should be made accessible and notably decriminalized. A decade later, the Committee appeared to take a clearer stance on the matter. In its general comment on health in 2013, the Committee declares that '[t]he interventions that should be made available across this continuum include, but are not limited to: . . . safe abortion services', and 'States should ensure that health systems and services are able to meet the specific sexual and reproductive health needs of adolescents, including family planning and *safe abortion services*'.[41] It goes further by referring to safe abortion in relation to the girl's right to consent to medical treatment without the permission of her parents or legal guardians, thereby addressing the interconnected issues of childism and paternalism:

> States should *review* and *consider* allowing children to consent to certain medical treatments and interventions *without the permission of a parent, caregiver, or guardian*, such as HIV testing and sexual and reproductive health services, including *education and guidance* on sexual health, contraception and *safe abortion*'.[42]

The Committee however appears to refer to 'education and guidance' on safe abortion rather than the treatment itself. Moreover, it only requires states to 'review' and 'consider' their legislation. The general comment also stipulates that '[t]he Committee recommends that States ensure access to safe abortion and post-abortion care services, irrespective of whether abortion itself is legal',[43] which does not place a duty on the State to legalize abortion, but rather to provide girls with access to a safe abortion. The two notions appear contradictory; indeed, if abortions are not legal, they cannot be provided in a safe environment. The Committee changed its position in 2016 by expressly requiring states to legalize abortion to protect girls' rights:

> The Committee *urges States to decriminalize abortion* to ensure that girls have *access to safe abortion and post-abortion services*, review legislation with a view to guaranteeing the best interests of pregnant adolescents and ensure that their views are always heard and respected in abortion-related decisions.[44]

Accordingly, it appears that while the Committee has not expressly prohibited PSS nor protected the unborn female, it has chosen to take a stance in this

40 Ibid.
41 CRC General Comment No. 15: 'Health' (2013), paras. 54, 56 (emphasis added).
42 Ibid., para. 31 (emphasis added).
43 Ibid., para. 70.
44 CRC General Comment No. 20: 'Adolescence' (2016), para. 60 (emphasis added).

debate twenty-seven years after the adoption of the CRC and recognize the pregnant girl's right to a safe abortion.

## 3 *ICCPR*

The Covenant does not refer to PSS in any provision. One could contend that PSS constitutes a discriminatory practice and is thereby prohibited under article 2, which states that the rights recognized in the Covenant shall be respected 'without distinction of any kind, such as ... sex':

> Each State Party to the present Covenant undertakes to respect and to ensure to all individuals within its territory and subject to its jurisdiction the rights recognized in the present Covenant, *without distinction of any kind, such as* race, colour, *sex*, language, religion, political or other opinion, national or social origin, property, birth or other status.[45]

Moreover, in its general comment on equality between men and women, the Human Rights Committee expressly refers to PSS and recognizes that this practice is underpinned by gender discrimination:

> Inequality in the enjoyment of rights by women throughout the world is deeply embedded in tradition, history and culture, including religious attitudes. The subordinate role of women in some countries is illustrated by the high incidence of *prenatal sex selection* and *abortion of female foetuses*.[46]

The Committee has also underscored the issue of PSS in its concluding observations, and recommends 'monitoring the scale of this phenomenon, addressing its root causes and long-term implications for the society ... and carrying out awareness-raising activities on the detrimental impact of sex selection and on the equal value of girls and boys'.[47] However, article 2 of the Covenant refers to the rights of 'individuals', and it is not clear whether the female unborn is included in this category. Likewise, the Covenant does not employ the terms 'unborn', 'fetus' and 'embryo' in any provision. Consequently, one cannot assert that the unborn is comprised in the 'individual' category. The ICCPR does not specify when life begins, including in article 6, its provision on the right to life. This provision nonetheless stipulates that a sentence of death shall not be carried out on a pregnant woman, which

[45] Emphasis added.

[46] ICCPR General Comment No. 28: 'Equality between Men and Women (2000), para. 5 (emphasis added).

[47] *Commentary ICCPR* (2020), 93. See for example Georgia (2014) UN Doc CCPR/C/GEO/CO/4, 7(f).

implies a concern to protect the life of her unborn child.[48] Yet the androcentric wording of article 6 whereby 'no one shall be arbitrarily deprived of his life' could be interpreted as signifying that the Covenant protects the right to life of men, or at least that States parties' duties are primarily focused on men.[49] Article 24 of the ICCPR stipulates that every child is entitled to protective measures 'as are required by *his* status as a minor':

> Every child shall have, *without any discrimination as to* race, colour, *sex*, language, religion, national or social origin, property or birth, the right to such measures of protection as are required by *his status as a minor*, on the part of his family, society and the State.[50]

Once again, the androcentric wording of article 24 is problematic as it could appear to refer solely to boys. The provision nevertheless specifies that such protection is granted without any discrimination, including on the basis of sex. One could therefore attempt to argue that PSS constitutes a discriminatory practice on the grounds of sex prohibited under article 24. Yet since the ICCPR fails to provide a beginning point for childhood, one cannot claim that the conceptual notion of 'child' in article 24 includes the unborn, notably the female unborn. The Committee nonetheless appears to address the issue of pregnant girls who are pressured into abortion following a sex diagnosis, noting that '[t]he States parties should also provide the Committee with information on measures to prevent *forced abortion* or forced sterilization'.[51]

The Human Rights Committee however seems cautious to tackle girls' right to a safe abortion. In 2000, it noted that 'States parties should give information on any measures taken by the State to help women prevent unwanted pregnancies, and to ensure that they do not have to *undergo life-threatening clandestine abortions*',[52] and thus did not expressly recognize the right to a safe abortion *per se*, as this statement could simply imply better access to contraception to prevent unwanted pregnancies. The Committee does refer to the issue of abortion when the pregnancy results from rape:

> The Committee needs to be *provided information* on national laws and practice with regard to domestic and other types of violence against women,

[48] ICCPR, art. 6(5): '[s]entence of death shall not be imposed for crimes committed by persons below eighteen years of age and shall not be carried out on pregnant women'.

[49] ICCPR, art. 6(1). For a discussion on androcentric wording in the ICCPR and the girl child, see *Feminicides Girl Children* (2018).

[50] ICCPR, art. 24(1) (emphasis added).

[51] ICCPR General Comment No. 28: 'Equality between Men and Women' (2000) (emphasis added), para. 11.

[52] Ibid., para. 10 (emphasis added).

> including rape. It also needs to know whether the State party gives *access to safe abortion to women* who have become pregnant *as a result of rape*.[53]

Yet the Committee only requires states to provide information as to whether or not access to safe abortions is granted in cases of rape, not to legalize abortion, and moreover, it solely refers to abortions when the pregnancy is the result of rape. It is also worthy of note that the Committee refers to women, not girl children, in this context. The Committee recognizes women's right to make decisions without their husband's consent:

> Another area where States may fail to *respect women's privacy* relates to their reproductive functions, for example, where there is a requirement for *the husband's authorization* to make a decision in regard to sterilization; where general requirements are imposed for the sterilization of women, such as having a certain number of children or being of a certain age, or where States impose a legal duty upon doctors and other health personnel *to report cases of women who have undergone abortion*.[54]

Once again, it is notable that the Committee refers exclusively to women, not to girls, in this context. The Human Rights Committee adopts a very mediated approach to girls' right to a safe abortion. While the Committee does not recognize the legal right to abortion *per se*, it outlines limitations to its prohibition. Firstly, the Committee specifies that restrictions to abortion should not jeopardize girls' right to life, subject them to physical or mental pain amounting to torture or inhuman treatment as per article 7, discriminate against them, nor violate their right to privacy.[55] It is notable that the Committee refers to both women and girls in this paragraph, thereby recognizing that adolescent girls can become pregnant and should be expressly protected under the Covenant. Secondly, the Committee goes further by stating that the State party should provide 'safe, legal and effective access to abortion' if 1) the girl's right to life or health is at risk; 2) carrying the pregnancy to term would cause pain or suffering, including if pregnancy is the result of rape, or is not viable.[56] Thirdly, states cannot regulate abortion if

[53] Ibid., para. 11 (emphasis added).

[54] Ibid., para. 20 (emphasis added).

[55] ICCPR General Comment No. 36: 'Right to Life' (2018), para. 8: 'restrictions on the ability of *women or girls* to seek abortion must not, inter alia, *jeopardize their lives, subject them to physical or mental pain or suffering* which violates article 7, *discriminate against them or arbitrarily interfere with their privacy*' (emphasis added).

[56] Ibid.: 'States parties must provide safe, legal and effective access to abortion where the life and health of the pregnant woman or girl is at risk, or where carrying a pregnancy to term would cause the pregnant woman or girl substantial pain or suffering, most notably where the pregnancy is the result of rape or incest or is not viable'.

it 'runs contrary' to their 'duty to ensure' that girls do not have to resort to unsafe abortions.[57] This last formulation is quite broad as any restriction could indeed lead to an unsafe abortion. Moreover, the Committee provides examples in this context, such as 'criminalizing pregnancies by unmarried women', and criminal sanctions to girls who undergo abortion or doctors who provide abortions.[58] It is worthy of note that the Committee refers exclusively to women in the context of 'unmarried women', which could infer that it does not recognize child marriage. Fourthly, states must remove barriers such as conscience objectors in the medical profession.[59] Of interest is the broad formulation that states should protect girls against 'the mental and physical health risks associated with unsafe abortions',[60] which could imply an obligation to provide safe abortions, although the Committee focuses on education and contraception in this context:

> In particular, they should ensure access for women and men, and, especially, girls and boys, to quality and evidence-based information and education on sexual and reproductive health and to a wide range of affordable contraceptive methods, and prevent the stigmatization of women and girls who seek abortion.[61]

Finally, states should ensure access to quality post-abortion services, which implies that abortion is not criminalized after the procedure takes place.[62] Hence, one can observe that the Human Rights Committee attempts to restrict the criminalization of abortion, although it does not go as far as to recognize the actual right of adolescent girls to a safe abortion in all circumstances. It is notable that while the CRC Committee took a clear stance on the matter in 2016, the Human Rights Committee was still reluctant to unambiguously do the same two years later.

57 Ibid.: 'States parties may not regulate pregnancy or abortion in all other cases in a manner that runs contrary to their duty to ensure that women and girls do not have to undertake unsafe abortions, and they should revise their abortion laws accordingly'.

58 Ibid.: '[f]or example, they should not take measures such as criminalizing pregnancies by *unmarried women* or apply criminal sanctions against women and girls undergoing abortion or against medical service providers assisting them in doing so, since taking such measures compel women and girls to resort to unsafe abortion' (emphasis added).

59 Ibid.: 'States parties should not introduce new barriers and should remove existing barriers that deny effective access by women and girls to safe and legal abortion, including barriers caused as a result of the exercise of conscientious objection by individual medical providers'.

60 Ibid.: 'States parties should also effectively protect the lives of women and girls against the mental and physical health risks associated with unsafe abortions'.

61 Ibid.

62 Ibid.: 'States parties should ensure the availability of, and effective access to, quality prenatal and post-abortion health care for women and girls, in all circumstances, and on a confidential basis'.

## 4 CEDAW

The CEDAW does not refer to PSS. It nevertheless embodies the principle of non-discrimination against women, and one could therefore argue that PSS constitutes a discriminatory practice on the basis of gender prohibited under article 1 of the Convention:

> Art 1: For the purposes of the present Convention, the term 'discrimination against *women*' shall mean any distinction, exclusion or restriction made on the basis of *sex* which has the effect or purpose of impairing or nullifying the recognition, enjoyment or exercise by women, irrespective of their marital status, on a basis of equality of men and women, of human rights and fundamental freedoms in the political, economic, social, cultural, civil or any other field.[63]

However, article 1 refers to 'discrimination against women' and as shall be discussed in Chapter 8, the CEDAW does not provide a boundary for the beginning of womanhood. Accordingly, one cannot assert that the unborn female is comprised in the 'woman' category. In addition, the CEDAW does not mention the unborn, the embryo or the fetus in any provision. Of particular relevance is the decision of the CEDAW Committee not to refer to the female unborn nor to PSS in any of its thirty-nine general recommendations. As a result, one cannot assert that the unborn female is a rights holder under the CEDAW. It could nonetheless be argued that PSS constitutes discrimination against women on the grounds that it impairs the recognition, enjoyment and exercise by women of their rights, reflects and reinforces gender stereotypes and causes gender imbalances which in turn lead to the violation of women's rights, such as kidnapping women for forced marriage and polyandry.[64] In this context, article 2 of the CEDAW, which stipulates that States parties 'pursue by all appropriate means and without delay a policy of eliminating discrimination against women',[65] could be invoked to adopt measures tackling PSS. In addition, the CEDAW stipulates as follows:

> Art 5: States Parties shall take all appropriate measures:
>
> (a) To modify the social and cultural patterns of conduct of men and women, with a view to achieving the elimination of prejudices and

[63] Emphasis added.

[64] Sneha Kumar and Nistha Sinha, 'Preventing More "Missing Girls": A Review of Policies to Tackle Son Preference' (2020) 35 *World Bank Research Observer* 87, 91.

[65] CEDAW, art. 2.

> customary and all other practices which are based on the idea of the inferiority or the superiority of either of the sexes or on stereotyped roles for men and women.

This provision could also be employed to place a duty on States parties to tackle PSS and the sexism that underpins this practice. Moreover, the CEDAW Committee addresses the coercion of a pregnant girl by her husband and larger family to undergo a gender-related abortion in several general recommendations from 1992 to this day. For example, in its 1992 general recommendation on violence, the Committee specifies that '*[c]ompulsory* sterilization or *abortion* adversely affects women's physical and mental health, and infringes the right of women to decide on the number and spacing of their children'.[66] The Committee expressly notes that her partner cannot pressure her: '[d]ecisions to have children or not, while preferably made in consultation with spouse or partner, *must not nevertheless be limited by spouse*, parent, partner or Government'.[67] However, the Committee refers to the 'woman', not the girl child, and it is not clear whether girl is comprised in 'woman' in this context, which could be explained by the Committee's decision not to condone child marriage.

The CEDAW does not expressly refer to abortion, and mentions 'family planning', not contraception nor abortion, under article 12 and thereby 'does not clearly take account of needs such as contraception ... or access to safe abortion'.[68] The CEDAW Committee has nonetheless progressively taken a stance on the right to safe abortion. The first general recommendation mentioning the issue was adopted in 1992, and refers to 'compulsory abortion'; it also requires states to ensure that women are not 'forced to seek unsafe medical procedures such as illegal abortion':

> States parties should ensure that measures are taken to prevent coercion in regard to fertility and reproduction, and to ensure that women are not forced to seek unsafe medical procedures such as *illegal abortion* because of lack of appropriate services in regard to fertility control.[69]

However, the Committee places an obligation on appropriate services in regard to fertility control, which could imply that it does not recognize the right to safe abortion *per se* but rather the right to contraceptive measures to prevent unwanted pregnancies. In 1999, the CEDAW Committee went a bit

66 CEDAW General Recommendation No. 19: 'Violence' (1992), para. 22.

67 CEDAW General Recommendation No. 21: 'Equality Marriage' (1994), para. 22 (emphasis added).

68 *Commentary CEDAW* (2012), 18.

69 CEDAW General Recommendation No. 19: 'Violence' (1992), para. 24(m) (emphasis added).

further by stating that '[w]hen possible, legislation criminalizing abortion should be amended, in order to withdraw punitive measures imposed on women who undergo abortion'.[70] The wording is nonetheless quite cautious as the Committee introduces this obligation with 'when possible', which offers a broad opportunity for States parties not to implement it. Moreover, although the Committee refers to punitive measures against women who underwent abortion, it does not require the legalization and accessibility of this procedure. In its 2008 recommendation on migrant women, the Committee, when describing discrimination, mentions that women may face 'coercive abortion or lack of access to safe reproductive health and abortion services', which could imply that limited access constitutes a prohibited form of discrimination under article 1 of the CEDAW.[71] The Committee goes further in its 2013 recommendation on women in conflict situations, as it lists 'safe abortion services' and 'post-abortion care' under sexual and reproductive health care:

> Ensure that sexual and reproductive health care includes access to sexual and reproductive health and rights information; psychosocial support; family planning services, including emergency contraception; maternal health services, including antenatal care, skilled delivery services, prevention of vertical transmission and emergency obstetric care; *safe abortion services*; post-abortion care.[72]

In its 2015 general recommendation on access to justice, the CEDAW Committee expressly states that the criminalization of abortion constitutes discrimination against women:

> Some criminal codes or acts and/or criminal procedure codes *discriminate against women* by:
>
> (b) Criminalizing forms of behaviour that can be performed only by women, such as *abortion*[73]

It further requires States parties to abolish the criminalization of behaviour performed only by women, and refers expressly to abortion in this context:

> *Abolish discriminatory criminalization* and review and monitor all criminal procedures to ensure that they do not directly or indirectly discriminate against women; decriminalize forms of behaviour that are not criminalized

[70] CEDAW General Recommendation No. 24: 'Women and Health' (1999), para. 31.

[71] CEDAW General Recommendation No. 26: 'Women Migrant Workers' (5 December 2008) UN Doc CEDAW/C/2009/WP.1/R, para. 18.

[72] CEDAW General Recommendation No. 30: 'Women in Conflict' (2013), para. 52(c) (emphasis added).

[73] CEDAW General Recommendation No. 33: 'Access Justice' (2015), para. 47 (emphasis added).

> or punished as harshly if they are performed by men; *decriminalize forms of behaviour that can be performed only by women, such as abortion.*[74]

The CEDAW Committee reiterates this obligation in its recommendation on rural women:

> That *laws and regulations* that place obstacles to rural women's access to health care, including to sexual and reproductive health services, are *repealed*, in particular *laws that criminalize* or require waiting periods or third party consent for *abortion*.[75]

Finally, in its updated general recommendation on violence against women, which it renamed 'gender-based violence against women' (2017), thereby underscoring the sexism underpinning violence experienced by women, the CEDAW Committee expressly states that the criminalization of abortion constitutes violence against women:

> Violations of *women*'s sexual and reproductive health and rights, such as forced sterilization, forced abortion, forced pregnancy, *criminalization of abortion, denial or delay of safe abortion and/or post abortion care*, forced continuation of pregnancy, and abuse and mistreatment of *women and girls* seeking sexual and reproductive health information, goods and services, *are forms of gender based violence* that, depending on the circumstances, *may amount to torture or cruel, inhuman or degrading treatment.*[76]

In fact, the Committee states that both the criminalization *and* the denial or delay when it comes to access to a safe abortion, and post abortion care, constitute violations of women's sexual and reproductive health and rights as well as forms of violence against women. It additionally states that such violations can amount to torture or inhuman or degrading treatment. However, the Committee once again refers to 'women', not to 'girls' in relation to the right to a safe abortion, and then mentions 'women and girls' solely as regards 'sexual and reproductive health information, goods and services', which could imply, *a contrario*, that solely adult women have the right to a safe abortion. The CEDAW Committee also recognizes the right to a safe abortion in its general recommendation on disaster:

> Accord priority to the provision of family-planning and sexual and *reproductive health* information *and services*, within disaster preparedness and response

[74] Ibid., para. 51(l) (emphasis added).
[75] CEDAW General Recommendation No. 34: 'Rural Women' (2016), para. 39(c) (emphasis added).
[76] CEDAW General Recommendation No. 35: 'Gender-based Violence' (2017), para. 18 (emphasis added).

> programmes, including access to emergency contraception, post-exposure prophylaxis for HIV, treatment for AIDS and *safe abortion*.[77]

Finally, in its recommendation on Indigenous women and girls (2022), the Committee expressly mentions girls as holders of the right to a safe abortion, as it requires States parties to:

> [g]uarantee that Indigenous women and *girls* receive prompt, comprehensive and accurate information, in accessible formats, on sexual and reproductive health services and *affordable access to such services, including safe abortion services* and modern forms of contraception.[78]

Hence, it appears that both the CEDAW and CRC Committees formally recognize the right to a safe abortion, whereas the CEDAW Committee has chosen not to mention nor address PSS and the unborn female. The Human Rights Committee, along with the CRC Committee, refers to the issue of PSS, yet adopts a more cautious approach concerning the right to abortion.

## II MEANING

### 1 *CRC*

The *travaux préparatoires* of the CRC indicate that both PSS and the girl's right to a safe abortion were not addressed by the delegates, including during the drafting of article 2 on the principle of non-discrimination, article 6 on the right to life and article 24 on the right to health.[79] However, during the drafting of article 1 on the definition of child, the World Association of Children's Friends suggested to protect the 'unborn child from genetic experiments and manipulations injurious to his physical, moral or mental integrity or to his health', and add the following to the Convention:

> The States Parties to the present Convention shall take all steps to prohibit, at the least:
>
> The selection of sex by genetic manipulation for non-therapeutic purposes.[80]

This demonstrates a concern for the procedure of sex selection, and the rights of the unborn to be protected against medical experimentation, although this

[77] CEDAW General Recommendation No. 37: 'Disaster Risk' (2018), para. 68(d) (emphasis added).

[78] CEDAW General Recommendation No. 39: 'Indigenous Women and Girls' (2022), para. 52 (b) (emphasis added).

[79] *Travaux préparatoires* CRC (1992); 'History CRC' (2007). See Chapter 5 for a discussion on negotiations concerning the girl child and issues specific to her.

[80] UN Doc E/CN.4/1988/WG.1/NGO/1 (emphasis added); 'History CRC' (2007), 310.

suggestion was not approved by the drafting committee.[81] Moreover, when examining article 24 on the right to health, Austria noted a 'possible inconsistency between "the child's" right to adequate prenatal care and the possibilities for legal abortion provided in some countries'.[82] The decision to disregard both PSS and girls' access to a safe abortion could be explained by substantial disagreements regarding the beginning point of childhood, and thus girlhood, between the drafters of the Convention. For example, Barbados questioned whether the definition of child and right to life should encompass the unborn:

> The child's right to life has not been articled. How far should this right go? *Does the child include the unborn child, or the foetus?* Under specified circumstances, should a foetus be aborted without an offence being committed or at the relevant time was the foetus a human life? All these are questions which should be considered before the child's right to life is articled.[83]

And New Zealand added that 'a point of some importance which this article, and indeed all the articles raise to some degree, is the definition of a child. Does the definition begin at conception, at birth, or at some point in between?'[84] In the revised Polish draft of the CRC (1979), the child was defined as 'every human being from the moment of *his birth* to the age of 18 years unless, under the law of his State, he has attained his age of majority earlier',[85] which indicated that childhood began at birth. Some delegates argued that childhood should be extended to include the entire period from the moment of conception.[86] Other delegates disagreed and stressed that the wording should be neutral to ensure compatibility with the wide variety of domestic legislation worldwide.[87] The representative of Morocco therefore proposed that the words 'from the moment of his birth' be deleted, a suggestion supported by several delegates.[88] The definition of the child was complicated by a paragraph ensuring protection to the child 'before as well as after birth' taken from the Declaration of the Rights of the Child,[89] and inserted in the preamble of the CRC at the request of the Holy See.[90] Several delegations

81 'History CRC' (2007), 310.
82 UN Doc E/CN.4/1324; 'History CRC' (2007), 581.
83 UN Doc E/CN.4/1324; 'History CRC' (2007), 301 (emphasis added).
84 UN Doc E/CN.4/1324/Add.5; 'History CRC' (2007), 303.
85 UN Doc E/CN.4/1349; 'History CRC' (2007), 305 (emphasis added).
86 UN Doc E/CN.4/1408, para 277; 'History CRC' (2007), 305.
87 Ibid.
88 Ibid.
89 Declaration of the Rights of the Child, preamble: '[w]hereas the child, by reason of his physical and mental immaturity, needs special safeguards and care, including appropriate legal protection, before as well as after birth'.
90 *Travaux préparatoires CRC* (1992), 102.

supported this addition on the grounds that their national legislation contained provisions protecting 'the rights of the unborn from the time of conception'.[91] It is worthy of note that these delegates underscored that their *meaning-intention* was not to criminalize abortion *per se*:

> The purpose of the amendment was not to preclude the possibility of abortion, since many countries had adopted legislation providing for abortion in certain cases, such as threat to the health of the mother.[92]

However, the drafters solely referred to safe abortion under certain circumstances, and did not consider the girl child. Other delegations disagreed and noted that 'the definition of "child" should be contained in article 1 and that nothing in the preamble should prejudge or slant the definition formulated in article 1'.[93] The delegates decided to leave this addition 'in brackets' until they could agree on a definition of child in article 1.[94] After the adoption of article 1, the drafting group revisited the preamble. The delegations of Italy, Venezuela, Senegal, Kuwait, Argentina, Austria, Colombia and Egypt supported the 'before as well as after birth' insertion.[95] Other delegations – including Norway, the Netherlands, India, China, the USSR, Denmark, Australia, Sweden, the German Democratic Republic and Canada – opposed it on the grounds that this paragraph might be used in interpreting the definition of childhood as beginning before birth.[96] Finally, these debates led to an open-ended definition in article 1, and a preambular paragraph that protects the child 'before as well as after birth', yet which is accompanied by an interpretative statement, in the *travaux préparatoires* of the CRC, stating that this wording ('before birth') cannot be used to interpret the provisions of the Convention – a rare occurrence in international law which had to be approved by the CRC Working Group Legal Counsel.[97] The Legal Counsel himself noted that this proposal was 'strange': 'it is at first sight *strange* that a text is sought to be included in the *travaux préparatoires* for the purpose of depriving a particular preambular paragraph of its usual purpose, i.e. to form part of the basis for the interpretation of the treaty'.[98] The Legal Counsel further explained that it would be more appropriate to include such a

91 UN Doc E/CN.4/1408, para 277; 'History CRC' (2007), 285.
92 Ibid.
93 Ibid.
94 Ibid.
95 UN Doc E/CN.4/1989/48, paras. 25–74; 'History CRC' (2007), 295.
96 Ibid.
97 *Travaux préparatoires* CRC (1992), 115–19; 'History CRC' (2007), 301–13.
98 'Report of the Working Group to the Commission on Human Rights' (9 December 1988) UN Doc E/CN.4./1989/48, 144.

statement in the final Convention or an accompanying instrument, rather than within the *travaux préparatoires*.[99] Hence, the decision to add an interpretative statement in the *travaux* rather than the Convention itself constitutes an important sign that should not be disregarded; it demonstrates that the drafters held significantly different views on the beginning of childhood, and therefore, girlhood.

## 2 *ICCPR*

As concerns the ICCPR, its *travaux préparatoires* reveal that PSS was not discussed, including during the drafting of article 2 which enshrines the principle of non-discrimination.[100] It is worthy of note that while contemplating whether to employ the terms 'individuals' or 'persons' in article 2, those who favoured the referent 'persons' argued that it would be more appropriate since 'the use of the term "persons" would stress that certain basic rights were shared by all human beings *from birth*',[101] which implies that they did not consider the unborn as a rights holder under this provision. Moreover, as is the case with the CRC, the drafters of the ICCPR purposefully chose to leave the issue of the beginning of life unaddressed and unresolved. This question was already a subject of contention in 1947 during the drafting of article 3 of the UDHR, which states that '(e)veryone has the right to life'.[102] On the one hand, several delegates suggested to explicitly protect the life of the unborn, such as the InterAmerican Juridical Committee: '(e)very person has the right to life. This right includes the right to life from the moment of conception'.[103] The Lebanese representative also suggested a provision stating that '[e]very *one* has the right to life and to bodily integrity from the moment of conception, regardless of physical or mental condition',[104] and the Chilean representative proposed the following specification: '[u)]nborn children and incurables, mentally defectives and lunatics shall have the right to life'.[105] On the other hand, the representative of the UN Commission on the Status of Women opposed this formulation for it would run counter to 'advanced

[99] Ibid.

[100] *Travaux préparatoires ICCPR* (1987).

[101] Ibid., 53 (emphasis added). The drafters finally chose the referent 'individuals' because the term 'persons' covered 'not only individuals but also juridical persons such as bodies corporate, with which the Covenant was not concerned'.

[102] 'Unborn Child' (1990), 159.

[103] Ibid., citing Verdoodt, *Naissance et signification de la Déclaration des droits de l'homme* (Birth and Significance of the Declaration of Human Rights) (1964), 95–96.

[104] UN Doc E/CN.4/21, 74.

[105] Ibid.

legislation: which envisaged, in certain cases, "the right to abortion"'.[106] The same debate arose during the very first session of the ICCPR draft committee when examining article 6 on the right to life.[107] Since the first draft version of article 6 did not refer to the beginning point of life,[108] Lebanon suggested an alternate text which protected the right to life from conception: '(i)t shall be unlawful to deprive any person, from the moment of conception, of *his* life or bodily integrity'.[109] The drafting committee thereafter considered adding the words 'at any stage of *his* human development' after 'any person', yet this proposal was refuted.[110] The working group of the Commission on human rights thereafter considered a first paragraph that would not refer to the beginning of life and simply state 'any person', and a second paragraph specifying that abortion is unlawful, except in special circumstances:

> It shall be unlawful to procure abortion except in a case in which it is permitted by law and is done in good faith in order to preserve the life of the woman, or on medical advice to prevent the birth of a child of unsound mind to parents suffering from mental disease, or in a case where the pregnancy is the result of rape.[111]

The drafting procedure of the ICCPR operated by vote rather than consensus,[112] and the distribution of votes is revealing. For example, the first paragraph was adopted, while the second paragraph prohibiting abortion except in certain cases, was deleted by ten votes to three.[113] During the third Committee meeting in 1957, Belgium, Brazil, El Salvador, Mexico and Morocco submitted an amendment to replace paragraph one with '(t)he right to life is inherent in the human person. From the moment of conception, this right shall be protected by law'.[114] These countries argued that since one of the provisions of article 6 protected the life of the unborn child whose mother is sentenced to death, such protection should be extended to all unborn children, which supports our argument in the *sense* section that the wording of article 6 which protects the pregnant woman from execution should not be

[106] UN Doc. E/CN.4Ac.2/SR.3, 7–8, cited in 'Unborn Child' (1990), 159.
[107] *Travaux préparatoires ICCPR* (1987), 113.
[108] Ibid.: '[i]t shall be unlawful to deprive any person of *his* life save in the execution of a sentence of a court following his conviction of a crime for which this penalty is provided by law' (emphasis added).
[109] Ibid., 113 (emphasis added).
[110] Ibid., 114 (emphasis added).
[111] *Travaux préparatoires ICCPR* (1987), 114.
[112] Ibid.
[113] Ibid.
[114] Ibid., 119.

disregarded.[115] Some representatives also noted that legislation in many countries accorded protection to the unborn child.[116] However, this amendment was opposed on the grounds that it is impossible for the State party to determine the moment of conception and therefore to undertake to protect life from that moment. In addition, Great Britain underlined that such a provision would involve the rights and duties of the medical profession. Finally, the delegates noted that countries had different positions on this issue and that it was therefore inappropriate to include such a provision in an international instrument. The amendment adding protection from conception was therefore rejected by thirty-one votes to twenty, with seventeen abstentions.[117] Lebanon had submitted another amendment to protect life from the moment of conception at the 6th Session of the Commission on Human Rights in 1950, however, it was not voted upon.[118] Lastly, the beginning point of childhood was discussed during the drafting of article 24 of the Covenant on the Rights of Children. On the one hand, the Chilean representative suggested to protect the rights of the child 'from the prenatal period until *his* coming of age',[119] and the Peruvian working paper suggested to specify that '(a)n unborn child shall be deemed to be already born in all respects in which *he* stands to benefit'.[120] On the other hand, Poland and Yugoslavia submitted a revised proposal, which stated that '(e)very child shall be entitled from *his* birth to a name and a nationality'.[121] The drafting committee decided to adopt the current article 6 which does not refer to the beginning of childhood.[122]

## 3 *CEDAW*

Although PSS constitutes a discriminatory practice embedded in sexism, this issue was not mentioned during the drafting of the very treaty designed to protect women's rights, the CEDAW.[123] The drafters did not contemplate whether or not the unborn female was included in the 'woman' category, and chose not to mention the right to a safe abortion, even though it expressly

[115] Ibid., 121.
[116] Ibid.
[117] Ibid.
[118] Ibid., 120.
[119] Ibid., 457 (emphasis added). Once again, the use of the masculine pronoun is notable.
[120] Ibid., 464 (emphasis added).
[121] Ibid., 464 (emphasis added).
[122] Ibid., 145.
[123] *Travaux préparatoires* CEDAW (1993). See Chapter 8 for a discussion on the CEDAW *Travaux préparatoires*.

concerns women and girls.[124] During the drafting of articles 1 and 2, which, respectively, define and prohibit discrimination against women, the drafters were silent as concerns the definition of womanhood and its boundaries, and they did not refer to specific discriminatory practices.[125] It is worthy of note that the draft CEDAW initially did not contain a separate provision on the right to health, a central right for women and girls, which was instead incorporated into articles 11 on employment, 10 on education and 14 on rural women.[126] Moreover, when the delegates subsequently examined article 12 on the right to health, some expressly opposed a provision recognizing 'family planning services' on the grounds that 'these did not exist everywhere and ... could result in refusal to ratify the convention',[127] which implies a reluctance for the right to contraception and safe abortion. The provision on 'family planning services' was nonetheless approved, although it was worded in broad terms and did not mention PSS nor contraception or safe abortion.[128] The drafters were however more open to education pertaining to family planning under article 10, and the Federal Republic of Germany suggested to add 'preparation for a responsible family life, especially the access to information and advice on family planning' and 'should specify that such information must be accessible to both men/boys and women/girls'.[129] Although abortion was not mentioned in this context, the International Federation of University Women recommended that 'family planning services respect the moral and personal attitudes of each married couple'.[130] Yet since 'family planning services' caused disagreements, it was decided to solely refer to 'information and advice' rather than to 'services'.[131] Finally, during the drafting of article 16 on women's rights in the private sphere, Finland stated that one of the aims of the CEDAW would be to achieve 'the right of women to choose whether to have children, and if so, how many, and the right of women to have access to birth control information and methods at little cost',[132] although it did not mention abortion nor PSS in this context. Belgium suggested to add a paragraph on family planning and the number and spacing of children, and the German Democratic Republic stated that

[124] Ibid., 42–61.
[125] Ibid.
[126] Ibid., 145. This could be explained by the fact that the DEDAW also did not contain a separate provision on the right to health.
[127] Ibid., 145.
[128] Ibid.
[129] Ibid., 120–21.
[130] Ibid., 121.
[131] Ibid.
[132] Ibid., 171.

both spouses should decide on this matter by mutual agreement yet 'failing such agreement, the decision was taken by the wife alone'. UNESCO proposed to add 'conception' along with 'the number and spacing', and the United Kingdom underscored that men and women should have the same rights to decide 'freely and responsibly' on the number and spacing of their children.[133] However, Egypt, Morocco and Bahrain expressed reservations, and the latter proposed a restriction that this decision would 'not run counter to the interests of the children and conforms with the rules and regulations of society derived from the provision of the applicable religious and positive laws prevailing in the society'.[134] Hence, one can observe that the notions of 'number and spacing' and 'family planning' were already subjects of contention, even without mentioning the right to safe abortion nor PSS. In this regard, Schulz et al. observe that 'unplanned and unwanted pregnancy as well as sexual education were largely a taboo subject; abortion was unmentionable in any international arena'.[135]

## III SIGNIFICANCE

The CRC does not mention PSS, and while the principle of non-discrimination applies to children, the latter category does not clearly include the unborn female. At the same time, the CRC does not expressly recognize the girl's right to a safe abortion. The *travaux préparatoires* of the CRC demonstrate that the drafters were not able to agree on a parameter for the beginning of childhood and purposefully left this issue unresolved. The CRC Committee nonetheless states in its general comments that selective abortions constitute a form of discrimination against girl children, and increasingly recognizes girls' right to a safe abortion, although these comments are not legally binding. The significance of the content of the CRC is that States parties are not expressly obliged to prohibit PSS as a discriminatory practice, nor to provide access to safe abortions to the pregnant girl child. Yet the wording of the preambular paragraph protecting children 'before as well as after birth', and the fact that its interpretative statement was incorporated in the *travaux* rather than the CRC itself, constitutes an important sign that should not be disregarded. The ICCPR does not refer to PSS, and although the principle of non-discrimination applies to all individuals, one cannot

[133] Ibid., 177–78.

[134] Ibid., 178.

[135] Patricia Schulz, Ruth Halperin-Kaddari and Beate Rudolf, 'Introduction' in Patricia Schulz et al. (eds.), *The UN Convention on the Elimination of All Forms of Discrimination against Women and Its Optional Protocol: A Commentary* (2nd ed., Oxford University Press 2022), 30.

assert that the unborn is comprised in the 'individual' category, as the Covenant does not specify when life begins, notably in article 6. The *travaux préparatoires* indicate that the drafters chose not to clarify the boundary for the beginning of life. In addition, although the Human Rights Committee acknowledges the issue of PSS, it does not prohibit this practice, and while it recognizes the issue of unsafe abortions, it does not clearly require girls' access to safe abortions in all circumstances. The significance of the content of the ICCPR is that States parties are not under a clear duty to prohibit PSS, nor to provide girls with access to a safe abortion. Finally, the CEDAW does not refer to PSS, and the CEDAW Committee fails to acknowledge this issue in its thirty-nine general recommendations. In addition, the Convention does not expressly include the unborn female in the woman category. The *travaux préparatoires* of the CEDAW reveal that the drafters avoided the issue of abortion and neglected PSS altogether. One can contend that the CEDAW Committee purposefully ignores the issue of PSS out of a concern that doing so might curtail the right of the pregnant girl child or woman to a safe abortion, which it progressively recognizes in several general recommendations since 1992. The wording of article 1 of the CEDAW could nevertheless imply that PSS is a form of discrimination as it impacts women. The significance of the content of the CEDAW is therefore that although PSS is not expressly mentioned in the CEDAW, States parties could be under a duty to tackle this issue on the grounds that it constitutes a distinction impairing the rights of women, and therefore a form of discrimination against women.

## IV SEMIOETHICS

The complexity and controversial aspect of PSS is illustrated by the decision of the drafters of the very instruments designed to protect children's rights – the CRC, women's rights – the CEDAW, as well as the main treaty protecting the right to life of all human beings – the ICCPR, to avoid clarifying the beginning of childhood, and any reference to the unborn, the fetus or the embryo. One can contend that the drafters of these treaties eluded this issue because it is located within the debate of the beginning of life, which impacts the potential right to life of the unborn girl as well as the right of pregnant girl children and women to a safe abortion, a matter which was left unresolved in all treaties. This book shall follow the approach of the drafters of these three treaties. Indeed, we consider that it is not possible to prohibit PSS without curtailing the pregnant girl's right to a safe abortion. Hence, contrarily to our approach in other chapters, we do not recommend to amend the provisions of the CRC, ICCPR and CEDAW to specifically prohibit the practice of PSS.

Instead, this book considers that PSS can solely be addressed by tackling its root causes identified in Chapters 3 and 4, notably the phenomenon of son preference and daughter devaluation, and thus gender-based discrimination as concerns civil and political rights as well as economic, social and cultural rights, such as patrilineal kinship structures, sexist inheritance laws, the practice of dowry, limited education and economic potential for girls and the inability for girl children to perform certain traditional religious and funeral rites, whereby girls are perceived as a burden, while boys constitute an asset, to their family.

# 7

# The End of Girlhood under International Law

The boundary separating girlhood and womanhood under international law raises several questions. First, does international law provide clear parameters for the end of girlhood, and do they coincide with the beginning of womanhood? Should girls remain under the umbrella of 'childhood' until they reach the yardstick of eighteen years? Or would they benefit from obtaining 'adult' rights earlier? In other words, should adolescent girls remain protected under the CRC as long as possible, or should they instead be covered under other treaties granting political and economic rights?

## I SENSE

The current definition of child in the CRC is characterized by the absence of a clear and uniform boundary for the end of girlhood. Article 1 of the CRC stipulates that:

> [f]or the purposes of the present Convention, a child means every human being below the age of eighteen years *unless under the law applicable to the child, majority is attained earlier.*[1]

One can observe that the CRC provides 'majority' as the parameter for the end of girlhood, under the upper age limit of eighteen years. This definition is notable on three grounds. Firstly, the CRC yardstick – eighteen years – for the upper limit of childhood is age-based rather than competence-based, and the Convention thereby adopts a conception of childhood grounded in age.[2] Secondly, the Convention allows for childhood to be terminated before

[1] Emphasis added.
[2] 'Definition of Child' (2019), 22. See Chapter 2.

eighteen years, once majority is reached. In this context, the CRC does not provide an age at which majority is attained. Moreover, the Convention refers solely to 'majority' and not to the 'age of majority', and thus neglects to indicate the parameter for majority: is it age, or other means, such as entering marriage, or reaching puberty? As previously noted, the conceptual notion of 'majority' is defined in terms of age in the English language, and thus article 1 of the CRC is less specific than dictionaries.[3] In fact, as shall be examined in the next section on the *meaning-intention*, the CRC drafters purposefully removed the 'age' qualifier of majority, allowing for a broader interpretation as to how majority can be attained. This leaves room for a competence-based attainment of majority under domestic law, and thus as an end of girlhood under the CRC. The CRC Committee attempts to clarify the outer limit of childhood in several general comments by specifying that the term 'child' comprises all persons under the age of eighteen years within the jurisdiction of a State party.[4] The Committee expressly states that 'adolescents up to 18 years old are holders of all the rights enshrined in the Convention',[5] which implies that the recommended boundary for the end of childhood is eighteen years. The Committee also requires States parties to provide health care to children 'until they reach 18 years of age'.[6] Moreover, in its general comment on adolescence, the Committee notes that the Convention 'recognizes the rights of all persons under 18 years'.[7] As discussed in Chapter 2, the Committee clarifies the divisions of childhood as early childhood (0–8 years),[8] middle childhood, and adolescence, the latter 'from 10 years until the 18th birthday',[9]

3 See Chapter 2.

4 CRC General Comments: 1) No. 3: 'HIV/AIDS' (2003), para. 20, referring to 'the needs of children under 18 years of age, in particular adolescents'; 2) No. 4: 'Adolescent Health' (2003), paras. 1, 6, 9, 20; 3) No. 5: 'Implementation' (2003), para. 48; 4) No. 7: 'Early Childhood' (2006), para. 39, noting that '[t]his system should cover all children up to the age of 18 years'; 5) No. 10: 'Juvenile Justice' (2007), paras. 31, 36, 37, 38, 67, 75, 76, 77, 86; 6) No. 11: 'Indigenous Children' (2009), para. 66; 7) No. 13: 'Violence' (2011), paras. 33, 72; 8) No. 14: 'Best Interests' (2013), para. 21; 9) No. 15: 'Health' (2013), paras. 1, 90; 10) Joint CEDAW-CRC GenRec/Com: 'Harmful Practices' (2014), paras. 20, 21, 55; 11) No. 19: 'Public Budgeting' (2016), para. 3; 12) No. 20: 'Adolescence' (2016), paras. 1, 5, 24, 40, 52, 86, 88; 13) No. 21: 'Street Situations' (2017), para. 16; 14) Joint CRC-CMW General Comment No. 23: 'Migration' (2017), paras. 3, 26; 15) No. 24: 'Child Justice' (2019), paras. 20, 29, 30, 31, 32, 35, 36, 70, 71, 79, 80, 81, 93, 95.

5 CRC General Comment No. 4: 'Adolescent Health' (2003), para. 1. It also notes that 'States parties have the obligation to ensure that all human beings *below* 18 enjoy all the rights set forth in the Convention without discrimination' (emphasis added): para. 6.

6 CRC General Comment No. 15: 'Health' (2013), para. 90.

7 CRC General Comment No. 20: 'Adolescence' (2016), para. 1.

8 CRC General Comment No. 7: 'Early Childhood' (2006), para. 4. See Chapter 2.

9 CRC General Comment No. 20: 'Adolescence' (2016), para. 5.

thereby inferring that the frontier of childhood is eighteen years. English dictionaries provide definitions of childhood, adolescence, youth, adulthood and majority, which as previously discussed, appear to overlap or constitute mutually exclusive periods of life, and thus tend to complicate rather than clarify the CRC open-ended definition.[10]

The Convention nevertheless comprises definite age boundaries for children involved in armed conflict as well as those in conflict with the law, which could shed light on the interpretation of article 1. Indeed, as previously mentioned, the Vienna Convention stipulates that each article should be interpreted in good faith in accordance with the ordinary meaning to be given to the terms of the treaty in their context and in the light of its object and purpose, and thus of the CRC as a whole.[11] Article 38 of the CRC provides the parameter of fifteen years for children to take a direct part in armed conflict, as it requires States parties to 'take all feasible measures to ensure that *persons* who have not attained the age of fifteen years do not take a direct part in hostilities',[12] and 'refrain from recruiting *any person* who has not attained the age of fifteen years into their armed forces'.[13] Additionally, the Convention stipulates that '[i]n recruiting among those *persons* who have attained the age of fifteen years but who have not attained the age of eighteen years, States Parties shall endeavour to give priority to those who are oldest'.[14] It is however notable that the CRC employs the expressions 'persons' and 'any person' rather than 'children' in this context. Indeed, it appears peculiar for a Convention dedicated to children to employ a descriptive other than 'child'. All CRC provisions, except for those relating to armed conflict and children in conflict with the law, exclusively refer to 'the child' and 'children', and the decision to use the expression 'persons' when specifying fifteen years therefore stands out. The *travaux préparatoires* reveal that earlier versions of article 38 employed the expressions 'child' and 'children'; however, the drafters noted that according to the 'majority' boundary under article 1, a person could cease to be a child *before* fifteen years, and thus chose the term 'person' instead of child in article 38.[15] This demonstrates that the language of article 1 has impacted parameters within other CRC provisions. The low threshold of fifteen years under article 38 has been heavily criticized and is 'the object of

[10] See Chapter 2.
[11] Vienna Convention (1969), art. 31(1). See Chapter 1.
[12] CRC, art. 38(2) (emphasis added).
[13] CRC, art. 38(3) (emphasis added).
[14] Ibid. (emphasis added).
[15] UN Doc E/CN.4/1989/WG.1/CRP.1, 40; 'History CRC' (2007), 792.

a concerted effort to augment its protective content'.[16] Several CRC member states have expressed declarations to increase the age to eighteen years under their domestic law.[17] Moreover, the CRC Committee has noted that 'States parties should not recruit into their armed forces persons below the age of 18',[18] and dedicated a day of general discussion to armed conflict in which it recommended an optional protocol to the CRC 'raising the age of recruitment of children into the armed forces to 18 years of age'.[19] The international community thereafter adopted an Optional Protocol to the CRC on Armed Conflict (OPAC) which raises the age of fifteen years to eighteen years for children in armed forces to take direct part in hostilities.[20] The OPAC also stipulates:

> Article 3:
> States Parties shall raise the minimum age for the voluntary recruitment of persons into their national armed forces from that *set out in article 38, paragraph 3, of the Convention on the Rights of the Child, taking account of the principles contained in that article and recognizing that under the Convention persons under 18 are entitled to special protection.*[21]

The wording of this provision is notable as it implies that the CRC offers special protection until eighteen years, not solely until majority is reached under the upper age limit of eighteen years, and the OPAC drafters thereby indicate a *meaning-intention* to compensate for the formulations of articles 1 and 38, although the protocol still refers to 'persons' in this context. Another notable CRC provision prohibits capital punishment and life imprisonment for children under the age of eighteen years. However, the wording of the provision is once again ambiguous, as it refers to 'persons' rather than 'children':

> Article 37:
> States Parties shall ensure that:
>
> (a) ... Neither capital punishment nor life imprisonment without possibility of release shall be imposed for offences committed by *persons* below eighteen years of age.[22]

16 Mark Drumbl and John Tobin, 'Article 38: The Rights of Children in Armed Conflict' in John Tobin (ed.), *The UN Convention on the Rights of the Child: A Commentary* (Oxford University Press 2019), 1505.
17 Reservations and Declarations to the CRC 1577 UNTS 3.
18 CRC Report (22 March 1996) UN Doc CRC/C/50, para. 251.
19 DGD (19 October 1992) UN Doc CRC/C/50, para. 75(e).
20 OPAC, art. 1.
21 Emphasis added.
22 Emphasis added.

Additionally, if one reads article 1 in combination with this provision, the formulation of article 37 could imply that 'person' and 'child' are two different identity categories: a 'person' under eighteen years who already reached majority is no longer a child, yet still protected against capital punishment and life imprisonment. The Committee has attempted to clarify that the 'child justice system should apply to all children above the minimum age of criminal responsibility but below the age of 18 years at the time of the commission of the offence',[23] and thus that 'persons' under eighteen years are in fact 'children'. From a semiotics perspective, it is worthy of note that while the CRC expressly covers girls in conflict with the law when it comes to protection against capital punishment and life imprisonment until they reach eighteen years, the actual provision on the right to life, article 6, which protects girls against murders, notably in the private sphere, such as feminicides and female infanticide, does not specifically cover girls until they reach eighteen years.[24] The Convention also requires States parties to establish a minimum age below which 'children shall be presumed not to have the capacity to infringe the penal law'; however, it does not specify a minimum age.[25] Also, while the CRC prohibits child labour, it does not specify a minimum age for admission to employment.[26] The *travaux préparatoires* indicate that the initial draft offered the threshold of fifteen years for employment, yet once again, the drafters chose not to provide a minimum age.[27]

Other international human rights treaties that refer to the concepts of minority and majority also do not offer an age nor explain how majority is attained. The ICCPR recognizes the right to measures of protection of children on account of their status as 'minors', yet does not specify an age nor explains how majority is reached. Indeed, article 24 of the Covenant stipulates:

> Every child shall have, without any discrimination as to race, colour, sex, language, religion, national or social origin, property or birth, the right to such measures of protection as are required by *his status as a minor*, on the part of his family, society and the State.[28]

[23] CRC General Comment No. 24: 'Child Justice' (2019), para. 29.

[24] For a discussion on the semiotics of art. 6 of the CRC, see 'Gendercide CRC' (2018).

[25] CRC, art. 40(3)(a): '[t]he establishment of a minimum age below which children shall be presumed not to have the capacity to infringe the penal law'.

[26] CRC, art. 32(2).

[27] UN Doc E/CN.4/1349; 'History CRC' (2007), 697.

[28] ICCPR, art. 24(1) (emphasis added).

As underscored by the Human Rights Committee in its general comment on the rights of the child, each state is at liberty to choose when the child reaches majority:

> The right to special measures of protection belongs to every child because of *his* status as a minor. Nevertheless, the Covenant does not indicate the age at which *he* attains majority. *This is to be determined by each State party in the light of the relevant social and cultural conditions.*[29]

Taylor observes in this context that the Human Rights Committee 'leaves the question open' as to the definition of child or minor, although the age of majority 'should not be set unreasonably low'.[30] The Committee nonetheless refers to an age of majority rather than 'majority', thereby implying that majority should be reached at a specific age rather than through other means, such as marriage or puberty. Also, the ICCPR specifies that the death penalty shall not be imposed for those under eighteen years: '[s]entence of death shall not be imposed for crimes committed by *persons* below eighteen years of age and shall not be carried out on pregnant women',[31] which could imply that eighteen years is the threshold for adulthood, although as in the CRC, the Covenant refers to 'persons' rather than children in this context. The ICESCR recommends that states establish age limits for child labour: '[c]hildren and young persons should be protected from economic and social exploitation ... *States should also set age limits* below which the paid employment of child labour should be prohibited and punishable by law'.[32] Yet it does not mention any age and refers to both children and young persons in this context. The ILO Worst Forms of Child Labour Convention offers eighteen years as the threshold for the end of childhood: '[f]or the purposes of this Convention, the term 'child' shall apply to all persons under the age of 18',[33] which could indicate that childhood ends at eighteen years. Yet it stipulates that the term child applies to persons under eighteen years solely 'for the purposes of this Convention', and thus exclusively as concerns 'the worst forms of child labour'. The latter notion is defined as comprising all forms of

29 ICCPR General Comment No. 17: 'Rights Child' (1989), para. 4 (emphasis added). The androcentric phrasing of the Human Rights Committee is notable, see Chapter 5.

30 *Commentary ICCPR* (2020), 660.

31 ICCPR, art. 6(5) (emphasis added).

32 ICESCR, art. 10(3).

33 Art. 2. Presently, 187 states are parties to this treaty, thus 9 less than the CRC. www.ilo.org/dyn/normlex/en/f?p=1000:11300:0::NO:11300:P11300_INSTRUMENT_ID:312327 (accessed 11 July 2023).

slavery, prostitution, pornography, trafficking of drugs and work 'which, by its nature or the circumstances in which it is carried out, is likely to harm the health, safety or morals of children'.[34] The ILO Minimum Age Convention also provides that eighteen years is the minimum age for employment or work 'which by its nature or the circumstances in which it is carried out is likely to jeopardize the health, safety or morals of young persons'.[35] However, it offers an exception for sixteen-year-olds 'on condition that the health, safety and morals of the young persons concerned are fully protected and that the young persons have received adequate specific instruction or vocational training'.[36] Moreover, it allows member states to set the minimum age for general employment at fifteen years, and even fourteen years for states 'whose economy and educational facilities are insufficiently developed', and offers exceptions to these thresholds for participation in 'artistic performances'.[37] It also permits employment of thirteen-year-olds for light work, described as 'not likely to be harmful to their health or development', nor prejudicial to attendance at school.[38] Moreover, while the Minimum Age Convention employs the expression 'child labour' under article 1, it uses the terms 'children and young persons' or 'young persons and children' in the same sentence within some provisions which could imply that they constitute separate identity categories.[39] Additionally, it solely uses the expression 'young persons' or even 'persons' when referring to persons below 18 years, over 16 years, over 15 years, and between 13–15 years,[40] which could imply that the latter are not children. Accordingly, under the Minimum Age Convention, the upper limit of childhood is not clarified, and could be thirteen, fourteen, fifteen or sixteen rather than eighteen years. The upper boundary of girlhood is therefore not clearly established in the CRC nor in the Twin Covenants and ILO Conventions. In this regard, Besson and Kleber underscore that the delineation of childhood from adulthood 'is still a very controversial question given CRC article 1's incomplete definition of the "child"'.[41]

34 Ibid., art. 3.
35 Convention No. 138 Concerning Minimum Age for Admission to Employment (Geneva, adopted 26 June 1973, entered into force 19 June 1976) ST/HR/1/Rev.6 (vol. I/part 1), art. 3 (1).
36 Ibid., art. 3(3).
37 Ibid., arts. 2(3), 2(4), 8.
38 Ibid., art. 7.
39 Ibid., arts. 5(4), 6.
40 Ibid., arts. 3, 6, 7, 9.
41 'Non-Discrimination' (2019), 42.

## II MEANING

The *travaux préparatoires* indicate that the definition of child in the first draft of the CRC comprised every human being from the moment of birth to the age of eighteen years unless the 'age of majority' was reached earlier:

> According to the present Convention a child is every human being from the moment of his birth to the age of 18 years unless, under the law of his state, he has attained his *age of majority* earlier.[42]

This open-ended definition of childhood, and thus girlhood, generated much debate between the delegates.[43]

### 1 *Terminal Point of Girlhood*

On one end of the spectrum, some state representatives argued that due to the high mortality rate and low life expectancy of children, the terminal point of childhood had to be established earlier than eighteen years.[44] They pointed out that many countries had set an age of fourteen for the end of compulsory education and that the UN General Assembly had agreed on the age limit of fifteen in connection with the International Year of the Child.[45] They also contended that setting the upper limit of childhood at fourteen would clearly distinguish it from the concept of minority, which was already protected under the domestic law of many nations.[46] It is worthy of note that these states also espoused this parameter on the grounds that fourteen was the legal age of marriage for girls in several countries,[47] which implies that they supported child marriage at this early age. These delegates also claimed that many states could not afford the measures required to protect children up to eighteen years. Nepal favoured the upper age limit of sixteen 'to take into account the concerns of poorer States who may not be able to shoulder the burdens imposed by this convention for children up to

42 UN Commission on Human Rights, 'Question of a Convention on the Rights of the Child' (17 January 1980) UN Doc E/CN.4/1349*, 2, art. 1 (emphasis added); *Travaux préparatoires CRC* (1992), 115. For a discussion on the androcentric phrasing of draft CRC provisions, see Chapter 5.

43 *Travaux préparatoires CRC* (1992), 115–18.

44 *International Law Child* (1998), 36.

45 *Travaux préparatoires CRC* (1992), 115.

46 Ibid.; Commission HR, 'Report of the 1980 Open-Ended Working Group on the Question of a Convention on the Rights of the Child' (10 March 1980) UN Doc E/CN.4/L.1542, 5–6.

47 *Travaux préparatoires CRC* (1992), 115.

18 years of age'.[48] On the other end of the spectrum, several delegates supported the standard age of eighteen as their domestic legislation protected children above the age of fifteen years.[49] They also considered that the CRC should apply to as large a group as possible.[50] Finally, other delegates stressed that:

> the need was felt for some flexibility, considering that the age of eighteen years is not necessarily consonant with the age of majority in various countries, and that the application of the rights recognized in the CRC to a person who is no longer a minor could be incompatible with his or her legal status.[51]

Hence, there was clearly a tension between cultural relativism and universalism, and thus whether a single age or threshold be applied in every state globally. It is noteworthy that Finland offered a compromise in this context. It suggested to set eighteen years as the parameter for the end of childhood, while providing that children between fifteen and eighteen years and who are no longer minors be granted specific 'adult' rights:

> Article 1:
>
> 1 For the purposes of the present Convention, a *child* means every human being who has not attained the age of 18 years.
> 2 No provision of the present Convention shall be applied to a child who has attained the age of [15] years and who no longer is a minor, where the application would be manifestly incompatible with the legal status of that child.
> 3 In terms of paragraph 2 of this article, *a child who no longer is a minor* means a child who:
> (a) has full legal capacity; or
> (b) has become emancipated in all matters relating to his or her person; or
> (c) has the right to determine his or her own residence; or
> (d) has the capacity to enter into certain contractual relationships; or
> (e) has the capacity to dispose of certain parts of his or her property.[52]

48 Commission HR, 'Question of a Convention on the Rights of the Child: Report of the Working Group on a Draft Convention on the Rights of the Child' (2 March 1989) UN Doc E/CN.4/1989/48, para. 82.
49 *Travaux préparatoires* CRC (1992), 116.
50 Ibid.
51 Sharon Detrick, A *Commentary on the United Nations Convention on the Rights of the Child* (Martinus Nijhoff 1999), 52–53.
52 Commission HR, 'Question of a Convention on the Rights of the Child: Report of the Working Group on a Draft Convention on the Rights of the Child' (6 April 1988) UN Doc E/CN.4/1988/28, para. 224, Proposal E/CN.4/1988/WG.1/WP.10.

In addition, Finland noted that 'the age of majority' as a parameter to delimit the scope of application of the Convention was problematic, and further argued that it 'could weaken the whole convention considerably'.[53] Finland nevertheless withdrew its proposal, although it still emphasized that the wording of article 1 should be revised in order to establish 'crucial links' with other provisions providing age parameters in the CRC, such as those regarding the participation of children in armed conflict.[54] The following year, the Finnish delegation made the following proposal:

> For the purpose of the present Convention a child means every human being who is a minor and has not attained the age of 18 years.[55]

One can observe that Finland attempted once again to clarify the relationship between minority and childhood, although this proposal was not approved by other delegates. India suggested to underscore that different age limits might be established for different purposes:

> According to the present Convention a child is every human being up to the age of 18 years unless, under the law of his State, he has ceased to be a child earlier *or different age limits for different purposes* are recognised.[56]

During the drafting negotiations, the observer for the International Union for Child Welfare suggested to eliminate the upper age limit of eighteen years altogether, which would have enabled States parties to establish *any* age for majority, including a very young age, or an age over eighteen years, since eighteen years would no longer be considered as a yardstick.[57] In this regard, this proposal clearly adopted a cultural relativist approach.[58] Several delegates, even those who preferred the parameter of majority, opposed the suggestion to eliminate the reference to the upper limit of eighteen years within the definition.[59] These delegates warned that the concept of 'majority age' varied greatly both between and within countries depending on the civil, penal and

53 Ibid., para. 225.

54 Ibid.

55 Commission HR, 'CRC Report Working Group' UN Doc E/CN.4/1989/48, para. 76; Proposal UN Doc E/CN.4/1989/WG.1/WP.12.

56 Commission HR, 'CRC Report Working Group' UN Doc E/CN.4/1989/48, para. 76; Proposal UN Doc E/CN.4/1989/WG.1/WP.14 (emphasis added).

57 *Travaux préparatoires CRC* (1992), 116; The text would have read as follows: '[a]ccording to the present Convention a child is every human being who has not attained the age of majority in conformity with the law of his state'.

58 See Chapter 3 for a discussion on cultural relativism.

59 *Travaux préparatoires CRC* (1992), 116.

political aspects at issue.[60] The debate was pursued until the very end of the drafting process; Kuwait suggested to remove the specific age limit of eighteen in the final text as late as 1989,[61] whereas Portugal insisted on the yardstick of eighteen years on the grounds that '[a] definition based on the simple notion of majority would not therefore seem to be desirable, taking into account the different solutions existing in various legal systems'.[62] Portugal further noted that the upper age limit of eighteen should be present in the definition of child to 'underline the recognition of the need to ensure special protection to human beings under that age'.[63]

### 2 *Majority or Age of Majority*

The second debate concerned the concept of majority itself. In the first draft, the definition of child referred to 'the age of majority' rather than 'majority',[64] which signifies that states had to establish an age at which majority was reached and were thus not at liberty to claim that majority was attained by other means, such as reaching puberty or entering a marriage. This draft definition ensured uniformity, at least within States parties, as all children, including girls, would reach majority at the same age within their respective jurisdictions. This definition also prevented states from establishing puberty or marriage as a means of attaining majority. In fact, the delegates favoured this parameter until the very end of the drafting process.[65] It is however notable that the drafters did not discuss the issue of child marriage in this context, even though it was a valid argument to support the 'age of majority' formulation as it prevented young girls from becoming adults through marriage.[66] Finland and India, with the support of the United States, expressed concern that the very concept of majority might be interpreted differently across nations, and argued

60 Ibid.

61 Commission HR, 'CRC Report Working Group' UN Doc E/CN.4/1989/48, para. 81.

62 Ibid., para. 82.

63 Ibid.

64 Commission HR, 'Question CRC' (17 January 1980) UN Doc E/CN.4/1349*, 2, art. 1; *Travaux préparatoires CRC* (1992), 115.

65 That is, until 1989. See for example Commission HR, 'CRC Report Working Group' UN Doc E/CN.4/1989/48, para. 75: '[f]or the purpose of the present Convention, a child means every human being to the age of 18 years unless, under the law of (his) the child's State, *the age of majority* is attained earlier' (emphasis added); Commission HR, 'CRC Report Working Group' (16 October 1987) UN Doc E/CN.4/1988/WG.1/WP.1, 5: '[a]ccording to the present Convention a child is every human being to the age of 18 years unless, under the law of his State, he has attained his *age of majority* earlier' (emphasis added).

66 *Travaux préparatoires CRC* (1992), 115–18.

that it should therefore not be present in the CRC.[67] These delegates recognized the role of the immediate, dynamical and final interpretants, including various communities worldwide, in 'meaning-making', and Welby's statement that there is no 'plain meaning' of words. It is also notable that this proposal was not solely coming from the Global North, as it included a significant Global South nation: India. Finally, not only did the term majority remain in article 1, but at the very end of the drafting process, the representative of the Netherlands argued that majority could be reached by 'satisfying criteria other than age', and his suggestion to delete the words 'the age of' was adopted by the drafters of the CRC.[68] In this context, he failed to specify which criteria other than age could be applied, notably marriage.[69] The *travaux* unfortunately do not shed light on the reasons that led other delegates to approve his suggestion. It is worthy of note that this proposal came from a Global North nation – the Netherlands – an imperialist state with a colonialist history, which ties into Rao's concern as to *who* speaks on behalf of communities and cultures, on *what* grounds, and *who* is impacted by those decisions, in the case at hand, the girl child.[70] The Dutch proposal also links to the observation from the African Committee on Traditional Practices that claims of cultural relativist terminology often come from the Global North, which speaks *for* instead of *with* the Global South.[71] In fact, the African Union adopted, one year after the CRC, a charter for children's rights that enshrines the age parameter of eighteen years for the end of childhood, thereby demonstrating that Global South states are not systematically in favour of lower thresholds.[72]

## III SIGNIFICANCE OF THE ABSENCE OF A UNIFORM BOUNDARY

The boundary of girlhood remains uncertain: when exactly is majority reached under the upper age limit of eighteen years? The current parameter of 'majority' for the end of girlhood in the CRC raises serious

67 Commission HR, 'CRC Report Working Group' UN Doc E/CN.4/1989/48, para. 79.

68 Ibid., para. 80; *Travaux préparatoires CRC* (1992), 118–19.

69 Commission HR, 'CRC Report Working Group' UN Doc E/CN.4/1989/48, para. 80; *Travaux préparatoires CRC* (1992), 118–19.

70 'Gender and Culture' (1995); see Chapter 3.

71 See glossary definition of FGM and Chapter 3.

72 African Charter on the Rights and Welfare of the Child, African Union (Addis Ababa, adopted 11 July 1990, entered into force 29 November 1999), art. 2: '[f]or the purposes of this Charter, a child means every human being below the age of 18 years'. The Charter also provides under art. 22(2) that 'no child shall take a direct part in hostilities', which according to its definition of child under art. 1, covers children until eighteen years.

questions relating to the protection and the empowerment of the girl child. The 'majority' parameter signifies that female human beings who reach majority before eighteen years under domestic law are no longer covered by the Convention. On the one hand, it could be argued that this is detrimental to girl children since they lose the protection offered by the CRC before the age of eighteen years. On the other hand, one could contend that the CRC comprises provisions that restrict girls' autonomy rights and it would be beneficial to reach the end of girlhood earlier than eighteen years, through majority. Hence, the boundary for the end of girlhood raises the debate between paternalism and child liberationism discussed in Chapter 3. Indeed, under a paternalistic approach, adults wish to protect children as long as possible, including against themselves, whereas child liberationists consider that children should be granted the same legal rights as adults.

## 1 *Positive Features of the CRC for Girl Children*

In his description of the CRC drafting process, Lopatka explains that the Convention is embedded in a contemporary conception of childhood that emerged between the two world wars, whereby:

> the child is an autonomous person who has his or her own needs, interests and rights; and that he or she is not only an object of care and concern but also a subject whose interests and rights should be respected.[73]

Indeed, the CRC adopts a rights approach and enshrines several provisions that are essential to the girl child. Accordingly, it would be important to ensure that she is covered under the Convention until she reaches eighteen years.

### 1.1 Most Widely Ratified Treaty Globally

It is important to bear in mind that the CRC is the most widely ratified international human rights treaty.[74] Consequently, girls who reach majority before eighteen years and who are living in countries that have not ratified other international treaties, are deprived of rights enshrined in the CRC that they cannot claim elsewhere. Presently, several countries are not member

[73] 'History CRC' (2007), xxxvii.

[74] Presently, 196 states are parties to the CRC. The United States is the only nation that has not yet ratified the CRC: 1577 UNTS 3.

states of the ICCPR (twenty-four),[75] ICESCR (twenty-six)[76] and CEDAW (eight),[77] and girls living in those jurisdictions are not accorded civil and political rights; economic, social and cultural rights; and rights essential to female human beings, under these three treaties, respectively. Moreover, several states that ratified the ICCPR, ICESCR and CEDAW entered reservations to provisions that are fundamental to girl children, for instance, the rights to education, participation and protection from violence in the private and public spheres.[78] Girls who reach majority before eighteen years are therefore stripped of rights granted in the CRC that are either not available because their country is not party to other human rights treaties, or significantly weakened as a result of reservations.

### 1.2 Unique and Comprehensive Rights

The CRC enshrines several rights that are either not recognized or not protected as extensively under other international human rights treaties. Firstly, the CRC guarantees, under article 19, the right of children to protection from all forms of violence, abuse, neglect, maltreatment and exploitation, while in the care of parents or legal guardians.[79] Likewise, the CRC enshrines the right of children, deprived of their family

75 The following eighteen countries neither signed nor ratified the ICCPR: Bhutan, Brunei Darussalam, Cook Islands, the Holy See, Kiribati, Malaysia, the Federated States of Micronesia, Myanmar (Burma), Niue, Oman, Saint Kitts and Nevis, Saudi Arabia, Singapore, Solomon Islands, South Sudan, Tonga, Tuvalu and the United Arab Emirates. The following six signed but did not ratify the ICCPR: China, Comoros, Cuba, Nauru, Palau and Saint Lucia: 999 UNTS 171.

76 The following twenty-two countries neither signed nor ratified the ICESCR: Principality of Andorra, Bhutan, Botswana, Brunei Darussalam, Cook Islands, the Holy See, Kiribati, Malaysia, the Federated States of Micronesia, Mozambique, Nauru, Niue, Saint Kitts and Nevis, Saint Lucia, Samoa, Saudi Arabia, Singapore, South Sudan, Tonga, Tuvalu, the United Arab Emirates and Vanuatu. The following four signed but did not ratify the ICESCR: Comoros, Cuba, Palau and the United States of America: 993 UNTS 3.

77 The following six countries neither signed nor ratified the CEDAW: the Holy See, Islamic Republic of Iran, Niue, Somalia, Sudan and Tonga. The following two signed but did not ratify the CEDAW: Palau and the United States of America: 1249 UNTS 13.

78 Reservations to the ICCPR, 999 UNTS 171; Reservations to the ICESCR, 993 UNTS 3; Reservations to the CEDAW, 1249 UNTS 13. See Chapter 5 for a discussion on reservations, notably on key rights enshrined in the CEDAW.

79 CRC, art. 19(1). This comprehensive provision enshrines a right to protection from 'all forms of physical or mental violence, injury or abuse, neglect or negligent treatment, maltreatment or exploitation, including sexual abuse, while in the care of parent(s), legal guardian(s) or any other person who has the care of the child'.

environment as a result of violence and neglect, to 'special protection and assistance' by the State and specifies that such measures shall include foster care and adoption.[80] Instead, the CEDAW does not enshrine a provision expressly prohibiting violence against women.[81] The ICCPR offers a broad right to 'such measures of protection as are required' by children,[82] and prohibits cruel, inhuman or degrading treatment,[83] and the ICESCR stipulates that 'special measures of protection and assistance should be taken on behalf of all children', especially as concerns economic and social exploitation.[84] However, these instruments do not offer the comprehensive protection of the CRC. Indeed, in addition to requiring States parties to protect children against all forms of violence, the CRC underscores their duty of due diligence to prevent and investigate acts of violence, which is especially pertinent for girl victims of abuse:

> Such protective measures should, as appropriate, include effective procedures for the establishment of social programmes to provide necessary support for the child and for those who have the care of the child, as well as for other forms of *prevention and for identification, reporting, referral, investigation, treatment and follow-up* of instances of child maltreatment ... and, as appropriate, for *judicial involvement*.[85]

The CRC Committee explains that this provision places a 'positive and active obligation' on States parties to prevent, investigate and punish those responsible, as well as redress human rights violations and abolish 'the widespread practice of de jure and de facto impunity, in particular of State actors'.[86] Girls who reach majority before eighteen years are therefore stripped of the protection against violence accorded in the CRC while not granted this right under the CEDAW and Twin Covenants. For example, girls who have reached majority and are separated from their family because of abuse and neglect, are denied special protection and assistance by the State that is provided in the CRC. In this regard, the CRC Committee underscores that the present

80 CRC, art. 20(1) and (3).

81 The CEDAW Committee produced three general recommendations on violence against women to address this gap, however, these are not legally binding: CEDAW General Recommendations: 1) No. 12: 'Violence against Women' (1989); (2) No. 19: 'Violence against Women' (1992); 3) No. 35: 'Gender-based Violence' (2017).

82 ICCPR, art. 24(1).

83 ICCPR, art. 7.

84 ICESCR, art. 10(3).

85 CRC, art. 19(2) (emphasis added).

86 CRC General Comment No. 13: 'Violence' (2011), paras. 5, 55.

boundary of childhood precludes adolescents between sixteen and eighteen years from accessing facilities, noting that:

> [a]dolescents in alternative care are commonly required to leave once they reach 16–18 years of age and are particularly vulnerable to sexual abuse and exploitation, trafficking and violence as they lack support systems or protection and have been afforded no opportunities to acquire the skills and capacities to protect themselves.[87]

The CRC Committee attempts to broaden the protection against violence of article 19 by specifying in its general comments that States parties are required to 'recognize that persons up to the age of 18 years are entitled to continuing protection from all forms of exploitation and abuse',[88] and that given the child's 'specific vulnerability to maltreatment', article 19 also applies to children under eighteen years who attained majority or emancipation through early or forced marriage.[89] The Committee thus appears to compensate for the general wording of article 1 to ensure that girl children are covered by the CRC until eighteen years, as no other treaty offers such comprehensive protection against violence.

Secondly, the CRC enshrines the right of child victims to physical and psychological recovery,[90] which is not guaranteed under the Twin Covenants and CEDAW. The definition of 'child victim' in the CRC is extensive as it includes those who experienced 'any form of neglect, exploitation, or abuse; torture or any other form of cruel, inhuman or degrading treatment or punishment; or armed conflicts'. Furthermore, the right to recovery is broad as it comprises 'physical and psychological recovery and social reintegration', that must take place 'in an environment which fosters the health, self-respect and dignity of the child'. The CRC also offers a comprehensive provision on the rights of children with disabilities. Accordingly, the girl child who has a mental or physical disability is entitled to special care and to enjoy 'a full and decent life, in conditions which ensure dignity, promote self-reliance and facilitate the child's active participation in the community'.[91] More specifically, she is accorded the right to effective access to 'education, training, health

87 CRC General Comment No. 20: 'Adolescence' (2016), para. 52.

88 Ibid., para. 40.

89 CRC General Comment No. 13: 'Violence' (2011), footnote 13.

90 CRC, art. 39: 'States Parties shall take all appropriate measures to promote physical and psychological recovery and social reintegration of a child victim of: any form of neglect, exploitation, or abuse; torture or any other form of cruel, inhuman or degrading treatment or punishment; or armed conflicts. Such recovery and reintegration shall take place in an environment which fosters the health, self-respect and dignity of the child'.

91 CRC, art. 23(1) and (2).

care services, rehabilitation services, preparation for employment and recreation opportunities'.[92] This protection is not offered in the Covenants and CEDAW, and since many states have yet to ratify the Convention on the Rights of Persons with Disabilities (2006), girls with disabilities who reach majority before eighteen years are deprived of essential measures for accessibility, including education and preparation for employment.[93]

Thirdly, the right to health is broader under the CRC than the ICESCR as the former comprises the right to 'facilities for the treatment of illness and rehabilitation of health',[94] and the provision of 'necessary medical assistance and health care to all children with emphasis on the development of primary health care'.[95] The CRC also requires States parties to develop family planning education and services, which is particularly relevant for adolescent girls as concerns the rights to contraception and safe abortion.[96] In this regard, it is notable that the CRC Committee had to clarify that the child's right to health under the CRC is protected until eighteen years:

> The Committee reminds the State party of their obligations to ensure that relevant government authorities and service providers are held accountable for maintaining the highest possible standards of children's health and health care until they reach 18 years of age.[97]

Moreover, the CRC recognizes the right to be protected from 'traditional practices prejudicial to the health of children'.[98] This provision is especially important to tackle violations such as FGM and child marriage that are specific to or predominantly experienced by girl children. Furthermore, although both treaties recognize the right to an adequate standard of living,[99] the CRC guarantees a standard of living 'adequate for the child's physical, mental, spiritual, moral and social development',[100] which is uniquely comprehensive.

[92] CRC, art. 23(3).

[93] Presently, nine states are not parties to the CRPD. The following four countries neither signed nor ratified the CRPD: Eritrea, the Holy See, Niue and South Sudan. The following five signed but did not ratify it: Bhutan, Lebanon, Tajikistan, Tonga and the United States of America.

[94] CRC, art. 24(1).

[95] CRC, art. 24(2)b).

[96] CRC, art. 24(2)(f): '[t]o develop preventive health care, guidance for parents and family planning education and services'.

[97] CRC General Comment No. 15: 'Health' (2013), para. 90.

[98] CRC, art. 24(3): 'States Parties shall take all effective and appropriate measures with a view to abolishing traditional practices prejudicial to the health of children'.

[99] ICESCR, art. 11; CRC, art. 27. Both treaties also enshrine the right to social security: ICESCR, art. 9; CRC, art. 26.

[100] CRC, art. 27(1).

Fourthly, the right to education is wider in the CRC than in the ICESCR since States parties are required to 'make educational and vocational information and guidance available and accessible to all children',[101] offer 'financial assistance in case of need[102] and 'take measures to encourage regular attendance at schools and the reduction of drop-out rates'.[103] The CRC also addresses the issue of the corporal punishment of girl children in an educational setting by stipulating that 'school discipline is administered in a manner consistent with the child's human dignity and in conformity with the present Convention'.[104] In addition, whereas the ICESCR provides that education shall be directed to the 'full development of the human personality and the sense of its dignity',[105] the CRC refers more comprehensively and holistically to the child's 'personality, talents and mental and physical abilities to their fullest potential'.[106] Furthermore, the right to rest and leisure in the ICESCR is only accorded as concerns work,[107] whereas the CRC guarantees this right independently from work. Indeed, the CRC recognizes the right of the child to rest and leisure *per se*, which comprises that of engaging 'in play and recreational activities appropriate to the age of the child',[108] and thereby also safeguards the right to rest and leisure of girl children as concerns their studies. Hence, the formulation of this right in the CRC addresses the double burden of girlhood whereby girls are often left with no time to rest after they complete their school hours and numerous household chores.[109] The ICESCR guarantees children and young persons, which one could assume includes girls who reached majority before eighteen years under the subgroup 'young persons', a certain safeguard against economic exploitation, notably against work harmful to their morals or health, life and normal development,[110] yet the protection offered under the CRC is more extensive as it also prohibits work that is likely to be hazardous or to interfere with the child's education, or be harmful to the child's health or physical, mental, spiritual, moral or social development,[111] and 'all other forms of

[101] CRC, art. 28(1)d).
[102] CRC, art. 28(1)b).
[103] CRC, art. 28(1)(e).
[104] CRC, art. 28(2).
[105] ICESCR, art. 13(1).
[106] CRC, art. 29(1)a).
[107] ICESCR, art. 7: 'the right of everyone to the enjoyment of just and favourable conditions of work which ensure, in particular ... d) rest, leisure and reasonable limitation of working hours and periodic holidays with pay, as well as remuneration for public holidays'.
[108] CRC, art. 31.
[109] See Chapter 3; *Burden Girlhood* (1995).
[110] ICESCR, art. 10(3): '[c]hildren and young persons should be protected from economic and social exploitation. Their employment in work harmful to their morals or health or dangerous to life or likely to hamper their normal development should be punishable by law'.
[111] CRC, art. 32(1).

exploitation prejudicial to any aspects of the child's welfare'.[112] In this regard, it is worthy of note that the CRC Committee specifies that children should be protected against hazardous work until eighteen years of age, thereby attempting once again to compensate for the wording of article 1.[113] The CRC also protects girls against the illicit use of narcotic drugs and psychotropic substances, and involvement in trafficking of such substances.[114] The Convention expressly tackles the issue of sexual exploitation for it places an obligation on States parties to prevent the inducement or coercion, and the exploitative use of children in prostitution and pornographic performances and material,[115] and thus offers a broader protection than the CEDAW which solely refers to 'all forms of traffic in women and exploitation of prostitution of women'.[116] The comprehensive protection in the CRC is crucial given the vulnerability of girls, notably adolescent girls, to sexualized social and dress codes, including on social media platforms such as Instagram and TikTok.[117] Moreover, the CEDAW does not clearly indicate whether the 'woman' category comprises 'girls' in this context, and thus does not unambiguously cover girls.[118]

Lastly, while both the ICCPR and the CRC comprise several articles on the rights of persons deprived of liberty and accused of having committed a crime, including the principle of the presumption of innocence,[119] and the rights to legal assistance and an interpreter,[120] the CRC offers additional protection to the girl child. Although the ICCPR stipulates that 'juvenile persons shall be … brought as speedily as possible for adjudication', the CRC states that detention shall be used as a measure of last resort and for the shortest appropriate period of time.[121] Also, whereas the ICCPR states that juvenile persons shall be segregated from adults in the penitentiary system, the CRC specifies that children shall be separated from adults and have the right to maintain contact with their families through correspondence and visits.[122] Furthermore, while the ICCPR states that the criminal procedure shall take account of the juvenile person's age and the desirability of promoting their

[112] CRC, art. 36.
[113] CRC General Comment No. 20: 'Adolescence' (2016), para. 86.
[114] CRC, art. 33.
[115] CRC, art. 34.
[116] CEDAW, art. 6.
[117] See Chapter 4.
[118] See Chapter 8.
[119] ICCPR, art. 14(2); CRC, art. 40, 2)b)i).
[120] ICCPR, art. 14(3)d) and f); CRC, art. 40 (2)b)ii) and vi).
[121] ICCPR, art. 10(2)b); CRC, art. 37(b).
[122] ICCPR, art. 10(2)b); CRC, art. 37c).

rehabilitation,[123] the CRC offers a much broader provision requiring States parties to treat children:

> in a manner consistent with the *promotion of the child's sense of dignity and worth, which reinforces the child's respect for the human rights and fundamental freedoms of others* and which takes into account the child's age and the desirability of promoting *the child's reintegration and the child's assuming a constructive role in society*.[124]

One can observe that this provision places a strong duty on States parties to strive for the reintegration of children and to assist them in assuming a constructive role in society, which implies significantly more measures than the ICCPR. It is also notable that the ICCPR employs the expression 'juvenile' in this context, which as discussed in Chapter 1, has a negative connotation. The CRC also provides for alternative measures to detention for children, including care, guidance, counselling, probation, foster care, education and vocational training programmes, and reiterates that the human rights and legal safeguards for children shall be fully respected.[125] The CRC Committee underscores that provisions concerning children in conflict with the law in the Convention should apply to children until they reach eighteen years, thereby once again attempting to compensate for the broad upper boundary of childhood under article 1.[126] Finally, the CRC is the most comprehensive instrument concerning child rights, as it enshrines civil and political rights as well as economic, social and cultural rights, comprised in the ICCPR and ICESCR.[127] Girl children living in a state which is a party to only one of the Twin Covenants will therefore be deprived of half of the rights accorded in the CRC.

### 2 *Positive Features of Majority before Eighteen Years*

The CRC nevertheless features certain concepts ensconced in paternalism and *childism*, and adolescent girls would thus benefit from being granted

[123] ICCPR, art. 14(4).
[124] CRC, art. 40(1) (emphasis added).
[125] CRC, art. 40(3)b).
[126] CRC General Comments No. 10: 'Juvenile Justice' (2007), paras. 31, 36, 37, 38, 67, 75, 76, 77, 86; No. 24: 'Child Justice' (2019), paras. 20, 29, 30, 31, 32, 35, 36, 70, 71, 79, 80, 81, 93, 95.
[127] CRC, art. 4: 'States Parties shall undertake all appropriate legislative, administrative, and other measures for the implementation of the rights recognized in the present Convention. With regard to economic, social and cultural rights, States Parties shall undertake such measures to the maximum extent of their available resources and, where needed, within the framework of international cooperation'.

certain 'adult' rights under treaties such as the CEDAW, ICCPR and ICESCR before reaching eighteen years.

### 2.1 'Childist' Provisions of the CRC

The CRC comprises provisions that could appear to constitute a form of paternalism or childism,[128] especially the concepts of the best interests of the child (BIC) and parental authority. It could be argued that while these principles may be problematic for all girl children, they are particularly difficult for adolescent girls who reached rational autonomy as they constitute clear limitations to their autonomy rights.

2.1.1 Best Interests of the Child The BIC principle is enshrined in article 3 of the CRC:

> Art 3(1) In all actions concerning children, whether undertaken by public or private social welfare institutions, courts of law, administrative authorities or legislative bodies, the best interests of the child shall be a primary consideration.

The BIC is closely linked to the concept of parental authority, which is located within the same article, in the following paragraph:

> Art 3(2) States Parties undertake to ensure the child such protection and care as is necessary for his or her well-being, *taking into account the rights and duties of his or her parents*, legal guardians, or other individuals legally responsible for him or her, and, to this end, shall take all appropriate legislative and administrative measures.[129]

One can observe that the text expressly requires States parties to take into consideration the rights and duties of the child's parents. The BIC constitutes one of the two principles of interpretation of the Convention, along with the evolving capacities of the child (article 5), and every provision of the treaty should therefore be interpreted in light of these twin principles.[130] The BIC is also one of the four guiding principles of the CRC, along with the principle of non-discrimination (article 2) and the rights to life (article 6) and participation (article 12).[131] The BIC is reiterated in other articles of the CRC as concerns children separated from their family

[128] See Chapter 3 for an examination of childism.
[129] Emphasis added.
[130] *International Law Child* (1998), 45.
[131] CRC General Comment No. 5: 'Implementation' (2003), para. 12.

environment (articles 9 and 20), the child's upbringing (article 18), adoption (article 21) and the justice system (articles 37 and 40). However, while the BIC is accorded such a central position in the Convention, the latter fails to clarify its content. It is worthy of note that during the drafting of the CRC, many delegates considered that the formulation of the BIC allowed each state to define its meaning, and many voiced concerns regarding subjectivity:[132]

> Because of its general nature, there is a danger that the concept of the best interests of the child as recognized in article 3 ... may induce States ... to give this concept a purely nationalist content and interpretation.[133]

Venezuela underscored the subjectivity of the BIC as formulated in the draft CRC: '[t]hat would mean leaving the interpretation of the "best interests of the child" to the judgement of the person, institution or organization applying the rule'.[134] The BIC is thus very difficult to implement. As noted by Mnookin, '[d]eciding what is best for a child poses a question no less ultimate than the purposes and values of life itself'.[135] Askari underscores the problematic terminology of article 3:

> [I]nterpretive problems plague the application of the best interest standard. These difficulties stem from the wording of the phrase itself, its open-endedness and its inconsistent usage in different settings and cultures.[136]

In this regard, Alston argues that '[i]f human rights norms in general can be said to be inherently indeterminate, the best interests principle is located by most of its critics at the most indeterminate outer margins even of that body of norms'.[137] It is noteworthy that the CRC Committee drafted a general

[132] For a discussion on the *meaning* behind the best interests of the child (BIC), see Clara Chapdelaine-Feliciati, 'Translating the Meaning-Intention behind the "Best Interests of the Child" Principle in the Convention on the Rights of the Child', in Meng Ji and Susan Petrilli (eds.), *Intersemiotic Perspectives on Emotions: Translating Across Signs, Bodies and Values* (Routledge 2022). For example, New Zealand presumed that the BIC would 'be open, through the general terms in which they are couched, to varied interpretations and will in fact be defined nationally': UN Doc E/CN.4/1324/Add.5; 'History CRC' (2007), 336. Others worried that the broad wording of art. 3 could drive states further apart: UN Doc E/CN.4/1984/WG.1/WP.6; 'History CRC' (2007), 341–42.

[133] UN Doc E/CN.4/1984/WG.1/WP.6; 'History CRC' (2007), 341.

[134] Commission HR, 'CRC Report Working Group' UN Doc E/CN.4/1989/48, para. 120.

[135] Robert Mnookin, 'Child-Custody Adjudication: Judicial Functions in the Face of Indeterminacy' (1975) *Law and Contemporary Problems* 226, 260.

[136] 'Jus Cogens' (1998), 18.

[137] Philip Alston, 'The Best Interests Principle: Towards a Reconciliation of Culture and Human Rights' (1994) 8 *International Journal of Law, Policy and the Family* 1, 18.

comment specifically for the purpose of clarifying the BIC principle almost twenty-five years after the adoption of the CRC, for it implies that States parties have had difficulties in interpreting the BIC, and that it has been wrongly construed in the past.[138] The CRC Committee itself states:

> The flexibility of the concept of the child's best interests allows it to be responsive to the situation of individual children and to evolve knowledge about child development. However, *it may also leave room for manipulation; the concept of the child's best interests has been abused by Governments and other State authorities* to justify racist policies, for example; by parents to defend their own interests in custody disputes; by professionals who could not be bothered, and who dismiss the assessment of the child's best interests as irrelevant or unimportant.[139]

Hence, it could be argued that the BIC constitutes a subjective test that will differ according to the conceptions of childhood in a given state, as well as that of the master signifiers who are in a position of authority towards girl children, both in the public and private spheres. The BIC could thus be employed as an instrument to strengthen the power of adults over girls in societies that adopt a paternalistic or childist approach. On the one hand, some scholars in the Anglo-Saxon Global North consider the BIC as a rather clear principle, or devised interpretative mechanisms to support this claim. For instance, Eekelaar distinguishes between decisions that concern children and those that affect children indirectly and employs 'dynamic self-determinism' as a means of ensuring that the BIC is applied appropriately: 'the very fact that the outcome has been, at least partly, determined by the child is taken to demonstrate that the outcome is in the child's best interests'.[140] However, these scholars appear to refer almost exclusively to jurisdictions such as the United Kingdom, Canada and Australia, and to some extent South Africa, which are not representative of domestic laws and practices

[138] CRC General Comment No. 14: 'Best Interests' (2013).
[139] Ibid., para. 34 (emphasis added).
[140] John Eekelaar, 'The Interests of the Child and the Child's Wishes: The Role of Dynamic Self-Determinism' (1994) 8 *International Journal of Law, Policy and the Family* 42, 48. See also John Eekelaar, 'The Role of the Best Interests Principle in Decisions Affecting Children and Decisions about Children' (2015) 23 *International Journal of Children's Rights* 3; John Eekelaar 'Two Dimensions of the Best Interests Principle: Decisions about Children and Decisions Affecting Children' in Elaine Sutherland and Lesley-Anne Barnes Macfarlane (eds.), *Implementing Article 3 of the United Nations Convention on the Rights of the Child: Best Interests, Welfare and Well-being* (Cambridge University Press 2016); John Eekelaar and John Tobin, 'Article 3: The Best Interests of the Child' in John Tobin (ed.), *The UN Convention on the Rights of the Child: A Commentary* (Oxford University Press 2019).

internationally.[141] On the other hand, several scholars, many from the Global South, underscore the different possible interpretations of the BIC, and how this principle intersects and interacts differently with various legal systems and cultures.[142] Already in 1994, Goonesekere warned that the BIC could be employed to revive empowering traditional practices, yet also questionable ones.[143] More recently, Moussa explains that the BIC is:

> decidedly subjective and may be interpreted differently depending on the cultural context. In practice, applying the 'best interests' standard is left to the discretion of domestic Judges and is therefore a principle whose application differs from one setting to another and from one culture to another.[144]

As is the case with the competence test, the subjectivity of the BIC is particularly problematic when examined in light of intersectionality theory whereby the conceptions of different groups of children vary according to a series of factors, such as gender.[145] The BIC could thus be shaped by conceptions of girlhood embedded in both childism and sexism that significantly curtail the rights of girl children, notably their autonomy rights. Halperin-Kaddari and Freeman note that '[l]egislatures, courts, or other family tribunals may determine that the "best interests of the child" is served, for example, by awarding custody to fathers in a patrilineal society, by applying discriminatory religious law, or by awarding custody to the parent who has greater financial resources (generally the father)'.[146] The subjectivity of the BIC is particularly problematic in the private sphere as most parents do not

[141] 'Article 3: The Best Interests of the Child' (2019); John Tobin, 'Judging the Judges: Are They Adopting the Rights Approach in Matters Involving Children?' (2009) 33 *Melbourne University Law Review* 579; Jason Pobjoy, 'The Best Interests of the Child Principle as an Independent Source of International Protection' (2015) 64 *International and Comparative Law Quarterly* 327.

[142] See for example Shabnam Ishaque and Muhammad Mustafa Khan, 'The Best Interests of the Child: A Prevailing Consideration within Islamic Principles and a Governing Principle in Child Custody Cases in Pakistan' (2015) 29 *International Journal of Law, Policy and the Family* 78; Harith Al-Dabbagh, 'Iraq' in Nadjma Yassari et al. (eds.), *Parental Care and the Best Interests of the Child in Muslim Countries* (Springer 2017); Jean-Philippe Dequen, 'India' in Nadjma Yassari et al. (eds.), *Parental Care and the Best Interests of the Child in Muslim Countries* (Springer 2017); Jasmine Moussa, 'Egypt' in Nadjma Yassari et al. (eds.), *Parental Care and the Best Interests of the Child in Muslim Countries* (Springer 2017).

[143] Savitri Goonesekere, 'The Best Interests of the Child: A South Asian Perspective' (1994) 8 *International Journal of Law and the Family* 117, 146.

[144] 'BIC Egypt' (2017), 2.

[145] See Chapter 4.

[146] Ruth Halperin-Kaddari and Marsha Freeman, 'Article 16' in Patricia Schultz et al. (eds.), *The UN Convention on the Elimination of All Forms of Discrimination against Women and Its Optional Protocol: A Commentary* (2nd ed., Oxford University Press 2022), 603.

receive special training in this field, unlike the judiciary or other institutions interacting with children, such as child protection agencies. Fortin notes:

> Unlike the exercise of paternalism by the judiciary, which is at least open to public scrutiny, parental paternalism is restrained only by the indeterminacy of the best interests test and hidden from view by the curtain of family privacy.[147]

She further argues that 'the best interests test is too subjective to deter bullying parents from seeing only their own point of view'.[148] Conversely, scholars who adopt a paternalistic approach criticize the BIC on the grounds that it could be employed by the State and the CRC Committee to impose a vision of child autonomy rights on parents. Wilkins et al. explain this fear instilled in parents: 'How are parents to evaluate an "evolving capacity"? What if they make a mistake? What if a parent's notion of "best interests" conflicts with the notions of the Committee of "ten experts" [the CRC Committee]?'[149] It is notable that in the latter case, the authors, referring to Hafen and Hafen, argue that the language employed to phrase autonomy rights in the CRC could be erroneous due to translations, an issue underscored in Chapter 1 of this book:

> It is quite possible that many members of the international community have simply not understood either the CRC's language or its conceptual novelty. Given the complexities of language translation in an area where nuanced phrasing and subtle legal distinctions are at the heart of the arguments, this is a believable interpretation.[150]

The BIC has been interpreted very differently in courts, both within the Global North and the Global South, leading Salter to observe that it has:

> become so diluted that it does no real heavy lifting and can offer no real guidance to families, decision makers, or health care professionals. To settle for this as the dominant standard for pediatric decision making is just that: settling.[151]

Hence, one can argue that it can be detrimental to apply the subjective BIC test to make decisions *for* adolescent girls who otherwise possess rational autonomy.

[147] *Children's Rights* (2009), 100.

[148] Ibid., 100.

[149] Richard Wilkins et al., 'Why the United States Should Not Ratify the Convention on the Rights of the Child' (2003) 22 *Saint Louis University Public Law Review* 411, 424–25.

[150] Ibid., 418; Bruce Hafen and Jonathan Hafen, 'Abandoning Children to Their Autonomy: The United Nations Convention on the Rights of the Child' (1996) 37 *Harvard International Law Journal* 449, 489.

[151] Erica Salter, 'Deciding for a Child: A Comprehensive Analysis of the Best Interest Standard' (2012) 33 *Theoretical Medicine and Bioethics* 179, 195.

2.1.2 Parental Authority Another provision that may appear paternalistic in the CRC is the concept of parental rights:

> States Parties shall respect the responsibilities, rights and duties of parents ... to provide, in a manner consistent with the evolving capacities of the child, appropriate direction and guidance in the exercise by the child of the rights recognized in the present Convention.[152]

As discussed in Chapter 3, the concept of parental rights or 'parental authority' is problematic for it can strengthen the public/private divide and deter the State from interfering in the family, except in extreme circumstances such as physical or sexual abuse. Fortin underscores the inherent weakness of this provision: 'the wording of article 5 itself is fraught with difficulty, since those obliged to fulfil it are the very individuals who may have a personal interest in ensuring that children do not exercise their rights'.[153] Conversely, it is notable that certain scholars have criticized article 5 for the opposite reason: they argue that its wording weakens the principle of parental authority. For instance, Smolin contends that:

> [b]ecause Article 5 purports to define the respect that States Parties must accord to parental rights and responsibilities, its awkward and ambiguous language can be viewed as distorting the Convention's entire treatment of children's rights ... this language appears to define parental rights as that of simply advising and facilitating the exercise of decisional autonomy by children.[154]

In this regard, there can be concerns that the CRC be employed by the State to remove children from loving homes based on arbitrary decisions, notably for political, economic and social gain, or for discriminatory purposes, such as the persecution of political dissenters, and/or on the grounds of race, class, gender, (dis)abilities and sexual orientation. From a semiotic perspective, the location of the principles of the BIC and parental authority at the very beginning of the CRC, within articles 3 and 5 respectively, thus in a privileged position, and before any child rights listed thereafter, that is, from article 6 onwards, is worthy of note. The decision-making power held over children by adults – either the State or parents – is symbolically given precedence in the very instrument designed to protect child rights.

[152] CRC, art. 5.
[153] *Children's Rights* (2009), 43.
[154] David Smolin, 'Overcoming Religious Objections to the Convention on the Rights of the Child' (2006) 20 *Emory International Law Review* 81, 91.

Another problematic provision of the CRC is article 12, which ironically promotes the participation rights of children. Indeed, this article ends with the phrase 'the views of the child being given due weight in accordance with the *age* and *maturity* of the child':

> Art 12(1) States Parties shall assure to the child who is *capable of forming his or her own views* the right to express those views freely in all matters affecting the child, the views of the child being given due weight *in accordance with the age and maturity of the child.*[155]

One can contend that the last section of the sentence weakens the participatory rights of the girl child for it provides that decision makers, often her own parents, are those who decide *when* and *if* she is capable of forming her views and whether she has the proper age and maturity to make a decision.[156] This two-part test: 1) whether she is capable of forming her own views and 2) decisions made in accordance with her age and maturity, can give way to several interpretations. In fact, the CRC Committee produced a general comment in which it expressly clarifies the meaning of this sentence in article 12(1):

> This phrase [capable of forming his or her own views] *should not be seen as a limitation,* but rather as an obligation for States parties to assess the capacity of the child to form an autonomous opinion to the greatest extent possible. This means that *States parties cannot begin with the assumption that a child is incapable of expressing her or his own views.* On the contrary, States parties should presume that a child has the capacity to form her or his own views and recognize that she or he has the right to express them; it is not up to the child to first prove her or his capacity.[157]

The Committee explains that children are presumed to have the capacity to form their views and further stresses that 'it is not up to the child to first prove her or his capacity',[158] thereby placing the burden of proof on master signifiers who wish to demonstrate that children cannot make their own decisions. The Committee also clarifies the second part of the test, that is, decisions made in accordance with the age and maturity of the child. First, it defines the notion of maturity as 'the ability to understand and assess the implications of a

155 Emphasis added.

156 *Children's Rights* (2009), 43.

157 CRC General Comment No. 12: 'Right to be Heard' (2009), para. 20 (emphasis added). The author wishes to thank child rights experts for discussions on the content of this draft general comment for which she provided input while serving at the UNICEF Office of Research.

158 Ibid.

particular matter'.[159] The Committee further notes that the child's age cannot be the sole factor, and that the main criterion should instead be the capacity to express one's views on issues in a reasonable and independent manner.[160] In this context, the Committee argues that the views of the child should be assessed on a case-by-case examination.[161] However, it is still up to the master signifiers, hence parents, institutions or courts, to determine whether, in their view, the girl child can express her views in a 'reasonable' and 'independent' manner, which as discussed in Chapter 3, constitutes a subjective exercise of its own, and may be impacted by their conceptions of childhood, especially girlhood. The formulation of the girl's right to participation in the CRC also raises the distinction between equality in the law and equality before the law. The CRC guarantees, under article 2, equality between children in the law – the equality the law guarantees between girls and boys, which imposes a negative duty on States parties to prevent discrimination when enacting laws and a positive duty to adopt special laws to address discrimination.[162] However, it does not guarantee equality between children and adults before the law which concerns equality in the application of the law by courts and administrative bodies, and refers to how legal subjecthood is distributed.[163] Indeed, contrarily to the CEDAW which accords women equality with men before the law, notably 'a legal capacity identical to that of men' in civil matters, in particular, to conclude contracts and administer property, the CRC does not expressly recognize the child's legal personality *per se*.[164] Additionally, as noted by Taylor, article 26 of the ICCPR, which protects equality before the law for 'all persons', does not 'preclude the imposition of reasonable legal disabilities upon certain categories of individuals such as minors', and thereby allows for differentiation between individuals or identity groups, notably between adults and children.[165] The child's legal personality can be derived indirectly through article 12 on the child's right to participation:

> Art 12(2) … the child shall in particular be provided the *opportunity to be heard* in any judicial and administrative proceedings affecting the child,

[159] Ibid., para. 30.
[160] Ibid., paras. 29–30.
[161] Ibid., para. 29.
[162] 'Non-Discrimination' (2019), 58; *Commentary ICCPR* (2020), 729–32.
[163] 'Non-Discrimination' (2019), 58; *Commentary ICCPR* (2020), 729–32.
[164] CEDAW, art. 15.
[165] ICCPR, art. 26: '[a]ll persons are equal before the law and are entitled without any discrimination to the equal protection of the law'; *Commentary ICCPR* (2020), 730. Taylor distinguishes 'equality before the law' with 'equal protection of the law', as per the terminology employed in art. 26 of the ICCPR: *Commentary ICCPR* (2020), 729–32.

> either directly, or through a representative or an appropriate body, in a manner consistent with the procedural rules of national law.[166]

This paragraph is nonetheless circumscribed to the child's right to be 'heard'. Accordingly, the CRC does not ensure equality before the law between children and adults as legal subjects in decision-making, notably in civil matters. Another provision which expressly enshrines parental authority concerns freedom of religion. The CRC stipulates:

> Art 14(2) States Parties shall respect the rights and duties of the parents and, when applicable, legal guardians, to provide direction to the child in the exercise of his or her right [to freedom of thought, conscience and religion] in a manner consistent with the evolving capacities of the child.

Fortin notes that '[t]his could imply that the CRC merely gives children the right to practice their own religion, rather than the freedom to "choose" it, thereby maintaining the parental right to impose a 'choice' of religion on their children'.[167] This provision is particularly meaningful for adolescent girls who reached rational capacity and yet whose autonomy rights might still be curtailed by their parents under the guise of parental authority. Hence, it might be beneficial for girls to attain majority before eighteen years and thereby no longer be subjected to paternalistic provisions of the CRC. Moreover, as noted by King, the CRC 'contains a wide range of rather vague political and economic rights and duties which require further precision and transformation at the national level if they are to become amenable to lawful/unlawful decisions'.[168] More broadly, Archard and Tobin explain that:

> it matters greatly *which* rights are accorded and which, correspondingly, are withheld. The holder of some set of rights may be excluded from the privileges and benefits afforded to those who hold some other set of rights. Thus, children may have children's rights; and adults, by contrast, may have rights that are exclusive to adults, which may be denied to children.[169]

Adolescent girls could therefore be significantly empowered if they were granted political and economic rights normally restricted to adults and majors *before* they turn eighteen years.

[166] Emphasis added.
[167] *Children's Rights* (2009), 44.
[168] Michael King, 'Children's Rights as Communication: Reflections on Autopoietic Theory and the United Nations Convention' (1994) 57 *Modern Law Review* 385, 395.
[169] 'Definition Child' (2019), 22.

### 2.2 Empowering Provisions of Other Treaties

The Twin Covenants comprise central political and economic rights that are not granted in the CRC nor accorded to minors under domestic law and which would be beneficial to the adolescent girl.[170] As concerns political rights, the ICCPR enshrines the rights to take part in the conduct of public affairs, vote and be elected.[171] The adolescent girl's right to vote is particularly important as elected officials might be more inclined to consider the issues faced by girl children if the latter constitute potential voters in their respective constituencies. Moreover, if adolescent girls were granted the right to run for office, they could become a voice for other girls. In other words, adolescent girls could become *master signifiers* of policies and laws promoting girls' rights at the domestic and international levels, which would contrast with the limited participation of children, including girl children, during the drafting of the CRC.[172] The CRC Committee recognizes that 'participation in work activities in accordance with international standards ... may be beneficial for the development of the adolescent',[173] and adolescent girls could acquire valuable skills in the proper environment, especially if allowed to contribute to policy-making. The right to freedom of thought, conscience and religion as worded in the ICCPR is not restricted, contrarily to the CRC which, as previously discussed, specifies that States parties shall 'respect the rights and duties of the parents ... to provide direction to the child' in this context.[174] Indeed, the ICCPR stipulates that '[t]his right shall include freedom to have or to adopt a religion or belief of his choice',[175] and furthermore that '[n]o one shall be subject to coercion which would impair his freedom to have or to adopt a religion or belief of his choice',[176] thereby expressly prohibiting any restriction to this fundamental freedom. The adolescent girl covered by the ICCPR could therefore choose to follow a different belief system than that of

[170] See Chapter 8 for an examination of important provisions for the girl child in the CEDAW.

[171] ICCPR, art. 25: '[e]very citizen shall have the right and the opportunity ... a) To take part in the conduct of public affairs, directly or through freely chosen representatives; b) To vote and to be elected at genuine periodic elections which shall be by universal and equal suffrage and shall be held by secret ballot, guaranteeing the free expression of the will of the electors'.

[172] See Chapter 3; 'History CRC' (2007).

[173] CRC General Comment No. 4: 'Adolescent Health' (2003), para. 18.

[174] CRC, art. 14(2).

[175] ICCPR, art. 18(1): 'Everyone shall have the right to freedom of thought, conscience and religion. This right shall include freedom to have or to adopt a religion or belief of his choice, and freedom, either individually or in community with others and in public or private, to manifest his religion or belief in worship, observance, practice and teaching'. It is however notable that this provision employs masculine possessive adjectives, see Chapter 5.

[176] ICCPR, art. 18(2).

her parents or legal guardians, or a more liberal interpretation of that belief system. This right is particularly important for girls raised in very conservative or fundamentalist communities in which interpretations of religion may be instrumentalized to impose restrictive social codes. Moreover, contrarily to the CRC, the ICCPR enshrines the right to liberty of movement and to choose a residence,[177] thus mobility rights, which is especially useful for an adolescent girl who wishes to escape a violent family environment.

However, one cannot affirm that all the rights comprised in the ICCPR are granted to girl children, notably while they are minors. Although the Human Rights Committee specifies that 'as individuals, children benefit from all the civil rights enunciated in the Covenant', general comments are not legally binding.[178] Furthermore, as noted in the previous section, children are not granted a legal capacity identical to that of adults in civil matters. Moreover, the decision of the Human Rights Committee to refer expressly to civil and not political rights in this context could infer *a contrario* that children are not allocated political rights.[179] The same issue arises with the ICESCR. The latter enshrines central rights for workers, such as the rights to just and favourable conditions of work, fair wages and equal remuneration,[180] safe and healthy working conditions[181] and the right to form trade unions, as well as to strike,[182] which would be essential for adolescent girls who are employed. The ICESCR nevertheless fails to provide a single age limit both for the right to work and corresponding workers' rights. Accordingly, States parties are at liberty to establish a low threshold for employment while not granting other workers' rights, such as the right to form and join trade unions. This is particularly problematic since, as previously examined, the Minimum Age Convention provides that the minimum age for admission to employment is fifteen years, and fourteen years if the State party does not have available resources, or thirteen years for light work,[183] yet does not clarify that

[177] ICCPR, art. 12(1): '[e]veryone lawfully within the territory of a State shall, within that territory, have the right to liberty of movement and freedom to choose his residence'.

[178] ICCPR General Comment No. 17: 'Rights Child' (1989), para. 2.

[179] Taylor notes that this statement from the Human Rights Committee 'implies that political rights may not be relevant': *Commentary ICCPR* (2020), 660.

[180] ICESCR, art. 7: '[t]he States Parties to the present Covenant recognize the right of everyone to the enjoyment of just and favourable conditions of work which ensure, in particular: a) Remuneration which provides all workers, as a minimum, with: i) Fair wages and equal remuneration for work of equal value'.

[181] ICESCR, art. 7 (b): '[s]afe and healthy working conditions'.

[182] ICESCR, art. 8 (1) (a): 'The right of everyone to form trade unions and join the trade unions of his choice'; d): 'The right to strike'.

[183] Minimum Age Convention, arts. 2(3), 2(4), 7.

adolescents shall automatically be accorded all the rights associated with employment, notably those in the ICESCR. The ICCPR also enshrines, within the right to freedom of association, 'the right to form and join trade unions', yet it does not specify whether this right is granted to all individuals, or solely to majors.[184] Since the right to freedom of association in the CRC does not comprise the right to form or join trade unions,[185] the girl child might be entitled to work and yet not accorded basic workers' rights under both the ICESCR and the ICCPR. Instead, it is argued that if adolescent girls were granted majority earlier under the CRC, for example at fifteen years, they would unequivocally be granted all the rights under the Covenants, including those concerning employment. Additionally, it would appear appropriate that adolescent girls be entitled to serve as elected officials and take part in the conduct of public affairs before eighteen years. Indeed, whether one considers that adolescent girls should be entitled to work full time or part-time, it would, in either case, appear unfair to allow their employment in low-paid jobs while prohibiting work in public policy or other fields of public life. In other words, if an adolescent girl can work in the garment industry, she should also be able to work as a member of a political organization at the local, regional or national level.

### 3 *Problematic Features of the Current Threshold of Majority*

Whether one adopts a paternalistic or child liberationist approach, the current upper boundary of girlhood in the CRC has seven key problematic features: 1) absence of minimum age for the end of girlhood, 2) discrepancy between the end of girlhood and emancipation, 3) possibility of unequal treatment on the grounds of national domicile, 4) possibility of unequal treatment on the grounds of gender, 5) possibility of unequal treatment between girl children within the same State party and issues concerning 6) monitoring and 7) data analysis.

#### 3.1 Absence of Minimum Age for End of Girlhood

Since the definition of child in the CRC does not offer, under the upper limit of eighteen years, a minimum age for majority and thus for the end of

[184] ICCPR, art. 22(1): '[e]veryone shall have the right to freedom of association with others, *including the right to form and join trade unions* for the protection of his interests' (emphasis added).

[185] CRC, art. 15(1): 'States Parties recognize the rights of the child to freedom of association and to freedom of peaceful assembly'.

childhood, States parties could establish that majority is reached at a very young age. As examined in Chapter 3, while child liberationists and child rights scholars criticize the political and social ramifications of paternalistic conceptions of childhood and suggest granting autonomy rights to children before adulthood, they generally do not contend that the boundary of childhood should be established at adolescence nor that states' duty to protect teenagers should cease. Several scholars in the field of child rights have thus attempted to compensate for the terminology employed in article 1 by arguing that children are protected until eighteen years save for exceptional circumstances. Archard and Tobin contend that:

> states can invoke domestic law to justify the end of childhood at a point less than 18 years of age, but the legitimacy of any alternative conception of childhood will only be justified in exceptional circumstances.[186]

Yet as previously discussed, this interpretative approach does not consider the semiotic notions of the immediate, dynamical and final interpretants.[187] Presently, several States parties to the CRC establish the end of childhood before eighteen years, either de jure or de facto.[188] The decision of the CRC Committee to clarify, in fifteen out of twenty-five general comments – thus in more than half of general comments – that children are protected under the Convention until they reach eighteen years is indicative that conflicting information stems from States parties' reports. The CRC Committee's clarifications certainly constitute a sign that it aims to address the ambiguous outer boundary of childhood. The Committee also attempts to counterweigh the wording of article 1 in its concluding observations, whereby it criticizes States parties that set a boundary before eighteen years, and urges them to review and modify their legislation accordingly.[189] The Committee notably explains that the boundary of sixteen years is not compatible with the CRC.[190] It underscores that a 'large number of children [are] still involved in child

[186] 'Definition Child' (2019), 24.

[187] See Chapters 1 and 5.

[188] See Chapters 2, 3 and 5; see also *Minimum Age* (2009).

[189] Concluding Observations: see for example Cuba (16 June 2022) UN Doc CRC/C/CUB/CO/3–6, para. 16; Vietnam (21 October 2022) UN Doc CRC/C/VNM/CO/5–6, para. 15; Pakistan (11 July 2016) UN Doc CRC/C/PAK/CO/5, para. 17; Albania (7 December 2012) UN Doc CRC/C/ALB/CO/2–4, paras. 25, 26; Namibia (16 October 2012) UN Doc CRC/C/NAM/CO/2–3, para. 28; Myanmar (14 March 2012) UN Doc CRC/C/MMR/CO/3–4, para. 34; Thailand (17 February 2012) UN Doc CRC/C/THA/CO/3–4, para. 32; Sudan (22 October 2010) UN Doc CRC/C/SDN/CO/3–4, paras. 27–28.

[190] For example, the Committee notes that the Law on Children adopted in 2016 in Vietnam defines a child as a person under sixteen years of age and urges the State to modify this threshold to eighteen years: Concluding Observations: Vietnam (21 October 2022) UN Doc

labour, including hazardous work' and urges States parties to 'explicitly prohibit the employment of all children under 18 years of age in harmful, hazardous, overtime and overnight work'.[191] The Committee is also concerned that 'children deprived of a family environment have to leave care institutions at the age of 15 and are left without any protection and financial support by the State party',[192] and that the criminal act of 'sexual abuse against children' does not cover children above fourteen years unless there is additional violence.[193] Furthermore, the absence of a minimum age signifies that States parties could determine that majority is reached *anytime* before eighteen years, and in theory, even once the girl child is *one day old*. Porterfield and Stanton have argued that the minimum age for the end of childhood should be established at the very earliest at fourteen years,[194] and McGoldrick suggests that the CRC should at least provide a minimum age limit for the declaration of majority by national laws.[195] The wording of article 1, which refers to 'majority' rather than 'age of majority', also allows States parties to establish that majority is reached through means other than age, such as reaching puberty or entering a marriage. In fact, several states have adopted this interpretation and allow puberty as the parameter for majority, either de jure or de facto, which has been criticized by the CRC Committee in its concluding observations.[196] Moreover, the parameter of puberty applies exclusively to girls and not to boys in some states, provinces or territories, both for protection in the child justice system and as victims of child sexual abuse.[197]

CRC/C/VNM/CO/5–6, para. 15. See also Nigeria (21 June 2010) UN Doc CRC/C/NGA/CO/3–4, para. 26.

191 CRC Concluding Observations: Vietnam (21 October 2022) UN Doc CRC/C/VNM/CO/5–6, paras. 47, 48.

192 CRC Concluding Observations: Albania (7 December 2012) UN Doc CRC/C/ALB/CO/2–4, para. 25.

193 Ibid., para. 45.

194 Timothy Porterfield and Gregory Stanton, 'The Age of Majority: Article 1' (1989) 16 *New York School Journal of Human Rights* 30, 33–34.

195 Dominic McGoldrick, 'The United Nations Convention on the Rights of the Child' (1991) *International Journal of Law, Policy and Family* 132, 133.

196 For example, CRC Concluding Observations: Nigeria (21 June 2010) UN Doc CRC/C/NGA/CO/3–4, para. 26; Sudan (22 October 2010) UN Doc CRC/C/SDN/CO/3–4, para. 27: 'adulthood is, in practice, determined by reference, inter alia, to the attainment of puberty in conformity with sharia law in the northern part of the State party, and according to custom in other parts of the country'; Pakistan (2 October 2009) UN Doc CRC/C/PAK/CO/3–4, para. 26: 'the definition of the girl child contained in the Zina and Hadood Ordinances (1979) (16 years or puberty)' and para. 27: '[i]t recommends … raising the minimum age of marriage for girls to 18 years'; Albania (7 December 2012) UN Doc CRC/C/ALB/CO/2–4, para. 25.

197 CRC Concluding Observations: Albania (7 December 2012) UN Doc CRC/C/ALB/CO/2–4, para. 25: '[t]he Committee is deeply concerned that under … the Criminal Code, girls are

Tobin and Archard support the CRC Committee endeavour to clarify the boundary:

> To hold otherwise would be to give license to a state to avoid its obligations under the Convention by simply reducing the age of majority for reasons of convenience as opposed to a need to respect and accommodate long standing cultural or customary conceptions of childhood and adulthood.[198]

They argue that the best approach is a constructive dialogue 'within groups whose customary practices have no historical links with an age-based conception of childhood that ends at 18',[199] and thereby acknowledge that several interpretants still apply different thresholds for the end of childhood. Finally, another issue of concern is that since the definition of 'child' offered in the CRC is the main description of child under international law, girls who reach majority before eighteen years are not systematically embraced by provisions of other international instruments referring to 'girls' and 'girl children'[200] and UN documents that expressly purport to improve the situation of the girl child, such as the resolutions on the girl child adopted by the General Assembly.[201]

## 3.2 Discrepancy between the End of Girlhood and Emancipation

The definition of child in the CRC does not clearly establish whether the girl child who reaches majority is automatically granted all the rights accorded to adults in other international treaties, notably political rights, such as the rights to vote and run for office; economic rights, such as the right to control one's finances, rent or buy property, obtain a mortgage or microcredit; family rights such as heading a household and raising children as well as reproductive rights, including access to contraception. The CRC does not require States parties to ensure that under domestic law, the girl child who reaches majority before eighteen years – and thereby ceases to be a child under the Convention – shall automatically obtain all the political and economic rights accorded to adults. The Twin Covenants refer to all human beings, which implies that they cover individuals regardless of age, yet enshrine certain rights that are not accorded to children, such as the rights to vote and manage

treated as adults from the age of puberty' and para. 45: 'children between the age of 14 and 18 years are only protected if there is violence and girls only up to the age of puberty'.

198 'Definition Child' (2019), 28.

199 Ibid., 28–29.

200 See Chapter 2 for an analysis of international instruments referring to the expressions 'girl' and 'girl child'.

201 See Introduction; UNGA Resolutions: 'The Girl Child'.

property.[202] Since the CRC and Twin Covenants fail to specify minimum thresholds for civil, political and legal rights, States parties are not clearly required to consider that girls who reach majority are granted all the rights comprised in these respective treaties. Accordingly, the girl child who reaches majority before eighteen years could be deprived of rights enshrined in the CRC while not granted all 'adult' rights under other treaties. Moreover, the same state may establish numerous age thresholds for activities, notably as regards emancipation, voting rights, consent to sexual relations or medical treatment, criminal responsibility and employment. For instance, some states report over twenty-five age limits and eleven age brackets.[203] In this regard, Fredman observes that adolescents are 'classified legally as adults or children depending on the issue at hand'.[204] Whilst domestic law may consider that a ten-year-old girl has the required *mens rea* to commit a crime, she might not be deemed sufficiently rational to give informed consent for medical treatment until she turns fourteen or sixteen, to drive until she reaches sixteen, or to vote for an additional two years, when she attains eighteen years.[205] Distinct age thresholds could be justified on the grounds that the capacities of children will vary according to the nature of the rights exercised. In this regard, Lansdown notes that 'children … require varying degrees of protection, participation and opportunity for autonomy in different contexts and across different areas of decision-making'.[206] However, the establishment of different age limits for activities that require similar levels of competency may not be so easily justified. For example, if an adolescent girl is deemed to enjoy the required rational autonomy to drive a vehicle at sixteen, which places the safety of drivers, cyclists and pedestrians literally 'in her hands', it may appear arbitrary that the same girl is not considered sufficiently capable of exercising the right to vote for another two years. In this regard, Cipriani notes that 'it is generally incoherent to argue that children at a given age are mature and responsible in one domain, yet unready to exercise rights on their own behalf in a comparable domain', and concludes that 'children's age limits … depend most heavily upon fluctuating social constructions of childhood, and not on

[202] See Chapter 2.

[203] *Minimum Age* (2009), 3. Fortin underscores this phenomenon also in the United Kingdom, where sixteen-year-old children can 'consent to surgical, medical or dental treatment, marry with the consent of their parents, join the army and consent to sexual intercourse', while still not allowed to vote, stand for Parliament, acquire a legal estate or make a will: *Children's Rights* (2009), 110–11.

[204] Sandra Fredman, 'The Age of Equality' in Sandra Fredman and Sarah Spencer (eds.), *Age as an Equality Issue: Legal and Policy Perspectives* (Hart 2003), 34.

[205] Ibid.

[206] 'Evolving Capacities' (2005), 3.

children themselves'.[207] Hence, it could be argued that the delimitation of age thresholds for distinct rights and activities relies more on the conceptions of childhood in a given society, and notably on master signifiers' willingness to grant children rights, than on the *actual capacities* of the latter.

3.2.1 Child Justice System The current boundary of childhood as 'majority' under the upper limit of eighteen years in the CRC is problematic for girls in conflict with the law who might lose significant protection offered in the Convention. Additionally, the current definition of child in the CRC allows for flexibility as concerns the minimum ages of criminal responsibility (MACR). Presently, the spectrum of MACR goes from the total absence of a minimum age to sixteen years, and some States parties offer parameters other than age, such as puberty.[208] The latter criterion might appear questionable as it implies that the development of physical and sexual attributes is automatically accompanied by the required cognitive capacity for the *mens rea*.[209] Thresholds such as puberty might not be based on the actual competencies of a given girl child but rather on conceptions of childhood and girlhood and the court's discretionary power which may be politically constructed, and gender-based. The CRC Committee shows concern that some States parties selected an age below eighteen years, and even below sixteen years, for children to be covered by the child justice system:

> The Committee recommends that those States parties that limit the applicability of their child justice system to children under the age of 16 years (or lower), or that allow by way of exception that certain children are treated as adult offenders (for example, because of the offence category), change their laws to ensure a non-discriminatory full application of their child justice system to all persons below the age of 18 years at the time of the offence.[210]

The Committee reiterates this concern in its concluding observations, noting moreover that in some cases, executions were established for offences

[207] *Minimum Age* (2009), 4.
[208] Ibid., 98–108.
[209] Ibid., 105: An interesting example offered by Cipriani is that of states where 'children who have reached puberty may face the death penalty for crimes including adultery, apostasy, "corruption on earth", drug trafficking, sabotage, (political) rebellion … as well as for actions within the broad category allowing courts' discretionary punishment … In addition, judges may consider physical characteristics of puberty at the time of trial or upon sentencing, rather than considering children's ages at the time of the alleged offenses, and may exercise significant discretion over which physical characteristics'.
[210] CRC General Comment No. 24: 'Child Justice' (2019), para. 30.

committed before eighteen years, or even on children below eighteen years.[211] The Committee also notes that according to the criminal law of some States parties, 'girls are treated as adults from the age of puberty'.[212]

### 3.3 Possibility of Unequal Treatment on the Grounds of National Domicile

The current definition of child allows States parties to establish the end of childhood at different ages under eighteen years, or via different parameters, such as puberty or marriage, thereby causing discrepancies for the end of childhood worldwide. On the one hand, as noted by Lansdown, since children acquire competencies according to diverse life experiences,[213] it could be argued that the required age to reach adulthood should be adjusted to each nation's socio-economic and cultural realities. For example, the abilities developed by a girl child belonging to an underprivileged social class in the Global South, who has the 'adult' responsibilities of raising her siblings and providing financially for her family, may differ from that of a girl raised in a privileged environment in the Global North. Moreover, it could be argued that certain state authorities do not have the financial resources to protect girl children over a certain age, and that lower thresholds should be established accordingly. In this regard, one could contend that allowance should be made for different understandings of the end of girlhood within differing national and cultural frameworks. This issue illustrates one of the problems of adopting international treaties enshrining rights and duties that might not reflect the distinct conceptions of human rights, and childhood, globally. As previously noted, international law has been criticized for imposing a conception of human rights stemming from the Global North.[214] More specifically, the CRC has been accused of 'attempting to impose on non-industrialized countries the ideas and values of the richer Western states' and enshrining rights which could be endorsed by the ruling elites of states in the Global South but not by their local populations.[215] Pupavac argues that the CRC imposes a 'modern Western childhood' and contends that '[c]hildhood remains a luxury that is unrealisable for the majority of the population in developing

[211] CRC Concluding Observations: Pakistan (11 July 2016) UN Doc CRC/C/PAK/CO/5, para. 24; Sudan (22 October 2010) UN Doc CRC/C/SDN/CO/3–4, paras. 35–36.

[212] CRC Concluding Observations: Albania (7 December 2012) UN Doc CRC/C/ALB/CO/2–4, para. 25.

[213] 'Evolving Capacities' (2005).

[214] See Chapter 3; 'Jus Cogens' (1998); 'HRs for Girls' (2014); 'Cutting Edge' (2015); 'Cultural Practices' (2002); *Burden Girlhood* (1995).

[215] *Children's Rights* (2009), 45.

countries'.[216] Hence, the dimensions, boundaries and divisions of childhood might not achieve consensus worldwide. Yet while it is acknowledged that the girl child develops abilities according to various personal and social factors, psychology studies have demonstrated that human beings mature at a relatively similar pace globally unless placed in exceptional surroundings. Archard notes:

> the acquisition by human beings of various skills and abilities proceeds according to a fairly standard and universal chronology. Indeed, the pattern of human sensory, motor, cognitive and linguistic development displays a significant degree of cultural invariance.[217]

The unique realities of states with distinct cultures and socio-economic circumstances might therefore not justify establishing significantly distinct age parameters worldwide. Indeed, the scientific argument that capacities are acquired at certain ages or within certain age gaps cannot be completely discarded. Also, the argument of flexible boundaries according to states' socio-economic and cultural situations could be criticized on the grounds that it views children in a given state as a monolithic group and thereby disregards the role played by other identity vectors in defining the situation of groups of children, such as sex, class, race, religion and culture. For instance, as concerns class, it could be argued that while many girl children who live in extreme poverty in the Global South shoulder significant adult responsibilities, the situation of girls from the middle and upper class in these states is closer to that of girls belonging to the same social class in the Global North. In other words, if one were to apply the argument of socio-economic relativity to justify distinct age limits for the end of childhood between the Global North and the Global South, it would be more appropriate to establish distinct age parameters between socio-economically privileged and oppressed girl children. A single uniform boundary for the end of childhood in a state would not account for the extremely different realities of lower, middle and upper-class girl children residing on its territory. Moreover, within the same state, distinct communities may have different conceptions of childhood on account of specific cultures, traditions, customs and beliefs: for instance, one community might adopt a paternalistic approach whereby children are not granted autonomy rights, while another might consider that children should shoulder adult responsibilities, such as working to support their family,

[216] Vanessa Pupavac, 'The Infantilization of the South and the UN Convention on the Rights of the Child', in Henry Steiner and Philip Alston (eds.), *International Human Rights in Context: Law, Politics, Morals* (2nd ed., Oxford University Press 2000), 518.

[217] *Childhood* (2015), 84.

during middle childhood and adolescence. Accordingly, if one were to adopt cultural relativism, girls would be considered children or adults depending on their family and community rather than the state in which they reside. It would be difficult to argue that within a single state all girls share the exact same cultural and religious characteristics.[218] Conversely, it should be acknowledged that states do not have the same level of available resources worldwide as a result of past and present colonization, imperialism and armed conflict.[219] Hence, the pragmatic argument that certain states simply cannot provide services for children cannot be disregarded. It is nevertheless argued that the absence of available resources in certain states is often due to the unequal distribution of resources within and between states as well as corporations rather than because of actual poverty.[220] Moreover, the CRC provides for international cooperation to assist states that have limited resources.[221]

Age thresholds also vary between states that have comparable characteristics. For instance, while England and Canada are common law countries that share similarities politically, economically and culturally, the required *mens rea* to commit a crime is established at ten years in England, with no presumption of doli incapax,[222] and twelve years in Canada.[223] This example could support the argument that distinct age thresholds for the end of childhood might not be correlated to states' social, economic, cultural and legal characteristics. Some scholars contend that the decision of the British government to abolish the presumption of doli incapax in 1998, almost 700 years after its inception, could be explained by a shift in society's conception of childhood after the Bulger case rather than a progressive change in the perception of children's capacities, or significant societal changes in the

[218] Except when a State party imposes specific interpretations and conceptions across its jurisdiction, although even in such cases, there can be inter and intra differences, both de jure and de facto.

[219] See Introduction and Chapter 3.

[220] See Philip Alston, Special Rapporteur, 'Report on Extreme Poverty and Extreme Inequality' (27 May 2015) UN Doc A/HRC/C/29/31, paras. 2, 8–32.

[221] CRC, art. 4.

[222] Children and Young Persons Act 1933 c. 12, section 50: the original age was eight years but it was increased to ten in the Children and Young Persons Act 1963 c. 37, section 16. See also Crime and Disorder Act 1998 c. 37, section 34: '[t]he rebuttable presumption of criminal law that a child aged 10 or over is incapable of committing an offence is hereby abolished'.

[223] Canada Criminal Code R.S.C. 1985, c. C-46, art. 13: '[n]o person shall be convicted of an offence in respect of an act or omission on his part while that person was under the age of twelve years'. It is worthy of note that the Criminal Code refers to a 'person', rather than a 'child' in this context. Also, the YCJA defines 'child' as a person less than twelve years, and 'young person' as between twelve and eighteen years, which implies that these are two exclusive categories: Canada Youth Criminal Justice Act SC 2002, c. 1 (YCJA), art. 2.

country, over the course of centuries.[224] It could be argued that while England and Canada share historical similarities, a single event – the violent murder of a two-year-old boy by two ten-year-old boys – might have in itself changed the conception of childhood in the former country. Moreover, the argument that differences should be established between states according to socio-economic, cultural and religious factors could be criticized on the grounds that it constitutes discrimination between children solely based on their national domicile. For example, it could be argued that denying children certain rights solely on the grounds that they live in the Global South violates the principle of non-discrimination between children that is recognized under international law.[225] In this regard, Porterfield and Stanton contend that:

> in such countries where children live in exceptionally difficult conditions, children need greater consideration, not less. Due to more adverse conditions, these children are in even greater need of protections of the Convention.[226]

Furthermore, as previously discussed, the Global South–North division is increasingly questionable, especially with regard to BRICS countries' economic development, contrasted with western Europe and North America's socio-economic crises.[227] The ability of States parties to the CRC to establish different ages for the end of childhood could thus be considered a form of discrimination between girl children according to their country of domicile. In their analysis of the definition of child in the CRC, conducted before its adoption (1989), Porterfield and Stanton underscored their concern that:

> to allow each and every country to arbitrarily decide at what age childhood ends and when adulthood begins could destroy the international uniformity of the Convention, and lead to unequal treatment of children based solely upon their national domicile.[228]

They further stress that 'the United Nations should not allow any country the legal flexibility to exploit its children for its own gain and still be in accordance with international law'.[229] In fact, they argue that this ambiguous threshold for the end of childhood threatens the goals of the entire Convention.[230] It is

[224] *Minimum Age* (2009), 117; R v. Secretary of State for the Home Department, ex parte Venables and Thompson (1998) AC 497 (Bulger case).
[225] See CRC, art. 2; ICCPR, arts. 2, 26; ICESCR, art. 2.
[226] 'Age of Majority' (1989), 32.
[227] See Chapter 3.
[228] 'Age of Majority' (1989), 31.
[229] Ibid.
[230] Ibid.

notable that at the time of their analysis, the draft CRC referred to the 'age of majority' and not 'majority' as is presently the case, and thus established a clearer parameter than the current version, which implies that Porterfield and Stanton's criticism would be more severe today. In fact, Besson and Kleber recently criticized 'the potential discrimination of "children" depending on their qualification as children from one state to the next'.[231]

### 3.4 Unequal Treatment on the Grounds of Gender

Another issue of concern is that the boundaries for the end of childhood may vary between girls and boys. The CRC does not specify that childhood terminates at the same moment for boys and girls. According to article 1, States parties can determine *when* and *how* majority is reached, under the upper limit of eighteen years. The wording of article 1 could thus be interpreted as signifying that states can establish distinct age limits for majority between girls and boys. As a result, a girl and a boy who are the same age may respectively be considered a child and an adult within the same country.[232] In addition, since the CRC does not offer a minimum age for majority, states could provide significantly different age limits for each sex. Technically, they could establish that majority is reached at *one day old* for girl children and *eighteen years* for boys. While such an extreme division seems unlikely, the present book examines signs at their extreme ramifications, including for the final interpretant, and the failure of the CRC to at least offer a minimum age for the end of childhood allows for this possibility. Moreover, since article 1 of the CRC does not require states to determine the same parameter for the attainment of majority by both sexes, majority could be reached by girls very early, for instance at puberty, and by boys much later, through other means, for instance when they join armed forces. The CRC however prohibits discrimination between groups of children, notably on the grounds of sex under article 2: 'States Parties shall respect and ensure the rights set forth in the present Convention to each child within their jurisdiction without discrimination of any kind, irrespective of … sex', which implies that states cannot establish a different age of majority for each gender and thereby strip boys or girls of their rights in the CRC at distinct ages. Yet, as previously examined, many States parties entered reservations to the CRC and CEDAW expressly stipulating that they would not apply rights equally to female and

[231] 'Non-Discrimination' (2019), 42.
[232] *Burden Girlhood* (1995), 1–2.

male human beings, notably girls and boys.[233] The CRC Committee underlines that minimum ages should be the same for boys and girls, for instance as concerns sexual consent, marriage and the possibility of medical treatment without parental consent.[234] In its more recent general comment on adolescence, the Committee expressly notes that states cannot establish different thresholds for girls and boys: '[t]he Convention prohibits any gender-based discrimination, and age limits should be equal for girls and boys'.[235] The decision of the Committee to clarify that states cannot adopt laws establishing different age limits for girls and boys demonstrates a concern that the wording of article 1 could lead to discriminatory laws on the grounds of gender. This is especially concerning for, as previously discussed, several states globally grant fewer rights to girls than boys, and adopt laws that directly and indirectly discriminate against girls.[236] For example, Cipriani notes that fourteen States parties to the CRC have established secondary criminal responsibility age limits for offences such as rape only for boys, and stresses that, as a result, 'such provisions discriminatorily assign criminal responsibility to girls for sex-related crimes'.[237] In their concluding observations, the CRC and CEDAW Committees underscore that several States parties provide different age limits for marriage for girls and boys, and in all cases, the threshold is lower for girl children; moreover, some states do not provide a minimum age for marriage at all, and in many states puberty is the threshold for the end of girlhood but not for the end of boyhood.[238] The minimum legal age for marriage can also be

[233] See Chapter 5.

[234] CRC General Comment No. 4: 'Adolescent Health' (2003), para. 9: 'States parties need to ensure that specific legal provisions are guaranteed under domestic law, including with regard to setting a minimum age for sexual consent, marriage and the possibility of medical treatment without parental consent. These minimum ages should be the same for boys and girls'.

[235] CRC General Comment No. 20: 'Adolescence' (2016), para. 38.

[236] See Chapter 3.

[237] *Minimum Age* (2009), 110.

[238] See for example CRC Concluding Observations: Pakistan (11 July 2016) UN Doc CRC/C/PAK/CO/5, paras. 16–17, whereby the CRC Committee reiterates the same concerns as its preceding report of 2009, demonstrating that its recommendations were not applied by the state, for example para. 16: 'the Committee remains concerned about the disparity between the minimum legal age for marriage for boys (18 years) and that for girls (16 years) in all other provinces, and that the Zina and Hahood Ordinances (1979) provide a definition of a "girl child" that only covers girls up to the age of 16 years or puberty'; CRC Concluding Observations: Albania (7 December 2012) UN Doc CRC/C/ALB/CO/2–4, paras. 25, 45. Freeman et al., *Commentary CEDAW* (2012), 438. The CEDAW Committee has noted that in some states, the vast majority of court-approved child marriages relate to girls, some as young as thirteen years, and showed concern for 'the high rate of approval of those authorizations': CEDAW Concluding Observations: 'Morocco' (8 April 2008) UN Doc CEDAW/C/MAR/CO/4, para. 34.

significantly lowered with parental consent, which can further widen the existing age limit differences for girls and boys.[239] In this regard, Sohoni criticizes the many distinct boundaries and divisions of girlhood and boyhood globally, and notes that '[t]here is a need in law, culture, and religion to establish a common definition of "girlhood", as well as to correct any disparities in relation to "boyhood", to achieve legal uniformity'.[240]

### 3.5 Unequal Treatment between Girl Children within the Same Jurisdiction

The definition of child refers to the concept of majority rather than the 'age of majority', and as indicated in the *travaux préparatoires*, the drafters expressly removed 'age' as the parameter of majority. Accordingly, states are at liberty to establish that girl children will attain majority in various ways, such as reaching puberty or when they enter marriage. As most domestic legal systems fail to articulate a uniform definition of the girl child, the same female person may be legally classified as a girl for some purposes and a woman for others.[241] The CRC Committee notes, in its concluding observations, the legal inconsistencies concerning the definition of child not only *between* but also *within* States parties at the federal, provincial and territorial levels.[242] Moreover, due to different conceptions of girlhood, the definition of 'girl child' in some States parties only covers girls up to sixteen years or puberty.[243] Hence, girls who marry or reach puberty early are stripped of their rights under the CRC, which places them at a disadvantage compared to other girls, and conversely, girls who acquire this status later will be submitted to childist provisions of the CRC, such as parental authority, for a longer period which also constitutes a disadvantage. A girl child who is not granted all adult rights when reaching majority might be considered a woman for the purposes of marriage and a girl child as regards legal capacity as well as political and economic rights.

[239] UN Women, 'Families Changing World' (2020), 84: 'two thirds of countries and territories allow girls to be married earlier [than 18 years] with parental or judicial consent'.

[240] *Burden Girlhood* (1995), 2.

[241] Kirsten Backstrom, 'The International Human Rights of the Child: Do They Protect the Female Child?' (1996) 30 *George Washington Journal of International Law and Economics* 541, 554; 'Age Equality' (2003), 34.

[242] See for example CRC Concluding Observations: Pakistan (11 July 2016) UN Doc CRC/C/PAK/CO/5, para. 16: '[i]t is also concerned about legal inconsistencies concerning the definition of child at the federal, provincial and territorial levels, and disparities in that regard between secular and sharia law'.

[243] Ibid., para. 16.

3.5.1 Child Marriage The present boundary for the end of girlhood in the CRC is particularly problematic as concerns child marriage. Since there is no minimum age for the end of childhood in the CRC, and that majority can be reached by any means, including through marriage, States parties are at liberty to determine that once girls marry, they enter majority and are no longer protected under the Convention. Moreover, the CRC fails to specify a minimum age for marriage, and is silent as concerns the issue of child marriage altogether. As discussed in Chapter 5, while the CRC was conceived as gender blind, its provisions fail to expressly tackle violations uniquely or predominantly affecting girls, notably child marriage.[244] Accordingly, marriage could occur at any time during girlhood, including at a very young age. Other treaties, such as the Convention on Marriage (1962), the CEDAW and the ICCPR also fail to provide a minimum age for marriage. For example, the ICCPR refers, under article 23, to '[t]he right of men and women of marriageable age to marry', yet does not specify the age in question. Taylor observes that '[i]n the Commission on Human Rights it was agreed that it should be left to States to determine marriageable age, which could refer to the age of legal majority or of physical maturity'.[245] Although some articles of the CRC indirectly address child marriage, such as article 24(3) regarding traditional practices prejudicial to the health of the child, they fail to expressly refer to this practice, thereby enabling states to deny that it falls within the Convention.[246] States can also argue that prohibiting traditional practices would be discriminatory against the girl child's family or larger community customs and traditions, and thus in violation of article 2(1) of the CRC.[247] Also, since the CRC enshrines – while failing to define – the 'best interests of the child' principle, states can contend that child marriage is appropriate on the grounds that it is in the girl's best interests, for example, because: 1) she is less likely to lose her virginity before marriage and thereby bringing dishonour upon her family, 2) her spouse's wealth will ensure her economic stability, 3) the marriage will remove her from a conflict zone or 4) a problematic

[244] 'CRC Child marriage' (1998), 124, 130, 137. For a discussion on the gender-neutral language of the CRC, see Chapter 5.

[245] *Commentary ICCPR* (2020), 647.

[246] 'CRC Child marriage' (1998), 124, 130, 137; CRC, art. 24(3): 'States Parties shall take all effective and appropriate measures with a view to abolishing traditional practices prejudicial to the health of children'.

[247] CRC, art. 2(1): 'States Parties shall respect and ensure the rights set forth in the present Convention to each child within their jurisdiction without discrimination of any kind, irrespective of the child's or *his or her parent's or legal guardian's* race, colour, sex, language, religion, political or other opinion, national, ethnic or social origin, property, disability, birth or other status' (emphasis added); 'CRC Child Marriage' (1998), 128–29.

home.[248] As previously discussed, a semiotic analysis requires an examination of the role of the immediate, dynamical and final interpretants: how individuals, communities and States parties might interpret the formulation of rights, including at its extremes.[249] Given that child marriage is prevalent globally, and that several States parties to the CRC entered reservations expressly to diminish the rights of girls,[250] the final interpretant should not be discounted. While the practice of child marriage has declined in South Asia due to India adopting measures to tackle this problem, it reaches the highest proportions in Africa, as well as the Middle East and Latin America.[251] Moreover, child marriage is not prohibited under the law in many states. Presently, in the 112 countries in which child marriage is prevalent, only 9 countries amended their laws to increase the minimum age of marriage.[252] The CRC Committee underscores the problematic outer boundary of childhood as concerns child marriage in its general comments, noting that '[b]oth the legal minimum age and actual age of marriage, particularly for girls, are still very low in several States parties'.[253] It further explains that children lose the protection of the CRC through marriage: 'in some States parties married children are legally considered adults, even if they are under 18, depriving them of all the special protection measures they are entitled under the Convention'.[254] In this regard, the Committee 'strongly recommends that States parties review and, where necessary, reform their legislation and practice to increase the minimum age for marriage with and without parental consent to 18 years, for *both girls and boys*'.[255] The decision of the Committee to clarify that states should provide minimum ages for both girls and boys constitutes a sign that it does not wish to allow states to fail to protect one sex, notably girls. The Committee also stresses that the protection against violence shall apply 'also to children under the age of 18 who have attained majority or emancipation through *early marriage and/or forced marriage*',[256] which demonstrates a concern that girls be removed from the CRC umbrella on account of child marriage. In their joint recommendation-comment, the CEDAW and CRC Committees

[248] 'CRC Child Marriage' (1998), 126–27; 'Jus Cogens' (1998), 19. See previous discussion on the subjectivity of the BIC principle.

[249] See Chapters 1 and 5.

[250] See Chapters 4 and 5.

[251] See UNFPA, 'Global Programme to Accelerate Action to End Child Marriage' (2019).

[252] Quentin Wodon et al., 'Ending Child Marriage: Child Marriage Laws and Their Limitations' (World Bank 2017), 3.

[253] CRC General Comment No. 4: 'Adolescent Health' (2003), para. 20.

[254] Ibid.

[255] Ibid. (emphasis added).

[256] CRC General Comment No. 13: 'Violence' (2011), footnote 13 (emphasis added).

attempt to at least restrict the phenomenon of child marriage by allowing for marriage at sixteen years instead of eighteen years and solely under special circumstances:

> As a matter of respecting the child's evolving capacities and autonomy in making decisions that affect her or his life, a marriage of a mature, capable child below 18 years of age may be allowed in exceptional circumstances, provided that the child is at least 16 years of age and that such decisions are made by a judge based on legitimate exceptional grounds defined by law and on the evidence of maturity, without deference to culture and tradition.[257]

One can observe that the Committees require that the decision be made by a judge, according to the law, and specify that culture and tradition cannot be invoked to justify marriage before eighteen years, thereby demonstrating their concern for cultural relativism, which ties into Rao's discussion on *who speaks* on behalf of a given culture, *who defines* the culture and who is instead *impacted* by this interpretation, namely the girl child. In its concluding observations, the CRC Committee has urged states to raise the minimum age of marriage to eighteen years.[258] It has criticized States parties in which the minimum age of marriage of eighteen years does not apply to customary marriages,[259] and those that recognize 'the legality of the marriage of girls as young as 14 years with parental consent',[260] or when they reach puberty,[261] which as previously mentioned, can be as early as nine years old, as well as those where the 'age limit can be lowered to 13 years in cases where children are sexually abused and may consequently marry the perpetrators, who in turn avoid any criminal prosecution for the crime'.[262]

[257] Joint CEDAW-CRC GenRec/Com: 'Harmful Practices' (2014), para. 20.

[258] CRC Concluding Observations: Thailand (17 February 2012) UN Doc CRC/C/THA/CO/3–4, para. 32. See also CRC Concluding Observations: Cuba (16 June 2022) UN Doc CRC/C/CUB/CO/3–6, para. 16.

[259] CRC Concluding Observations: Namibia (16 October 2012) UN Doc CRC/C/NAM/CO/2–3, para. 28.

[260] CRC Concluding Observations: Myanmar (14 March 2012) UN Doc CRC/C/MMR/CO/3–4, para. 33.

[261] CRC Concluding Observations: Nigeria (21 June 2010) UN Doc CRC/C/NGA/CO/3–4, para. 26: 'the Child Rights Act at state level sets the age at 16 years (Akwa-Ibom state) or defines the child not by age but by "puberty" (Jigwa state), reportedly for the purposes of early marriages'; CRC Concluding Observations: Pakistan (11 July 2016) UN Doc CRC/C/PAK/CO/5, paras. 16–17.

[262] CRC Concluding Observations: Thailand (17 February 2012) UN Doc CRC/C/THA/CO/3–4, para. 31.

### 3.6 Monitoring

The current definition of 'child' in the CRC may create complications for treaty bodies when they evaluate the implementation of the Convention and other treaties relevant to the girl child at the domestic level. The absence of a uniform boundary for the end of childhood propelled the CRC Committee to 'remind' States parties, in its general comment on general measures of implementation, that 'data collection needs to extend over the whole period of childhood, up to the age of 18 years'.[263] The CRC Committee also 'urges' states to develop a system of data collection and indicators that covers all children up to the age of eighteen years, and disaggregated by gender, thereby distinguishing between girls and boys.[264] Additionally, the Committee stresses that States parties, when making decisions concerning public budgeting, are required to consider children until eighteen years to ensure that adolescents who reach majority earlier will not be left behind, and underscores that states should consider children 'of any gender', thus comprising girls.[265] Moreover, several States parties to the CRC fail to examine children up to eighteen years, as noted by the Committee in its concluding observations.[266] The Human Rights Committee has also had to specify, in its general comment on the rights of the child, that 'a State party cannot absolve itself from its obligations under the Covenant regarding persons under the age of 18, notwithstanding that they have reached the age of majority under domestic law'.[267] The decision of the Human Rights Committee to make this clarification demonstrates that the absence of a definite and uniform boundary for the end of childhood under international law impacts the monitoring of the implementation of children's rights in the ICCPR, and notably that it may be invoked by States parties to absolve themselves from their obligations under the Covenant. In this regard,

[263] CRC General Comment No. 5: 'Implementation' (2003), para. 48.

[264] CRC General Comment No. 7: 'Early Childhood' (2006), para. 39: '[t]he Committee urges all States parties to develop a system of data collection and indicators consistent with the Convention and disaggregated by gender, age, family structure, urban and rural residence, and other relevant categories. This system should cover all children up to the age of 18 years, with specific emphasis on early childhood, particularly children belonging to vulnerable groups'.

[265] CRC General Comment No. 19: 'Public Budgeting' (2016), para. 3: '[w]hen referring to a "child" or "children", the general comment includes all persons of any gender under the age of 18 whose rights are or can be directly or indirectly, positively or negatively, affected by public budget-related decisions'.

[266] See for example CRC Concluding Observations: Albania (7 December 2012) UN Doc CRC/C/ALB/CO/2–4, para. 18; CRC Concluding Observations: Cuba (16 June 2022) UN Doc CRC/C/CUB/CO/3–6, para. 47; CRC Concluding Observations: Namibia (16 October 2012) UN Doc CRC/C/NAM/CO/2–3, para. 18.

[267] ICCPR General Comment No. 17: 'Rights Child' (1989), para. 4.

it is noteworthy that the issue of the absence of a uniform boundary for the end of childhood was underscored by the Human Rights Committee in a general comment produced the very same year that the CRC was adopted (1989), and yet this did not incite the drafters of the CRC to reconsider the parameter of majority which can be reached at any time before eighteen years.[268]

## 3.7 Research Data on Girls

The absence of a uniform boundary for the end of girlhood signifies that the research and data on the girl child produced by international agencies exclude an important percentage of female persons under eighteen years who are no longer considered girl children under the CRC because they reached majority earlier. An illustration of this problem is that the UN Population Fund data qualify the distinct category 'married women' as comprising female persons between 15–49 years, which implies that married girl children fifteen years and over are considered 'women'.[269] Moreover, the UNDP classifies persons over the age of fifteen years both as 'adults' as concerns 'adult literacy rates',[270] and 'youth' as concerns 'youth literacy rates'.[271] Girls who are fifteen years and over are thereby simultaneously placed in the youth and adult categories for statistical purposes, instead of the 'child' class. Likewise, in its data on HIV prevalence, the UNDP places girls over fifteen years in both the 'youth' (15–24 years old),[272] and 'adult' (15–49 years old)[273] categories.[274] As a result, girl children over fifteen years are merged with 'women up to 24 years', 'women up to 49 years' and 'youth' according to the issue examined, and

268 The CRC was adopted in November 1989, and the Human Rights Committee expressed its concern about the absence of a boundary of eighteen years for childhood in its general comment published earlier the very same year (April 1989). The decision of the Human Rights Committee to underscore this problem in a general comment appears to indicate that it had attracted their attention for some time.

269 UNDP, Human Development Reports (HDR), 'Sustainability and Equity: A Better Future for All' (Palgrave Macmillan 2011), 139–42; 'The Real Wealth of Nations: Pathways to Human Development' (Palgrave Macmillan 2010), 156–60: as concerns 'contraceptive prevalence, any method'. It also identifies 'women' as persons between 15–49 years as concerns data on pregnancy with anemia: HDR, 'Gender Equality' (Oxford University Press 1995), 168–69: 'pregnant women aged 15–49 years with anemia'.

270 UNDP, 'Sustainability' (2011), 158–61; UNDP, HDR, 'Millennium Development Goals: A Compact among Nations to End Human Poverty' (Oxford University Press 2003), 318–21, 354–55: '[l]iteracy rate, adult: The percentage of people aged 15 and above'.

271 UNDP, 'Millennium' (2003), 318–21, 355: '[l]iteracy rate, youth: The percentage of people aged 15–24'.

272 UNDP, 'Real Wealth' (2010), 197–201.

273 Ibid.

274 UNDP, 'Sustainability' (2011), 158–61.

even as concerns the same issue, within different Human Development Reports,[275] which demonstrates discrepancies both between and within the reports of the same UN agency.[276] The UNDP itself laments the lack of disaggregated data for girl children between 15–19 years to examine adolescent fertility rates.[277] Other international agencies refer to 'women aged between 15 and 44 years,[278] thereby implying that persons fifteen and over are 'women', or classify 'young people' as comprising persons between 15–24.[279] Moreover, 'young people' are also identified as persons between 14–25 years.[280] Lastly, the category 'young women' refers to persons aged 15–19 years.[281] The publications of UN agencies may therefore miss significant data on the situation of girl children between the ages of 15–18 worldwide, which in turn impacts their findings and diagnoses. Indeed, the adolescent girl over fifteen is subsumed within the 'youth', 'young woman' and 'adult' categories and her vulnerability to violations due to childism is not taken into consideration. Hence, while the situation of adolescent girls differs from that of adult women, as the former often have fewer civil and political rights, participatory rights, economic rights and reproductive rights than the latter, these two identity groups are still merged in data and statistics. Girl children between fifteen and eighteen years, and the unique issues they face, thereby become invisible within international research.

## IV SEMIOETHICS: RECOMMENDED BOUNDARY

This chapter has noted that since the CRC comprises unique rights and as it is the most widely ratified treaty, it would be beneficial for girl children to be covered by the Convention. At the same time, certain provisions of the CRC weaken autonomy rights, which is especially problematic for adolescent girls. This chapter also underscored that the lack of uniformity for the end of girlhood adversely impacts monitoring and data analysis. It is argued that the

[275] It is notable that the HDRs of 2010 and 2011, published within a year of each other, do not offer uniform age groups, for example as regards HIV prevalence: See UNDP, 'Real Wealth' (2010), 197–201; UNDP, 'Sustainability' (2011), 158–61.

[276] UNDP, 'Sustainability' (2011), 139–42, 158–61; UNDP 'Millennium' (2003), 86, 198–202.

[277] UNDP, 'Real Wealth' (2010), 123: '[w]e use the adolescent fertility rate for girls ages 15–19. Fertility for girls below age 18 would be preferable, but these data are not available'.

[278] 'Gender Mental Health' (2004), 8.

[279] UNFPA, 'Young People' (2011), 1: 'young people age 15–24'.

[280] ILO, 'Give Girls a Chance: Tackling Child Labour, a Key to the Future' (2009), 5: 'young people in the 14–25 age group'.

[281] WHO, 'Multi-Country Study on Women's Health and Domestic Violence against Women' (2005), 8.

silence concerning the minimum age for the end of childhood and the meaning of 'majority', is in any case problematical. This raises the question of how the definition of 'child' in the CRC could be amended to promote the rights of the girl child.[282]

### 1 *Separate Majority and the End of Girlhood*

One potential solution could be to separate the concepts of majority and the end of girlhood. Rather than link majority to the end of girlhood, an adolescent girl could be considered a 'child' and thus covered by the CRC until eighteen years, and also a 'major' accorded autonomy rights and thereby no longer submitted to 'childist' provisions in the CRC. In this regard, it is pertinent to refer to the proposal of article 1 submitted by the observer for Finland during the drafting of the CRC, who suggested eighteen years as the threshold for the end of childhood while allowing that children between the ages of fifteen and eighteen be considered both a 'child' and a 'major' so that they would not be submitted to provisions of the CRC 'manifestly incompatible' with their status as a major.[283] While all individuals below the age of eighteen years are protected under the CRC according to paragraph 1 of the Finnish proposal, the provisions of the Convention that are incompatible with the rights of a major will not apply, according to paragraph 2 of this proposal, once a child reaches fifteen years. Accordingly, it could be argued that 'childist provisions' such as the concepts of parental authority and BIC would no longer apply to girl children once they turn fifteen years old. This formulation also reproduces the compromise solution supported by Askari, Goonesekere, Coomaraswamy, Archard, Fortin and Guercio to distinguish between young girls and adolescent girls and grant the latter autonomy rights.[284] More specifically, the Finnish proposal appears to address the seven main criticisms of the current definition of girlhood under the CRC previously examined in this chapter. First, it solves the current problem of the absence of a minimum age for majority and thus for the end of girlhood: under this proposal, the boundary of childhood is set at eighteen years, and that of majority at fifteen years. Second, it ensures that girl children are holders of the rights enshrined

[282] This book proposes to address weaknesses in the formulation of provisions by amending relevant treaties. As discussed in Chapter 5, Section IV: 'Semioethics: Recommended Definition', art. 50 of the CRC enables States parties to amend the Convention, and the general rules on the amendment of treaties are comprised in the Vienna Convention (1969), arts. 39–41.

[283] See the Finnish proposal in Section II: Meaning of this chapter.

[284] See Chapter 3.

in the CRC until they reach eighteen years, notably unique rights which are not otherwise provided for in the Twin Covenants. This aligns with Fortin's compromise of setting the parameter for the end of childhood at eighteen years to ensure that 'adolescents still prone to youthful recklessness gain a few extra years of legal protection', while granting more rights during adolescence.[285] Third, this proposal specifies that provisions 'manifestly incompatible' with girls' status as majors, notably childist provisions, would not be imposed upon them as soon as they reach fifteen years. It tackles the issue of girl children who reach majority under domestic law and yet are not automatically granted all adult rights enshrined in the Twin Covenants, while also no longer protected under the CRC. According to this proposal, adolescent girls are covered both by the CRC and the provisions of the other treaties normally attributed to adults, such as the ICCPR and the ICESCR. Lastly, this proposal would ensure uniformity worldwide. Accordingly, it would attend to the issue of the discrepancy in the boundary of childhood leading to discrimination on the grounds of gender and national domicile, and between girls within the same jurisdiction. Moreover, it would strengthen uniformity as concerns data analysis and treaty implementation.

The Finnish proposal therefore appears to strike a balance between the paternalistic and child liberationist approaches. More specifically, this proposal would empower adolescent girls within the private sphere. For example, an adolescent girl submitted to restrictive social codes who lives in a controlling family environment and fears to become the victim of an honour-related killing would become a major at fifteen years old under domestic law and entitled to autonomy rights, such as emancipation. She would not be under the authority of a court of law and a master signifier, notably a judge or social worker, who can determine whether it is in her best interests to be emancipated. The adolescent girl who reaches majority at fifteen years could move out of her parents' home, city or region if her safety were threatened, and she could earn a living, sign a lease and be in the love relationship of her choice, without being arrested by State authorities and sent back home. In this regard, it is worthy of note that many victims of honour-related killings, notably in Canada and the United Kingdom, had contacted authorities, and for example, attempted to leave their family home, or asked the State to be emancipated and move away from their parents' care, or to be placed in child protection housing; however, child protection authorities and law enforcement that had received no training on the dynamics of 'dishonour', dismissed or

[285] *Children's Rights* (2009), 89.

underestimated the severity of their situation, which led to their deaths.[286] At the same time, this proposal would ensure that girls are still protected under the CRC until they reach eighteen years, and for example afforded housing, financial support and access to education, including vocational training. Such an approach is thereby closely related to qualified liberal paternalism or justified paternalism,[287] as adolescent girls would be allocated 'adult' rights while continuing to benefit from rights enshrined in the CRC, such as the rights to health, education, protection against sexual exploitation and the use of narcotic drugs.[288] The State would still hold the power to protect the adolescent girl against 'self-destructive choices',[289] especially non-reversible changes, such as undergoing cosmetic plastic surgery and FGM such as labiaplasty, or consuming drugs such as heroin or fentanyl, until she reaches eighteen years, on account of her right to health.[290] The State would also protect her against sex trafficking and sexual exploitation, including partaking in online pornography.[291] For example, the State could protect girl performers against sexual and economic exploitation at the hands of their parents, legal guardians, managers or any other agent, while promoting their right to education, until they reach eighteen years.[292]

## 2 *Challenges*

The Finnish proposal could be criticized on four grounds. Firstly, it fails to specify, in paragraph 2, which provisions of the CRC would be considered 'manifestly incompatible' with the legal status of a major:

> (2) No provision of the present Convention shall be applied to a child who has attained the age of 15 years and who no longer is a minor,

[286] See for example R v. Shafia, 2012 ONSC 1548; R v. Ahmed and Ahmed [2012] Chester Crown Court (unreported); R v. Mahmod Babakir Mahmod [2009] EWCA Crim 775.

[287] See Chapter 3; *Children's Rights* (2009), 28.

[288] CRC, arts. 24 (health), 19 (sexual abuse), 34 (sexual exploitation), 33 (narcotic drugs and psychotropic substances), 35 (trafficking) and 36 (all forms of exploitation).

[289] *Children's Rights* (2009), 28.

[290] These drugs have recently been legalized in some jurisdictions: Dr Jeremy Devine, *Toronto Star*, 'The Federal Drug Strategy is Not Helping the Addicts' (17 July 2023). www.thestar.com/opinion/contributors/2023/07/17/the-federal-drug-strategy-is-not-helping-the-addicts.html?rf (accessed 20 July 2023); Ashleigh Stewart, *The Independent*, 'Free Cocaine, Meth and Heroin for Everyone: One City's Plan to Tackle Its Drug Problem' (17 July 2021). www.independent.co.uk/news/world/americas/vancouver-free-drugs-cocaine-heroin-canada-b1885905.html (accessed 20 July 2023).

[291] 'Cam Girls Business' (2023); 'Aggression Pornography' (2020).

[292] CRC, arts. 19 (sexual abuse), 32 (economic exploitation), 34 (sexual exploitation), 28 and 29 (right to education) and 31 (right to leisure).

where the application would be *manifestly incompatible with the legal status of that child.*

The Finnish proposal as formulated could enable a State party to remove any right enshrined in the CRC which it considers 'manifestly incompatible' with the status of an adolescent girl. For instance, it could remove the protection against sexual and economic exploitation under articles 32–36 on the grounds that as a major, the adolescent girl no longer needs protection. Moreover, it could remove State protection against violence in the home provided for under article 19, which is particularly problematic since the CEDAW fails to offer this protection to adult women. At the same time, the State party could still keep the two main problematic provisions of the CRC for adolescent girls identified in this book: the BIC principle (article 3), and parental authority (articles 3 and 5).

Secondly, the definition of 'a child who no longer is a minor' in the Finnish proposal offers a list of possible criteria which are listed as options, as indicated by the conjunction 'or' between each paragraph. This appears to indicate that the criterion for majority might differ between states and thus a girl child who can dispose of parts of her property under domestic law is considered a major according to the CRC, while she might not be automatically granted the other rights listed, such as emancipation. This problem could be addressed by adding a clarification that a child who becomes a major shall be granted emancipation as well as *all the rights* listed in the legal, political and economic spheres. However, such a provision might not appeal to states adopting a paternalistic approach that might therefore refuse to support the amended definition of child on the grounds that it grants autonomy rights too early. Thirdly, as previously discussed, it is very difficult to establish a single age for the end of childhood or girlhood worldwide as the realities of children differ greatly. Any age limit, including eighteen years for adulthood and fifteen years for majority, may appear arbitrary and unfair, and any fixed definition of childhood or girlhood, inappropriate. States parties might disagree as to the age of majority: some might favour a child liberationist approach and suggest a lower age within the adolescent category, such as twelve years, while others might argue for fourteen, sixteen, seventeen or simply eighteen years. Also, setting eighteen years as the uniform age for the end of childhood might be difficult for States parties that do not have the available resources to provide for the rights enshrined in the CRC. Hence, an amendment to article 1 inspired by the Finnish proposal might not appear feasible for states in the Global South or the Global North that might refuse to ratify it. In this regard, for such an age threshold to be established, the provision of the CRC for international state cooperation in article 4 would be essential to ensure that assistance:

> States Parties shall undertake all appropriate legislative, administrative, and other measures for the implementation of the rights recognized in the present Convention. With regard to economic, social and cultural rights, States Parties shall undertake such measures to the maximum extent of their available resources and, where needed, *within the framework of international co-operation*.[293]

This is however easier said than done as various geopolitical factors might come into play. Fourthly, states might prefer the current dichotomy between childhood and majority, and thus the either/or approach whereby an individual is either a girl child and protected under the CRC, or a major and granted rights in the Twin Covenants. Accordingly, they might not agree with the proposal that adolescents, including adolescent girls between the ages of fifteen and eighteen years, be considered both children and majors.

As discussed in Chapter 1, one of the great challenges of semioethics is that contrarily to other semiotic theories, such as Welby's Meaning Triad, which exclusively focuses on examining the sense, meaning and ultimate significance of signs, this novel approach also attempts to explore how signs could be modified to address their possible detrimental repercussions. Yet the ability of the semiotician to achieve the first step of the semioethic analysis – the diagnosis of a given sign – does not necessarily signify that s/he can uncover a new sign to replace it. This book has identified weaknesses in the terminology employed to frame the boundary of girlhood in the CRC as concerns the protection and empowerment of girl children, as well as research and monitoring. However, the second step of finding a suitable amended definition is problematic. In this regard, one could contend that the boundary for the end of childhood in article 1 of the CRC should remain unchanged. It is nevertheless argued that the current boundary of childhood is very problematic as it fails to establish a minimum age for the end of girlhood which could technically be set as young as *one-day old*, strips girl children who reach majority before eighteen years of important rights enshrined in the CRC and conversely submits adolescent girls who reached rational autonomy to childist provisions in the Convention. It also creates significant discrepancies in data analysis and monitoring worldwide. In other words, it is argued that while a definition of 'child' addressing every limitation examined in this book

[293] Emphasis added.

is yet to be found, the current definition of childhood under the CRC is more detrimental to the protection and promotion of girl child rights than an amended definition that would address some of the most serious abovementioned limitations.

## 3 *Proposed Amendment*

This book recommends to adapt the Finnish proposal according to the issues previously raised. We suggest to remove the term 'unless under the law applicable to the child, majority is attained earlier' in article 1 to ensure that all children, including girl children, are covered under the CRC until they reach eighteen years. In addition, the current formulation of article 1 which employs the wording 'below the age of 18 years' would be maintained, rather than the Finnish proposal which stated 'who has not attained the age of 18 years', in order to avoid unnecessary modifications. The proposed amendment would employ fifteen years, as in the Finnish proposal, although it is acknowledged that identifying a specific age is problematic. The present book's proposal would keep the two paragraphs from the Finnish proposal, while suggesting some amendments to these paragraphs (see in italics), and adding proposals from Chapter 5 to ensure the visibility of the girl child:

1 For the purposes of the present Convention, a child means every human being – *girl and boy* – below the age of eighteen years. *The rights in the present Convention apply equally to the girl-child and the boy-child.*[294]
2 *The provisions* of the present Convention *enshrining the best interests of the child (article 3) and parental authority (articles 3 and 5) shall not be applied* to a child who has attained the age of 15 years and who *thereby reaches majority for these provisions* would be manifestly incompatible with the legal status of that child.
3 In terms of paragraph 2 of this article, a child who *reached majority shall be granted all the following rights under domestic law*:
   (a) full legal capacity;
   (b) *emancipation* in all matters relating to *her/his* person;
   (c) the right to determine *her/his* own residence;
   (d) the capacity to enter into *contractual* relationships; and
   (e) the capacity to dispose of parts of *her/his* property.

First, this proposed amended article stipulates in paragraph 2 that the two provisions that are incompatible with the status of the child as a major, that is,

[294] See Chapter 5, Section IV: 'Semioethics: Recommended Definition', to ensure the visibility and thereby the 'presence' of the girl child in the CRC.

the BIC and parental authority, shall no longer apply to a child who turns fifteen as s/he will automatically reach majority at that age. According to this amended proposal, States parties are not able to choose which provisions of the CRC they shall consider 'incompatible' with the status of a major and thereby strip adolescent girls of essential rights enshrined in the Convention. Second, this proposed provision indicates that once children reach fifteen years, they automatically attain majority and are granted autonomy rights: 'a child who has attained the age of 15 years and who *thereby reaches majority*'. Instead, the Finnish proposal stated that 'a child who has attained the age of fifteen years *and* who no longer is a minor', which could imply that a child might simultaneously be fifteen years and a minor, since the sentence does not clarify that the two are interconnected, for instance by specifying that a child 'has attained 15 years and who thereby is no longer a minor'. The proposed amendment expressly stipulates that once a child reaches majority, s/he shall be granted all the autonomy rights enumerated in paragraph 3, and the 'or' between each paragraph would thus be deleted: '[i]n terms of paragraph 2 of this article, a child who reached majority shall be granted *all* the following rights under domestic law'. This amendment also removes the qualifier 'certain' in paragraphs (d) and (e) as they restrict the ability of majors to enter contractual relationships and dispose of parts of their property. For instance, under the Finnish proposal, majors are solely entitled to enter 'certain' contractual agreements, and thus might not be able to sign a lease, obtain microcredit or buy property. Lastly, this amendment employs the possessive adjective 'her/his' with a slash in paragraph 3 rather than 'his or her' to ensure that States parties do not misinterpret the 'his or her' as signifying that the right applies either to males *or* females. Moreover, this formulation further strengthens the visibility of the girl child as the female possessive adjective appears first: 'her/his'.

This new provision would have four significant positive repercussions for the identification of the girl child in the CRC. Firstly, it tackles the issue of the invisibility of the girl child in the Convention, and ensures that States parties undoubtedly acknowledge that she is a rights holder under the Convention for she is expressly mentioned in paragraph 1 and the suggested paragraphs 3b), c) and e) employ the possessive adjectives 'her/his', thereby placing the feminine before the masculine, contrarily to all CRC provisions that give precedence to the masculine.[295] Secondly, this amended provision offers a uniform and objective parameter worldwide for the end of childhood – eighteen years – and thereby attends to the problem of discrimination on the

[295] See Chapter 5.

grounds of gender within and between states as well as discrimination on the basis of national domicile. It also addresses the concern that there is presently no minimum age for the end of childhood. Thirdly, this provision ensures that girl children are granted essential rights enshrined in the CRC until they reach eighteen years, and thus offers protection to more girl children than the current definition. Fourthly, the second and third paragraphs stipulate that adolescent girls are granted autonomy rights once they attain fifteen years and are thereby no longer submitted to the 'childist' provisions of the CRC, that is, the BIC and parental authority. This amended provision also prevents States parties from removing rights enshrined in the CRC when an adolescent girl reaches fifteen years, as the suggested proposal expressly stipulates that the only provisions that shall not apply to majors between fifteen and eighteen years are the BIC and parental authority. It is argued that if girl children are covered under the provisions of the CRC until they reach eighteen years, they may be granted autonomy rights at fifteen years, such as entering a contract, because they will still be protected under the CRC, and thus against adults or other adolescents who might intend to take advantage of them, for example under articles 32–36 on economic and sexual exploitation and article 24 on the right to health. Hence, this proposed amendment would address the concerns of both paternalists and child liberationists.

The age limit for majority is however still debatable and fifteen years is offered solely as a suggestion, not as a final recommendation. States parties could reach an agreement on a different age that they find more suitable within adolescence. It is acknowledged that the amended definition would still comprise inherent weaknesses, since the imposition of an age threshold for majority as well as for the end of childhood does not account for the unique capacities and circumstances of each individual girl child. Furthermore, states might not reach a consensus in agreeing to such a proposed amendment as they may adopt a more extreme paternalistic or child liberationist approach, and some nations might not agree to provide for and protect children until they reach eighteen years. In this regard, the proposed amendment does not constitute an ideal solution, but rather an attempt at the most suitable definition under difficult circumstances and a complex international setting.

# 8

# Girlhood and Womanhood in the CEDAW

Since the current definition of child under international law fails to clarify the boundary separating girlhood and womanhood, perhaps the definition of woman can shed light on the distinction between girls and adult women. Yet the expression 'woman' is not defined under international law, and more significantly, instruments pertaining to women's rights, such as the CEDAW, the Convention on the Political Rights of Women (1953),[1] the Declaration on the Elimination of Violence Against Women (1993),[2] and the Beijing Declaration (1995), do not delineate the boundaries of girlhood and womanhood.

## I SENSE OF WOMAN

The CEDAW does not provide a definition of the term 'woman', nor does it clarify that the 'womanhood' umbrella encompasses girl children, or that girlhood constitutes a division within womanhood. In fact, some CEDAW provisions refer to women *and* girls or women *and* children, as distinct identity groups. Whereas the Convention refers to women throughout its provisions, girls are mentioned solely once, as a separate entity, under article 10(f) as concerns '[t]he reduction of female student drop-out rates and the organization of programmes for *girls* and *women* who have left school prematurely'.[3] One can contend that if the term 'woman' were perceived as all-inclusive of girls, the CEDAW would not need to mention girls specifically in this one provision. Moreover, this article refers to 'girls' and 'women' as distinct groups

1 (New York, adopted 31 March 1953, entered into force 7 July 1954) 193 UNTS 135.
2 (New York, adopted 20 December 1993) UN Doc A/RES/48/104.
3 Emphasis added.

within the same sentence, which seems to indicate that women *exclude* girls. Indeed, from a semiotic perspective, when a sentence refers to two identity groups and connects them with the conjunction 'and', one expects these two groups to constitute mutually exclusive entities. It could be argued that if 'women' were intended to include girls under article 10(f) of the CEDAW, this provision would simply refer to 'women', or 'females, including younger and older women', or 'women, including girls and older women'. Also, the few CEDAW provisions comprising the term 'children' refer to 'children' and 'women' in a context which clearly indicates that they are perceived as mutually exclusive entities. Indeed, article 5 recognizes 'the common responsibility of men and *women* in the upbringing and development of their *children*',[4] and article 9 on nationality stipulates that 'States Parties shall grant *women* equal rights with men with respect to the nationality of their *children*'.[5] Additionally, its provision prohibiting child marriage refers to '[t]he betrothal and the marriage of a *child*',[6] not that of 'a woman', which could indicate once again that 'woman' refers solely to adult women and not to girl children in the context of the CEDAW. In fact, the decision to refer to a 'child' rather than a 'girl child' further stresses the distinction between an adult woman and a 'child'. It is also notable that many provisions of the CEDAW enshrine rights accorded to adult women and not girls. The CEDAW guarantees the right to political and public life, such as the right to vote and be eligible for election,[7] which is not available to girls. The Convention also protects economic rights such as access to bank loans, mortgages and other forms of financial credit,[8] which are usually not available to children, thus girls. Furthermore, the CEDAW enshrines the legal capacity of women,[9] which is usually not accorded to girls. And although the CEDAW, contrarily to the CRC, refers to the issue of child marriage, it does not mention gender-based violence nor several violations specific to or predominantly experienced by girl children, such as female infanticide. In this regard, Schulz et al. observe that 'key terms are not defined and some issues that are critical to women's full enjoyment of their human rights are not mentioned or are addressed only in general and indeterminate language'.[10] This absence of

4 CEDAW, art. 5b) (emphasis added).
5 CEDAW, art. 9(2) (emphasis added).
6 CEDAW, art. 16(2): '[t]he betrothal and the marriage of a child shall have no legal effect' (emphasis added).
7 CEDAW, art. 7.
8 CEDAW, art. 13.
9 CEDAW, art. 15.
10 Patricia Schulz, Ruth Halperin-Kaddari and Beate Rudolf, 'Introduction' in Patricia Schulz et al. (eds.), *The UN Convention on the Elimination of All Forms of Discrimination against Women and Its Optional Protocol: A Commentary* (2nd ed., Oxford University Press 2022), 22.

definitions, including that of the key term 'woman', therefore leaves room for interpretation as to whether or not girls are covered under the CEDAW. In comparison, the Protocol on the Rights of Women in Africa provides a definition of women as 'persons of female gender, including girls', and thus clearly covers girl children.[11]

## 1 *Definition of 'Discrimination against Women' in the CEDAW*

While the International Bill of Rights refers to the age- and gender-neutral concepts of 'distinction' and 'discrimination',[12] the only treaty that offers a definition of discrimination on the grounds of sex is the CEDAW, although it employs instead the expression 'discrimination against women', defined as:

> any distinction, exclusion or restriction made on the basis of sex which has the effect or purpose of impairing or nullifying the recognition, enjoyment or exercise by *women*, irrespective of their marital status, on a basis of equality of men and *women*, of human rights and fundamental freedoms in the political, economic, social, cultural, civil or any other field.[13]

It is notable that the CEDAW uses the expression 'discrimination against women' in article 1 rather than the age-neutral denominations 'discrimination on the basis of sex' or 'discrimination on the basis of gender'. The definition of 'discrimination against women' nonetheless refers to 'any distinction … made on the basis of sex', which would encompass all distinctions made between female and male human beings. However, immediately after mentioning 'any distinction … made on the basis of sex', article 1 exclusively refers to the effect this distinction has on 'women' without defining the term woman and thus whether it comprises girls. As a result, this definition could be interpreted as signifying that it refers solely to the sexism experienced by *adult women* in relation to *adult men*. Moreover, when referring to the concept of equality in other provisions, the CEDAW uses the expressions 'equality of rights of men and women',[14] 'equality between men and women',[15] 'equality of men and

[11] Protocol to the African Charter on Human and People's Rights on the Rights of Women in Africa (Maputo, adopted 11 July 2003, entered into force 25 November 2005), art I(k). It is also noteworthy that the Protocol comprises – under its very first article – a list of definitions to avoid misinterpretations, thereby adopting Welby's approach to the importance of clarifying terms in a glossary, as applied in our Meaning Glossary in this book.

[12] UDHR, art. 2: 'distinction of any kind, such as … sex'; ICCPR, art. 2(1): 'distinction of any kind, such as … sex'; ICESCR, art. 2(2): 'discrimination of any kind as to … sex'.

[13] CEDAW, art. 1 (emphasis added).

[14] CEDAW, preamble.

[15] CEDAW, preamble, arts. 4(1), 23.

women'[16] and 'equality with men',[17] instead of age-neutral terms such as 'female and male persons' or 'persons of the two sexes'. It is worthy of note that the CEDAW refers to 'sex' instead of 'gender'. The Committee adopted the term 'gender' in addition to sex in several general recommendations since the late 1980s-early 1990s, and underscores that the CEDAW aims at 'eliminating all forms of discrimination against *women* on the basis of sex *and* gender'.[18] It notes that '[a]lthough the Convention only refers to sex-based discrimination, interpreting article 1 together with articles 2(f) and 5(a) indicates that the Convention covers gender-based discrimination against *women*'.[19] One can observe that the Committee once again refers to the undefined term 'woman' in this context. The Committee often mentions sex- and gender-based discrimination grouped together, and notably refers to 'discrimination against women on the basis of sex and gender', 'discrimination of women based on sex and gender', 'the concept of non-discrimination on the basis of sex and gender', 'the principles of equality and non-discrimination on the basis of sex and gender', 'structural sex and gender-based discrimination' and 'sex non-discrimination and gender equality', and further employs the expression 'sex- and gender-based human rights'.[20] It distinguishes between

16 CEDAW, arts. 1, 2, 10, 11(1), 12(1), 13, 14(2), 16(1).

17 CEDAW, arts. 3, 15(1).

18 CEDAW General Recommendation No. 28: 'Obligations', art. 2 (2010), para. 3 (emphasis added). See also General Recommendations No. 19: 'Violence' (1992), paras. 1, 4, 5, 6, 7, 11, 12, 17, 21, 24; No. 24: 'Women and Health' (1999), paras. 15, 18, 25, 31; No. 26: 'Migrant Women' (2008), paras. 2, 5, 8, 11, 13, 14, 15, 21, 23, 24, 25, 26, 28; No. 27: 'Older Women and Protection of Their Human Rights' (16 December 2010) UN Doc CEDAW/C/GC/27, paras. 5, 11, 13, 16, 20, 21, 25, 29, 31, 33, 35, 41, 47, 50; No. 28: 'Obligations', art. 2 (2010), paras. 3, 5, 16, 17, 18, 19, 22, 37; No. 29: 'Article 16 Economic Consequences of Marriage, Family Relations and Their Dissolution' (30 October 2013) UN Doc CEDAW/C/GC/29, paras. 1, 8, 18, 43; No. 30: 'Conflict Situations' (2013), paras. 2, 7, 17, 18, 22, 23, 27–35, 37–39, 41–44, 50, 52, 53, 55–57, 59, 65–70, 72–74, 76–79, 81; Joint CEDAW-CRC GenRec/Com: 'Harmful Practices' (2014), paras. 4, 6, 7, 9, 11, 15, 17, 18, 29, 54, 55, 61, 62, 67, 69, 74, 83, 87; No. 32: 'Refugee Women' (2014), paras. 1, 3, 5, 6, 10, 11, 13–16, 19, 21–23, 25, 27, 28, 30, 31, 34, 36–38, 40, 44, 45, 50, 54, 57; No. 33: 'Access Justice' (2015), paras. 3, 6, 7, 8, 11, 13–15, 17, 18, 20, 21, 25–27, 29–31, 33–35, 37, 41, 42, 44, 46, 48, 51, 60; No. 35: 'Gender-based Violence' (2017), (throughout); No. 36: 'Education' (2017), paras. 1, 3, 4, 9, 13, 16, 17, 27, 29, 30, 31, 37, 43, 57, 62–66, 68, 73, 75, 76, 78–81; No. 37: 'Disaster Risk' (2018), paras. 2–5, 7, 8, 12, 13, 16–18, 20, 21, 24, 26, 28, 29, 36, 38–42, 44–48, 51–53, 55, 57, 60–62, 64, 65, 68, 69, 72, 75, 76, 78–81; No. 39: 'Indigenous Women and Girls' (2022), paras. 2–5, 9, 10, 12, 15–18, 20, 22–24, 26, 27, 29, 31–36, 38–42, 45–53, 56, 59. Also, No. 17: 'Domestic Activities' (10th session, 1991), refers to 'statistics disaggregated by gender', para. a); No. 9: 'Situation of Women' (8th session, 1989): 'data can be disaggregated according to gender', para. 4.

19 CEDAW General Recommendation No. 28: 'Obligations', art. 2 (2010), para. 5 (emphasis added).

20 See for example CEDAW General Recommendations: No. 26: 'Migrant Women' (2008), paras. 2, 11, 14, 15, 24, 28; No. 28: 'Obligations', art. 2 (2010), paras. 3, 17, 18, 19, 37; No. 30:

sex which 'refers to biological differences between men and women', and gender as:

> socially constructed identities, attributes and roles for *women and men* and society's social and cultural meaning for these biological differences resulting in hierarchical relationships *between women and men* and in the distribution of power and rights favouring men and disadvantaging *women*.[21]

The CEDAW Committee thus adopts the binary distinction between females and males, and the hybrid conception of females on biological and social grounds discussed in Chapter 2. As noted by Byrnes and Kapai:

> The Convention uses the term 'sex' as the central marker for deciding what types of differential treatment or disparate impact are (im)permissible. Underpinning the Convention are the assumptions both of (binary) sexual difference – that there exist two different sexes and that there are biological differences of significance between men and women as well as culturally constructed differences – and of shared humanity.[22]

However, once again, the Committee refers to the 'attributes and roles for *women and men*', the 'hierarchical relationships *between women and men*' and the distribution of power 'disadvantaging *women*', and does not clarify that discrimination against women, whether based on sex, gender, or sex and gender, applies to all females throughout the life cycle in this context. It is therefore notable that the current definition of discrimination in the CEDAW is age-centric whereas the expressions 'gender discrimination', 'sexism' or 'discrimination on the basis of sex' are age-neutral and would clearly encompass all female beings, including girl children. In this regard, Price Cohen argues that '[a]lthough the definition of "discrimination against women" possibly could be interpreted as including girls, the purpose of the Women's Convention is to equalize relationships between adult men and women'.[23]

'Conflict Situations' (2013), para. 77; Joint CEDAW-CRC GenRec/Com: 'Harmful Practices' (2014), paras. 6, 74; No. 32: 'Refugee Women' (2014), paras. 5, 6, 11, 54; No. 39: 'Indigenous Women and Girls' (2022), para. 24.

21 CEDAW General Recommendation No. 28: 'Obligations', art. 2 (2010), para. 5 (emphasis added).

22 Andres Byrnes and Puja Kapai, 'Article 1' in Patricia Schulz et al. (eds.), *The UN Convention on the Elimination of All Forms of Discrimination against Women and Its Optional Protocol: A Commentary* (2nd ed., Oxford University Press 2022), 87.

23 Cynthia Price Cohen, 'The United Nations Convention on the Rights of the Child: A Feminist Landmark' (1997) 3 *William and Mary Journal of Women and the Law* 29, 37.

## 2 *The Life-Cycle Approach*

Conversely, one can contend that since the CEDAW makes no distinction as to age, it applies equally to the girl child and the adult woman. This view is supported by the CEDAW Committee which has adopted, since 1999, a life-cycle approach in its general recommendations whereby womanhood includes all the stages of development, from infancy to old age.[24] The Committee states that the CEDAW 'reflects a life-cycle approach', thereby covering girls.[25] It specifies that 'girls are part of the larger community of women', and accordingly, States parties must enact legislation prohibiting discrimination in all fields of women's lives throughout their lifespan.[26] In its general recommendation on older women, the Committee emphasizes that girlhood is a stage of life within womanhood:

> The full development and advancement of women can only be achieved through a life-cycle approach that recognizes and addresses the different stages of women's lives – *from childhood through adolescence, adulthood and old age* – and the impact of each stage on the enjoyment of human rights by older women. The rights enshrined in the Convention are applicable to all stages of a woman's life.[27]

In addition, the CEDAW Committee notes, when addressing special issues such as prostitution and poverty,[28] and health needs,[29] that girls are included

[24] Also referred to as 'the lifespan', see CEDAW General Recommendations: 1) No. 24: 'Women and Health' (1999), paras. 2, 7, 8, 29; 2) No. 27: 'Older Women' (2010), paras. 11, 15, 30, 31; 3) No. 28: 'Obligations', art. 2 (2010), para. 31; 4) No. 30: 'Women in Conflict' (2013), para. 7; 5) No. 35: 'Gender-based Violence' (2017), para. 14; 6) No. 36: 'Education' (2017), paras. 20, 24, 58; 7) No. 39: 'Indigenous Women and Girls' (2022), paras. 4, 17, 42.

[25] CEDAW General Recommendation No. 30: 'Women and Conflict' (2013), para. 7: '[g]iven that the Convention reflects a *life-cycle approach*, States parties are also required to address the rights and distinct needs of conflict-affected *girls* that arise from gender-based discrimination' (emphasis added).

[26] CEDAW General Recommendation No. 28: 'Obligations', art. 2 (2010), para. 21: 'States parties in particular are obliged to promote the equal rights of girls since *girls are part of the larger community of women* and are more vulnerable to discrimination in such areas as access to basic education, trafficking, maltreatment, exploitation and violence' (emphasis added); para. 31.

[27] CEDAW General Recommendation No. 27: 'Older Women' (2010), para. 15 (emphasis added).

[28] CEDAW General Recommendation No. 19: 'Violence against Women' (1992), para. 15: '[p]overty and unemployment force many women, *including young girls*, into prostitution' (emphasis added).

[29] CEDAW General Recommendation No. 24: 'Women and Health' (1999), para. 6: 'special attention should be given to the health needs and rights of women belonging to vulnerable and disadvantaged groups, such as migrant women, refugee and internally displaced women, *the*

in the woman class. The Committee observes that States parties must tackle discrimination against women and girls throughout the lifespan:

> State action to prevent and address discrimination against Indigenous women and girls throughout their lifespan must integrate a gender perspective, an intersectional perspective, an Indigenous women and girls perspective, an intercultural perspective and a multidisciplinary perspective.[30]

UN specialized agencies, such as the UNFPA and UNICEF, also consider that the provisions of the CEDAW 'apply to females throughout the life cycle – from infancy to old age'.[31] The CEDAW Committee moreover adopts an intersectional discrimination perspective in several general recommendations, and notably identifies 'girls' as constituting a group of women experiencing intersecting forms of discrimination.[32] Many of these recommendations nonetheless refer to gender and 'age' without specifying girls or girlhood, which could imply that the term 'woman' comprises solely younger and older adult women; moreover, some recommendations solely refer to other grounds, such as race.[33] The general recommendation on disaster risk mentions 'adolescents

*girl child* and older women, women in prostitution, indigenous women and women with physical or mental disabilities' (emphasis added).

[30] CEDAW General Recommendation No. 39: 'Indigenous Women and Girls' (2022), para. 4.

[31] UNFPA and UNICEF, 'Women's and Children's Rights: Making the Connection' (2010), 24; Savitri Goonesekere and Rangita de Silva-de Alwis, 'Women's and Children's Rights in a Human Rights Based Approach to Development' (UNICEF 2005), 16.

[32] CEDAW General Recommendation No. 30: 'Conflict Situations' (2013), para. 7: 'intersecting forms of discrimination ... address the rights and distinct needs of conflict-affected girls'; para. 57: 'different groups of internally displaced and refugee women who are subjected to multiple and intersecting forms of discrimination, including women with disabilities, older women, *girls*, widows, women who head households, pregnant women, women living with HIV/AIDS, rural women, indigenous women' (emphasis added); Joint CEDAW-CRC GenRec/Com: 'Harmful Practices' (2014), para. 6; No. 36: 'Education' (2017), para. 18; No. 39: 'Indigenous Women and Girls' (2022), which almost systematically refers to Indigenous women and girls in this context, paras. 2, 3, 4, 23, 26, 33, 39, 42.

[33] CEDAW Recommendations: No. 28: 'Obligations', art. 2 (2010), para. 18, 'intersectionality ... discrimination of women ... is inextricably linked with other factors that affect women, such as ... age'; No. 33: 'Access Justice' (2015), para. 8: '[g]rounds for intersecting or compounded discrimination may include ethnicity/race, indigenous or minority status, colour, socioeconomic status and/or caste, language, religion or belief, political opinion, national origin, marital and/or maternal status, age': one can observe that age is among the last prohibited grounds mentioned, and age does not signify childhood; No. 32: 'Refugee Women' (2014), para. 6: '[d]iscrimination against women based on sex and/or gender is often inextricably linked with and compounded by other factors that affect women, such as ... age'; No. 34: 'Rural Women' (2016), para. 94, refers to disaggregated data by sex and age; No. 35: 'Gender-based Violence' (2017), para. 34(b): 'intersecting forms of discrimination against women and other relevant sociodemographic characteristics, including the age of the victim/survivor'; No. 38: 'Trafficking' (2020), para. 28, solely refers to racial discrimination.

and older women', which implies that the conceptual notion 'woman' comprises adolescent girls, yet possibly excludes young girls.[34] It is worthy of note that the Committee refers to 'girls (including the girl child and adolescent girls, where appropriate)'[35] and 'girl children and adolescent girls',[36] thereby recognizing the divisions of girlhood. Yet the use of the expressions 'girl child' and 'adolescent girl' separately in the same sentence implies that adolescents are no longer girl children, which is why this book prefers the divisions 'young girl' and 'adolescent girl', both under the 'girl' - 'girl child' category.[37]

It is also notable that the Committee only applied the life cycle in 1999, in its 24th general recommendation, thus twenty years after the adoption of the CEDAW. As a result, States parties were not incited to adopt a life-cycle approach during the first two decades of the CEDAW's existence. Moreover, only seven out of thirty-nine general recommendations refer to the life-cycle approach, thus less than one-fifth, and in less than half of the recommendations adopted since 1999. It is also worthy of note that the CEDAW Committee refers to 'women and girls' and 'girls and women',[38] or 'women and the girl child',[39] or 'girl or woman', 'women or girls' or 'a woman or a

[34] No. 37: 'Disaster Risk' (2018), para. 2: 'intersecting forms of discrimination against, among others ... adolescents and older women, who are often disproportionately affected compared with men or other women'.

[35] CEDAW General Recommendation No. 33: 'Access Justice' (2015), para. 24.

[36] CEDAW General Recommendation No. 24: 'Women and Health' (1999), para. 12(b): '[g]irl children and adolescent girls are often vulnerable to sexual abuse by older men and family members, placing them at risk of physical and psychological harm and unwanted and early pregnancy'.

[37] See Chapter 2.

[38] See CEDAW General Recommendations referring to 'women and girls' and 'girls and women': 1) No. 24: 'Women and Health' (1999), paras. 18, 28; 2) No. 30: 'Women in Conflict' (2013), paras. 4, 22–24, 34, 35, 36, 38–41, 48, 50, 52, 53, 57, 58, 60–62, 65–69, 78, 81; 3) Joint CEDAW-CRC GenRec/Com: 'Harmful Practices' (2014), paras. 6, 9, 11, 17–19, 24, 25, 27, 29, 42, 53, 54, 56, 60–63, 65, 66, 68, 69, 72, 73, 77, 82, 83, 85; for example, para. 6: 'the Committees draw States parties' attention to the fact that sex- and gender-based discrimination intersects with other factors that affect women and girls; 4) No. 32: 'Refugee Women' (2014), paras. 10, 27, 34, 45, 51, 53, 63; 5) No. 33: 'Access Justice' (2015), paras. 1, 18, 25, 35; 6) No. 34: 'Rural Women' (2016), paras. 2, 8, 10, 12, 22, 23, 25, 26, 27, 34, 39, 42, 43, 75, 76, 81–85; 7) No. 35: 'Gender-based Violence' (2017), paras. 18, 26, 30, 35; 8) No. 36: 'Education' (2017), paras. 2, 4, 5, 7, 12, 13, 18–25, 27–29, 31–33, 35, 38–40, 42–44, 46–48, 50, 51, 55–57, 60–63, 65, 69, 72, 81–83; for example, para. 18: 'multiple and intersecting forms of discrimination that prevent girls and women from enjoying rights to, within and through education are addressed and ultimately eliminated'; 9) No. 37: 'Disaster Risk' (2018), paras. 2–7, 15, 19, 26, 29–32, 36, 38, 46, 55, 57, 59, 60, 62, 66, 68, 69, 75, 78; 10) No. 38: 'Trafficking' (2020), paras. 1, 2, 4–6, 10, 12–22, 24, 25, 30, 31, 33, 34, 40, 42, 45, 47–50, 52, 54–56, 65, 67, 71, 75, 76, 79–82, 84, 86–89, 93, 95, 97–102, 104, 106, 107–109, 112, 114, 117–119; 11) No. 39: 'Indigenous Women and Girls' (2022), all paras. except 14, 24, 32.

[39] CEDAW General Recommendation No. 25: 'Temporary Measures' (2004), paras. 19, 26.

girl',[40] within the same sentence in several general recommendations, which as previously discussed, could imply that they constitute distinct categories. The Committee also refers to 'women and adolescent girls' in the same sentence,[41] which implies that adolescent girls located at the frontier of adulthood are not included in womanhood. More specifically, the Committee mentions 'girls and young women'[42] and 'girls, young women and women',[43] which clearly implies a distinction between girls and young women as, respectively, belonging to 'girlhood' and 'womanhood'. The Committee further strengthens this distinction by referring to 'young girls, adolescent girls and adult women'.[44] Additionally, the CEDAW Committee specifies in certain general recommendations that '[f]or the purposes of the present general recommendation … "women" *includes* girls and adolescents',[45] which could indicate *a contrario* that under other circumstances, the woman class *excludes* girls. Furthermore, the Committee appears to refer to girls as 'women in becoming' rather than as actual women: '[a]n Indigenous women and girls perspective … involves considering the status of *Indigenous girls as developing women*, which requires interventions to be appropriate to their age, development and condition'.[46] The next section shall therefore explore the description of woman in the English language to assess whether it clarifies the boundaries separating girlhood and womanhood.

40 Joint CEDAW-CRC GenRec/Com: 'Harmful Practices' (2014), paras. 55, 82, 84; No. 36: 'Education' (2017), para. 24.

41 CEDAW General Recommendation No. 24: 'Women and Health' (1999), para. 18: '[t]he issues of HIV/AIDS and other sexually transmitted diseases are central to the rights of women and adolescent girls to sexual health'; Joint CEDAW-CRC GenRec/Com: 'Harmful Practices' (2014), para. 68.

42 CEDAW General Recommendation No. 36: 'Education' (2017), para. 68; No. 37: 'Disaster Risk' (2018), para. 32.

43 CEDAW General Recommendation No. 37: 'Disaster Risk' (2018), para. 36.

44 CEDAW General Recommendation No. 38: 'Trafficking' (2020), para. 7: '[t]he Committee acknowledges that the causes, consequences and experiences of trafficking differ for young girls, for adolescent girls and for adult women'.

45 CEDAW General Recommendation No. 24: 'Women and Health' (1999), para. 8. See also No. 33: 'Access Justice' (2015), para. 1: '[f]or the purposes of the present general recommendation, all references to "women" should be understood to include women and girls, unless otherwise specifically noted'; No. 35: 'Gender-based Violence' (2017), para. 14: '[g]ender based violence affects women throughout their life cycle and, accordingly, references to women in the present document include girls'.

46 CEDAW General Recommendation No. 39: 'Indigenous Women and Girls' (2022), para. 5 (emphasis added). It further notes that '[t]he [CEDAW] Committee recognizes … the status of Indigenous girls as developing women, which calls for a State response tailored to their best interests and needs and the adaptation of government procedures and services to the age, development, evolving capacities, and condition of Indigenous girls': para. 14.

## 3 English Definition

The definitions of 'woman', 'girl', 'boy' and 'man' shed light on the meanings associated with these comparative identity groups in the English language. The OED defines the term woman as '[w]omen considered collectively; the female sex',[47] and '[a]n adult female human being. The counterpart of man',[48] and the Webster as 'a female human being – distinguished from man'. These definitions indicate that the term 'woman' shares the parameters of sex and femalehood with the girl child, and that it is described in contrast to males, which seems to indicate that the woman class comprises girls. The term boy shares the parameter of age and childhood with girls as 'a male child or youth', while it is also identified with 'malehood'.[49] However, the expression woman is also described as a comparative negative to both men and girls: '[a]n adult female person, as opposed to a man or girl or both',[50] and 'an adult female human being – distinguished from girl',[51] which implies that the expression 'woman' excludes girls. It is also defined as 'a female person who has reached adulthood, esp. in legal contexts; a female person who is considered mature', thereby distinguishing this identity group from the girl child on the grounds of adulthood and 'maturity'. Woman is moreover defined as follows: '[f]requently contrasted with girl'.[52] The latter citation underscores that the concepts of womanhood and girlhood can be viewed as mutually exclusive in the OED. One can therefore question whether the girl child, especially when she is near adulthood, is incorporated in the definition of woman. In addition, since the expression 'womanhood' is defined as '[t]he state of being a woman rather than a girl' in the OED,[53] and as it is offered as a synonym to 'adulthood' in the Thesaurus, the notion of womanhood does not appear to unequivocally and systematically embrace the girl child.

While the OED contains this historical and traditional definition of woman in terms of sex and femalehood, including biological traits, it is noteworthy that in recent years, the notions of self-identification, gender and trans-identity have expanded in the Global North whereby individuals may be viewed as

47 The SOEDHP defines her as 'the female human person, esp. viewed as a type; the female sex'.

48 OED.

49 OED.

50 SOEDHP.

51 Webster.

52 OED.

53 OED. The term womanhood is also defined in terms of adulthood in the SOEDHP: '[t]he state of being a grown woman', linked to adulthood. The definition of womanhood in the Webster does not offer any clarification: 'the State of being a woman: the distinguishing character or qualities of a woman or of womanhood'.

having joined other sex, race and ableism identity categories.[54] Accordingly, individuals who were born male may self-identify as female, and vice versa, and while some undergo gender reassignment surgeries, including genital surgical reconstruction, to acquire similar physical features of the opposite sex, others may fully keep their biological traits – for instance, of a male – while identifying as a female in society. This phenomenon was enshrined in the 2022 modification to the Cambridge English Dictionary (CED), which offers, after the classical definition of woman as 'an adult female human being', the new addition of 'an adult who lives and identifies as female though they may have been said to have a different sex at birth'.[55] This new definition provided in the CED demonstrates that the definition of woman has been extended to cover persons born male who identify as women, which implies that 'women' could also be extended to cover girl children. However, this argument raises two issues. First, one must bear in mind that this new definition and some other tenets of gender identity scholarship have not reached consensus globally, especially in the Global South, on cultural, traditional and religious grounds, as well as within feminists, LGBT groups and transactivists, including detransitioners.[56] Secondly, this new definition refers to 'an adult who identifies as

[54] See for example Alessandra Lemma, *Transgender Identities: A Contemporary Introduction* (Routledge 2021); Emily Rose, *Translating Trans Identity: (Re)Writing Undecidable Texts and Bodies* (Routledge 2021); Spencer Garrison, 'On the Limits of "Trans Enough": Authenticating Trans Identity Narratives' (2018) 32 *Gender & Society* 613; Laura Erickson-Schroth (ed.), *Trans Bodies, Trans Selves: A Resource by and for Transgender Communities* (2nd ed., Oxford University Press 2022); Nathan Rothenbaum, 'The Transracial Subject and the Emotive Regime: Rachel Dolezal, Racial Phronêsis, and Inverted Miscegenation' (2023) 20 *Communication and Critical/Cultural Studies* 252; Jasbir Puar, 'Bodies with New Organs: Becoming Trans, Becoming Disabled' (2015) 33 *Social Text* 45; Sarah Boesveld, *The National Post*, 'Becoming Disabled by Choice, Not Chance: "Transabled" People Feel Like Impostors in Their Fully Working Bodies' (3 June 2015). https://nationalpost.com/news/canada/becoming-disabled-by-choice-not-chance-transabled-people-feel-like-impostors-in-their-fully-working-bodies (accessed 29 July 2023).

[55] CED (addition made in December 2022).

[56] This scholarly and policy approach is mostly present in the Global North; see Jami Taylor et al., *The Remarkable Rise of Transgender Rights* (University of Michigan Press 2018); Kimberley Manning, 'Attached Advocacy and the Rights of the Trans Child' (2017) 50 *Canadian Journal of Political Science* 579; Damian Gonzalez-Salzberg, *Sexuality and Transsexuality under the European Convention on Human Rights: A Queer Reading of Human Rights Law* (Hart Publishing 2019), and much less so in the Global South, see 'Right to Change Legal Gender by Country' (Equaldex). www.equaldex.com/issue/changing-gender (accessed 29 July 2023). Also, several feminists, LGBT, transactivists and detransitioners – that is, persons who transitioned to another sex and thereafter detransitioned and returned to their original sex – have questioned some of its manifestations, such as gender reassignment surgeries performed on children below the age of eighteen years: see for example Alison Clayton et al., 'Commentary: The Signal and the Noise – Questioning the Benefits of Puberty Blockers for Youth with Gender Dysphoria – A Commentary on Rew et al. (2021)' (2022) 27 *Child and Adolescent Mental Health* 259; Clare Dyer, 'Children are "Highly Unlikely" to be

female', and thus a girl child who identifies as an adult woman does not appear covered by this wording. Finally, the term 'man' is defined as 'an adult male human being … contrasted with a woman',[57] thus by opposition to woman, and 'a male person who has reached adulthood (spec. the age of majority); a male person who shows maturity',[58] thus by opposition to childhood and youth. Hence, one can observe that as is the case with the girl child, the expressions 'boy', 'woman' and 'man' are described in relation to the parameters of sex and age, and by opposition to one another, and the term woman therefore does not appear to systematically cover girls.[59]

## II MEANING

The analysis of the *meaning-intention* behind the CEDAW is hindered by a significant obstacle: its *travaux préparatoires* appear to have been lost in transit between New York and Vienna.[60] The UN apparently had not made copies of the documentation before it was moved.[61] As a result, the UN libraries in Vienna, New York and Geneva contain incomplete collections, and cannot offer a comprehensive examination of the negotiations leading to the adoption of the CEDAW. Moreover, when exploring the *meaning-intention* behind the terminology selected in the CEDAW, it is important to understand the context of its adoption. The CEDAW came into existence in 1979, thus a decade before the adoption of the CRC, which is the first legally binding international instrument recognizing children as rights holders, and at a time when the expression 'girl' had only been mentioned in a single legally binding instrument – the Marriage Convention (1962). This could signify that the CEDAW drafters assumed that the term 'woman' comprised all female persons, and therefore girl children, or conversely, that girls' rights, to the exception of specific issues such as child marriage, were not their central focus. The working

Able to Consent to Taking Puberty Blockers, Rules High Court' (2020) *BMJ* 371; Cal Horton, 'Experiences of Puberty and Puberty Blockers: Insights From Trans Children, Trans Adolescents, and Their Parents' (2024) 39 *Journal of Adolescent Research* 77; Michael Irwig, 'Detransition among Transgender and Gender-Diverse People – An Increasing and Increasingly Complex Phenomenon' (2022) 107 *Journal of Clinical Endocrinology & Metabolism* 4261; Ruth Pearce et al., 'TERF Wars: An Introduction' (2020) 68 *Sociological Review* 677; Annie Pullen Sansfaçon et al., 'A Nuanced Look into Youth Journeys of Gender Transition and Detransition' (2023) 32 *Infant and Child Development* 2402.

57 OED.

58 OED.

59 OED. It should also be noted that the definition of girl, in the *Cambridge English Dictionary*, does not, as yet, include children who were born male and self-identify as girls, although these definitions could be modified in accordance with that of woman in the near future.

60 *Travaux Préparatoires* CEDAW (1987), vii, 3.

61 Ibid., vii, 3.

group of the CEDAW based its drafting on the DEDAW, and therefore employed the same terminology as the latter, without questioning whether or not 'women' included 'girls'.[62] The *travaux préparatoires* indicate that the drafters debated whether the convention should focus on sex-based discrimination or rather on discrimination experienced by women, as they were:

> divided between those who felt that the convention should deal only with discrimination against women (stressing women's position in society, their dual role at home and at work and their maternal functions) and those who felt it should deal with discrimination on the grounds of sex as a whole.[63]

It appears that the drafters adopted the expression 'discrimination against women' to underscore that women, rather than men, have historically experienced sexism, rather than to exclude girls *per se*. Indeed, Freeman et al. explain:

> A number of States would have preferred that the Convention address discrimination on the ground of sex generally, thereby also covering discrimination against men on the basis of sex, rather than focusing only on discrimination against women. However, the overwhelming view was that such a symmetrical approach would fail to recognize the pervasive discrimination against women on the basis of their sex, and that an asymmetric guarantee was needed in the form of a sex-specific instrument.[64]

Coomaraswamy notes in this regard that overall '[w]omen are adults and their main quest is for empowerment and equality with men',[65] which could explain the limited attention paid by the drafters to girl children. Goonesekere moreover argues that the division, among feminists, between universality and cultural relativism has 'discouraged consistency in making the link between women's human rights and the rights of girl children as a continuum of discrimination in a life-cycle approach', which could account, in part, for the focus on adult women rather than girls.[66]

## 1 *Girls in Article 10(f)*

The inclusion of the term 'girls' in article 10(f) as concerns school drop-out rates appears however to have generated discussions.[67] The ILO suggested to

[62] Ibid., 6–12, 29, 42–49.
[63] Ibid., 44.
[64] *Commentary CEDAW* (2012), 52.
[65] 'Cutting Edge' (2015), 4.
[66] 'HRs Girls' (2014), 489.
[67] *Travaux préparatoires CEDAW* (1987), 118–20.

expressly refer to girls in this context, and Belgium proposed a sub-paragraph specifically mentioning girls,[68] which could imply that the drafters did not consider that the girl child belonged to the woman category for the purposes of the CEDAW, although it could simply signify that they wished to underscore the importance of protecting girls in the context of education. Argentina thereafter recommended to replace 'girls' with 'women', which could either indicate that it wished to ensure conformity within the Convention, or its awareness that mentioning the girl child solely in one provision could *a contrario* imply that she is not covered elsewhere in the CEDAW.[69] Iran preferred the expression 'female' followed by 'young girls' and 'women',[70] which demonstrates a concern for a more inclusive term. However, the use of the term 'female' to refer to both 'women' and 'young girls' in this provision could have further implied that the last two categories are mutually exclusive, and thus adolescent girls might be covered under the umbrella of womanhood, but not young girls. These discussions seem to indicate that the drafters were aware of the distinction between women and girls, and that according to them, the former did not automatically include the latter.

### 2 *Child Marriage: Article 16(2)*

The negotiations leading to the adoption of the provision prohibiting child marriage demonstrate that the drafters considered that 'woman' does not systematically include 'girls'. While certain nations debated between the expressions 'children', 'girl' and 'young girls', none argued that the CEDAW could employ the term 'woman' or 'young woman', in this provision.[71] Moreover, as regards the boundary separating girlhood and womanhood, the provision concerning child marriage initially prohibited the betrothal of girls solely 'before puberty' and thereby would have provided puberty as the perimeter for the end of girlhood.[72] The term 'puberty' was deleted at the request of the United States, yet it was not replaced by another parameter. In this regard, Rehof notes that '[t]he problem of "when is a child not a child?" resulted from deleting the qualification "before puberty"' found in a previous draft.[73] As discussed in Chapter 2, certain girls reach puberty as young as nine

68 Ibid.

69 Ibid., 119.

70 Ibid., 120: '[r]eduction of the female drop-out rate, and the provision of programmes for young girls and women who left school too early'.

71 Ibid., 184.

72 Ibid.

73 Ibid.

years old, at an age when they cannot physically have sexual relations and bear a child, and the US amendment was therefore beneficial. It is however unfortunate that the drafters of the CEDAW did not seize this opportunity to specify when girlhood ends and whether it constitutes a division within womanhood.

## III SIGNIFICANCE

Since the parameter for the end of childhood is open-ended under the upper age limit of eighteen years in the CRC, and as the terms 'girl' and 'woman' are not defined in international instruments, including within the CEDAW, one cannot categorically assert that girls are comprised within the concept of 'women' under international law. More specifically, as the CEDAW does not provide a parameter for the beginning of womanhood, it is not clear whether girls of all ages – young girls and adolescent girls – are covered by this treaty. Feminist legal scholars have argued that the CEDAW does cover girls, noting that '[a]lthough [the CEDAW] does not spell out that "women" includes girls under the age of eighteen …, this is evidently the case'.[74] However, as previously explained, the present book examines signs as potentially decoded by the immediate, dynamical and final interpretants, and the ambiguous terminology employed in the CEDAW should therefore not be disregarded. The *travaux préparatoires* of the CEDAW demonstrate that the drafters considered girls distinct from adult women under certain circumstances, notably as concerns child marriage and the right to education. The CEDAW Committee has attempted to clarify that the expression 'women' does cover girls by adopting the life-cycle approach in some general recommendations since 1999, yet the latter are not legally binding on States parties. Moreover, the Committee has referred to girls and women as mutually exclusive identity groups in many recommendations since adopting the life-cycle approach, or to girls as 'developing women', thereby further confusing its application. The ambiguous delimitation of the upper boundary of girlhood in the CRC and the uncertain coverage of girls as 'women' in the CEDAW are particularly significant as these could imply that female human beings located at the intersection of girlhood and womanhood fall short of the protection of both the CRC and many provisions of the CEDAW, the two central instruments promoting children's rights and women's rights.

[74] *Commentary CEDAW* (2022), 23.

As noted by Freeman et al., '[m]any of the concerns addressed in the Convention ... have immediate and important consequences for girls'.[75] The CEDAW provides that political and economic rights shall be granted equally to women and men, and thus constitutes a central instrument to combat sexism against girl children in these two fields. Article 7 of the CEDAW requires States parties to eliminate discrimination against women in the political and public life of the country, and notably to ensure that the rights to vote and be eligible for elections, formulate government policies and perform public functions shall be granted to women on equal terms with men.[76] Moreover, the CEDAW enshrines women's right to represent their government at the international level and to participate in the work of international organizations,[77] which would give adolescent girls the opportunity to contribute to policy-making globally. The CEDAW also recognizes women's right to apply for and obtain bank loans, mortgages and other forms of financial credit,[78] which is especially important for adolescent girls who act as the head of the household and raise their younger siblings, and those who work to support their family. The CEDAW moreover enshrines several provisions that are essential to protect adolescent girls who are employed as concerns equal remuneration, the right to promotion, job security, benefits, vocational training and apprenticeships as well as social security.[79] Additionally, the CEDAW comprises provisions that protect women's right to health and safety in employment, including as concerns reproductive function, thereby prohibiting any work that is hazardous for the pregnant girl,

[75] Ibid., 14.

[76] CEDAW, art. 7: 'States Parties shall take all appropriate measures to eliminate discrimination against women in the political and public life of the country and, in particular, shall ensure to women, on equal terms with men, the right: a) To vote in all elections and public referenda and to be eligible for election to all publicly elected bodies; b) To participate in the formulation of government policy and the implementation thereof and to hold public office and perform all public functions at all levels of government'.

[77] CEDAW, art. 8.

[78] CEDAW, art. 13: 'States Parties shall take all appropriate measures to eliminate discrimination against women in other areas of economic and social life in order to ensure, on a basis of equality of men and women, the same rights, in particular: a) The right to family benefits; b) The right to bank loans, mortgages and other forms of financial credit'.

[79] CEDAW, art. 11(1) b): '[t]he right to the same employment opportunities, including the application of the same criteria for selection in matters of employment; c) ... the right to promotion, job security and all benefits and conditions of service and the right to receive vocational training and retraining, including apprenticeships, advanced vocational training and recurrent training; d) The right to equal remuneration, including benefits, and to equal treatment in respect of work of equal value, as well as equality of treatment in the evaluation of the quality of work; e) The right to social security, particularly in cases of ... unemployment, sickness, invalidity ... the right to paid leave'.

or which could impair her reproductive capacity.[80] Furthermore, the CEDAW requires states to pay for maternity leave and develop childcare facilities,[81] which would enable adolescent mothers to support themselves after giving birth and possibly to pursue their studies thereafter, especially if provided access to affordable childcare or daycare facilities. While as discussed in Chapter 7, the Minimum Age Convention offers a threshold for the right of the child to work at thirteen, fourteen or fifteen,[82] the ICCPR, ICESCR and CEDAW fail to specify an age at which a person is entitled to political and economic rights and granted legal capacity, and while the CRC recognizes the child's right to participation, it does not enshrine those other rights. Accordingly, states are not expressly required to grant these rights to girls, notably adolescent girls, under domestic law. In addition, since the CEDAW is the main instrument protecting women's rights, the ambiguity in this treaty as to whether or not the girl child is comprised in the woman category may imply that girls are not protected under provisions referring to women's rights within other instruments pertinent to female human beings, such as the Declaration on the Elimination of Violence against Women. This uncertainty has concrete ramifications for the girl child. For example, although adolescent girls are entitled to employment in the public sphere under instruments such as the Minimum Age Convention, they might not be eligible to perform public functions or hold positions in unions. In other words, whereas they may be considered sufficiently competent to work in a factory, farm or household, they are not granted the right to participate in decision-making with their adult counterparts. Furthermore, although an increasing number of households are headed by girls, the latter still do not have the legal capacity to administer property at the domestic level, nor the right to obtain bank loans, mortgages and other forms of financial credit, in several states globally.[83] Thus, while girls may be required to work outside the home to support their family, the fruit of their labour might be dilapidated by the legal guardians who control their finances, as is often the case for girl child performers.[84] This

[80] CEDAW, art. 11(1)f): '[t]he right to protection of health and to safety in working conditions, including the safeguarding of the function of reproduction'; CEDAW, art. 11(2)d): '[t]o provide special protection to women during pregnancy in types of work proved to be harmful to them'.

[81] CEDAW, art. 11(2).

[82] See Chapter 7.

[83] 'Discrimination Girl Child' (2006), para. 19; 'Women, Business, Law' (2023); 'Equality, Law, Women, Girls' (2019).

[84] 'Striking a Pose' (2014); 'Underage Fashion Models' (2017); 'Changing Childhood' (2005), 17; Kimberlianne Podlas, 'Does Exploiting a Child Amount to Employing a Child: The FLSA's Child Labor Provisions and Children on Reality Television' (2010) 17 *UCLA*

ambiguity also impacts monitoring and data analysis. Goonesekere argues that the CEDAW Committee can at times disregard the specificity of girl children, including in its Concluding Observations, which negatively impacts the monitoring of this Convention at the domestic level:

> [T]he situation of girl children has yet to be recognised as a necessary dimension and first stage in eliminating discrimination against adult women. The near universal ratification of the CRC is sometimes referred to by members of the CEDAW Committee in their internal discussions as a reason for not addressing the rights of girl children in the constructive dialogue with States Parties or in Concluding Observations.[85]

As discussed in Chapter 7, adolescent girls situated at the frontiers of girlhood and womanhood are often not covered in data regarding girl children within research studies published by international specialized agencies, and the unique condition of girls is disregarded by international studies that examine children as a homogenous group and fail to disaggregate data by sex. Moreover, it is not always clear whether the expression 'woman' covers the girl child in data and research. The UN Human Rights Council recently extended the mandate of the Special Rapporteur on violence against women to that of violence against women *and girls*, noting that girls are often at greater risk of being exposed to and experiencing various forms of discrimination and violence and requests the Rapporteur 'to examine the specific ways that girls are impacted by violence'.[86] This implies that the term 'woman' was not perceived as systematically covering girls, or that the unique situation of girls was overlooked and subsumed within a 'woman class' perceived as homogenous. Yet, since the term woman is not defined in the CEDAW, the decision to rename the Special Rapporteur on violence against women to that of *violence against women and girls* could further infer that the two identity groups constitute distinct categories. Furthermore, as the definition of childhood is open-ended in the CRC, it is not clear which female human beings would be considered girls or women in the Special Rapporteurs' reports. This begs the question as to how the CEDAW could be modified to tackle the abovementioned problems.

*Entertainment Law Review* 39; John Shannon and Richard Hunter, 'Principles of Contract Law Applied to Entertainment and Sports Contracts: A Model for Balancing the Rights of the Industry with Protecting the Interests of Minors' (2015) 48 *Loyola Los Angeles Law Review* 1171.

85 'HRs Girls' (2014), 488.

86 UNGA Resolution 'Mandate of Special Rapporteur on Violence against Women and Girls, Its Causes and Consequences' (18 July 2022) UN Doc A/HRC/RES/50/7, preamble, para. 2.

## IV SEMIOETHICS: RECOMMENDED DEFINITION

This book proposes to clarify that girls are comprised in the woman category and thus covered in the CEDAW. We suggest to insert a second paragraph into article 1 of the CEDAW, which currently enshrines the definition of discrimination against women. The second paragraph would stipulate that the term 'woman' includes female human beings throughout the lifespan, and thus the girl child:

> Art 1(2) The term 'woman' comprises female human beings throughout the lifespan, including young girls, adolescent girls, young women and older women.

Girl children are usually not accorded all adult women's rights as concerns political and economic rights, and one could thus contend that girls should not be included in the woman category in the CEDAW. However, since the CEDAW tackles discrimination based on sex, thus discrimination between males and females, it is argued that the inclusion of girls in the definition of woman in the CEDAW would not be problematic, as young girls would simply be granted the same rights as boys their age, not those of adult men and women, while adolescent girls would obtain legal, political and economic rights granted at majority, as per our recommended definition of 'child' in Chapter 7. Indeed, when one combines our current proposal with that of Chapter 7, the girl child would be covered by the CRC until eighteen years and granted rights afforded to adult women under the CEDAW as soon as she reaches majority, possibly at fifteen years (tentative age to be negotiated),[87] notably political rights, such as the right to vote, and economic rights, such as the right to manage her finances. In other words, the adolescent girl would be protected under the CRC while empowered under the CEDAW.

The CEDAW comprises a revision clause under article 26 which provides that a State party can request a revision by notification in writing addressed to the UN Secretary-General, and empowers the UN General Assembly to establish the procedure for this amendment.[88] It is important to acknowledge

[87] See Chapter 7.

[88] CEDAW, art. 26: '(1) A request for the revision of the present Convention may be made at any time by any State Party by means of a notification in writing addressed to the Secretary General of the United Nations. (2) The General Assembly of the United Nations shall decide upon the steps, if any, to be taken in respect of such a request'. See Susann Kroworsch, 'Article 26' in Patricia Schulz et al. (eds.), *The UN Convention on the Elimination of All Forms of Discrimination against Women and Its Optional Protocol: A Commentary* (2nd ed., Oxford University Press 2022), 776–79.

that this provision is not as straightforward as its equivalent, article 50 in the CRC. The procedure under article 26 of the CEDAW notably differs in that it is the UN General Assembly that decides upon the steps, rather than the States parties negotiating the terms of the amendment as provided under article 40 (2) of the Vienna Convention and article 50 of the CRC.[89] Indeed, Kroworsch explains that under article 26 of the CEDAW, 'it is up to the discretion of the UNGA to decide on the measures to be taken to enact the amendment, including delegating the amendment process to another body'.[90] The Vienna Convention provides that where a treaty is silent on particular issues, the subsidiary rules of its article 40 may be applied, and accordingly, rules such as those under article 40(2) which stipulate that the proposal must be notified to all contracting states, could be employed.[91] Also, while the Vienna Convention and the CRC specify that the amendment only binds states that agree to become a party to the treaty as amended, the CEDAW does not contain such a provision.[92] In this regard, Kroworsch notes that revisions under the CEDAW may appear 'cumbersome', as illustrated by the amendment to modify the duration of CEDAW Committee meetings, which was noted with approval by the UN General Assembly nearly thirty years ago and yet has not formally entered into force, and thereby remains dependent on the repeated authorization from the General Assembly.[93] Hence, while this book proposes to revise the CEDAW, it notes that the procedure could be more complex than that under the CRC.

89 Vienna Convention (1969), art. 40(2): '[a]ny proposal to amend a multilateral treaty as between all the parties must be notified to all the contracting States, each one of which shall have the right to take part in: (a) the decision as to the action to be taken in regard to such proposal; (b) the negotiation and conclusion of any agreement for the amendment of the treaty'.

90 Kroworsch, 'Article 26', *Commentary CEDAW* (2022), 776–79.

91 The Vienna Convention (1969) stipulates under art. 40(1) that '[u]nless the treaty otherwise provides, the amendment of multilateral treaties shall be governed by the following paragraphs', and thus some of the Vienna Convention subsidiary rules can apply in the context of the CEDAW; Kroworsch, 'Article 26', *Commentary CEDAW* (2022), 776–79.

92 Vienna Convention (1969), art. 40(4): '[t]he amending agreement does not bind any State already a party to the treaty which does not become a party to the amending agreement'.

93 Amendment to art. 20, paragraph 1 of the Convention on the Elimination of All Forms of Discrimination against Women (New York, 22 December 1995); 'Report of the Eighth Meeting of the States Parties to the Convention on the Elimination of All Forms of Discrimination against Women (2 June 1995) UN Doc CEDAW/SP/1995/2; UNGA Resolution 50/202 (23 February 1996) UN Doc A/RES/50/202; it has not yet been accepted by a two-thirds majority of States parties; see Kroworsch, 'Article 26' in Patricia Schulz et al. (eds.), *Commentary CEDAW* (2022), 776–79.

# Conclusion

The legal significs and semioethics methodology adopted in this book constitutes a valuable tool to interpret the content of international human rights treaties. This method has allowed for a demonstration that the terminology employed to identify the girl child in international law (sense) is carefully pondered by the drafters of treaties (meaning-intention), and considerably impacts the conceptions of girlhood globally as well as girls' rights and their implementation at the domestic level (significance). Our analysis has underscored that the first obstacle to the protection of the girl child lies in the silence concerning the boundaries and divisions of girlhood and womanhood internationally. The terminology employed in international human rights treaties is insufficient to clearly identify the girl child and protect her rights. The CRC, CEDAW, ICCPR and ICESCR, even if read as complementary treaties protecting the rights of children, women and human beings, fail to address the unique condition of the girl child. This book argues that the first step in improving the protection of girl child rights under international law rests in amending the definitions of 'child' in the CRC and 'woman' in the CEDAW. The new definition of 'child' in the CRC would simultaneously guarantee the visibility of the girl child and confirm that girls as well as boys are covered by the CRC and its optional protocols until the age of eighteen years. It would also ensure that adolescent girls, once reaching majority, are granted key political and economic rights enshrined in instruments such as the Twin Covenants and the CEDAW, while no longer submitted to childist CRC provisions. This proposal would provide consistency within States parties as all female human beings under the age of eighteen would be considered girls within their territories. This would in turn facilitate the monitoring of the implementation of the CRC. The proposed definition of 'child' would also require international agencies to cover girls separately from boys, and adolescent girls below eighteen years separately from adult women, in their research and data, which would promote the visibility of girl children at the international and domestic levels. The research and data would thence offer significant information on specific problems faced by girls, especially adolescent girls located at the frontier of womanhood, and allow for the adoption of targeted measures. The new definition of 'woman' in the CEDAW would clarify that girls of all ages are holders of the rights it enshrines, to the exception of certain 'adult' rights, such as political and economic rights, which would be attributed to adolescent girls once they reach majority, which would be set at fifteen years (tentative age to be negotiated),[1] according to the definition of child in the CRC proposed in this book. In future studies, semiotics, significs and semioethics of law could be employed to examine the wording of provisions pertaining to the rights of the girl child, as identified by Leblanc in the survival, protection and empowerment categories of rights,[2] to assess whether they sufficiently address issues uniquely or predominantly faced by girls, such as female infanticide, honour-related killings, sex trafficking, FGM, child marriage, limited access to reproductive care, restrictive social and dress codes, sexualized social and dress codes, health and education, and possibly recommend modifications to the content of international treaties accordingly.[3] Legal semiotics and semioethics could also be used to study the content of international human rights as concerns boys, adult men and adult women, and more broadly individuals located at the intersection of several vectors of identity, for the purpose of improving their status internationally.

[1] See Chapter 7.

[2] Lawrence Leblanc, *The Convention on the Rights of the Child: United Nations Lawmaking on Human Rights* (University of Nebraska Press 1995).

[3] See for example *Feminicides Girl Children* (2018); 'Gendercide CRC' (2018); 'Reservations Education CRC' (2022); 'Sex Trafficking Girls' (2023).

# Bibliography

## I INTERNATIONAL TREATIES


Charter of the United Nations (San Francisco, adopted 26 June 1945, entered into force 24 October 1945) 33 UNTS 993.

Convention against Torture and Other Cruel, Inhuman or Degrading Treatment or Punishment (New York, adopted 10 December 1984, entered into force 26 June 1987) 1465 UNTS 85.

Convention Concerning the Prohibition and Immediate Action for the Elimination of the Worst Forms of Child Labour (Geneva, adopted 17 June 1999, entered into force 19 November 2000) 2133 UNTS 161.

Convention No. 138 Concerning Minimum Age for Admission to Employment (Geneva, adopted 26 June 1973, entered into force 19 June 1976) ST/HR/1/Rev. 6 (Vol. I/Part 1).

Convention on Consent to Marriage, Minimum Age for Marriage and Registration of Marriage (New York, adopted 10 December 1962, entered into force 9 December 1964) 521 UNTS 231.

Convention on the Elimination of All Forms of Discrimination against Women (New York, adopted 18 December 1979, entered into force 3 September 1981) 1249 UNTS 13.

Convention on the Political Rights of Women (New York, adopted 31 March 1953, entered into force 7 July 1954) 193 UNTS 135.

Convention on the Rights of Persons with Disabilities (New York, adopted 13 December 2006, entered into force 3 May 2008) 2515 UNTS 3.

Convention on the Rights of the Child (New York, adopted 20 November 1989, entered into force 2 September 1990) 1577 UNTS 3.

International Convention on the Elimination of All Forms of Racial Discrimination (New York, adopted 7 March 1966, entered into force 4 January 1969) 660 UNTS 195.

International Covenant on Civil and Political Rights (New York, adopted 16 December 1966, entered into force 23 March 1976) 999 UNTS 171.

International Covenant on Economic, Social and Cultural Rights (New York, adopted 16 December 1966, entered into force 3 January 1976) 993 UNTS 3.

Optional Protocol to the CEDAW (New York, adopted 6 October 1999, entered into force 22 December 2000) 2131 UNTS 83.

Optional Protocol to the Convention on the Rights of the Child on the Involvement of Children in Armed Conflict (OPAC) (New York, adopted 25 May 2000, entered into force 12 February 2002) 2173 UNTS 222.

Optional Protocol to the Convention on the Rights of the Child on the Sale of Children, Child Prostitution and Child Pornography (OPSC) (New York, adopted 25 May 2000, entered into force 18 January 2002) 2171 UNTS 227.

Optional Protocol to the CRC on a Communications Procedure (New York, adopted 19 December 2011, entered into force 14 April 2014) 2983 UNTS 135.

Optional Protocol to the ICCPR (New York, adopted 16 December 1966, entered into force 23 March 1976) 999 UNTS 171.

Optional Protocol to the ICESCR (New York, adopted 10 December 2008, entered into force 5 May 2013) 2922 UNTS 29.

Rome Statute (Rome, adopted 17 July 1998, entered into force 1 July 2002) 2187 UNTS 3.

Vienna Convention on the Law of Treaties (Vienna, adopted 23 May 1969, entered into force 27 January 1980) 1155 UNTS 331.

## II UNITED NATIONS DOCUMENTS

Alston P, Special Rapporteur on Extreme Poverty and Human Rights, 'Report on Extreme Poverty and Extreme Inequality' (27 May 2015) UN Doc A/HRC/C/29/31.

Cappa C, 'New Global Estimates of Child Marriage' (UNICEF 2018).

Chapdelaine-Feliciati C et al., 'United Nations Handbook on the Optional Protocol to the Convention on the Rights of the Child on the Sale of Children, Child Prostitution and Child Pornography' (UNICEF Office of Research 2009).

Commission on the Status of Women, 'Agreed Conclusions on the Elimination and Prevention of All Forms of Violence against Women and Girls' (2013) UN Doc E/CN.6/2013/11.

Coomaraswamy R, Special Rapporteur on Violence against Women, 'Cultural Practices in the Family That Are Violent Towards Women' (31 January 2002) UN Doc E/CN.4/2002/83.

Ertürk Y, Special Rapporteur on Violence against Women, 'Intersections between Culture and Violence against Women' (17 January 2007) UN Doc A/HRC/4/34.

Giammarinaro G, Special Rapporteur on Trafficking in Persons, Especially Women and Children, 'Report' (6 April 2020) UN Doc A/HRC/44/45.

Goonesekere S, 'Elimination of All Forms of Discrimination and Violence against the Girl Child' (2006) EGM/DVGC/2006/BP.1.

Goonesekere S and de Silva-de Alwis R, 'Women's and Children's Rights in a Human Rights Based Approach to Development' (UNICEF 2005).

Grover A, Special Rapporteur on the Right to Health, 'The Right of Everyone to the Enjoyment of the Highest Attainable Standard of Physical and Mental Health' (3 August 2011) UN Doc A/66/254.

Hart R, 'Children's Participation, from Tokenism to Citizenship' (UNICEF 1992).

International Labour Organization (ILO), 'Give Girls a Chance: Tackling Child Labour, a Key to the Future' (2009).

'Ending Child Labour by 2025: Review of Policies and Programmes' (2017).

'Global Estimates of Child Labour: Results and Trends 2012–2016' (2017).

Practical Guide to Ending Child Labour and Protecting Young Workers in Domestic Work (2017)

ILO and UNICEF, 'Child Labour Global Estimates, Trends and the Road Forward' (2020).

International Law Commission, Yearbook, 'Preparation of Multilingual Treaties: Memorandum by the Secretariat' (1966) Vol. II, UN Doc A/CN.4/187.

Joint United Nations Programme on HIV/AIDS (UNAIDS), 'Women and HIV: A Spotlight on Adolescent Girls and Young Women' (2019).

Lansdown G, 'The Evolving Capacities of the Child' (UNICEF 2005).

Manjoo R, Special Rapporteur on Violence against Women, 'Gender-Related Killings' (25 May 2012) UN Doc A/HRC/20/16.

Muñoz Villalobos V, Special Rapporteur on the Right to Education, 'Girl's Right to Education' (8 February 2006) UN Doc E/CN.4/2006/45.

Office of the United Nations High Commissioner for Human Rights (OHCHR), 'Legislative History of the Convention on the Rights of the Child' (2007).

'Report: Good Practices and Major Challenges in Preventing and Eliminating Female Genital Mutilation' (27 March 2015) UN DOC A/HRC/29/20.

Patel V, 'Gender in Mental Health Research' (WHO 2004).

Pinheiro PS, 'UN Study World Report on Violence against Children' (2006).

Singhateh MF, Special Rapporteur on the Sale and Sexual Exploitation of Children, Including Child Prostitution, Child Pornography and Other Child Sexual Abuse Material, 'Impact of Coronavirus Disease on Different Manifestations of Sale and Sexual Exploitation of Children' (22 January 2021) UN Doc A/HRC/46/31.

United Nations Children's Fund (UNICEF), 'A Study on Violence against Girls: Report of the International Girl Child Conference' (2009).

'Programme Brief: Child Marriage' (2012).

'WASH in Schools Empowers Girls' Education' (2013).

'A Familiar Face – Violence in the Lives of Children and Adolescents' (2017).

'Progress for Every Child in the SDG Era' (2018).

'Children, Food, Nutrition' (2019).

'Gender Counts – East and Southeast Asia: A Quantitative Assessment of Gender Equality and Its Impact on Girls and Boys' (2019).

'Gender Programmatic Reviews in UNICEF Officers in South Asia – Afghanistan, Bangladesh, Bhutan, Maldives, Nepal, Sri Lanka' (2019).

'Guidance on Menstrual Health and Hygiene' (2019).

'A New Era for Girls: Taking Stock of 25 Years of Progress' (2020).

'Research on the Sexual Exploitation of Boys: Findings, Ethical Considerations and Methodological Challenges' (2020).

'Gender Equality: Global Annual Results Report 2021' (2022).

'Improving Data for Women and Children: Guidance on Strengthening Administrative Data Systems for Gender Statistics' (2022).

United Nations Development Programme (UNDP), Human Development Reports (HDR), 'Gender Equality' (Oxford University Press 1995).
'Millennium Development Goals: A Compact among Nations to End Human Poverty' (Oxford University Press 2003).
'The Real Wealth of Nations: Pathways to Human Development' (Palgrave Macmillan 2010).
'Sustainability and Equity: A Better Future for All' (Palgrave Macmillan 2011).
'Making the Law Work for Women and Girls in the Context of HIV' (2020).
United Nations Educational, Scientific and Cultural Organization (UNESCO), 'Guidelines on Gender-Neutral Language' (1999).
'Good Policy and Practice in Health Education: Puberty Education & Menstrual Hygiene Management' (2014).
Institute for Statistics, 'Fact Sheet No. 48' (2018).
UNESCO and Plan International, and French Ministry, 'Beijing + 25: Generation Equality Begins with Adolescent Girls' Education' (2020).
UNESCO and United Nations Girls' Education Initiative (UNGEI), 'Teaching and Learning: Achieving Equality for All, Global Monitoring Report' (2013–2014).
United Nations Office on Drugs and Crime (UNODC), 'Global Study on Homicide: Gender-Related Killing of Women and Girls' (2018).
UN Population, 'Living Arrangements of Older Persons Around the World' (2019).
United Nations Population Fund (UNFPA), 'Young People: Forging the Future' (2011).
'Child Marriage in Kosovo' (2012).
'Sex Imbalances at Birth: Current Trends, Consequences and Policy Implications' (2012).
'Implementation of the International and Regional Human Rights Framework for the Elimination of Female Genital Mutilation' (2014).
'The State of the World Population: How Our Future Depends on a Girl at This Decisive Age' (2016).
and UNICEF 'Global Programme to Accelerate Action to End Child Marriage' (2019).
'Kingdom of Saudi Arabia: Gender Justice and the Law' (2019).
'My Body is My Own: Claiming the Right to Autonomy and Self-determination' (2021).
UNFPA and UNICEF, 'Women's and Children's Rights: Making the Connection' (2010).
Joint Programme on the Elimination of Female Genital Mutilation: Accelerating Change, 'Measuring Effectiveness of Female Genital Mutilation Elimination: A Compendium Of Indicators' (2020).
United Nations Secretary General, 'In-Depth Study on All Forms of Violence against Women', Report of the Secretary General (6 July 2006) UN Doc A/61/122/Add.1.
'Multilingualism' (4 October 2010) UN Doc A/65/488.
United Nations Women, 'Progress of the World's Women: In Pursuit of Justice' (2012).
'Female Genital Mutilation/Cutting and Violence against Women and Girls: Strengthening the Policy between Different Forms of Violence' (2017).
'Families in a Changing World' (2020).
'Women's Rights 25 Years After Beijing' (2020).

World Health Organization (WHO), 'Multi-Country Study on Women's Health and Domestic Violence against Women' (2005).

'Care of Girls and Women Living with Female Genital Mutilation: A Clinical Handbook' (2018).

'Guidelines on the Management of Health Complications from Female Genital Mutilation' (2018).

'Adolescent Pregnancy: Evidence Brief' (2019).

and UNICEF, 'Protect the Progress: Report on the Every Woman Every Child Global Strategy' (2022).

## III CASES

DeGraffenreid *v.* General Motors Assembly Div 413 F Supp 142 (E D Mo 1976).

Gillick *v.* West Norfolk and Wisbech Area Health Authority (1986) AC 112.

R *v.* Ahmed and Ahmed [2012] Chester Crown Court (unreported).

R *v.* Mahmod Babakir Mahmod [2009] EWCA Crim 775.

Re R (A Minor) (Wardship: Consent to Treatment) (1992) Fam 11.

R *v* Secretary of State for the Home Department, ex parte Venables and Thompson (1998) AC 497 (Bulger case).

R *v.* Shafia, 2012 ONSC 1548.

Re W (A Minor) (Medical Treatment: Court's Jurisdiction) (1993) Fam 64.

## IV DICTIONARIES

*Cambridge English Dictionary* (Online Updated Version).

*Chambers Dictionary of Etymology* (Chambers [1988] 2002).

Collins Online Dictionary.

Gifi S, *Barron's Dictionary of Legal Terms: A Simplified Guide to the Language of Law* (1993).

*Merriam-Webster Comprehensive International Dictionary of the English Language* (1995).

*Merriam-Webster Dictionary of the English Language*, Eleventh Edition (2003) Online Updated Edition (Webster).

*Morris Dictionary of Word and Phrase Origins: A Comprehensive Reference Book on the Origins and Meanings of Thousands of Words and Expressions, Presented with Wit and Authority* (Second Edition Harper Collins 1988).

Online Etymology Dictionary.

*Oxford Concise Medical Dictionary* (2020).

*Oxford Dictionary of English Etymology* (Oxford Clarendon Press 1966).

*Oxford English Dictionary*, Second Edition (1989), Online Updated Edition (OED).

*Short Oxford English Dictionary on Historical Principles* (Sixth Edition, 2007) (SOEDHP).

*The Concise Oxford Dictionary of Current English* (First Edition 1911)

## V SECONDARY SOURCES

Abegaz ST, 'The Influence of Human Rights Instruments on Children's Rights Jurisprudence: An Appraisal of the Ethiopian Federal Cassation Court' (2016) 30 *International Journal of Law, Policy and the Family* 197.
Adarsh H and Sahoo S, 'Pornography and Its Impact on Adolescent/Teenage Sexuality' (2023) 5 *Journal of Psychosexual Health* 35.
Al-Dabbagh H, 'Iraq' in Yassari N et al. (eds.), *Parental Care and the Best Interests of the Child in Muslim Countries* (Springer 2017), 81–119.
Alderson P and Goodwin M, 'Contradictions within Concepts of Children's Competence' (1993) 1 *International Journal of Children's Rights* 303.
Alston P, 'The Unborn Child and Abortion under the Draft Convention on the Rights of the Child' (1990) 12 *Human Rights Quarterly* 156.
'The Best Interests Principle: Towards a Reconciliation of Culture and Human Rights' (1994) 8 *International Journal of Law, Policy and the Family* 1.
'The Historical Origins of the Concept of "General Comments" in Human Rights Law' in Boisson de Chazournes L and Gowlland-Debbas V (eds.), *The International Legal System in Quest of Equity and Universality* (Kluwer 2001), 763–76.
Alston P and Simma B, 'The Sources of Human Rights Law: Custom, Jus Cogens, and General Principles' (1989) 12 *Australian Year Book of International Law* 82.
American Psychological Association, 'Report of the APA Task Force on the Sexualization of Girls' (2010).
Amoah J, 'The World on Her Shoulders: The Rights of the Girl Child in the Context of Culture and Identity' (2007) 4 *Essex Human Rights Review* 1.
Andro A and Lesclingand M, 'Female Genital Mutilation. Overview and Current Knowledge' (2016) 71 *Population* 217.
Archard D, *Children: Rights and Childhood* (3rd ed., Routledge 2015).
Archard D and Tobin J, 'Article 1: The Definition of Child' in Tobin J (ed.), *The UN Convention on the Rights of the Child: A Commentary* (Oxford University Press 2019), 21–40.
Arnstein S, 'A Ladder of Citizen Participation' (1969) 35 *Journal of the American Institute of Planners* 216.
Aroni G, *The Semiotics of Architecture in Video Games* (Bloomsbury Advances in Semiotics 2022).
'Semiotics in Architecture and Spatial Design' in Jamin P (ed.), *Bloomsbury Semiotics Anthology* (Bloomsbury 2023), 277–96.
'Games as Authorial Platforms? An Exploration of the Legal Status of User-Created Content from Digital Games' (2023) 36 *International Journal for the Semiotics of Law* 2021.
Asian Centre for Human Rights, 'Female Infanticide Worldwide: The Case for Action by the UN Human Rights Council' (2016).
Askari L, 'Girls' Rights under International Law: An Argument for Establishing Gender Equality as a Jus Cogens' (1998–99) 8 *Southern California Review of Law and Women's Studies* 3.
'The Convention on the Rights of the Child: The Necessity of Adding a Provision to Ban Child Marriages' (1998–99) 5 *ILSA Journal of International and Comparative Law* 123.

Atrey S, *Intersectional Discrimination* (Oxford University Press 2019).
Backstrom K, 'The International Human Rights of the Child: Do They Protect the Female Child?' (1996) 30 *George Washington Journal of International Law and Economics* 541.
Bagchi SS and Das A., *Human Rights and the Third World: Issues and Discourses* (Lexington Books 2014).
Baigorri Jalón J, *Interpreters at the United Nations. A History* (Universidad de Salamanca 2004).
Barthes R, 'Une problématique du sens', *Œuvres complètes* (Complete Works of Roland Barthes), (Éditions du Seuil 2002)
Bayefsky A, 'The Principle of Equality or Non-Discrimination in International Law' (1990) 11 *Human Rights Law Journal* 1.
*UN Human Rights Treaty System: Universality at the Crossroads* (Springer 2001).
Behm-Morawitz E, 'Sext up KIDS: How Children are Becoming Hypersexualized' (2013) 7 *Journal of Children and Media* 530.
Bercroft A, 'Children and Young People in Conflict with the Law: Asking the Hard Questions' (2009) 57 *Juvenile and Family Court Journal* 1.
Besson S, 'The Principle of Non-Discrimination in the Convention on the Rights of the Child' (2005) 13 *International Journal of Children's Rights* 433.
Besson S and Kleber E, 'Article 2: The Right to Non-Discrimination' in Tobin J (ed.), *The UN Convention on the Rights of the Child: A Commentary* (Oxford University Press 2019), 41–72.
Bissonette D et al., 'TikTok Use and Body Dissatisfaction: Examining Direct, Indirect, and Moderated Relations' (2022) 43 *Body Image* 205.
Bohlander M, 'Language, Intellectual Culture, Legal Traditions and International Criminal Justice' (2014) 12 *Journal of International Criminal Justice* 491.
Bond J, 'International Intersectionality: A Theoretical and Pragmatic Exploration of Women's International Human Rights Violations' (2003) 52 *Emory Law Journal* 71.
Bonfantini M, *Le tre tendenze semiotiche del novecento* (The Three Semiotic Trends of the Twentieth Century) (Versus 1981).
Bongaarts J and Guilmoto C, 'How Many More Missing Women? Excess Female Mortality and Prenatal Sex Selection 1970–2050' (2015) 41 *Population and Development Review* 241.
Bossuyt M, *Guide to the "Travaux Préparatoires" of the International Covenant on Civil and Political Rights* (Martinus Nijhoff 1987).
Bouquet S and Engler R (eds.), *Ferdinand de Saussure: Writings in General Linguistics* (Oxford University Press 2006).
Boyd S, 'Challenging the Public/Private Divide: An Overview' in Boyd S (ed.), *Challenging the Public/Private Divide: Feminism, Law and Public Policy* (Toronto University Press 1997).
Broekman J and Catá Backer L (eds.), *Lawyers Making Meaning: The Semiotics of Law in Legal Education II* (Springer 2013).
Broekman J, Mootz III F and Pencak W, 'Preface – Semiotics in the Seminar' in Broekman J and Mootz III F (eds.), *The Semiotics of Law in Legal Education* (Springer 2011), v–xiv.
Brown Z and Tiggemann M, 'Attractive Celebrity and Peer Images on Instagram: Effect on Women's Mood and Body Image' (2016) 19 *Body Image* 37.

Bull B et al., 'Parents of Non-Binary Children: Stories of Understanding and Support' (2022) 34 *Journal of Feminist Family Therapy* 125.

Burke R, *Decolonization and the Evolution of International Human Rights* (University of Pennsylvania Press 2010).

Byrnes A and Kapai P, 'Article 1' in Schulz P et al. (eds.), *The UN Convention on the Elimination of All Forms of Discrimination against Women and Its Optional Protocol: A Commentary* (2nd ed., Oxford University Press 2022), 79–108.

Cantwell N, 'Origins, Development and Significance of the United Nations Convention on the Rights of the Child' in Detrick S (ed.), *The United Nations Convention on the Rights of the Child: A Guide to the* Travaux Préparatoires (Martinus Nijhoff 1992), 19–30.

Carpenter M, 'The "Normalization" of Intersex Bodies and "Othering" of Intersex Identities in Australia' (2018) 15 *Journal of Bioethical Inquiry* 487.

Chapdelaine-Feliciati C, 'Restorative Justice for the Girl Child in Post-Conflict Rwanda' (2006) 7 *Journal of International Women's Studies* 14.

'Child Justice in Canada and the Four Ps: Protection, Prosecution, Prevention and Participation' (2007) 15 *Critical Criminology: An International Journal* 267.

'The Sense, Meaning, and Significance of the Twin International Covenants on Political and Economic Rights' (2013) 196 *Semiotica* Special Issue: On and Beyond Significs: Centennial Issue for Victoria Lady Welby (1837–1912) 325.

'Deconstructing the Convention on the Rights of the Child: Semiotics, Significs and Semioethics of Gendercide' (2018) 7 *Cambridge International Law Journal* 29.

*Feminicides of Girl Children in the Family Context: An International Human Rights Law Approach* (Brill 2018).

'The Semiotic Puzzle: Authentic Languages and International Law' (2020) 5 *International Journal of Legal Discourse* 317.

'Les réserves en droit international ont-elles des limites? Étude sémioéthique du droit à l'éducation de la Convention relative aux droits de l'enfant' (Do Reservations Have Limits under International Law? Semioethic Study of the Child's Right to Education under the Convention on the Rights of the Child) (2022) 35 *Revue internationale de sémiotique juridique* 309.

'Semiotics in Law and Jurisprudence' in Pelkey J (ed.), *Bloomsbury Semiotics Anthology* (Bloomsbury 2023), 259–76.

'Translating the Meaning-Intention behind the "Best Interests of the Child" Principle in the Convention on the Rights of the Child' in Ji M and Petrilli S (eds.), *Intersemiotic Perspectives on Emotions: Translating Across Signs, Bodies and Values* (Routledge 2022), 116–29.

Encyclopedia Entry 'Semiotics of Law', SEMIOTICON SEO-Semiotics Encyclopedia Online.

'Sex Trafficking of Girl Children: A Legal Semiotics Study of the Convention on the Rights of the Child' in Marusek S and Wagner A (eds.), *Research Handbook on Legal Semiotics* (Elgar 2023), 300–12.

Charlesworth H, 'Feminist Methods in International Law' (1999) 93 *American Journal of International Law* 379.

Cipriani D, *Children's Rights and the Minimum Age of Criminal Responsibility: A Global Perspective* (Ashgate 2009).

Clarke J, 'Sex Assigned at Birth' (2022) 122 *Columbia Law Review* 1821.

Clayton A et al., 'Commentary: The Signal and the Noise – Questioning the Benefits of Puberty Blockers for Youth with Gender Dysphoria – A Commentary on Rew et al. (2021)' (2022) 27 *Child and Adolescent Mental Health* 259.

Coggon J, 'Varied and Principled Understandings of Autonomy in English Law: Justifiable Inconsistency or Blinkered Moralism?' (2007) 15 *Health Care Analysis* 235.

Conklin A and Meier B, 'A "Vector" of Rights Approach for Public Health: Towards an Intersectional Human Rights Framework for Considering the Prevention and Treatment of Harms to Girl Child Soldiers' (2008) 13 *Australian Journal of Human Rights* 65.

Connell R et al., *Making the Difference: Schools, Families and Social Division* (Routledge 1982).

Coomaraswamy R, 'Women and Children: The Cutting Edge of International Law' (2015) 30 *American University International Law Review* 1.

Crenshaw K, 'Demarginalizing the Intersection of Race and Sex: A Black Feminist Critique of Antidiscrimination Doctrine, Feminist Theory and Antiracist Politics' (1989) 1989 *University of Chicago Legal Forum* 139.

'Mapping the Margins: Intersectionality, Identity Politics, and Violence against Women of Color' (1991) 43 *Stanford Law Review* 1241.

Cyran E, 'Common Law Lawyers Should Mind Their Trial Practices: Understanding, Identifying, and Correcting a Semiotic Imbalance' in Broekman J and Mootz III F (eds.), *The Semiotics of Law in Legal Education* (Springer 2011), 115–28.

Darbyshire P, 'Childhood: Are Reports of Its Death Greatly Exaggerated?' (2007) 11 *Journal of Child Health Care* 85.

Dawson M and Mobayed Vega S, 'Femicide and Feminicide: A Growing Global Human Rights Movement' in Dawson M and Mobayed Vega S (eds.), *The Routledge International Handbook on Femicide and Feminicide* (Routledge 2023), 3–14.

Dequen JP, 'India' in Yassari N et al. (eds.), *Parental Care and the Best Interests of the Child in Muslim Countries* (Springer 2017), 29–61.

Detrick S (ed.), *The United Nations Convention on the Rights of the Child: A Guide to the Travaux Préparatoires* (Martinus Nijhoff 1992).

*A Commentary on the United Nations Convention on the Rights of the Child* (Martinus Nijhoff 1999).

Diamond-Smith N et al., 'Too Many Girls, Too Much Dowry': Son Preference and Daughter Aversion in Rural Tamil Nadu, India' (2008) 10 *Cultural Health* 1.

Dines G, 'Growing Up With Porn: The Developmental and Societal Impact of Pornography on Children' (2017) 2 *Dignity: A Journal of Analysis of Exploitation and Violence* 1.

Dinstein Y, 'Discrimination and International Human Rights' (1985) 15 *Israel Yearbook on Human Rights* 11.

Dorais M, *Don't Tell: The Sexual Abuse of Boys* (McGill-Queen's University Press 2007).

Doyle J (ed.), *The Conimbricenses: Some Questions on Signs* (Marquette University Press 2001).

Drolet C and Drolet A, 'Self-Objectification, System Justifying Beliefs, and the Rise of Labiaplasty' (2019) 32 *Social Justice Research* 318.

Drumbl M and Tobin J, 'Article 38: The Rights of Children in Armed Conflict' in Tobin J (ed.), *The UN Convention on the Rights of the Child: A Commentary* (Oxford University Press 2019), 1503–60.

Duivenbode R and Padela A, 'Female Genital Cutting (FGC) and the Cultural Boundaries of Medical Practice' (2019) 19 *American Journal of Bioethics* 3.

Dwyer J, *Moral Status and Human Life: The Case for Children's Superiority* (Cambridge University Press 2011).

Dyer C, 'Children are "Highly Unlikely" to Be Able to Consent to Taking Puberty Blockers, Rules High Court' (2020) 371 *BMJ*.

Earp B and Johnsdotter S, 'Current Critiques of the WHO Policy on Female Genital Mutilation' (2021) 33 *International Journal of Impotence Research: Your Sexual Medicine Journal* 196.

Eekelaar J, 'The Emergence of Children's Rights' (1986) 6 *Oxford Journal of Legal Studies* 161.

'The Interests of the Child and the Child's Wishes: The Role of Dynamic Self-Determinism' (1994) 8 *International Journal of Law, Policy and the Family* 42.

'The Role of the Best Interests Principle in Decisions Affecting Children and Decisions about Children' (2015) 23 *International Journal of Children's Rights* 3.

'Two Dimensions of the Best Interests Principle: Decisions about Children and Decisions Affecting Children' in Sutherland E and Barnes Macfarlane LA (eds.), *Implementing Article 3 of the UN Convention on the Rights of the Child* (Cambridge University Press 2016), 99–111.

Eekelaar J and Tobin J, 'Article 3: The Best Interests of the Child' in Tobin J (ed.), *The UN Convention on the Rights of the Child: A Commentary* (Oxford University Press 2019), 73–107.

End Prostitution and Child Trafficking (ECPAT), 'Protecting Children from Online Sexual Exploitation' (2016).

Endong FP, 'Pornography and Objectification of Women in Nollywood Films: A Study of Nigerian Actresses' Perception of Acting Sex and Nudity Scenes' (2019) 20 *Journal of International Women's Studies* 58.

Erickson-Schroth L (ed.), *Trans Bodies, Trans Selves: A Resource by and for Transgender Communities* (2nd ed., Oxford University Press 2022).

Ertan S and Yol F, 'Forced Marriage' in Romaniuk S and Marton P (eds.), *The Palgrave Encyclopedia of Global Security Studies* (Palgrave MacMillan 2019).

Ertürk Y and Purkayastha B, 'Linking Research, Policy and Action: A Look at the Work of the Special Rapporteur on Violence against Women' (2012) 60 *Current Sociology* 142.

European Union, 'Discriminatory Laws Undermining Women's Rights' (2020).

Farson R, *Birthrights* (Macmillan 1974).

Flood M, 'The Harms of Pornography Exposure among Children and Young People' (2009) 18 *Child Abuse Review* 384.

Fortin J, *Children's Rights and the Developing Law* (3rd ed., Cambridge University Press 2009).

Frade C, 'Power Dynamics and Legal English' (2007) 26 *World Englishes* 48.

Fredman S, 'Beyond the Dichotomy of Formal and Substantive Equality: Towards a New Definition of Equal Rights' in Boerefijn I et al. (eds.), *Temporary Special*

*Measures: Accelerating De Facto Equality of Women under Art 4 CEDAW* (Intersentia 2003), 111–18.

'The Age of Equality' in Fredman S and Spencer S (eds.), *Age as an Equality Issue: Legal and Policy Perspectives* (Hart Publishing 2003), 21–69.

'Engendering Socio-Economic Rights' (2009) 25 *South African Journal of Human Rights* 410.

*Discrimination Law* (Oxford University Press 2011).

'Women and Poverty – A Human Rights Approach' (2016) 24 *African Journal of International and Comparative Law* 494.

Freeman M, Chinkin C and Rudolf B (eds.), The UN Convention on the Elimination of All Forms of Discrimination against Women: A Commentary (1st ed., Oxford University Press 2012).

Friedman L et al., 'Physical Abuse of Elderly Adults: Victim Characteristics and Determinants of Revictimization' (2017) 65 *Journal of the American Geriatrics Society* 1420.

Fritz N et al., 'A Descriptive Analysis of the Types, Targets, and Relative Frequency of Aggression in Mainstream Pornography' (2020) 49 *Archives of Sexual Behaviour* 3041.

García-Del Moral P and Dersnah M, 'A Feminist Challenge to the Gendered Politics of the Public/Private Divide: On Due Diligence, Domestic Violence, and Citizenship' (2014) 18 *Citizenship Studies* 661.

Gardiner R, *Treaty Interpretation* (Oxford University Press 2015).

Garland J and Slokenberga S, 'Protecting the Rights of Children with Intersex Conditions from Nonconsensual Gender-Conforming Medical Interventions: The View from Europe' (2019) 27 *Medical Law Review* 482.

Garrison S, 'On the Limits of "Trans Enough": Authenticating Trans Identity Narratives' (2018) 32 *Gender & Society* 613.

Gendercide Watch, 'Case Study: Female Infanticide' (2007).

Gerding S and Stevens J, 'Sexualization, Youthification, and Adultification: A Content Analysis of Images of Girls and Women in Popular Magazines' (2018) 95 *Journalism and Mass Communication Quarterly* 625.

Ghanea N, 'Rights, Women and Human Rights Change in Iran' in MacLean M and Eekelaar J (eds.), *Managing Family Justice in Diverse Societies* (Hart 2013), 247–62.

Ghaznavi J et al., 'Increasingly Violent but Still Sexy: A Decade of Central Female Characters in Top-Grossing Hollywood and Bollywood Film Promotional Material' (2017) 11 *International Journal of Communication* 23.

Gill A et al., 'Violence between Female In-laws in India' (2013) 14 *Journal of International Women's Studies* 147.

Gill A and Mitra-Kahn T, 'Explaining Daughter Devaluation and the Issue of Missing Women in South Asia and the UK' (2009) 57 *Current Sociology* 684.

Girija K and Basavaraja G, 'Globalization and Commodification of Beauty – How Setting Beauty Standards Have Violated Women's Rights?' (2019) 8 *Political Science* 37.

González Moreno MJ et al., 'Fear for All Women: European Women's Fear of Harassment and Aggression in Public Spaces' (2022) 37 *Journal of Interpersonal Violence* 160.

Gonzalez-Salzberg D, *Sexuality and Transsexuality under the European Convention on Human Rights: A Queer Reading of Human Rights Law* (Hart Publishing 2019).
Goonesekere S, 'The Best Interests of the Child: A South Asian Perspective' (1994) 8 *International Journal of Law, Policy and the Family* 117.
'From Social Welfare to Human Rights for Girls – A Path to Achieving Gender Equality' (2014) 10 *International Journal of Law in Context* 478.
Greasley K, Arguments about Abortion: Personhood, Morality, and Law (Oxford University Press 2017).
Guercio L, 'Establishing the Social and Legal Categories for "Girls" and "Girl Children"' (2022) 28 *Violence against Women* 1842.
Gunnarsson L, 'A Defense of the Category "Women"' (2011) 12 *Feminist Theory* 23.
Guttmacher Institute, 'Abortion Worldwide: Uneven Progress and Unequal Access' (2017).
Hafen B and Hafen J, 'Abandoning Children to Their Autonomy: The United Nations Convention on the Rights of the Child' (1996) 37 *Harvard International Law Journal* 449.
Hale B, 'Understanding Children's Rights: Theory and Practice' (2006) 44 *Family Court Review* 350.
Halperin-Kaddari R and Freeman M, 'Article 16' in Patricia Schulz et al. (eds.), *The UN Convention on the Elimination of All Forms of Discrimination against Women and Its Optional Protocol: A Commentary* (2nd ed., Oxford University Press 2022), 577–626.
Hancock AM, 'When Multiplication Doesn't Equal Quick Addition: Examining Intersectionality as a Research Paradigm' (2007) 5 *Perspectives on Politics* 63.
Harb C et al., 'Motivators and Barriers to Accessing Sexual Health Care Services for Transgender/Genderqueer Individuals Assigned Female Sex at Birth' (2019) 4 *Transgender Health* 58.
Harde R, 'Girls and Rape Culture' (2021) 14 *Girlhood Studies* vii.
Hardwick C and Cook J (eds.), Semiotics and Significs: The Correspondence between Charles S Peirce and Lady Victoria Welby (Indiana University Press 1977).
Hargitt S, 'What Could be Gained in Translation: Legal Language and Lawyer-Linguists in a Globalized World' (2013) 20 *Indiana Journal Global Legal Studies* 425.
Harris J, 'Liberating Children' in Leahy M and Cohn-Sherbok D (eds.), *The Liberation Debate: Rights at Issue* (Routledge 1996), 135–46.
Hartshorne C and Weiss P (eds.), *The Collected Papers of Charles Peirce* (Harvard University Press 1931-35).
Hazen E et al., 'Child, Adolescent and Adult Development' in Stern T et al. (eds.), *Massachusetts General Hospital Comprehensive Clinical Psychiatry* (Elsevier 2016), 47–62.
Heinze E, 'The Myth of Flexible Universality: Human Rights and the Limits of Comparative Naturalism' (2019) 39 *Oxford Journal of Legal Studies* 624.
Hendrick H, 'Constructions and Reconstructions of British Childhood: An Interpretative Survey, 1800 to the Present' in James A and Prout A (eds.), *Constructing and Reconstructing Childhood: Contemporary Issues in the Sociological Study of Childhood* (Routledge 2015), 29–53.
Herring J, 'Children's Rights for Grown-ups' in Fredman S and Spencer S (eds.), *Age as an Equality Issue: Legal and Policy Perspectives* (Hart 2003) 145–74.

'Vulnerability, Children, and the Law' in Freeman M (ed.), *Law and Childhood Studies: Current Legal Issues* (Oxford University Press 2012), 243–63.

Herring J and Gilmore S, '"No" is the Hardest Word: Consent and Children's Autonomy' (2011) 23 *Child and Family Law Quarterly* 3.

Hohfeld W, *Fundamental Legal Conceptions as Applied in Judicial Reasoning* (Yale University Press 1923).

Holt J, *Escape from Childhood: The Needs and Rights of Children* (Penguin 1974).

Horton C, 'Experiences of Puberty and Puberty Blockers: Insights from Trans Children, Trans Adolescents, and Their Parents' (2024) 39 *Journal of Adolescent Research* 77.

Hosseinnejad K, 'On the Nature of Interpretation in International Law' (2015) 4 *UCL Journal of Law and Jurisprudence* 225.

Human Rights Watch, 'Everything I Have to Do is Tied to a Man' (2021).

'World Report: Events' (2021).

Humphrey J, 'The International Bill of Rights: Scope and Implementation' (1976) 17 *William and Mary Law Review* 527.

Infrastructure and Cities for Economic Development (ICED), 'Violence against Women and Girls, Infrastructure and Cities' (2017).

International Law Association (ILA), Committee on International Human Rights Law and Practice, 'Final Report on the Impact of the Findings of the United Nations Human Rights Treaty Bodies', Berlin Conference (2004).

Irwig M, 'Detransition among Transgender and Gender-Diverse People – An Increasing and Increasingly Complex Phenomenon' (2022) 107 *Journal of Clinical Endocrinology & Metabolism* 4261.

Ishaque S and Khan MM, 'The Best Interests of the Child: A Prevailing Consideration within Islamic Principles and a Governing Principle in Child Custody Cases in Pakistan' (2015) 29 *International Journal of Law, Policy and the Family* 78.

Jackson B, 'Legal Semiotics and Semiotic Aspects of Jurisprudence' in Wagner A and Broekman J (eds.), *Prospects of Legal Semiotics* (Springer 2010).

Jain P et al., 'Sexuality and Substance Abuse Portrayals in Item Songs in Bollywood Movies' (2019) 17 *South Asian Popular Culture* 15.

James A and Prout A, 'Re-Presenting Childhood' in James A and Prout A (eds.), *Constructing and Reconstructing Childhood: Contemporary Issues in the Sociological Study of Childhood* (Routledge 2015), 202–19.

Jones M, 'Intersex Genital Mutilation – A Western Version of FGM' (2017) 25 *International Journal of Children's Rights* 396.

Joseph R, *Human Rights and the Unborn Child* (Martinus Nijhoff 2009).

Kadelbach S, 'Interpretation of the Charter' in Simma B et al. (eds.), *The Charter of the United Nations: A Commentary* (Oxford University Press 2012), 71–99.

Kassa GM et al., 'Prevalence and Determinants of Adolescent Pregnancy in Africa: A Systematic Review and Meta-Analysis' (2018) 15 *Reproductive Health* 195.

Kaya S, 'Gender and Violence: Rape as a Spectacle on Prime-Time Television' (2019) 58 *Social Science Information* 681.

Keller H and Grover L, 'General Comments of the Human Rights Committee and Their Legitimacy' in Keller H and Ulfstein G (eds.), *UN Human Rights Treaty Bodies: Law and Legitimacy* (Cambridge University Press 2012), 116–98.

Kelly T, 'Two Cheers for Ritual: The UN Committee against Torture' (2018) 9 *Humanity* 93.

Kelly J and Garmon L, 'Perceptions of Child Beauty Pageants and Their Impacts: What Really Lies Behind the Tiara?' (2016) 24 *Atlantic Journal of Communication* 201.

Kevelson R, *Peirce, Science, Signs* (Peter Lang 1996).

Khaitan T, *A Theory of Discrimination Law* (Oxford University Press 2015).

Kim G, 'Between Hybridity and Hegemony in K-Pop's Global Popularity: A Case of Girls' Generation's American Debut' (2017) 11 *International Journal of Communication* 2367.

King M, 'Children's Rights as Communication: Reflections on Autopoietic Theory and the United Nations Convention' (1994) 57 *Modern Law Review* 385.

Kishore J, *The Vanishing Girl Child* (Century Publications 2005).

Kleemans M et al., 'Picture Perfect: The Direct Effect of Manipulated Instagram Photos on Body Image in Adolescent Girls' (2018) 21 *Media Psychology* 93.

Kloesel C (ed.), *Writings of Charles S Peirce: A Chronological Edition* (Indiana University Press 1982–2000).

Kolb R, 'Is There a Subject-Matter Ontology in Interpretation of International Legal Norms?' in Andenas M and Bjorge E (eds.), *A Farewell to Fragmentation: Reassertion and Convergence in International Law* (Cambridge University Press 2015), 473–85.

Kon A, 'Transgender Children and Adolescents' (2014) 14 *American Journal of Bioethics* 48.

Koo GY and Han HE, 'To Veil or Not to Veil: Turkish and Iranian Hijab Policies and the Struggle for Recognition' (2018) 24 *Asian Journal of Women's Studies* 47.

Kroworsch S, 'Article 26' in Schulz P et al. (eds.), *The UN Convention on the Elimination of All Forms of Discrimination against Women and Its Optional Protocol: A Commentary* (2nd ed., Oxford University Press 2022), 777–80.

Kumar S and Sinha N, 'Preventing More "Missing Girls": A Review of Policies to Tackle Son Preference' (2020) 35 *World Bank Research Observer* 87.

La Fornara L, 'Islam's (In)compatibility with the West?: Dress Code Restrictions in the Age of Feminism' (2018) 25 *Indiana Journal of Global Legal Studies* 463.

Lagarde M, 'Una feminista contra el feminicidio' (2005) 278 *Revista Envio* 1.

'Introducción: Por la vida y la libertad de las mujeres. Fin al feminicidio' (Introduction: For the Life and Freedom of Women: End Feminicide) in Russell D and Harmes R (eds.), *Feminicidio: Una perspectiva global (Femicide in Global Perspective)*, Spanish ed., Teachers College Press 2006), 15–42.

Lauterpacht H, 'De l'interprétation des traités: Rapport' (Treaty Interpretation: Report) (1950-II) 43 *Annuaire de l'Institut de Droit International – Yearbook, Institute of International Law*, 366.

Laws J, 'The Limitations of Human Rights' (1998) *Public Law* 254.

Leblanc L, *The Convention on the Rights of the Child: United Nations Lawmaking on Human Rights* (University of Nebraska Press 1995).

Lemma A, *Transgender Identities: A Contemporary Introduction* (Routledge 2021).

Lewis H, 'Female Genital Mutilation and Female Genital Cutting', *Encyclopedia of Human Rights* (Oxford University Press 2009), 200–13.

Liberman A, *An Analytic Dictionary of English Etymology: An Introduction* (University of Minnesota Press 2008).

Linderfalk U, *On the Interpretation of Treaties: The Modern International Law as Expressed in the 1969 Vienna Convention on the Law of Treaties* (Springer 2007).

Lindley R, 'Teenagers and Other Children' in Scarre G (ed.), *Children, Parents, and Politics* (Cambridge University Press 1989), 72–93.

Locke J, 'Two Treatises of Government' in Shapiro I (ed.), *Two Treatises of Government and A Letter Concerning Toleration* (Yale University Press 2003 [1689]).

'Some Thoughts Concerning Education' in Adamson JW (ed.), *The Educational Writings of John Locke* (Cambridge University Press 2011 [1922], [1693]).

Logrieco G et al., 'The Paradox of Tik Tok Anti-Pro-Anorexia Videos: How Social Media Can Promote Non-Suicidal Self-Injury and Anorexia' (2021) 18 *International Journal of Environmental Research and Public Health* 1041.

Lowe P, 'The Rise of the BRICS in the Global Economy' (2016) 41 *Teaching Geography* 50.

Lücker-Babel MF, 'Les réserves à la Convention des Nations Unies relative aux droits de l'enfant et la sauvegarde de l'objet et du but du traité international' (Reservations to the UN Convention on the Rights of the Child and Safeguarding the Object and Purpose of the International Treaty) (1997) 8 *European Journal of International Law* 664.

Maddocks S, 'Feminism, Activism and Non-Consensual Pornography: Analyzing Efforts to End "Revenge Porn" in the United States' (2022) 7 *Feminist Media Studies* 1641.

Maki S et al., 'An Analysis of Vulva Appearance in Video Pornography' (2023) 27 *Sexuality and Culture* 310.

Manetti G, 'Ancient Semiotics' in Cobley P (ed.), *The Routledge Companion to Semiotics* (Routledge 2009), 13–28.

Manning K, 'Attached Advocacy and the Rights of the Trans Child' (2017) 50 *Canadian Journal of Political Science* 579.

Manzoor Ahmed Hanifi S et al., 'Where Girls are Less Likely to be Fully Vaccinated than Boys: Evidence from a Rural Area in Bangladesh' (2018) 36 *Vaccine* 3323.

Marcdante K et al., 'Overview and Assessment of Adolescents' in Marcdante K et al. (eds.), *Nelson Essentials of Pediatrics* (9th ed., Elsevier 2018), 267–72.

Martino W and Meyenn B, 'What About the Boys?': Issues of Masculinity in Schools (Open University Press 2001).

McCall L, 'The Complexity of Intersectionality' (2005) 30 *Signs: Journal of Women in Culture and Society* 1771.

McGoldrick D, 'The United Nations Convention on the Rights of the Child' (1991) 5 *International Journal of Law, Policy and the Family* 132.

Menjívar C and Drysdale Walsh S, 'The Architecture of Feminicide: The State, Inequalities, and Everyday Gender Violence in Honduras' (2017) 52 *Latin American Research Review* 221.

Merrell F, 'Charles Sanders Peirce 's Concept of the Sign' in Cobley P (ed.), *The Routledge Companion to Semiotics and Linguistics* (Routledge 2001), 28–39.

Mgbako C et al., 'Penetrating the Silence in Sierra Leone: A Blueprint for the Eradication of Female Genital Mutilation' (2010) 23 *Harvard Human Rights Journal* 111.

Mibenge CS, *Sex and International Tribunals: The Erasure of Gender from the War Narrative* (University of Pennsylvania Press 2014).

Mill JS, *The Subjection of Women* (Longmans, Green, Reader and Dyer 1869).
Minority Rights Group International, 'Beyond the Veil: Discrimination against Women in Iran' (2019).
Minow M, 'Rights of the Next Generation: A Feminist Approach to Children's Rights' (1986) 9 *Harvard Women's Law Journal* 1.
Mintz S, 'Children, Families and the State: American Family Law in Historical Perspective' (1992) 69 *Denver University Law Review* 635.
Mnookin R, 'Child-Custody Adjudication: Judicial Functions in the Face of Indeterminacy' (1975) 39 *Law and Contemporary Problems* 226.
Moeckli D, 'Equality and Non-Discrimination' in Moeckli D et al. (eds.), *International Human Rights Law* (Oxford University Press 2018), 151–68.
Moloo R, 'Changing Times, Changing Obligations? The Interpretation of Treaties over Time' in *Proceedings of the Annual Meeting, American Society of International Law 106 Confronting Complexity* (Cambridge University Press 2012).
Monárrez J, 'Morir por ser mujeres, Femicidio/Feminicidio. La violencia máxima' (Murdered because We are Women, Femicide/Feminicide. The Extreme Violence) (2008) 4 *Revista Mujer Salud* (Journal of Women's Health) 27.
Morris C, *Signification and Significance: A Study of the Relations of Signs and Values* (MIT Press 1964).
Mortenson J, 'The Travaux of the Travaux: Is the Vienna Convention Hostile to Drafting History?' (2013) 107 *American Journal of International Law* 780.
Moussa J, 'Egypt' in Nadjma Yassari et al. (eds.), *Parental Care and the Best Interests of the Child in Muslim Countries* (Springer 2017), 1–28.
Mowbray J, 'Language in the UN and EU: Linguistic Diversity as a Challenge for Multilateralism (2010) 8 *New Zealand Journal of Public and International Law* 91.
Muehlenhard C et al., 'Evaluating the One-in-Five Statistic: Women's Risk of Sexual Assault While in College' (2017) 54 *Journal of Sex Research* 549.
Mujuzi JD, 'Female Genital Mutilation in Uganda: A Glimpse at the Abolition Process' (2012) 56 *Journal of African Law* 139.
Murthy R, 'Fighting Female Infanticide by Working with Midwives: An Indian Case Study' (1996) 4 *Gender and Development* 20.
Muthulakshmi R, *Female Infanticide: Its Causes and Solutions* (Discovery Publishing House 1997).
Myhre J et al., 'Elder Abuse and Neglect: An Overlooked Patient Safety Issue. A Focus Group Study of Nursing Home Leaders' Perceptions of Elder Abuse and Neglect' (2020) 20 *BMC Health Services Research* 199.
Nash J, 'Re-Thinking Intersectionality' (2008) 89 *Feminist Review* 1.
Nathwani N, 'Islamic Headscarves and Human rights: A Critical Analysis of the Relevant Case Law of the European Court of Human Rights' (2007) 25 *Netherlands Quarterly of Human Rights* 221.
Oberleitner G, *Human Rights in Armed Conflict: Law, Practice, Policy* (Cambridge University Press 2015).
Obreja LD, 'Intimate Partner Violence in Childhood: Human Rights Implications in Multiple Exposure Scenarios' (2019) 27 *International Journal of Children's Rights* 99.

O'Flaherty M and Fisher J, 'Sexual Orientation, Gender Identity and International Human Rights Law: Contextualizing the Yogyakarta Principles' (2008) 8 *Human Rights Law Review* 207.

Ogden C and Richards I, *The Meaning of Meaning: A Study of the Influence of Language upon Thought and the Science of Symbolism* (Harcourt 1923).

Okongwu O, 'Are Laws the Appropriate Solution: The Need to Adopt Non-Policy Measures in Aid of the Implementation of Sex Discrimination Laws in Nigeria' (2021) 21 *International Journal of Discrimination and the Law* 26.

Olaitan A and Ifeoluwayimika B, 'The Menace of Domestic Violence: Improving the Lives of Women in Nigeria' (2016) 9 *African Journal of Legal Studies* 177.

Olsen F, 'Children's Rights: Some Feminist Approaches to the United Nations Convention on the Rights of the Child' (1992) 6 *International Journal of Law, Policy and the Family* 192.

Oransky M and Marecek J, '"I'm Not Going to Be a Girl": Masculinity and Emotions in Boy's Friendships and Peer Groups' (2009) 24 *Journal of Adolescent Research* 218.

Organization for Economic Co-operation and Development (OECD), 'A Long Way before Turning Promises into Progress: Discriminatory Laws and Social Norms Still Hamper Gender Equality' (2019).

'SIGI Global Report: Transforming Challenges into Opportunities' (2019).

Ortega K, 'Striking a Pose: Protecting the Welfare of Child Models' (2014) 35 *Cardozo Law Review* 2535.

Otto D, 'Lost in Translation: Re-Scripting the Sexed Subjects of International Human Rights Law' in Orford A (ed.), *International Law and Its Others* (Cambridge University Press 2006).

Paccione A, 'On Trend: Continuing the Effort to Inspire Fashion Industry Reform and Protect Underage Fashion Models' (2017) 41 *Seton Hall Legislative Journal* 417.

Pearce R et al., 'TERF Wars: An Introduction' (2020) 68 *Sociological Review* 677.

Pedalino F and Camerini AL, 'Instagram Use and Body Dissatisfaction: The Mediating Role of Upward Social Comparison with Peers and Influencers among Young Females' (2022) 19 *International Journal of Environmental Research and Public Health* 1543.

Pedersen L, 'Moving Bodies as Moving Targets: A Feminist Perspective on Sexual Violence in Transit' (2020) 3 *Open Philosophy* 369.

Peroni L, 'Violence against Migrant Women: The Istanbul Convention Through a Postcolonial Feminist Lens' (2016) 24 *Feminist Legal Studies* 49.

Petrilli S, *Signifying and Understanding: Reading the Works of Victoria Welby and the Signific Movement* (De Gruyter Mouton 2009).

*Sign Crossroads in Global Perspective: Semioethics and Responsibility* (Transaction Publishers 2010).

*The Self as a Sign, the World, and the Other: Living Semiotics* (Transaction Publishers 2013).

*Sign Studies and Semioethics: Communication, Translation and Values* (De Gruyter Mouton 2014).

*Victoria Welby and the Science of Signs: Significs, Semiotics, Philosophy of Language* (Transaction Publishers 2015).

Petrilli S and Ponzio A, 'Semioethics' in Cobley P (ed.), *The Routledge Companion to Semiotics* (Routledge 2009), 150–62.

Piaget J, *Science of Education and the Psychology of the Child* (Viking 1970).
et al., *Epistemology and Psychology of Functions* (Reidel Publishing Company 1977).
Pierce C and Allen G, 'Childism: The Basic Oppression' (1975) 5 *Psychiatric Annals* 266.
Pilgrim K and Bohnet-Joschko S, 'Selling Health and Happiness: How Influencers Communicate on Instagram about Dieting and Exercise: Mixed Methods Research' (2019) 19 *BMC Public Health* 1054.
Pobjoy J, 'The Best Interests of the Child Principle as an Independent Source of International Protection' (2015) 64 *International and Comparative Law Quarterly* 327.
Podlas K, 'Does Exploiting a Child Amount to Employing a Child? The FLSA's Child Labor Provisions and Children on Reality Television' (2010) 17 *UCLA Entertainment Law Review* 39.
Pogge T, 'Recognized and Violated by International Law: The Human Rights of the Global Poor' (2005) 18 *Leiden Journal of International Law* 717.
Ponzio A and Petrilli S, *Semioetica* (Meltemi 2003).
Population Research Institute, 'Sex-Selective Abortion in India: Estimates on the Occurrence of Sex Selective Abortion in India and Some Possible Solutions to Eliminate the Practice' (2019).
Porterfield T and Stanton G, 'The Age of Majority: Article 1' (1989) 16 *New York Law School Journal of Human Rights* 30.
Prasad E and Songwe V, 'Monetary Meld: A Currency Union Encompassing All of West Africa Promises Benefits but Faces a Multitude of Obstacles' (IMF 2021).
Price Cohen C, 'The United Nations Convention on the Rights of the Child: A Feminist Landmark' (1997) 3 *William and Mary Journal of Women and the Law* 29.
Puar J, 'Bodies with New Organs: Becoming Trans, Becoming Disabled' (2015) 33 *Social Text* 45.
Pullen Sansfaçon A et al., 'A Nuanced Look into Youth Journeys of Gender Transition and Detransition' (2023) 32 *Infant and Child Development* 2402.
Pupavac V, 'The Infantilization of the South and the UN Convention on the Rights of the Child' in Steiner H and Alston P (eds.), *International Human Rights in Context: Law, Politics, Morals* (2nd ed., Oxford University Press 2000), 517–518.
Purdie-Vaughns V and Eibach R, 'Intersectional Invisibility: The Distinctive Advantages and Disadvantages of Multiple Subordinate-Group Identities' (2008) 59 *Sex Roles* 377.
Radačić I, 'Human Rights of Women and the Public/Private Divide in International Human Rights Law' (2007) 3 *Croatian Yearbook of European Law and Policy* 443.
Ramcharan B, 'Equality and Non-Discrimination' in Henkin L (ed.), *The International Bill of Rights: The Covenant on Civil and Political Rights* (Columbia University Press 1981), 246–69.
Rana U, 'Increased Female Criminality in India: A Statistical Perception' (2016) 5 *Journal of Global Research and Analysis* 221.
Rao A, 'The Politics of Gender and Culture in International Human Rights Discourse' in Peters J and Wolper A (eds.), *Women's Rights, Human Rights: International Feminist Perspectives* (Routledge 1995), 167–75.

Rehof L, *Guide to the* Travaux Préparatoires *of the United Nations Convention on the Elimination of All Forms of Discrimination against Women* (Martinus Nijhoff 1993).
Rhineberger-Dunn G, 'Myth versus Reality: Comparing the Depiction of Juvenile Delinquency in Metropolitan Newspapers with Arrest Data' (2013) 83 *Sociological Inquiry* 473.
Ringrose J et al., 'A Qualitative Study of Children, Young People and "Sexting": A Report Prepared for the National Society for the Prevention of Cruelty to Children' (Institute of Education London, King's College London & LSE 2012).
Ris M, 'Treaty Interpretation and ICJ Recourse to Travaux Préparatoires: Towards a Proposed Amendment of Articles 31 and 32 of the Vienna Convention on the Law of Treaties' (1991) 14 *Boston College International and Comparative Law Review* 111.
Roberts N et al., 'Gendered Landscapes of Safety: How Women Construct and Navigate the Urban Landscape to Avoid Sexual Violence' (2022) 22 *Criminology and Criminal Justice* 287.
Robinson F, 'European Clothing Names and the Etymology of Girl' in Arndt W et al. (eds.), *Studies in Historical Linguistics in Honor of George Sherman Lane* (University of North Carolina Press 1967), 233–40.
Rodeschini S, 'New Standards of Respectability in Contemporary Pornography: Pornhub's Corporate Communication' (2021) 8 *Porn Studies* 76.
Rose E, Translating Trans Identity: (Re)Writing Undecidable Texts and Bodies (Routledge 2021).
Rosenne S, 'Interpretation of Treaties in the Restatement and the International Law Commission's Draft Articles: A Comparison' (1966) 5 *Columbia Journal of Transnational Law* 205.
Rossi-Landi F, *Significato, comunicazione, e parlare comune* (Meaning, Communication and Common speech), (Marsilio 1998 [1961]).
Language as Work and Trade: A Semiotic Homology for Linguistics and Economics (Bergin & Garvey Publishers 1983 [1968]).
Rothenbaum N, 'The Transracial Subject and the Emotive Regime: Rachel Dolezal, Racial Phronêsis, and Inverted Miscegenation' (2023) 20 *Communication and Critical/Cultural Studies* 252.
Royal College of Psychiatrists, 'Child Defendants Occasional Paper OP 56' (UK 2006).
'Position Statement on Early Intervention for Eating Disorders PS03/9' (UK 2019).
Rubattu V et al., 'Cam Girls and Adult Performers are Enjoying a Boom in Business' (2023) 12 *Social Sciences* 62.
Runacres S and Wood P, 'Cosmetic Labiaplasty in an Adolescent Population' (2016) 29 *Journal of Pediatric and Adolescent Gynecology* 218.
Russell D, 'Defining Femicide and Related Concepts' in Russell D and Harmes R (eds.), *Femicide in Global Perspective* (Teachers College Press 2001), 12–28.
Russell D and Caputi J, 'Femicide: Speaking the Unspeakable' (1990) 1 *Ms: The World of Women* 34–37.
Russell D and Radford J (eds.), *Femicide: The Politics of Woman Killing* (Twayne 1992).
Salter E, 'Deciding for a Child: A Comprehensive Analysis of the Best Interest Standard' (2012) 33 *Theoretical Medicine and Bioethics* 179.

Sanford V, 'From Genocide to Feminicide: Impunity and Human Rights in Twenty-First Century Guatemala' (2008) 7 *Journal of Human Rights* 104.
Save the Children, 'Global Childhood Report' (2019).
Schabas W, 'Reservations to the Convention on the Rights of the Child' (1996) 18 *Human Rights Quarterly* 472.
Schulz P, Halperin-Kaddari R and Rudolf B, 'Introduction' in Schulz P et al. (eds.), *The UN Convention on the Elimination of All Forms of Discrimination against Women and Its Optional Protocol: A Commentary* (2nd ed., Oxford University Press 2022), 2–60.
de Schutter O, *International Human Rights Law* (Cambridge University Press 2014).
Sebeok T, *Global Semiotics* (Indiana University Press 2001).
Seekis V and Barker G, 'Does #beauty have a Dark Side? Testing Mediating Pathways between Engagement with Beauty Content on Social Media and Cosmetic Surgery Consideration' (2022) 42 *Body Image* 268.
Shannon J and Hunter R, 'Principles of Contract Law Applied to Entertainment and Sports Contracts: A Model for Balancing the Rights of the Industry with Protecting the Interests of Minors' (2015) 48 *Loyola Los Angeles Law Review* 1171.
Shelton D, 'Reconcilable Differences? The Interpretation of Multilingual Treaties' (1997) 20 *Hastings International and Comparative Law Review* 611.
'Prohibited Discrimination in International Human Rights Law' in Constantinides A and Zaikos N (eds.), *The Diversity of International Law* (Martinus Nijhoff 2009), 259–92.
Shereshevsky Y and Noah T, 'Does Exposure to Preparatory Work Affect Treaty Interpretation? An Experimental Study of International Law Students and Experts' (2018) 28 *European Journal of International Law* 1287.
Shier H, 'Pathways to Participation: Openings, Opportunities and Obligations: A New Model for Enhancing Children's Participation in Decision-Making, in Line with Article 12.1 of the United Nations Convention on the Rights of the Child' (2001) 15 *Children and Society* 107.
Skjeie H and Langvasbråten T, 'Intersectionality in Practice? Anti-Discrimination Reforms in Norway' (2009) 11 *International Feminist Journal of Politics* 513.
Smith A, 'Interpreting and Supporting Participation Rights: Contributions from Sociocultural Theory' (2002) 10 *International Journal of Children's Rights* 73.
Smolin D, 'Overcoming Religious Objections to the Convention on the Rights of the Child' (2006) 20 *Emory International Law Review* 81.
Smolka J and Pirker B, 'International Law and Pragmatics: An Account of Interpretation in International Law' (2016) 5 *International Journal of Law and Language* 1.
Sohoni N, *The Burden of Girlhood: A Global Inquiry into the Status of Girls* (Third Party Publishing Company 1995).
Sorin R, 'Changing Images of Childhood – Reconceptualizing Early Childhood Practice' (2005) 1 *International Journal of Transitions in Childhood* 12.
South African Development Committee, 'Model Law on Eradicating Child Marriage and Protecting Children Already in Marriage' (2016).
Stark L, 'Early Marriage and Cultural Constructions of Adulthood in Two Slums in Dar es Salaam' (2018) 20 *Culture, Health, and Sexuality* 888.

Sumner M, 'The Unknown Genocide: How One Country's Culture is Destroying the Girl Child' (2009) 15 *International Journal of Nursing Practice* 65.

Tabe Tabe S, 'Traditional Law and Discriminatory Customary Practices against Women in Cameroon: A Critical Perspective' (2020) 28 *African Journal of International and Comparative Law* 418.

Taefi N, 'The Synthesis of Age and Gender: Intersectionality, International Human Rights Law and the Marginalization of the Girl Child' (2009) 17 *International Journal of Children's Rights* 345.

Tamer C, 'Toddlers, Tiaras, and Pedophilia? The Borderline "Child Pornography" Embraced by the American Public' (2011) 13 *Texas Review Entertainment and Sports Law* 85.

Tandon SL and Sharma R, 'Female Foeticide and Infanticide in India: An Analysis of Crimes against Girl Children' (2006) 1 *International Journal of Criminal Justice Sciences* 1.

Taylor J et al., *The Remarkable Rise of Transgender Rights* (University of Michigan Press 2018).

Taylor PM, *A Commentary on the International Covenant on Civil and Political Rights* (Cambridge University Press 2020).

Taylor R, 'Reversing the Retreat from Gillick? R (Axon) v. Secretary of State for Health (2007) 19 *Child and Family Law Quarterly* 81.

'Parental Responsibility and Religion' in Probert R, Gilmore S and Herring J (eds.), Responsible Parents and *Parental Responsibility* (Bloomsbury 2009), 123–41.

Terre des Hommes, INDIFESA Campaign, 'The Condition of the Girl Child Worldwide' (2019).

Thomas Reuters Foundation, 'The Law and FGM: An Overview of 28 African Countries' (2018).

Tiefenbrun S, *Decoding International Law: Semiotics and the Humanities* (Oxford University Press 2010).

Tobin J, 'Judging the Judges: Are They Adopting the Rights Approach in Matters Involving Children?' (2009) 33 *Melbourne University Law Review* 579.

'Introduction: The Foundation for Children's Rights' in Tobin J (ed.), *The UN Convention on the Rights of the Child: A Commentary* (Oxford University Press 2019), 1–20.

Tomuschat C, 'The (Hegemonic?) Role of the English Language' (2017) 86 *Nordic Journal of International Law* 196.

Truchot C, 'The Spread of English: From France to a More General Perspective' (1997) 16 *World Englishes* 65.

Van Bueren G, *The International Law on the Rights of the Child* (Martinus Nijhoff 1998).

Vandenbosch L et al., '"I Might Get Your Heart Racing in My Skin-Tight Jeans": Sexualization on Music Entertainment Television' (2013) 64 *Communication Studies* 178.

Vandenhole W, *Non-Discrimination and Equality in the View of the UN Human Rights Treaty Bodies* (Intersentia 2005).

Verrastro V et al., 'Fear the Instagram: Beauty Stereotypes, Body Image and Instagram Use in a Sample of Male and Female Adolescents' (2020) 15 *Qwerty – Open and Interdisciplinary Journal of Technology, Culture and Education* 31.

Vierdag B, *The Concept of Discrimination in International Law* (Martinus Nijhoff 1973).
Voloshinov V, *Freudianism: A Critical Sketch* (Indiana University Press 1987 [1927]).
Wagner A, 'Promises and Prospects' in Wagner A and Broekman J (eds.), *Prospects of Legal Semiotics* (Springer 2010).
Walkerdine V, 'Popular Culture and the Eroticization of Little Girls' in Jenkins H (ed.), *The Children's Culture Reader* (New York University Press 1998), 254–64.
Wallbank J and Bryan I, 'The Lore of Sexual Difference in Social and Legal Discourse on "Date Rape"' (2004) 15 *Law and Critique* 183.
Wallbank J and Cave E, 'Minors' Capacity to Refuse Treatment: A Reply to Gilmore and Herring' (2012) 20 *Medical Law Review* 423.
Wallner C et al., 'Digital Media Play a Key Role in Influencing Female Breast Perception' (2023) 26 *Cyberpsychology, Behavior and Social Networking* 11.
Waring M, 'Gender and International Law: Women and the Right to Development' (1989) 12 *Australian Yearbook of International Law* 177.
Warren MA, *Gendercide: The Implications of Sex Selection* (Rowman and Allanfield 1985).
Welby V, 'Meaning and Metaphor' (1893) 3 *The Monist* 510.
*Grains of Sense* (JM Dent & Co 1897).
*What is Meaning? Studies in the Development of Significance* (MacMillan 1903, reprint in Foundations of Semiotics, John Benjamins 1983).
Letter from Welby to Peirce (24 May 1903), Victoria Lady Welby Correspondence, Clara Thomas Archives and Special Collections, York University Libraries File 1970-101/021(7).
Letter from Welby to Charles Peirce (22 December 1903), Victoria Lady Welby Correspondence, Clara Thomas Archives and Special Collections, York University Libraries File 1970-010/012(7), Inventory No. 443.
Significs and Language: The Articulate Form of Our Expressive and Interpretative Resources (MacMillan 1911, reprint in Foundations of Semiotics, John Benjamins 1985).
Wessel J, 'International Law as Language – Towards a "Neo" New Haven School' (2010) 23 *International Journal for the Semiotics of Law* 123.
Wheeler D, 'Saudi Women Driving Change? Rebranding, Resistance, and the Kingdom of Change' (2020) 11 *Journal of the Middle East and Africa* 87.
Whitehorn J, Ayonrinde O and Maingay S, 'Female Genital Mutilation: Cultural and Psychological Implications' (2002) 17 *Sexual and Relationship Therapy* 161.
Wilkins R et al., 'Why the United States Should Not Ratify the Convention on the Rights of the Child' (2003) 22 *Saint Louis University Public Law Review* 411.
Wodon Q et al., 'Ending Child Marriage: Child Marriage Laws and Their Limitations' (World Bank 2017).
World Bank, 'Disease Control Priorities, Reproductive, Maternal, Newborn, and Child Health' (2016).
'Ending Violence against Women and Girls: Global and Regional Trends in Women's Legal Protection against Domestic Violence and Sexual Harassment' (2018).
'Preventing More 'Missing Girls': A Review of Policies to Tackle Son Preference' (2018).

'Women, Business and the Law' (2023).
Yelle R, *Semiotics of Religion: Signs of the Sacred in Religion* (Bloomsbury Advances in Semiotics 2012).
Young-Bruehl E, *Childism: Confronting Prejudice against Children* (Yale University Press 2012).
Zachariah M, 'Letter to the Editor' (1992) 36 *Comparative Education Review* 551.
Zampas C and Gher J, 'Abortion as a Human Right – International and Regional Standards' (2008) 8 *Human Rights Law Review* 249.
Zarbiyev F, 'The Cash Value of the Rules of Treaty Interpretation' (2019) 32 *Leiden Journal of International Law* 33.
Zeeman L and Aranda K, 'A Systematic Review of the Health and Healthcare Inequalities for People with Intersex Variance' (2020) 17 *International Journal of Environmental Research and Public Health* 6533.

# Index


best interests of the child, 31, 125, 132, 145, 200–1, 203, 224, 235

childhood, xviii–xix, xxii, xxix, 2–3, 5, 11–12, 26, 54–57, 60–63, 66, 68–69, 72, 74, 77, 83–84, 88–90, 92, 94–95, 109, 111–12, 114–15, 132, 146, 148–49, 154, 156–59, 163, 171–72, 175, 177–78, 180, 185, 187–89, 191–92, 195, 199, 202, 207, 212, 214–20, 224, 227–28, 230, 233–34, 236–37, 243–44, 247, 249, 252, 255, 272–73
childism, 4, 12–13, 43, 51, 63, 67, 77, 84–85, 87, 90, 96, 103, 108–9, 114, 116–19, 123, 154, 161, 199–200, 203, 229
cultural relativism, 13, 99, 102–5, 116, 134, 137, 188–89, 219, 226, 250

discrimination, xix, xxiii, xxvii, 1–2, 4–7, 12–13, 39, 48, 50–52, 56, 77, 79–82, 84, 89, 96, 104, 107–9, 111–14, 123, 125, 127–31, 139–40, 142–43, 145, 147–50, 154, 156–57, 159, 162–63, 166, 168, 170, 173, 176–78, 181, 184, 186, 200, 207, 220–21, 224, 231, 236, 240, 242–45, 250, 253, 255–56, 262, 267, 276–78, 280–81

equality, 7, 31, 48, 52, 77–80, 82, 103, 106, 113–14, 117, 119, 122, 126–28, 140, 142–44, 147, 149–50, 162, 166, 207–8, 240, 250, 253, 263, 266, 272

female genital mutilation, xviii, xxiv–xxvi, xxxi, 2, 60, 106, 121, 153, 264, 270
female infanticide, xviii–xix, xxii, 2, 60, 80, 114, 126, 135, 152, 160, 184, 239, 259
femalehood, xviii, 57
feminicide, xx–xxi, 126, 152

interpretant, 22–24, 26–28, 30, 139, 221, 225

legal semiotics, 12, 16, 19, 40, 125, 152

marriage, xviii–xix, xxviii–xxx, 2, 7, 31, 39, 52–53, 60, 71, 83, 91, 102, 108, 116–17, 126–27, 135–36, 141–44, 152–53, 160, 165–67, 181, 185, 187, 190, 195–96, 213, 217, 222–24, 226, 239, 249, 251–52, 259, 280
Meaning Triad, xv, 12, 26–27, 30, 38, 40, 124, 139

paternalism, 85, 87–89, 91, 161, 192, 199, 204, 232
Peirce, Charles, 16, 18, 21, 23–25, 27, 31, 36, 39–40, 43, 139, 272, 274–75, 282
prenatal sex selection, xix, xxiii, 2, 13, 60, 114, 154, 159, 162, 166, 178
puberty, 13, 58, 60–61, 68, 70–72, 108, 158, 181, 185, 190, 213, 216–17, 221, 223, 226, 251

semioethic, 11, 19, 43, 46, 77, 108, 152, 234
sexism, xx, xxiii, 4, 12–13, 43, 67, 77, 81, 83, 85, 88, 90, 96–97, 103, 108–9, 114, 116–17, 119, 123, 139, 150, 154, 169, 175, 203, 240, 242, 250, 253

sexualized social and dress codes, xxxi, 3–4, 6, 13, 102, 108, 121, 123, 138, 152, 198, 259
significs, 12, 22, 24–26, 40–41, 80, 125, 138, 268, 272, 277, 282
son preference, xix, 114
Welby, Victoria, xv, xvii, 12, 21–23, 25–27, 30, 33, 38–43, 104, 124–25, 127, 138–39, 191, 234, 240, 268, 272, 277, 282

For EU product safety concerns, contact us at Calle de José Abascal, 56–1°,
28003 Madrid, Spain or eugpsr@cambridge.org.

www.ingramcontent.com/pod-product-compliance
Lightning Source LLC
LaVergne TN
LVHW010055220926
848484LV00005BA/1083
* 9 7 8 1 3 1 6 5 1 2 7 8 4 *